SAMIR HUSNI'S GUIDE TO
NEW CONSUMER
MAGAZINES

Volume 11

Hearst Magazines Enterprises • *New York*

EDITOR
Samir A. Husni

MANAGING EDITORS
William P. (Parke) Cochran, John C. Niederschmidt II

SENIOR EDITORS
Elaine R. Abadie, Philip B. Cooper, Shu-ling Ko

EDITORIAL ASSISTANTS
Amy Bannon, Terri Thompson, Leah Stokes

PHOTOGRAPHERS
Holly Barker, Kevin Bain

ASSISTANTS TO THE EDITOR
Judy Baker, Telly Flemons

HEARST MAGAZINES ENTERPRISES

PRESIDENT
John Mack Carter

SENIOR VICE PRESIDENT
Thomas W. Wolf

EDITORIAL DIRECTOR
Thomas O'Neil

TEXT EDITORS
Michael Bath, E. Alexander Saenz

ART DIRECTOR
Mike Medina

OPERATIONS MANAGER
Aleksi Suvanto

BUSINESS COORDINATOR
Erika Larsen

ASSOCIATE ART DIRECTOR
Paulette Orlando

ART ASSOCIATES
Matt Schwenk, Michael Guralnik

To order individual copies, telephone 1-800-288-2131

ISBN: 0-688-14846-8

Printed in the United States of America
First edition

1 2 3 4 5 6 7 8 9 10

SAMIR HUSNI'S GUIDE TO NEW CONSUMER MAGAZINES

	Page
Foreward by John Mack Carter	5
Introduction by Samir Husni	7
Statistics	9
Statistics: Categories at a Glance	11
The 50 Most Notable Launches	25
New Consumer Magazines of 1995	77

NEW 1995 MAGAZINES BY CATEGORY

Category	Page
Art & Antiques	79
Automotive	81
Aviation	87
Babies	89
Black/African American	90
Bridal	92
Business & Finance	93
Camping & Outdoor Recreation	96
Children's	97
Comics & Comic Technique	98
Computers	101
Crafts, Games, Hobbies & Models	109
Dogs & Pets	121
Dressmaking & Needlework	122
Education & Teacher	123
Entertainment and Performing Arts	124
Epicurean	129
Fashion, Beauty & Grooming	135
Fishing & Hunting	137
Fitness	141
Gaming	144
Gardening (Home)	145
Gay Publications	147
General Editorial	148
Health	149
Home Service & Home	151
Horses, Riding & Breeding	158
Literary, Book Reviews & Writing Techniques	159
Mature Market	162
Media/Personalities	163
Men's	171
Metropolitan/Regional/State	172
Military & Naval	180
Motorcycle	182
Music	185
Mystery, Adventure & Science Fiction	189
Nature & Ecology	190
Photography	191
Political & Social Topics	193
Popular Culture	194
Religious & Denominational	197
Science/Technology	200
Sex	202
Special Interest Publications	216
Sports	221
Teen	233
Travel	234
TV, Radio/Communications & Electronics	236
Women's	238
CD-ROM Magazines	240
CD-ROM Addendum	241
Addendum	242
Index	248

It was, by *George*, another milestone year for new magazines. Not only did rocketing postal rates and paper costs fail to stop the number of new titles from hitting another record high, but the most-watched start-up of the year turned out to be not just publishing

The Year of *George,* Martha & Those Adorable Ferrets

as usual when John Kennedy introduced a new kind of magazine offering "not just politics as usual." Media baron Rupert Murdoch also mounted an attack on Washington, D.C., when he unfurled his conservative *Weekly Standard*.

Beyond the political category, there were lots of banner start-ups, too. *Parade* proclaimed "the largest magazine launch in history" when it introduced 4 million copies of *react*, its news and entertainment magazine for young people ages 12 to 15, into 75 newspapers. Young people in their 20s saw a shift from the kind of new magazines offered to them in 1994, from general interest titles like *Swing* and *Troika*, to publications that suddenly got down to business. The new financial magazines like *P.O.V.*, *Fast Company* and *Your Future* suggested that the young swingers were finally facing their bar tabs.

For twentysomethings still at the party, though, there were start-ups like *Speak*, "a survival guide for a generation on the brink of a new era," which was full of gritty fashions, loud-mouth music reviews and interviews with hip-hop deejays, reclusive abstract painters and drag queens who prefer to be called "performance artists." Speaking of drag queens, they got *two* new magazines in 1995 (*Transformation, Popcorn*) compared

to only one the previous year, southpaws got their first ever (*Lefthander*), and hedonists could celebrate the launch of *Juice*, the unabashed "journal of eatin', drinkin' and screwin' around."

Other 1995 trends worth noting included lots of general interest publications targeted to ethnic groups: *Sí, Urban* and *America Latina* for the Hispanic market; *Niko* and *Zasshi* for Japanese-Americans; and *Vietnow* for U.S. readers of Vietnamese descent. Regional magazines staged a surprising rally as they continued to become more specialized with new titles like *Alabama Teen Sports* and *New York Bar Guide*. Shelter magazines also became more focused, climbing to new heights in *Mountain Living* and heading to the beach in *Coastal Home*.

The pundits predict that very soon Americans will be spending more money on renovating existing homes than building new ones, a trend that has caused a boom in home remodeling tiles, including Time Inc.'s *This Old House* and Meredith's *Traditional Home Renovation Style*. Showing a concern for accent landscaping while also contributing to the recent huge crop of gardening titles, Meredith also introduced *Home Garden*.

The most successful new titles tend to be created by daring entrepreneurs with a vision.

Beyond the publishing behemoths, though, some of the most daring new magazines of the year were created by entrepreneurs with a vision who went after a niche — like the young Long Island, N.Y., couple, the Sheffermans, whose love of an animal that loves niches caused them to spawn *Modern Ferret*. Or consider another animal lover, the deputy features editor of the *Lafayette Journal & Courier* in Indiana who trots home every night after work to create another publication, *The Stable Companion*, filling its pages with poems, essays and short fiction expressing her and her contributors' unbridled love of horses.

Does anyone else still publish poetry? What's happened to the grand tradition of literary publishing in America? Well, 1995 revealed that it's alive and well, albeit sometimes with a 1990s twist. Surfer dudes and other modernday Moondoggies can now read sonnets while riding the waves and flipping through the pages of *The Surfwriters' Quarterly*. There's also the new *Bookcase*, billing itself as "a conversation between book enthusiasts," and *DoubleTake*, which delivered the double wallop of superb articles by literary stars like Joyce Carol Oates and startling photos by major lens artists. *The Village Voice* singled out *DoubleTake* as "the most promising magazine debut in years."

But there were so many other promising new magazines introduced in 1995, too, that Professor Husni simply couldn't fit them all into his "50 Most Notable Launches" section. Let me flag a few that didn't make the cut, but also deserve mention: *Brooklyn* *Bridge* and *Tribe* for creating metro magazines worthy of worldwide attention; *ZD Internet Life* for making cyberspace so welcoming; *Time for Kids* for making today's headlines mean something to those who will soon be making tomorrow's; and *Martha Stewart Living Weddings* for putting life, romance and cornflower boutonnieres back into a ceremony that once meant *everything*.

John Mack Carter
President
Hearst Magazines Enterprises

The publishing industry reached an historic milestone in 1995 when the 4,000 mark was passed. Wholesalers ended up distributing approximately 4,100 titles to the nation's newsstands. The record number represents a 150% increase over the total distributed just a decade ago.

Year in Review: Micro Publishing Goes Macro

The increase is attributed to two factors: a more or less steady climb in the number of new titles, and a higher survival rate. The number of new magazines has *not* gone up consistently each year during that same 10-year period — it dipped marginally in the late 1980s, for example — but the rallies that followed the downturns have always made up for the setbacks. In 1995, the new total climbed to 838, up from 832 the year before. The new total still represents nearly a quadruple jump over the 234 magazines that premiered a decade ago. The survival rate has also increased significantly. In 1985, 2 out of 10 new magazines were still around after 4 years of publishing. Now 3 out of 10 make it.

There are now 4,100 magazine titles on the nation's newsstands — a new record.

The new record number of titles in 1995 is surprising considering the one-two punch that nearly took the wind out of the whole publishing industry in 1995: a double-digit hike in postal rates and a staggering increase of more than 50% in paper prices. Starting in October, we saw some of the first casualties occur when more than a dozen planned launches suddenly got scrapped. Others followed. Now it looks like the slackened rate seems to be creeping over into 1996. We will learn next year whether the slowdown will halt another record number of startups from occurring.

One of the major changes in the industry is what I like to refer to as the "Micro Magazine Market." A host of magazines ranging from *Modern Ferret* to *The Stable Companion* are breaking loose from the old confines of such general categories as "Horses" and "Dogs & Pets" to the new terrain of ultra-specialization. They are magazines with micro content in a micro subject area directed to a micro audience. The editor of *The Stable Companion*, for example, is quite content to believe her circulation is moving forward at a healthy gallop since it's already reached 1,000.

MORE MASS MARKETING FOR SPECIALIZED TITLES

The channels of distribution are changing rapidly. Major chain bookstores are once again recognizing the important role magazines play in generating traffic to their door. Books-a-Million, Barnes & Noble and others are devoting more room to larger newsstands carrying more titles than ever. One sales outlet, the City News Newsstand in Chicago, prides itself on carrying 4,000 titles. Smaller retailers are getting more magazines, too, since more independent national distributors such as IPD, Fine Print and Ingram Periodicals are by-passing the wholesalers to get to them directly. In the past five years, IPD has almost tripled the number of publications it carries.

With the increase of larger sales outlets and the rise of smaller national distributors, titles that once would never have had a chance to reach the nation's newsstands are now finding their way.

MORE CIRCULATION-DRIVEN MAGAZINES

Magazines seem more reluctant than ever to cut their cover prices or offer discount subscription deals. Total magazine ad revenues for 1995 may have climbed 5.1% over 1994, but most of those dollars went to the top 150 titles. Circulation dollars are more precious than ever and more publishers are now pursuing new titles that will likely make most of their money off newsstand sales and subs. Two notable examples from 1995 include Hearst's *ESPN Total Sports* and Meredith's *Home Garden*.

Publishers also discovered the advantages of repackaging in 1995. Selling at such hefty cover prices as $5.95, the year saw quite a few retro roundups like *The Best of Low Rider* and *The Best of PC Computing*.

Some of the other more curious trends of 1995 include:

- Sex has reclaimed the number one spot after being sacked last year by sports. In 1994, the ranking was: 66 sports, 44 sex. The new score: 79 for sex, 70 for sports.
- Metropolitan and regional titles are back among the top 10 categories, making them the biggest gainers of the year. They're also good examples of the trend toward micro-marketing, since we're seeing more regional titles devoted to specific subjects such as sports, travel, gardening, and weddings.
- For the first time ever, more than half of the new magazines introduced had an intended frequency of at least four issues a year.
- The average cover price continued to rise, reaching a record $4.65
- The average number of pages in new magazines rose slightly, and the number of ad pages declined in a similar manner.
- Only 317 magazines offered subscriptions at an average price of $20.89, a decrease in both the numbers and the rate.

- The number of both annual publications and specials have dropped from their 1994 mark.

Samir A Husni, Ph.D.
Director, Magazine Service Journalism Program
The University of Mississippi

P.S. *Every effort was made to include all of the new consumer magazines launched and distributed on the nation's newsstands or through the mail. If we've overlooked one, please send us a copy of its premiere issue and we'll include it in the addendum section of next year's edition. The author assumes sole responsibility for the inclusions of magazines in the guide.*

Editorial Address:

Samir Husni's Guide to New Magazines
P.O. Box 2906
University, MS 38677
Telephone: (601) 232-7147
Fax: (601) 232-7765

Federal Express/UPS Mail:

Department of Journalism
University of Mississippi
331 Farley Hall
University, MS 38677

	1985	1990	1995
Total Number of Consumer Magazines:	2,500	3,000	4,100
Total Number of New Consumer Magazines:	234	557	838
Average Number of Pages in New Consumer Magazines:	82	90	92
Average Number of Ad Pages in New Consumer Magazines:	18	18	17
Average Cover Price of New Consumer Magazines:	2.60	3.60	4.65
Average Subscription Price of New Consumer Magazines:	16.50	18.50	21.00

NEW MAGAZINES RANK BY CATEGORY

Category	Total	Rank
Art and Antiques	7	29
Automotive	35	8
Aviation	8	26
Babies	2	46
Black/African American	8	26
Bridal	3	42
Business & Finance	14	17
Camping & Outdoor Recreation	5	38
CD-ROM	6	33
Children's	6	33
Comics & Comic Technique	15	16
Computers	48	4
Crafts, Games, Hobbies & Models	72	2
Dogs & Pets	3	42
Dressmaking & Needlework	6	33
Education & Teacher	1	49
Entertainment and Performing Arts	28	10
Epicurean	33	9
Fashion, Beauty & Grooming	9	25
Fishing & Hunting	20	12
Fitness	14	20
Gaming	6	33
Gardening (Home)	10	21
Gay Publications	6	33
General Editorial	2	46
Health	9	21
Home Service & Home	44	6
Horses, Riding & Breeding	3	42
Literary, Book Reviews & Writing Techniques	14	17
Mature Market	1	49
Media/Personalities	43	7
Men's	4	40
Metropolitan/Regional/State	48	4
Military & Naval	7	29
Motorcycle	16	15
Music	19	13
Mystery, Adventure & Science Fiction	3	42
Nature & Ecology	2	46
Photography	7	29
Political & Social Topics	5	38
Popular Culture	18	14
Religious & Denominational	14	17
Science/Technology	8	26
Sex	79	1
Special Interest Publications	25	11
Sports	70	3
Teen	4	40
Travel	10	21
TV, Radio/Communications & Electronics	7	29
Women's	10	21

NEW MAGAZINES BY RANK

1. Sex	79	9.42%	6. Media/Personalities	43	5.13%
2. Sports	70	8.35%	7. Home Service & Home	44	5.25%
3. Crafts, Games, Hobbies & Models	72	8.60%	8. Automotive	35	4.17%
4. Computers	48	5.72%	9. Epicurean	33	3.93%
5. Metropolitan/Regional/State	48	5.72%	10. Entertainment & Performing Arts	28	3.34%
				500	**59.7%**

MAGAZINE AVERAGE COVER PRICE BY RANK*

1. Literary, Book Reviews & Writing Techniques	$5.96	6. Travel	$4.60
2. Sex	$5.51	7. Crafts, Games, Hobbies & Models	$4.59
3. Computers	$5.27	8. Motorcycle	$4.38
4. Entertainment and Performing Arts	$5.14	9. Fishing & Hunting	$4.24
5. Media/Personalities	$5.09	10. Automotive	$4.21

MAGAZINE AVERAGE SUBSCRIPTION PRICE BY RANK*

1. Comics & Comic Techniques	$33.82	6. Media Personalities	$22.45
2. Computers	$31.60	7. Music	$20.93
3. Sex	$30.40	8. Gardening (Home)	$19.74
4. Entertainment and Performing Arts	$24.74	9. Special Interest Publications	$19.42
5. Literary, Book Reviews & Writing Techniques	$22.99	10. Travel	$19.14

MAGAZINE AVERAGE PAGES BY RANK*

1. Home Service & Home	132.42	6. Literary, Book Reviews & Writing Techniques	99.42
2. Sex	113.39	7. Computers	98.70
3. Motorcycle	105.50	8. Fitness	97.57
4. Sports	103.27	9. Business & Finance	96.71
5. Automotive	101.00	10. Epicurean	91.18

MAGAZINE AVERAGE AD PAGES BY RANK*

1. Business & Finance	37.46	6. Health	22.75
2. Computers	28.40	7. Sex	21.52
3. Metropolitan/Regional/State	27.81	8. Sports	19.33
4. Motorcycle	25.28	9. Automotive	18.50
5. Travel	23.33	10. Fishing & Hunting	18.37

TOP 10 STATES IN MAGAZINE LAUNCHES*

1. New York	233	7. Florida	28
2. California	176	8. Texas	20
3. New Jersey	46	9. Wisconsin	13
4. Illinois	45	10. Georgia	10
5. Iowa	29	10. Virginia	10
5. Pennsylvania	29		

FREQUENCY

Four Times or Higher	457	54.5%	Annuals/Semiannuals	86	10.2%
Specials	242	28.9%	Frequency Not Available	53	6.32%
				838	**100%**

Including only those categories with 10 or more new launches.

ARTS & ANTIQUES

Total Number: 7	Cover Price	Subscription Price	Pages	Ad Pages
Average	$5.79	$22.65	91.14	9.83
Median	$5.97	$20.00	84	10.5
Mode	$3.95	$19.95	84	4
Minimum	$3.95	$19.95	16	4
Maximum	$7.95	$28.00	164	13
Valid Cases	6	3	7	6

AUTOMOTIVE

Total Number: 35	Cover Price	Subscription Price	Pages	Ad Pages
Average	$4.21	$17.32	101	18.5
Median	$3.95	$17.47	86	14.5
Mode	$4.95	$8.00	76	13
Minimum	$2.95	$8.00	40	2
Maximum	$6.99	$25.00	202	51
Valid Cases	35	6	35	35

AVIATION

Total Number: 8	Cover Price	Subscription Price	Pages	Ad Pages
Average	$5.01	0	80.5	9.87
Median	$5.45	0	86	6.5
Mode	$5.95	0	88	5
Minimum	$2.95	0	48	3
Maximum	$5.95	0	96	24
Valid Cases	8	0	8	8

BABIES

Total Number: 2	Cover Price	Subscription Price	Pages	Ad Pages
Average	$2.95	0	76	9.5
Median	$2.95	0	76	9.5
Mode	$2.95	0	52	1
Minimum	$2.95	0	52	1
Maximum	$2.95	0	100	18
Valid Cases	1	0	2	2

BLACK/AFRICAN AMERICAN

Total Number: 8	Cover Price	Subscription Price	Pages	Ad Pages
Average	$3.41	$11.64	63.75	16.37
Median	$3.95	$12.00	67	18.5
Mode	$3.95	$12.00	40	24
Minimum	$1.95	$7.00	40	3
Maximum	$5.00	$15.00	92	24
Valid Cases	8	6	8	8

BRIDAL

Total Number: 3	Cover Price	Subscription Price	Pages	Ad Pages
Average	$4.15	0	148	79.50
Median	$3.95	0	84	79.50
Mode	$3.95	0	84	5
Minimum	$2.95	0	84	5
Maximum	$5.50	0	276	154
Valid Cases	3	0	3	2

BUSINESS & FINANCE

Total Number: 14	Cover Price	Subscription Price	Pages	Ad Pages
Average	$3.96	$15.61	96.71	37.46
Median	$3.95	$13.50	99	39
Mode	$3.95	$10.00	52	39
Minimum	$2.50	$10.00	48	9
Maximum	$7.00	$25.00	178	94
Valid Cases	14	8	14	13

CAMPING & OUTDOOR RECREATION

Total Number: 5	Cover Price	Subscription Price	Pages	Ad Pages
Average	$3.76	$16.95	127.2	42
Median	$3.95	$16.95	108	46
Mode	$3.95	$16.95	96	12
Minimum	$3.00	$16.95	96	12
Maximum	$3.95	$16.95	202	67
Valid Cases	5	1	5	5

CD-ROM

Total Number: 6	Cover Price	Subscription Price	Pages	Ad Pages
Average	$11.78	$49.95	n/a	n/a
Median	$9.95	$49.95	n/a	n/a
Mode	$9.95	$49.95	n/a	n/a
Minimum	$9.95	$49.95	n/a	n/a
Maximum	$15.95	$49.95	n/a	n/a
Valid Cases	6	1	n/a	n/a

CHILDREN'S

Total Number: 6	Cover Price	Subscription Price	Pages	Ad Pages
Average	$2.72	$10.35	44	12.2
Median	$2.50	$11.23	42	10
Mode	$2.50	$3.95	36	5
Minimum	$1.95	$3.95	8	5
Maximum	$3.95	$14.97	72	23
Valid Cases	4	4	6	5

COMICS & COMIC TECHNIQUE

Total Number: 15	Cover Price	Subscription Price	Pages	Ad Pages
Average	$3.32	$33.82	69.57	10.75
Median	$3.95	$34.00	52	4
Mode	$2.95	$20.00	52	1
Minimum	$1.25	$20.00	34	1
Maximum	$4.95	$59.40	138	51
Valid Cases	15	7	15	12

COMPUTERS

Total Number: 48	Cover Price	Subscription Price	Pages	Ad Pages
Average	$5.27	$31.60	98.70	28.40
Median	$4.95	$29.00	91	20
Mode	$4.95	$23.95	100	12
Minimum	$2.95	$7.90	36	3
Maximum	$14.95	$79.94	400	282
Valid Cases	46	25	48	48

CRAFTS, GAMES, HOBBIES & MODELS

Total Number: 72	Cover Price	Subscription Price	Pages	Ad Pages
Average	$4.59	$18.59	86.94	12.15
Median	$4.24	$19.57	88	9
Mode	$4.95	$10.00	100	3
Minimum	$1.25	$8.00	8	1
Maximum	$11.00	$35.40	212	49
Valid Cases	72	33	72	64

DOGS & PETS

Total Number: 3	Cover Price	Subscription Price	Pages	Ad Pages
Average	$3.80	$19.97	46	10
Median	$3.50	$18.00	38	10
Mode	$2.95	$16.98	32	6
Minimum	$2.95	$16.98	32	6
Maximum	$4.95	$24.95	68	14
Valid Cases	3	3	3	2

DRESSMAKING & NEEDLEWORK

Total Number: 6	Cover Price	Subscription Price	Pages	Ad Pages
Average	$4.54	$20.24	67	7.5
Median	$4.72	$20.24	66	7.5
Mode	$4.95	$18.49	68	4
Minimum	$3.95	$18.49	52	3
Maximum	$4.95	$22.00	100	12
Valid Cases	6	2	6	6

EDUCATION & TEACHER

Total Number: 1	Cover Price	Subscription Price	Pages	Ad Pages
Average	0	0	42	1
Median	0	0	42	1
Mode	0	0	42	1
Minimum	0	0	42	1
Maximum	0	0	42	1
Valid Cases	0	0	1	1

ENTERTAINMENT & PERFORMING ARTS

Total Number: 28	Cover Price	Subscription Price	Pages	Ad Pages
Average	$5.14	$24.74	80.14	13.75
Median	$4.97	$18.20	75	11
Mode	$4.95	$18.00	68	5
Minimum	$2.95	$15.00	24	1
Maximum	$9.99	$38.00	188	39
Valid Cases	28	7	28	26

EPICUREAN

Total Number: 33	Cover Price	Subscription Price	Pages	Ad Pages
Average	$3.60	$18.47	91.18	13.25
Median	$3.00	$14.42	96	8
Mode	$2.99	$8.00	100	1
Minimum	$2.00	$8.00	16	1
Maximum	$6.95	$44.95	162	26
Valid Cases	33	10	33	7

FASHION, BEAUTY & GROOMING

Total Number: 9	Cover Price	Subscription Price	Pages	Ad Pages
Average	$3.46	$19.98	93.11	12.85
Median	$3.50	$22.00	86	10
Mode	$3.95	$9.95	84	6
Minimum	$2.95	$9.95	52	6
Maximum	$3.95	$26.00	162	26
Valid Cases	9	4	9	7

FISHING & HUNTING

Total Number: 20	Cover Price	Subscription Price	Pages	Ad Pages
Average	$4.24	$17.76	89	18.37
Median	$3.95	$17.95	94	15.50
Mode	$3.95	$14.95	100	11
Minimum	$2.95	$14.95	52	3
Maximum	$5.95	$20.00	100	47.5
Valid Cases	19	5	20	20

FITNESS

Total Number: 14	Cover Price	Subscription Price	Pages	Ad Pages
Average	$3.40	$16.46	97.57	14.65
Median	$2.99	$16.46	96	7
Mode	$2.95	$12.95	100	2
Minimum	$1.95	$12.95	68	2
Maximum	$4.99	$19.97	174	39
Valid Cases	14	2	14	9

GAMING

Total Number: 6	Cover Price	Subscription Price	Pages	Ad Pages
Average	$3.84	$18.46	90.33	20.40
Median	$3.95	$18.46	83	24
Mode	$5.95	$6.95	148	3
Minimum	$1.50	$6.95	32	3
Maximum	$5.95	$29.97	148	39
Valid Cases	6	2	6	5

GARDENING (HOME)

Total Number: 10	Cover Price	Subscription Price	Pages	Ad Pages
Average	$3.82	$19.74	82.60	14.77
Median	$3.97	$18.90	84	13
Mode	$2.95	$16.98	84	2.2
Minimum	$2.95	$16.98	32	2.2
Maximum	$5.50	$26.00	140	38
Valid Cases	10	6	10	8

GAY PUBLICATIONS

Total Number: 6	Cover Price	Subscription Price	Pages	Ad Pages
Average	$5.62	$30.53	68	15
Median	$4.45	$28.25	66	14
Mode	$3.95	$20.00	32	11
Minimum	$3.00	$20.00	32	4
Maximum	$11.95	$43.00	116	27
Valid Cases	6	6	6	6

GENERAL EDITORIAL

Total Number:2	Cover Price	Subscription Price	Pages	Ad Pages
Average	$2.73	0	74	5
Median	$2.73	0	74	5
Mode	$2.50	0	48	3
Minimum	$2.50	0	48	3
Maximum	$2.95	0	100	7
Valid Cases	2	0	2	2

HEALTH

Total Number: 9	Cover Price	Subscription Price	Pages	Ad Pages
Average	$3.35	$15.48	89.45	22.75
Median	$2.95	$15.48	68	12.50
Mode	$2.95	$12.97	68	3
Minimum	$2.95	$12.97	36	3
Maximum	$4.95	$18.00	180	57
Valid Cases	9	2	9	8

HOME SERVICE & HOME

Total Number: 44	Cover Price	Subscription Price	Pages	Ad Pages
Average	$3.91	$17.27	132.42	17.68
Median	$3.95	$16.00	127	16
Mode	$3.50	$12.00	84	2
Minimum	$0.95	$9.99	60	1
Maximum	$7.00	$29.95	322	52
Valid Cases	44	13	44	37

HORSES, RIDING & BREEDING

Total Number: 3	Cover Price	Subscription Price	Pages	Ad Pages
Average	$4.46	$29.70	69.33	14
Median	$3.95	$29.70	60	17
Mode	$2.95	$24.00	48	2
Minimum	$2.95	$24.00	48	2
Maximum	$6.50	$35.40	100	23
Valid Cases	3	2	3	3

LITERARY, BOOK REVIEWS & WRITING TECHNIQUES

Total Number: 14	Cover Price	Subscription Price	Pages	Ad Pages
Average	$5.96	$22.99	99.42	5.42
Median	$5.47	$18.00	102	3
Mode	$6.00	$6.00	36	1
Minimum	$1.50	$6.00	24	1
Maximum	$20.00	$59.95	210	18
Valid Cases	14	11	14	13

MATURE MARKET

Total Number: 1	Cover Price	Subscription Price	Pages	Ad Pages
Average	$2.99	0	68	16
Median	$2.99	0	68	16
Mode	$2.99	0	68	16
Minimum	$2.99	0	68	16
Maximum	$2.99	0	68	16
Valid Cases	1	0	1	1

MEDIA/PERSONALITIES

Total Number: 43	Cover Price	Subscription Price	Pages	Ad Pages
Average	$5.09	$22.45	76.24	8.61
Median	$4.95	$22.00	80	8
Mode	$4.99	$22.00	68	4
Minimum	$2.50	$15.85	16	1
Maximum	$9.95	$29.95	138	26
Valid Cases	43	4	43	25

MEN'S

Total Number: 4	Cover Price	Subscription Price	Pages	Ad Pages
Average	$8.21	$24.95	132	26
Median	$7.45	$24.95	143	36
Mode	$3.00	$24.95	48	2
Minimum	$3.00	$24.95	48	2
Maximum	$14.95	$24.95	194	40
Valid Cases	4	1	4	3

METROPOLITAN/REGIONAL/STATE

Total Number:48	Cover Price	Subscription Price	Pages	Ad Pages
Average	$4.08	$16.88	80.40	27.81
Median	$3.72	$16.24	72	24
Mode	$2.95	$12.00	64	1
Minimum	$1.95	$7.95	16	1
Maximum	$12.95	$29.95	180	122
Valid Cases	45	24	48	43

MILITARY & NAVAL

Total Number: 7	Cover Price	Subscription Price	Pages	Ad Pages
Average	$5.60	0	88.57	9.85
Median	$5.95	0	88	10
Mode	$3.95	0	84	3
Minimum	$3.95	0	68	3
Maximum	$6.99	0	100	17
Valid Cases	7	0	7	7

MOTORCYCLE

Total Number: 16	Cover Price	Subscription Price	Pages	Ad Pages
Average	$4.38	$13.98	105.5	25.28
Median	$3.95	$13.95	100	21.5
Mode	$3.95	$10.00	100	12
Minimum	$1.75	$10.00	74	1
Maximum	$6.95	$18.98	164	97
Valid Cases	16	5	16	16

MUSIC

Total Number: 19	Cover Price	Subscription Price	Pages	Ad Pages
Average	$3.78	$20.93	82.10	17
Median	$3.95	$19.00	74	18
Mode	$4.95	$12.97	72	8
Minimum	$1.50	$12.97	36	4
Maximum	$5.95	$30.00	210	32
Valid Cases	19	10	19	19

MYSTERY, ADVENTURE & SCIENCE FICTION

Total Number: 3	Cover Price	Subscription Price	Pages	Ad Pages
Average	$4.96	$15.00	112	6
Median	$5.00	$15.00	90	6
Mode	$3.95	$15.00	68	6
Minimum	$3.95	$15.00	68	6
Maximum	$5.95	$15.00	178	6
Valid Cases	3	2	3	2

NATURE & ECOLOGY

Total Number: 2	Cover Price	Subscription Price	Pages	Ad Pages
Average	$4.45	$14.95	74	5
Median	$4.45	$14.95	74	5
Mode	$3.95	$14.95	48	5
Minimum	$3.95	$14.95	48	5
Maximum	$4.95	$14.95	100	5
Valid Cases	2	1	2	1

PHOTOGRAPHY

Total Number: 7	Cover Price	Subscription Price	Pages	Ad Pages
Average	$5.20	$36.00	141.71	40.85
Median	$4.95	$32.00	116	28
Mode	$3.95	$16.00	28	6
Minimum	$3.00	$16.00	28	6
Maximum	$10.00	$60.00	304	110
Valid Cases	7	3	7	7

POLITICAL & SOCIAL TOPICS

Total Number: 5	Cover Price	Subscription Price	Pages	Ad Pages
Average	$2.83	$33.72	100	70.33
Median	$2.95	$22.47	50	28
Mode	$2.95	$9.97	16	8
Minimum	$2.50	$9.97	16	8
Maximum	$2.95	$79.96	284	175
Valid Cases	5	5	5	4

POPULAR CULURE

Total Number: 18	Cover Price	Subscription Price	Pages `	Ad Pages
Average	$3.46	$14.78	75.41	11.81
Median	$3.00	$14.97	66	9.5
Mode	$3.95	$12.00	84	7.5
Minimum	$1.95	$6.00	28	2
Maximum	$8.95	$30.50	170	27
Valid Cases	18	12	18	16

RELIGIOUS & DENOMINATIONAL

Total Number: 14	Cover Price	Subscription Price	Pages	Ad Pages
Average	$2.90	$15.96	50	10.27
Median	$2.95	$15.00	48	12
Mode	$2.95	$12.95	48	13
Minimum	$1.35	$10.97	32	2
Maximum	$4.95	$24.95	68	14
Valid Cases	12	11	14	9

SCIENCE/TECHNOLOGY

Total Number: 8	Cover Price	Subscription Price	Pages	Ad Pages
Average	$6.39	$29.50	78.75	10.04
Median	$5.45	$29.50	76	9
Mode	$4.95	$21.00	68	4
Minimum	$3.95	$21.00	68	4
Maximum	$9.95	$38.00	104	25
Valid Cases	8	2	8	7

SEX

Total Number: 79	Cover Price	Subscription Price	Pages	Ad Pages
Average	$5.51	$30.40	113.39	21.52
Median	$5.95	$30.00	100	21
Mode	$5.99	$30.00	100	32
Minimum	$2.50	$18.25	32	4
Maximum	$6.99	$50.00	292	60
Valid Cases	79	17	79	77

SPECIAL INTEREST PUBLICATIONS

Total Number: 25	Cover Price	Subscription Price	Pages	Ad Pages
Average	$4.14	$19.42	73.44	14.69
Median	$3.47	$17.47	60	13.75
Mode	$2.95	$25.00	32	7
Minimum	$1.50	$8.95	16	2
Maximum	$9.95	$40.00	244	52
Valid Cases	24	16	25	24

SPORTS

Total Number: 70	Cover Price	Subscription Price	Pages	Ad Pages
Average	$4.13	$16.04	103.27	19.33
Median	$3.95	$15.00	93	18.62
Mode	$4.95	$9.95	100	5
Minimum	$2.50	$5.95	28	2
Maximum	$6.95	$35.00	290	82
Valid Cases	70	23	70	66

TEEN

Total Number: 4	Cover Price	Subscription Price	Pages	Ad Pages
Average	$3.28	$15.98	49.5	8.25
Median	$2.95	$15.98	41	9.50
Mode	$2.95	$15.97	16	12
Minimum	$2.95	$15.97	16	2
Maximum	$3.95	$16.00	100	12
Valid Cases	3	2	4	4

TRAVEL

Total Number: 10	Cover Price	Subscription Price	Pages	Ad Pages
Average	$4.60	$19.14	77.40	23.33
Median	$3.97	$19.45	84	21
Mode	$3.95	$19.95	84	8
Minimum	$2.50	$9.00	16	8
Maximum	$9.95	$36.00	142	53
Valid Cases	10	6	10	9

TV, RADIO/COMMUNICATIONS & ELECTRONICS

Total Number: 7	Cover Price	Subscription Price	Pages	Ad Pages
Average	$5.04	$19.47	119.71	35.57
Median	$4.95	$19.47	100	25
Mode	$4.95	$17.95	100	4
Minimum	$3.50	$17.95	32	4
Maximum	$6.95	$21.00	216	76
Valid Cases	6	2	7	7

WOMEN'S

Total Number: 10	Cover Price	Subscription Price	Pages	Ad Pages
Average	$3.91	$18.48	80	14.13
Median	$3.72	$14.99	80	12.65
Mode	$2.95	$9.97	64	1
Minimum	$2.95	$9.97	52	1
Maximum	$5.95	$36.00	114	32
Valid Cases	10	5	10	10

NEW CONSUMER MAGAZINES OF 1995

Total Number: 838	Cover Price	Subscription Price	Pages	Ad Pages
Average	$4.65	$20.89	92.45	18.69
Median	$3.99	$18.00	84	15
Mode	$4.95	$15.00	100	12
Minimum	$0.95	$3.95	8	1
Maximum	$20.00	$79.96	400	282
Valid Cases	822	317	838	742

The 50
MOST NOTABLE
LAUNCHES

NOTE: The information in this section was the latest available at press time.

American Cheerleader

PUBLISHED BY: Lifestyles Publications Inc.

350 W. 50th St., Suite 2AA

New York, NY 10019

TEL: (212) 861-8108 **FAX:** (212) 988-0621

DATE: February

FREQUENCY: Bimonthly

COVER PRICE: $2.95

SUBSCRIPTION PRICE: $23.70

DISCOUNT SUBSCRIPTION PRICE: $14.95

TOTAL NUMBER OF PAGES: 80

TOTAL NUMBER OF AD PAGES: 18

PUBLISHER: Michael Weiskopf

EDITOR: Julie Davis

Here's just what the sport of cheerleading needed: its own ra-ra publication full of spirited fan kicks, twinkling faces, arms splayed out into victorious "V" poses and an overall sense of teenage seriousness that could make you think you're reading about future Miss America contestants leading the fight for world peace. The broad reach of its articles — pompon to pompon — spans profiles of model squads and cheerleaders of the month; how-to's on such technical manuevers as partner stunts and straddle jumps; tips on health, nutrition, skin care and coping with damp gyms and buses; plus advice on how to be a team player. A calendar in each issue gives date and location details on related events coast to coast, and celebrity profiles reveal such nuggets as the fact that actress Sandra Bullock ("a real life varsity cheerleader at Washington-Lee High School in Arlington, Virginia") was voted "Most Likely to Brighten Your Day" by her classmates of 1982.

American Cheerleader celebrates the "extraordinary dedication and fierce determination demonstrated by the 1.2 million teenagers who are members of squads throughout the country ... [and is designed] to address their interests in a sophisticated, fun and informative way." Its mission is to promote cheerleading as "a bona-fide athletic activity and encourage the recognition that it deserves." Circulation targets: 200,000 by the end of 1995; 300,000 within five years.

MediaWeek notes: "AC is the brainchild of former *Chemical Week* executive VP Michael Weiskopf, who says, 'Like all good ideas, it jumped up at me. I was watching that Holly Hunter movie about the Texas cheerleader's mom [*The Positively True Adventures of the Alleged Texas Cheerleader-Murdering Mom*].'

"Weiskopf took a long hard look at cheering and found that there are about 3 million cheerleaders in the country, about half of whom are committed enough to attend camps to hone their skills. Using his knowledge of niche publishing, Weiskopf has eschewed the standard strategy of building a subscriber base through direct mail. He has instead struck deals with several cheerleading camps to market his magazine directly to their attendees, often in person. 'I wouldn't have launched the magazine without these arrangements,' says Weiskopf."

READERSHIP PROFILE: N/A

EDITORIAL CONCEPT: *All aspects of cheerleading — from competitions to celebrity practitioners.*

Aveda

PUBLISHED BY: Hachette Filipacchi

1633 Broadway

New York, NY 10019

TEL: (212) 767-5611

FREQUENCY: n/a

COVER PRICE: $3.95

SUBSCRIPTION PRICE: n/a

TOTAL NUMBER OF PAGES: 100

TOTAL NUMBER OF AD PAGES: 8

PUBLISHER: Beth-Ann Burzon

EDITOR: Corynne Corbett

*A*veda is really a "magalog" since it pushes its own beauty and health products as well as its corporate philosophy on healthy living amongst articles expressing concern for the global environment. A paper-thin PR ploy? Perhaps, but at least the magazine is printed on recycled paper and its inks are vegetable-based.

To draw an analogy to another notable advertising publication of recent years that had lofty editorial aspirations: whereas Benetton's magazine used shocking photos to awaken readers to social hipness, *Aveda* takes more of a Liberal Lite approach to awaken readers to ecological and New Age concerns. Inside are photos of happy tree huggers, illustrations of evil Republicans intent on poisoning the planet, a picture of a daisy serving as the definition of one's "(self)" and articles promising that human salvation lies in the secrets of herbs (that lie inside Aveda's products, of course).

Throughout its slick 100 pages of articles on aging and saving the Brazilian rain forests are obvious entreaties to buy Aveda products for — the magazine's tag line here — "The Beauty of a Balanced Life." Readers who want their hairdos "a cut above the rest" are told to finish them off with Aveda Plant Pure-Fume Anti-Humectant Pomade. The fashion section touts coats of "polar fleece" that claim by name to be "eco-spun" by "indigenous people" with whom the company works "respectfully," the magazine promises us, while "insisting on fair labor practices."

The magazine's international feel is underscored by the overriding spirit of Aveda's Austrian-born founder and CEO, Horst Rechelbacher, who states in a letter to readers: "Our objective is to foster a deep understanding and respect for the Earth, through both responsible manufacturing and community education. By relying on plants and other sustainable resources — rather than petrochemicals — to create our products, and by tapping into the wisdom of indigenous people, we hope to contribute to the bettering of the planet and to its preservation for future generations. This magazine is part of that commitment."

READERSHIP PROFILE: *Adults 18-54 interested in community/civic activities, health/natural foods, self-improvement and environmental concerns.*

EDITORIAL CONCEPT: *A new world of information that provides fresh, environmentally-sound concepts for every aspect of your life.*

Baywatch

PUBLISHED BY: Starlog Entertainment Inc.

475 Park Ave. S.

New York, NY 10016

TEL: (212) 689-2830 **FAX:** (212) 889-7933

DATE: September

FREQUENCY: 3/ year

COVER PRICE: $4.99

SUBSCRIPTION PRICE: n/a

TOTAL NUMBER OF PAGES: 76

TOTAL NUMBER OF AD PAGES: 9

PUBLISHER: Norman Jacobs

EDITOR: Len Canter

The hit TV show watched by a billion viewers in 140 countries worldwide now has an official fanzine.

The publishers of *Baywatch* promise: "Each 76-page issue will feature color photos and star interviews, on-set coverage, behind-the-scenes activities, exciting contests — plus six full-color fold-outs which open to become giant-sized 16-inch by 22-inch pinups." So that crazed fans won't accidentally destroy their treasured new magazine in their frenzy to tear out the paper icons inside, these instructions appear: "Open magazine to center, carefully open staples, lift out pinups, rebend staples to preserve magazine."

Inside the premiere issue are further intimate portraits of those brave babes and boys who somehow find time to rescue drowning kiddies and grannies in between fits over who borrowed who's Coppertone. Photos reveal lots of skimpy red beachwear, acres of sun-kissed sand and surf and as much skin as primetime American TV allows. The text invites readers to "sit back, get comfy and get to know some of your favorite actors and actresses in the most important role they play — real life." But how real is it?

Sample articles include "Pamela Anderson's Wedding In Her Own Words," describing the juicy details of how she got hitched in Cancun with Motley Crue rocker Tommy Lee: "The wedding wasn't planned at all. We woke up in the morning, put on our bathing suits and went down to the beach and got married. I was wearing a white bikini and Tommy was wearing shorts. Afterwards we jumped into the ocean!"

In "Up Close With David Hasselhoff," readers learn that the star originally turned down his part on *Baywatch*: "I didn't want to be 'Michael Knight [his *Knight Rider* character] in a bathing suit.' But then they came back to me with an offer I couldn't refuse!"

A contest invites fans to submit a story line, in 100 words or less, for a future script, "the most dramatic rescue you can imagine for Mitch and company to execute at the beach or on the pier." The prize: "Our grand champion will have a memento to cherish forever when David Hasselhoff signs his name on one of his actual *Baywatch* scripts and sends it to you!"

READERSHIP PROFILE: N/A

EDITORIAL CONCEPT: *The official magazine for lovers of the* Baywatch *television series.*

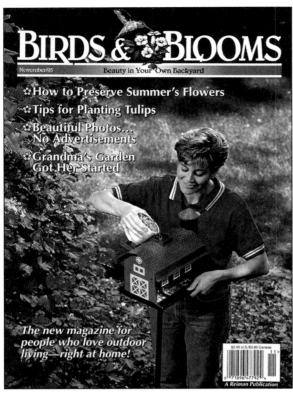

Birds & Blooms

PUBLISHED BY: Reiman Publications L.P.

5925 Country Ln.

Greendale, WI 53129

TEL: (414) 423-0100

DATE: January

FREQUENCY: Bimonthly

COVER PRICE: $2.95

SUBSCRIPTION PRICE: $16.98

DISCOUNT SUBSCRIPTION PRICE: $10.98

TOTAL NUMBER OF PAGES: 68

TOTAL NUMBER OF AD PAGES: 0

PUBLISHER: Roy Reiman

EDITOR: Tom Curl

Publisher Roy Reiman has made an amazing success out of a brave publishing philosophy: accept no ads in your magazine, assign your readers to write the contents and then just have your editors open the mail all day.

His seven titles, *Taste of Home, Reminisce, Country, Country Woman, Canadian Country Women, Farm & Ranch Living* and *Crafting Traditions*, generate yearly circulation revenues estimated at more than $75 million. Now he has added *Birds & Blooms*, which celebrates bird feeding and backyard living, in addition to *Talk About Pets* (see separate listing).

On the inside front cover of *Birds & Blooms'* premiere issue is a letter introducing the new title to its future contributors: "Each issue will take you on a 'photo-tour' of other people's 'outdoor living rooms.' These friendly folks will open their garden gates and invite you 'around back.' There they'll show you how they attract an abundance of birds and how their landscaping projects add the kind of colorful, 'homey' feeling that draws oohs and aahs from the neighbors.

"This is a sharing magazine," it adds, "providing a means for backyard enthusiasts to chat with each other and exchange personal experiences."

Throughout its pages, the writing is charming and the amateur photography reveals quite a few budding professionals. Its text reads like folksy chitchat exchanged over the backyard fence.

A homeowner from Hanover, Massachusetts, introduces readers to her private retreat: "In May, my cottage garden becomes a magical place. It erupts with flowering quince, bridal wreath and rhododendrons. Birds and butterflies return from their long travels south, and the sun warms me as I kneel on the ground to work with my hands in the soil."

A dabbler in dried flowers from Tacoma, Washington, reveals her hobby secrets: "Pink fireweed always dries purple and bell-shaped flowers such as lily of the valley do not hold their color," she warns. An "amiable grandmother from McCook, Nebraska" offers her edible-petals recipe for Nasturtium Nibbles.

Under the heading "Nest Best Thing," there's a photo of a mischievous feathered family nesting atop a Des Moines homeowner's electrical junction box.

Other photos reveal an equally whimsical spirit. The smiling face of one young girl in a blue bonnet "floats in a sea of bluebonnets," notes its caption. In another picture, an unnamed girl cuddles her pet kitten amidst a forest of black-eyed Susans. A Pennsylvania grandmother sends in the snapshot of her giddy grandson playing with the wounded hummingbird he nursed back to life.

READERSHIP PROFILE: *N/A*

EDITORIAL CONCEPT: *Welcome to the world of new sounds, scents and scenes right in your own backyard.*

April 1995
Volume I, No.2
$3.50

THE JOY OF READING & COLLECTING

INTERVIEW:
Whitney Otto

Children's Book Author
Arthur Yorinks

San Francisco Classic
City Lights

Plus: Calendar Of National Book Events!

Bookcase

PUBLISHED BY: Tumbleweed Productions

1447 Campus Rd.

Los Angeles, CA 90042

TEL: (213) 257-9269 **FAX:** (213) 256-1600

DATE: March

FREQUENCY: Monthly

COVER PRICE: $3.50

SUBSCRIPTION PRICE: $40.00

TOTAL NUMBER OF PAGES: 24

TOTAL NUMBER OF AD PAGES: 4

PUBLISHER: Angela Maria Ortiz

EDITOR: Kathleen Lawrence

"We think of *Bookcase* as a monthly conversation between writers, collectors, booksellers, and enthusiasts," says editor Kathleen Lawrence. "It's full of useful information about upcoming book releases, book fairs, signings and author tours, and it gives novice and experienced collectors basic 'how-to' information on starting a collection, finding out-of-print books, and preserving their collections, large or small. But most important it's about people who read, write, enjoy books — their enthusiasms, experiences, passions."

The first issue contains a tribute to the literary career of the late James Clavell, the author of *Shogun, King Rat* and *Noble House*, "who resembles Dickens more than DeLillo," insists its writer. "He knew how to grab you on the first page and hold you for 600 or more." A tour through the rare book collection of the Los Angeles Public Library uncovers 18th-century works advising Mexican friars on how to preach to New World natives and how to interact with them personally, too, asking, "Have you deflowered a virgin?"

In an introductory letter to readers, editor Lawrence notes that *Bookcase* is "off to a rousing start with a cracking good conversation with mystery writers Sue Grafton and Linda Barnes" when it caught up with them at a signing at Dutton's Book Shop in Brentwood, California. These two "good friends" and "comrades in crime" offer personal glimpses into their everyday lives. Grafton notes that she begins her day by walking, swimming or riding a stationary bike. "Otherwise, if you're a writer, your butt gets *this* big," she insists. Barnes notes that she winds down her day with works by other writers, which she reads to her young son "whether he wants me to or not."

Bookcase names its pick for Bookstore of the Month: the Much Ado Shop in Marblehead, Massachusetts, operated by an Anglophile couple who hang a shingle outside depicting a portrait of the Bard. Inside are 35,000 "old, rare and out-of-print books, many of them purchased on trips to England," and first editions of more recent titles like Gabriel Garcia Marquez's *Love in the Time of Cholera*.

At 24 pages, the publication is a thin book full of wide-ranging info: a new-products section reveals "a cushy idea" for reading in bed — a pillow bookstand; a column discusses financial thrillers as being a curious new trend in mysteries. Most curiously, *Bookcase* does not review books.

READERSHIP PROFILE: *N/A*

EDITORIAL CONCEPT: *"The joy of reading and collecting."*

Brew Your Own

PUBLISHED BY: Niche Publications

216 F St., Suite 160

Davis, CA 95616

TEL: (916) 758-4596 **FAX:** (916) 758-7477

DATE: May

FREQUENCY: Monthly

COVER PRICE: $3.95

SUBSCRIPTION PRICE: $44.95

DISCOUNT SUBSCRIPTION PRICE: $29.95

TOTAL NUMBER OF PAGES: 76

TOTAL NUMBER OF AD PAGES: 31

PUBLISHER: Carl B. Landau

EDITOR: Craig Bystrynski

Brew Your Own is "designed to reach the exploding consumer homebrew market" with tips on "old favorite and offbeat" techniques to produce the full range of beers from all-grain varieties to malt extracts.

How big is the trend? According to publisher Carl Landau, between 1 million and 1.5 million Americans have adopted the hobby ever since home brewing became legal in 1979, allowing the production of up to 200 gallons per household per year. Today there are more than 400 home-brewing clubs nationwide and 1,500 companies that sell supplies. The audience seemed large enough to convince the 38-year-old Californian to spend $100,000 to concoct his own magazine to tap into it. He had previously started up two successful publications: *Computer Language* for professional software designers and *AI Experience*, a magazine about artificial intelligence.

The Sacramento Bee describes his latest publishing brew as if it were a night out with the boys at the corner tavern, noting that the magazine is "filled with light-hearted stories as well as down-to-earth home-brewing tips and advice." Readers relate their own personal experiences and are given tours of leading microbreweries where master brewers offer expert advice.

The magazine also has its own expert on staff to answer readers' brewing questions, and the pages are full of "people pictures, reader forums and interesting homebrew setups."

Included in the first issue is Al Capone's recipe for bootleg brew. Upcoming issues promise to spill the secret recipes of such other famous home brewers as George Washington and Thomas Jefferson.

The magazine was launched in May with a direct-mail campaign of 150,000 letters that yielded 11,000 subscribers. An additional 14,000 single issues were sold on 1,600 newsstands nationwide. Publisher Landau projects a circulation of 100,000 after three years. Refering to 1995, he told the *Bee*, "I would expect to be in the black by the end of the year."

READERSHIP PROFILE: *95 % male; 41 % ages 30-39; 90 % graduated or attended college; average household income of $61,300. Average reader spends $355 per year on homebrew equipment and supplies and $465 on microbrew and import beers.*

EDITORIAL CONCEPT: *"To celebrate the art and science of brewing."*

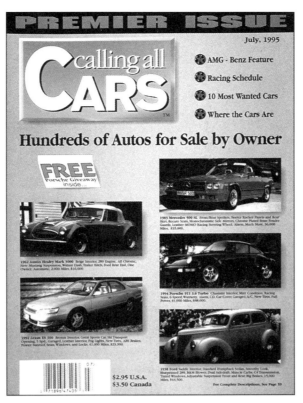

Calling All Cars

PUBLISHED BY: Calling All Cars

10824 Old Mill Rd., #2

Omaha, NE 68154

TEL: (402) 333-6191 **FAX:** (800) 546-8459

DATE: July

FREQUENCY: Bimonthly

COVER PRICE: $2.95

SUBSCRIPTION PRICE: $14.99

TOTAL NUMBER OF PAGES: 82

TOTAL NUMBER OF AD PAGES: 18

PUBLISHER: David Haggart

EDITOR: Andrew Haggart

Publisher Dave Haggart has been calling all cars since 1985, when he first began helping auto owners sell their wheels beyond local markets by forming a service that offered the vehicles through regional mailings and ads in *Car & Driver, Road & Track* and even *The Wall Street Journal.*

Now Haggart is taking his road show onto the info superhighway (http://www.cacars.com) and has created a new publishing vehicle to enhance the service and to offer, notes the magazine's tag line, "Hundreds of Autos for Sale By Owner." It's a family outing. "My son Andy edits the magazine and does the website," Haggard says. "Andy's wife's a graphic artist — she's got a great eye — so she designs the magazine."

The designer's job is somewhat easy since the magazine's layout is highly formatted: each page contains seven to eight photos of antique, luxury, sports and other exotic cars. Accompanying captions give detailed info on each one plus the name and telephone number of the owner. The offers are hard to size up — readers can't kick these tires — but *Calling All Cars* promises some real deals on wheels: a 1956 Rolls Royce Bentley Silver Cloud Convertible on page 5 of the premiere issue, for instance, is said to be in "excellent condition," yet sells for only $15,800. That's a steal compared to the 1958 Silver Cloud hardtop for sale on the next page for $30,000.

The many choices in this magazine could drive a car-lover mad with joy: a 1931 Ford "A" Sedan ("over $25,000 invested," says its owner who is selling it for $27,500); a 1951 Denzel Roadster 1500 (for only $68,000 thanks to its "vintage race history"); lots of mid-1960s Mustangs put up for sale by Baby Boomers who have now moved on to Tauruses and Accords; and a fleet of 1980s Mercedes, Porsches and BMWs offered by owners who probably now own newer models with built-in cell phones.

Calling All Cars names the models it gets the most calls about (Porsche 911s from 1986 to 1994 top the list, followed by BMW 740s from 1993 and 1994). It also lists upcoming auto racing events, car shows and auctions, a profile of its car-of-the-month (AMG Benz in the premiere issue), plus information on car preservation techniques.

Owners typically pay the Haggards about $200 to market their cars through newspaper ads and direct mail campaigns targeted to dealers, brokers and collectors. Now owners can pay an additional amount ("very reasonable!" insists the senior Haggart) to appear in the pages of their new magazine.

READERSHIP PROFILE: *95% male; average age 43; 70% married, 20% single, 10% divorced or separated; 85% attended college, 55% graduated from college and 20% hold a post-graduate degree; 85% employed, 10% retired, 65% hold a professional position; $80,000 median household income, $110,000 average household income.*

EDITORIAL CONCEPT: *A colorful registry of fine and classic automobiles.*

Coastal Home

PUBLISHED BY: Thomasson Publishing Corp.

203 Lookout Pl., Suite C

Maitland, FL 32751

TEL: (407) 740-6199 **FAX:** (407) 740-7459

FREQUENCY: Bimonthly

COVER PRICE: $3.00

SUBSCRIPTION PRICE: $24.00

TOTAL NUMBER OF PAGES: 138

TOTAL NUMBER OF AD PAGES: 31

PUBLISHER: Jack Thomasson

EDITOR: Sharon Cobb

When dreaming up new magazine startups, what should a publisher do to create a whole new one to compete with the many home-design titles already crowding the market? Relax, lay back, stretch out and just add water. Create a new publication that's like *Architectural Digest* on a day at the beach.

Coastal Home is an elegant chronicle of some of America's most idyllic sand castles. Within its pages the editors invite readers to breathe the salt air, marvel at regal furnishings accentuated with conch shells and exotic sponges discovered on the nearby sands and behold indoor beauty rivaled only by the views just over the window sills.

Overlooking a sapphire expanse of Long Island Sound, for example, one home featured is a contemporary, two-story villa on Pratt Island filled with antiques and such eccentric touches as a ruin-like frieze over the fireplace. The walls have a modernist slant, angled to focus attention on the sea. Another home forsakes walls for vast windows that welcome in Galveston Bay.

A French-styled contemporary chateau on an exclusive barrier island off the California coast, however, was clearly designed for owners less preoccupied by views. Inside is a home theater where a 100-inch-long film screen drops from the ceiling to cover an aquarium. Housed in the nearby cabinetry are two TVs and a highly sensitive sound system designed not to disturb the fish.

The magazine also invites readers to step outside these coastal homes and go beyond the deck chairs. A landscaping article explores the barren shore of Maine where Rockefellers have managed to make daylilies and peonies bloom through granite and where Beatrix Potter once distinguished herself as an "icon in American garden design history" when she wasn't penning *Peter Rabbit* to the sounds of the surf.

For readers who like to live near the water but not muddy their hands, the magazine features condos, too: one near Miami that's owned by European businessmen is appointed with purple Italian sofas that rest on sleek gray floors made of marble cut from the floor of the Aegean.

Ancillary sections tell readers of a new wicker chaise for sale ($1,600), how to make salmon mousse in the shape of a seashell, and the phone numbers to call to buy many of the furnishings featured in the magazine.

Donald Trump purchased his 18-acre Palm Beach estate Mar-a-Lago for $5 million in 1985 and added $3 million in lavish decor. A future edition of *Coastal Home* promises a peek inside.

READERSHIP PROFILE: *60% ages 35 to 49; 43% with household income between $100,000 and $199,000, 28% above $200,000; 57% live in the U.S. Southeast.*

EDITORIAL CONCEPT: *"Stylish interiors, extraordinary architecture, inspirational gardening, irresistible coastal cuisine, tantalizing travel, and gracious living."*

Coffee Journal

PUBLISHED BY: Tiger-Oak Publications Inc.

119 N. 4th St., Suite 211,

Minneapolis, MN 55401

TEL: (612) 338-4125   **FAX:** (612) 338-0532

DATE: June

FREQUENCY: Quarterly

COVER PRICE: $3.95

SUBSCRIPTION PRICE: $12.97

DISCOUNT SUBSCRIPTION PRICE: $22.77 (2 years)

TOTAL NUMBER OF PAGES: 84

TOTAL NUMBER OF AD PAGES: 21.5

PUBLISHER: R. Craig Bednar

EDITOR: Susan Bonne

How hot is coffee? Those new java salons percolating up across America and its TV screens are now joined by *Coffee Journal*, the stimulating new publication for "the coffee and tea lifestyle."

"We're a cross between *Martha Stewart Living* and *The Atlantic Monthly*," says founder Craig Bednar, describing how his publication captures a sophisticated, trendy lifestyle while also including thoughtful articles about contemporary concerns.

Bednar, 31, is also the publisher of *Minnesota Bride*. He started *Coffee Journal* "as a reaction to elements I see going on," he says. "People are again entertaining at home, and you can see that in the plethora of cooking and gardening titles. Gourmet coffees are a part of that kind of lifestyle."

The colorful, 84-page premiere issue is filled to the brim with ads for such upscale products as Godiva Liqueurs, Nikon cameras and popular compact discs, as well as articles about great coffeehouses, Kenyan beans, antique espresso machines and modern automatic coffeemakers. Name contributors include *New York Times* food writer Florence Fabricant, who discusses the impact that East African coffees have had on the world's drinking habits.

"We're definitely about more than a beverage," writes editor Susan Bonne. "There has been a concurrent groundswell in this country to focus on simple, yet quality pleasures: dark bread, organic vegetables, a perfect chair, a luxuriant bath. So another facet of *Coffee Journal*'s mission is to offer editorial that speaks to these values: easy yet rewarding recipes, intriguing fiction, and recommendations for truly worthwhile new products, books and music."

"The interest in coffee that started in the Northwest and has now gone nationwide certainly helped to provide the inspiration for *Coffee Journal*," Bonne adds. "People are eager to explore every permutation of this popular beverage, which has been a part of humanity's diet since the 12th century."

A writer for *The Boston Globe* gave this critique: "When the premiere issue of *Coffee Journal* appeared in the office, a quipping colleague asked if it would keep readers up at night. The straight answer is probably not — we're not talking espresso-strength writing here — but with its handsome design, elegant photos and thoughtful assortment of articles, the slick quarterly may, like a good cup of joe, be a way to ease into the morning. It's a natural for the coffee table."

READERSHIP PROFILE: *60% female; median age 40; 65% married; 83 percent attended college; mean household income $62,000.*

EDITORIAL CONCEPT: *A journal that focuses on the coffee and tea lifestyle.*

Create

PUBLISHED BY: Create Magazine

751 Laurel Street, #335

San Carlos, CA 94070

TEL: (415) 508-9526

DATE: Summer

FREQUENCY: Quarterly

COVER PRICE: $4.95

SUBSCRIPTION PRICE: n/a

TOTAL NUMBER OF PAGES: 100

TOTAL NUMBER OF AD PAGES: 35

PUBLISHERS: Roger Strukhoff, John A. Barry,

Dee Cravens, Chip Woerner

EDITORIAL DIRECTOR: John A. Barry

C*reate* was created for those whose job it is to translate the latest break-throughs in digital technology to film screens, TV tubes, magazine pages and other media.

Articles in the premiere issue offer dramatic stories of the digital revolution. *The San Francisco Examiner* had created its Sunday magazine insert *Image* in 1989, but folded it four years later due to high production costs. In an article titled "Deadline, Flatline, Lifeline," *Create* relates how a new *Examiner Magazine* was born in its place with half the staff of *Image* and costing 80 percent less in production expenses. "Desktop Downhill" tells how a Denver firm that produces ski movies ploughed new terrain in TV shows, magazines, books and on-line services after it learned how to manipulate digital imagery. A profile of video artist Flavio Kampah relates the technological tricks he used to produce the intro to the *American Gladiators* TV show (he captured "original footage on Hi8 video, digitized it with VideoVision Studio and then imported it into Adobe Premiere for compositing"). *Create* also spans more vanguard media: noting that "the average soup-to-nuts cost to develop a good-quality CD-ROM is between $1 million to $4 million," it offers advice on how to use technology to make CD-ROMs more efficiently. A section billed as "Tools of the Trade" offers shorter news items about what else is happening in the digital field, including new software and hardware introductions.

"*Create* is the answer to creative professionals who want to read about and see the work of members of their community," says its publishers. "It's also the answer to technology providers who want to reach the creative community at the creative level. It features top artists doing their best work. It reaches the top tier of design professionals."

As should be expected, the magazine is nicely designed with hip computer graphics (crumpled paper appears as a background to the *Examiner Magazine* article, appropriately), vivid photography (shown at various sizes and scanner resolutions to edify art directors) and text type that can be read easily.

READERSHIP PROFILE: *N/A*

EDITORIAL CONCEPT: *"The resource for integrating digital technology and design."*

DoubleTake

PUBLISHED BY: Center for Documentary Studies

at Duke University

1317 W. Pettigrew St.

Durham, NC 27705

TEL: (919) 660-3669 **FAX:** (919) 681-7600

DATE: Summer

FREQUENCY: Quarterly

COVER PRICE: $10.00

SUBSCRIPTION PRICE: $32.00

DISCOUNT SUBSCRIPTION PRICE: $24.00

TOTAL NUMBER OF PAGES: 128

TOTAL NUMBER OF AD PAGES: 12

EDITORS: Robert Coles, Alex Harris

READERSHIP PROFILE: *N/A*

EDITORIAL CONCEPT: *Photographic essays, fiction, poetry and book reviews make this magazine "a home where image and word have equal weight."*

Just based on its lofty definition, this new literary magazine might have been dismissed as another inaccessible indulgence for the pointy-headed. *DoubleTake* is so named because it's "devoted to the written word and to the visual image, to renderings of the world as it is and as it might be." But when critics picked up the first issue, they did their own double take. *The Village Voice* called it "the most promising magazine debut in years." *Newsweek* found it to be "blunt, unaffected," adding, "it is the young magazine at its best: a snapshot of a culture taken when no one was looking."

DoubleTake was founded by Harvard professor and child psychiatrist Robert Coles and photographer Alex Harris, the team that founded the Center for Documentary Studies at Duke University in 1989. Now they've doubled up to launch a new publication under its auspices. It's a "documentary magazine" chronicling the world in words by such literary icons as Nadine Gordimer and Joyce Carol Oates and in photos that reveal a lot about America: on one coast we see a heartless L.A. street gang; on the other, the heart of a North Carolina town is ripped out when its furniture factory is shut down.

"We chose the name *DoubleTake* because it suggests surprise and reappraisal," Coles says. "Also, it hints at the connection between viewer and subject, reader and renderer. And, we hope, the name implies two distinct modes of observation — image and text."

Newsstand browsers probably did their own double take when they saw the hefty cover price of $10, but inside they got 128 pages of their money's worth. *USA Today* said: "There's some truly excellent writing here, especially Steven Stern's magical story about the flying rabbi of Memphis and novelist Francine Prose's piece on Latin American author Felisberto Hernandez. And don't miss photographer Lee Friedlander's series of wry photos of workers (and nonworkers) at the Dreyfus Fund." *Newsweek* applauded another photo section: "Most striking is a 16-page collection of photos by children documenting their dreams."

DoubleTake has the two-fold mission of promoting the documenters' work and expanding "people's notions of what the word 'documentary' means: creating a vital, enduring record of people from every variety of background; presenting the most ambitious and skillful attempts to render the world, places odd and familiar, and the various ways in which we all struggle to get by and to get along." It contains about 50 pages of photos and 50,000 words of text encompassing fiction, essays and poetry.

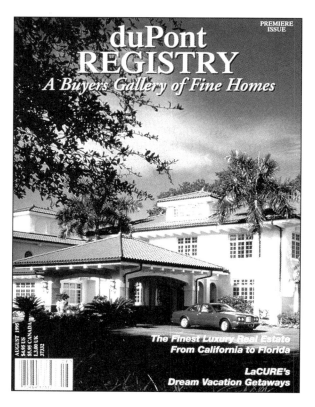

The duPont Registry: A Buyer's Gallery of Fine Homes

PUBLISHED BY: duPont Publishing

P.O. Box 25237

Tampa, FL 33622

TEL: (800) 233-1731 **FAX:** (813)-572-5523

DATE: August

FREQUENCY: Bimonthly

COVER PRICE: $4.95

SUBSCRIPTION PRICE: $29.92

DISCOUNT SUBSCRIPTION PRICE: $24.97

TOTAL NUMBER OF PAGES: 180

TOTAL NUMBER OF AD PAGES: n/a

PUBLISHER: Thomas L. duPont

EDITOR: Eric V. Kennedy

Real-estate guides for the rich and famous don't have to be local. Since the jet set can land anywhere, the typical realtor's credo of "Location! Location! Location!" can easily be answered with "Riviera! Rio! Palm Beach!"

Enter this global real-estate guide published by the editors of *The duPont Registry: A Buyer's Gallery of Fine Automobiles*, which for 10 years has featured cars for sale with sticker prices ranging from $60,000 to $15 million. "Having already driven after the Bentleys and Rolls Royces, duPont Publishing is now pursuing owners of the upper-crust dwellings where you would most likely find such pricey vehicles parked," noted *Inside Media*.

"Our readers kept asking us when we were planning to do similar publications about houses, yachts and planes," elaborates editor Eric Kennedy. "So we decided to test a line extension with this first publication on homes."

Now the entry price tag is a million dollars and the homes are predictably palatial. Readers may not be able to buy the famed Brooklyn Bridge, but for $4 million they can pick up the 40-room home built by its famed engineer Donald Roebling in Clearwater, Florida. On the cover of the premiere issue is another Clearwater home: the Mediterranean-style mansion of former Indy 500 champ Nigel Mansell, which rests on four acres and comes with two guest houses. Price: $13.9 million.

Usually, the identity of owners is kept top secret. "Celebrities insist on privacy," Kennedy adds. "We often can't say who owns what." But star homes do shine in its pages. Ann-Margret and Barry Manilow had properties featured in the premiere issue. Subsequent editions included Eddie Murphy's $5 million Brentwood estate and properties put up for sale by Madonna and Chevy Chase.

Owners and realtors pay to be featured ("We're really a catalog that publishes advertorial," notes Kennedy), but they get lots of room for text and photos. In one case, readers toying with spending $2.5 million for a manor house outside Chicago get more than just a glimpse of the 13-acre estate; they get a 400-word, 9-photo tour. Other properties are shown only in a single photo-with-caption and readers are left wondering why that 1-1/2 acres in California's Pacific Palisades is priced $50,000 cheaper than those two acres in Beverly Hills selling for $2.4 million.

For readers who can't afford luxury full time, there's a section featuring rental properties, some quite reasonable. Faringdon House, a Georgian mansion with a private lake, boathouse and pool in England, seems like a steal at $995 a night considering it includes 7 bedrooms.

Upon seeing the premiere issue, a columnist for *The Chicago Sun-Times* wrote: "Seeing that much pricey real estate is plenty disorienting. As you flip through the pages, pretty soon you start scoffing at anything under a couple of million."

READERSHIP PROFILE: *N/A*

EDITORIAL CONCEPT: *"Real estate for the elite."*

Eligible

PUBLISHED BY: Eligible Inc.

P.O. Box 17625

Encino, CA 91416-7625

TEL: (818) 709-1736

DATE: Summer

FREQUENCY: Quarterly

COVER PRICE: $2.95

SUBSCRIPTION PRICE: $11.50

TOTAL NUMBER OF PAGES: 74

TOTAL NUMBER OF AD PAGES: 18

PUBLISHER: Katherine Duliakas

EDITOR: Sada Volkoff

A good man is not really so hard to find, according to this new magazine, *Eligible*, formerly *L.A. Eligible*. Many bachelors are simply — what else? — misunderstood if we're to believe the likes of one man profiled in its pages, Neil Balter, who offers women not only hope, but millions if he finds the right one. "Most people see me as this playboy, when I'd rather be the family man," the entrepreneurial tycoon insists.

Publisher Kathy Duliakas believes that enough people are looking for serious relationships to justify her starting a publication for them. She came up with the idea while clerking at a California supermarket where she daydreamed of finding Mr. Right as she straightened out the magazine racks when things were slow. The answer to her quest, she decided, was right in her hands.

To find a man, she decided to found a magazine, which she accomplished by raising $50,000 in private investment funds and then adding her own life's savings. In 1994, she launched *L.A. Eligible*. One year later she dropped the magazine's regional Los Angeles focus and relaunched it as a national publication. Soon it was sold on the same magazine racks she used to straighten out at the supermarket.

"My message is that it's OK to be single," Duliakas says. "Women like myself are looking for men to share our lives, not make them."

But what are men looking for? *Eligible* asked one bachelor, David Silverman, and got an answer that's somewhat predictable for an animator of *The Simpsons*: "A sense of humor." Anthony Domino Giovanni, "a tough-talking, rapid-fire DJ," said he likes women "who aren't afraid to do things." His idea of a great first date is to take a woman balloon-riding and jet-skiing.

Duliakas insists that "eligible" refers to the women who read the magazine, not the men profiled inside it, so *Eligible* includes career and lifestyle articles for female readers, a fashion section, a horoscope and personals. But it's also full of lots of eligible men who reveal what they're really looking for in a mate.

Eligible scored a coup in its first national issue by securing an interview with Latin soul singer Jon Secada, who bared his soul. "I am not particular to skin color or even a certain look," he says. "It is the entire package, the way a person carries oneself." What kind of woman is he looking for? "Someone who is smart and who I can communicate with. Someone who is honest, sincere, who loves me for who I am and not for what I have. I will give my all." In return, he would like to have children with the woman he marries and someday he'd like to take them all to visit his native Cuba after Castro falls.

READERSHIP PROFILE: N/A

EDITORIAL CONCEPT: *Formerly LA's Eligible, the magazine features articles and information for the independent woman.*

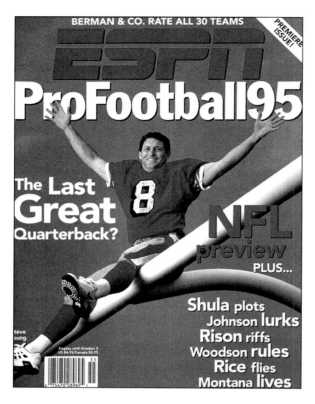

ESPN ProFootball '95
ESPN ProBasketball '95
ESPN College Basketball
ESPN: The Year in Sports

PUBLISHED BY: The Hearst Corp.

959 Eighth Ave.

New York, NY 10019

TEL: (212) 649-2000

FREQUENCY: Specials

COVER PRICE: $4.95

TOTAL NUMBER OF PAGES 164 (Pro Football),

156 (Pro Basketball), 156 (College Basketball),

156 (Year in Sports)

TOTAL NUMBER OF AD PAGES: 26 (Pro Football),

21 (Pro Basketball), 26 (College Basketball),

22 (Year in Sports)

PUBLISHER: John Mack Carter

EDITOR: Gary Hoenig

Testing the muscle of the *ESPN* brand name, Hearst, a 20 percent owner of the sports cable network, published special previews to the 1995 NFL football, NBA basketball and college basketball seasons, plus a wrap-up of the year in sports.

According to their editorial game plan, the new magazines promised to recruit "some of the best sports writers in the country, *ESPN* experts, former players and on-air personalities to tell fans what happens in the locker room, on the field and in the huddle." Once the finished product hit the newsstands in mid-summer, *The Baltimore Sun* prophesized that the new publications "could provide an interesting challenge to the venerable *Sports Illustrated* down the road."

Sun writer Milton Kent added that the first magazine, the NFL preview, is "slickly packaged with dazzling graphics and heavy on analysis and features from freelance writers, the best of which are profiles of Pittsburgh Steelers cornerback Rod Woodson, Cleveland Browns receiver Andre Rison and Miami Dolphins coach Don Shula."

An often playful editorial spirit helped to distinguish the new *ESPN* title from the competition. "Drew Learns to Read" read a sassy headline to an article on how New England Patriot QB Bledsoe "has become adept at reading defenses, at the cat-and-mouse game quaterbacks play with defensive coordinators." "There are 53 players on the Chicago Bears," noted another headline, adding the in-your-face dare: "Name one."

The heart of each preview magazine was its team-by-team sneak peaks. In the NBA issue, editors warned the Chicago Bulls to "just keep the straitjacket handy." In its college hoops edition, editors picked Kansas to carry the ball and did so without apology, noting that since the magazine isn't *Sports Illustrated*, "There's no jinx here — yet."

Looking back over 1995, the year-end issue noted that "U.C.L.A. had been upstaged by UConn women and the Mariners had outfought Mike Tyson."

Contributors include *ESPN GameDay* host Chris Berman and analyst Chris Mortensen, as well as an impressive team of leading sports writers from the nation's top dailies, such as *The Washington Post, Chicago Sun-Times* and *Detroit Free Press.*

READERSHIP PROFILE: *90% male; median age 30; 50% married; 55% graduated college, 85% attended and/or graduated college; median household income $40,000; 50% in professional and/or managerial jobs.*

EDITORIAL CONCEPT: *The complete resource for those seeking the inside line on NFL football, NBA basketball and college basketball, with previews and scouting reports.*

Fast Company

PUBLISHED BY: Fast Company Inc.

2400 N. St., NW

Washington, DC 20037-1196

TEL: (617) 927-2240

FREQUENCY: Bimonthly

COVER PRICE: $3.95

SUBSCRIPTION PRICE: n/a

TOTAL NUMBER OF PAGES: 178

TOTAL NUMBER OF AD PAGES: 94

PUBLISHER: Thomas R. Evans

EDITOR: Bill Breen

Disgruntled by their jobs at the *Harvard Business Review* and dissatisfied by what they were reading in competitive publications, two young editors decided to go into business for themselves by founding a new "handbook for the business revolution" for the next generation of corporate leaders.

Alan Webber and William Taylor raised enough private capital in 1993 to get *Fast Company* off the ground, printing 30,000 copies of a pilot test issue. They quickly realized they needed a large company as partners, however, and took *Fast Company*'s test results to Mortimer B. Zuckerman and Fred Drasner, publishers of *U.S. News & World Report* and *The Atlantic Monthly*.

Zuckerman and Drasner relaunched *Fast Company* by giving 800,000 subscribers of *U.S. News & World Report* a condensed 32-page preview in its October 31 issue, followed up seven days later by a newsstand drop of 250,000 copies, each thick with 96 ad pages that were the result of a spirited assault on Madison Avenue led by the *U.S. News* sales team. Four issues were planned for 1996; a regular monthly frequency was set for 1997.

"Our target audience is business people who are old enough to make a difference, but young enough to be different," says Taylor, describing his readers, aged 25 to 45. He and Webber wanted *Fast Company* to have a characteristically zippy, youthful design. "The look of FC is pure *Rolling Stone* right down to the James Pendergast cartoon," *MediaWeek* said about the result. Webber acknowledged that, when he and his art director were preparing the premiere issue, his instructions were "to make it caffeinated."

The articles are pretty perky, too. One describes how factories can best be run on the chaos theory, and there's a profile of at least one truly fast company ("Netscape has one strategy: speed"). A personality profile relates how the manager of the world's largest superconductor factory bounced back from a heart attack that hit him at age 36. And forget corporate climbing: *Fast Company* eggs on young professionals to scale Wyoming's Grand Teton under the headline "The Higher You Go, The Farther You See." Tips are also included on how to utilize career counselers, negotiate everyday business terms and field brainbusters tossed out during job interviews.

Webber and Taylor positioned their publication to compete more with business management magazines like *Fortune* than the newsy *BusinessWeek* or the financial advice titles like *SmartMoney*. To distinguish *Fast Company* from *Fortune*, the duo employ all the brashness and bravado of youth to diss the latter's editors. "They're living in the old world," Taylor griped to *The Boston Globe*, "and every so often they go on vacation to the new world. We really want to live in that new world."

When *Fast Company* hit the newsstands, *MediaWeek* contacted *Fortune*'s new editor-in-chief John Huey for comment. "I'm going to run out and take a look at it," he said. "And you can rest assured that if there's anything good in it, we'll appropriate it."

READERSHIP PROFILE: N/A

EDITORIAL CONCEPT: *"The new rules of business" for fast-paced, young professionals.*

Figurines & Collectibles

PUBLISHED BY: Cowles Magazines

6405 Flank Dr.

Harrisburg, PA 17112

TEL: (717) 657-9555 **FAX:** (717) 540-6728

DATE: May

FREQUENCY: Bimonthly

COVER PRICE: $3.95

SUBSCRIPTION PRICE: $23.70

TOTAL NUMBER OF PAGES: 100

TOTAL NUMBER OF AD PAGES: 28

PUBLISHER: David L. Miller

EDITOR: David L. Miller

When the first issue of *Figurines & Collectibles* hit newsstands in May, it contained the hottest news in the figurine scene: the availability of new porcelain reproductions of the covered bridges of Madison County, Iowa. The figurines — and the magazine — scooped the Clint Eastwood/Meryl Streep movie.

Elsewhere in the issue were porcelain, resin, crystal and glass renderings of mischievous children, fat cats, overdressed Victorians, frowning sisters, smiling pigs, frogs, penguins, raccoons and Dumbos, and a surprisingly swank Barbie in a black gown with plunging neckline.

How lucrative is such collecting? The magazine notes that Disney's Big Bad Wolf, the figurine traded most frequently in 1994, was originally issued for $295 and now is reportedly worth $750 to $895. The seventh-most traded "Little Pals" had a much better return on investment. Issued for only $95 in 1985, the figurine of a clown with two puppies poking out of his pants "now commands $2,200 to $3,500 on the secondary market," the magazine maintains.

Figurines & Collectibles features works from such top manufacturers as Lladro, Swarovski, M.I. Hummel, Royal Doulton, Enesco, Department 56 and others. Articles include profiles of top-selling artists. Charts reveal figurines' original issue prices and quotes on their current value.

Figurines & Collectibles supplies "both the advertiser and the reader with a vehicle to sell and buy figurines, and to establish a network of information," says its promotional material. "It is the only magazine available on the newsstands today that appeals directly to the heart of the figurine collector."

Figurines & Collectibles was launched by Cowles Magazines Collectibles Group, which also publishes *Doll Reader* and *Teddy Bear and Friends*. It was designed as a competitor to *Collector's Edition* and *Collector's Mart*, two publications that are "still crossing trade and consumer interests," *Figurines* publisher and editor David L. Miller told *Inside Media*. "Those magazines have from three to seven pages concerning figurines. Our whole magazine [100 pages] is figurines, so, if you are a collector, go figure which magazine will best suit your interest."

Miller maintains that there are millions of people who belong to figurine clubs and who regularly attend shows held every weekend across the country.

The magazine is distributed at these shows and is sold at newsstands, supermarkets, specialty gift and collectible stores and Barnes & Noble and Walden bookstores. Two special issues appeared in 1995 with a rate base of 80,000. A regular bimonthly publishing frequency was planned for the spring of 1996.

READERSHIP PROFILE: *91.4% female; average age 46; average household income $60,000; 22.4% reside in the U.S. Northeast, 19.4% in the Pacific region.*

EDITORIAL CONCEPT: *"The first magazine devoted exclusively to the world of figurine collectors."*

Fusion

PUBLISHED BY: Decker Publications Inc.

1920 Highland Ave., Suite 222

Lombard, IL 60148

TEL: (708) 916-7222 **FAX:** (708) 916-7227

DATE: August

FREQUENCY: Monthly

COVER PRICE: $3.99

SUBSCRIPTION PRICE: $23.95

TOTAL NUMBER OF PAGES: 116

TOTAL NUMBER OF AD PAGES: 27

PUBLISHER: Steve Harris

EDITOR: Bill Kunkel

What do the '80s punk rock group Devo (remember "Whip It"?), Bob Dylan and Pope John Paul II all have in common? They're all featured on new CD-ROMs. How about the Rolling Stones, Michael Jordan and Bart Simpson? In the Internet Age, remember, everyone has a website.

"Multimedia, electronic entertainment, the Internet and pop culture are all merging together, transforming traditional entertainment," reports the publishers of *Fusion*, which is anticipating a nuclear-sized reaction from readers since it dares to "investigate it all under one title."

In the premiere issue, the editors insist that *Fusion* is "more than just video games and computer curios. It is the first magazine to address all aspects of electronic entertainment — from the alternate realities living inside your PC to the man-made realities in film."

Fusion fuses together a broad range of opposing subjects. The cover story chronicles the battle between telephone companies and cable systems to become the king of broadband transmission and an inside piece reports on new groups formed to protect consumer interests ("Don't ignore the business behind the static curtain!" its writer cries). A sidebar asks industry leaders the provocative question "Will broadband replace the Internet?" but then the answers turn out to be anti-climatic when readers learn that none of them think it will.

Other features include a profile of Atari founder Nolan Bushnell, whose new venture E2000 is "halfway between Atari and Chuck E. Cheese," his other previous success. There's also a history of the 3DO Company, which has so far failed in its mission to "create a universal hardware and software standard for interactive media." Disney's Buena Vista Movie Web gets the nod from the editors for being Hollywood's top web site, beating out *Batman Forever* and *The Simpsons* site that's still probing the cliffhanger "Who Shot Mr. Burns?"

Reviews of games come with grades: Comix Zone scores an "A," beating out other video console games like Judge Dredd, which loses points not only for technical difficulties, but also because of "the greater issue of Dredd as an inappropriate role model." A CD focusing on the use of computer technology to alter photographs scores highest among computer offerings.

READERSHIP PROFILE: *N/A*

EDITORIAL CONCEPT: *"The magazine of interactive entertainment."*

Gambero Rosso

PUBLISHED BY: Gambero Rosso Inc.

5 East 22nd St.

New York, NY 10010

TEL: 212-388-9449 **FAX:** 212-388-9453

DATE: Winter

FREQUENCY: Quarterly

COVER PRICE: $4.95

SUBSCRIPTION PRICE: $15.85

TOTAL NUMBER OF PAGES: 100

TOTAL NUMBER OF AD PAGES: 14

PUBLISHER: Stefano Bonilla

EDITOR: Stefano Bonilla

"Gambero rosso" means "red shrimp," the most common name of restaurants and pizzerie throughout Italy. It was also the name of the fictional tavern where Pinocchio was scammed out of his gold coins by two devious conmen (conanimals?) known as the Cat and the Fox. According to *Gambero Rosso*'s editor-in-chief Stefano Bonilli, "The mission of this magazine is to protect Pinocchio's real-life counterparts — innocents abroad as well as trusting customers at home — from finding themselves at the mercy of padded bills, lumpy beds, gruff service, watery wine or mediocre food."

The new quarterly U.S. magazine is an addition to Gambero Rosso Inc.'s menu of publications, which includes a monthly counterpart in Italy and numerous guides to Italian wines, eateries, food stores and cities. Recognized as "a voice of authority" in Italy, the company figures that Americans with an amore for the Italian lifestyle will be interested in hearing what it has to say.

The Washington Post had this to say: "We caught up with the second issue and are still happily wandering vicariously through the neighborhoods of Rome." Readers won't get lost making their way through the magazine. Each issue is laid out in three parts: food, wine and travel.

The premiere issue picks cabbages as the vegetable of focus and serves up more than a half dozen recipes using such cabbage offspring as broccoli and brussels sprouts. A day spent with the owner of a Manhattan restaurant visiting his suppliers introduces readers to a former computer engineer who now works as a cheese artisan, a landscape-architect-turned-vegetable-farmer and a marine-biologist-turned-oyster-grower. (His process involves "inseminating the oysters in a tank.")

The next course in the first issue is a review of the 92 Italian wines to be awarded Tre Biccheri, or "Three Glasses," its greatest toast. According to Bonilli, "The 'three glasses' rating we award to only a handful of the thousands of wines we review on a yearly basis is a coveted and influential laurel." The reviews include suggested serving temperatures and meals to accompany the wines.

The journey through the first issue ends up in Tuscany, as the editors chart the "warm sea, rolling hills and gentle weather" of Bolgheri and visit the small hotel L'oroscopo, with 12 restaurant tables and 12 guest rooms to match the signs of the zodiac.

READERSHIP PROFILE: *N/A*

EDITORIAL CONCEPT: *Exporing wine, travel and food in Italy.*

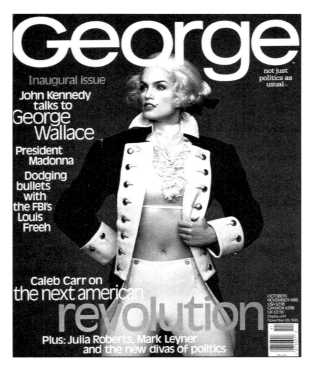

George

PUBLISHED BY: Hachette Filipacchi

1633 Broadway

New York, NY 10019

TEL: (212) 767-6000

DATE: September

FREQUENCY: Bimonthly

COVER PRICE: $2.95

SUBSCRIPTION PRICE: $9.97

TOTAL NUMBER OF PAGES: 284

TOTAL NUMBER OF AD PAGES: 175

PUBLISHER: Michael J. Berman

EDITOR: John F. Kennedy, Jr.

It may have been called *George*, but the new magazine was really about a man named John — or John-John as he had been called back in the days when he was still the Prince of Camelot.

George was named after America's first president and founded by the son of its 35th. The senior John Kennedy had once worked as a reporter for Hearst newspapers when he was still a young man. Now his only male offspring was trailblazing a new form of journalism in a magazine that wed politics with show-biz. "Many experts doubt the *George* concept can work," wrote *BusinessWeek*, echoing a widespread skepticism that JFK Jr. could launch such a hybrid of a new magazine, even though he was backed with an estimated $20 million from Hachette Filipacchi. Undaunted, the budding editor-in-chief traversed the nation while writing an article (an interview with former Alabama Governor George Wallace), assigning others and making ad sales calls. His peers in the press hovered at every turn. So did admirers of the opposite sex. When Kennedy called on ad agencies in Detroit, it was reported that young female account executives postponed their honeymoons and vacations just to meet him.

When Kennedy and partner/ publisher Mike Berman finally unveiled the "inaugural issue," 200 reporters packed Federal Hall in New York City where George Washington once took the presidential oath of office. The new magazine was equally packed with ads — 175, a near record. Only one magazine — *PC Sources* — had ever been introduced with more. *George* was also packed with noteworthy editorial.

On the cover, just under the tag line "Not Just Politics As Usual," was a provocative photo of supermodel Cindy Crawford dressed like a rather becoming George W. in drag. Inside were revealing articles tattling on who in Washington D.C. spouts the most news leaks (George Stephanopoulos) and profiling who causes Newt Gingrich the most angst (his lesbian half-sister Candace). Comedian Al Franken offered a "modest proposal" for cutting the federal budget ("Why not shoot the elderly into space?") and Madonna spouted off on what she'd do if she were president ("Howard Stern would get kicked out of the country and Roman Polanski would be allowed back in").

What was the final vote on *George?* Magazine buyers loved it, buying 97% of the first 550,000 copies. Some of Kennedy's editorial peers scoffed at the heavy dash of Hollywood in a political magazine, but he begged for more time for the fledging publication to prove itself.

"I expected some attention," Kennedy told *Newsday* after the blockbuster launch, "but the degree of it has surprised me. I mean, it's not like we've invented a new form of transportation or a cure for a major disease. We're only doing a magazine."

READERSHIP PROFILE: *Ages 25-44; $47,299, median household income; 61% attended college.*

EDITORIAL CONCEPT: *"Not just politics as usual," this magazine blends the worlds of politics and entertainment to form a new niche.*

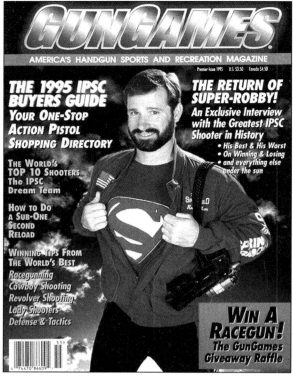

Gun Games

PUBLISHED BY: Wallyworld Publishing Inc.

P.O. Box 516

Moreno Valley, CA 92556

TEL: (909) 485-7986 **FAX:** (909) 485-6628

DATE: June

FREQUENCY: Bimonthly

COVER PRICE: $3.50

SUBSCRIPTION PRICE: $16.95

DISCOUNT SUBSCRIPTION PRICE: $44.95 (3 Years)

TOTAL NUMBER OF PAGES: 90

TOTAL NUMBER OF AD PAGES: 22

PUBLISHER: Wally Arida

EDITOR: Wally Arida

Gun Games aims to prove wrong the admonishment that people should never play with firearms. It bills itself as "America's handgun and recreation magazine" and is devoted to covering shooting games. It also publishes profiles of notable marksmen and gun industry leaders, a directory of shooting clubs, a calendar of championship shooting events, a buyer's guide to various models, and performance tips such as how to improve one's single-action revolver grip written by world champs.

Firearms Business notes: "Publisher Wally Arida sees his magazine as a route for the industry to take a new direction in promotion and marketing — a direction that presents a more positive image for gun owners. He sees a magazine that glorifies the games instead of the gore in the gun business."

"Shooting is more exciting than golf or television," insists Arida. "There's a major shooting event going on every weekend in this country, yet the only shooting that gets publicity in major newspapers is the weekend drive-bys."

His solution is this new magazine aimed at the fun-loving side of the 80 million handgun owners in America.

Games featured in the magazine include Western Fast Draw (you'll need to modify your Colt, Colt-clone or Ruger single-action revolver to achieve the best score, say the experts), cowboy action shooting (try a shotgun) and shooting bowling pins off tables (knock 'em down with a Smith & Wesson Model 27 using 200-grain, .38 Special bullets). The editors even play their own games, one of them inviting readers to identify a "celebrity" by a photo of a tattoo that depicts a man with a Beneli shotgun blasting through a window. "Could it be the 1994 U.S. Limited Ladies Champion with her trademark stars-and-stripes baseball cap?" the editors asked teasingly. Nope. Readers are supposed to know what grandmaster Jamie Craig looks like without a shirt.

The premiere issue hit the newsstands on June 6. "Arida claims the 88-page issue broke even or made a little money, a near-unprecedented feat in the magazine publishing business," *Firearms Business* said. Arida described his goal for the future: "I believe we can have professional shooters just as we have professional golfers, and I hope that by the end of next year, there's a circuit of major shooting events like golf or tennis."

READERSHIP PROFILE: *N/A*

EDITORIAL CONCEPT: *"America's handgun sports and recreation magazine."*

Home Garden

PUBLISHED BY: Meredith Corp.

1716 Locust St.

Des Moines, IA 50309-3023

TEL: (515) 284-2335

DATE: March/April

FREQUENCY: Bimonthly

COVER PRICE: $3.99

SUBSCRIPTION PRICE: $19.97

TOTAL NUMBER OF PAGES: 140

TOTAL NUMBER OF AD PAGES: 38

PUBLISHER: Catherine Potkay Westberg

EDITOR: Douglas A. Jaimerson

Gardening titles seem to be sprouting up everywhere in the 1990s: Hearst created *Country Living Gardener* in 1992; Meigher Communications relaunched *Garden Design* in 1994, the same year Rodale tested *Organic Flower Gardening*; in 1995, Gruner & Jahr repositioned *American Homestyle* by adding *Gardening* to its title. The top budding new title of 1995 was *Home Garden*, introduced by Meredith one year before Condé Nast planned to dig up its old *House & Garden*.

What's behind the boom in blooms? Baby boomers, now grown up and putting down roots, are suddenly more than just interested in eating arugala; they want to grow it. More than 78 million Americans dirtied their hands in 1994, a dramatic 28 percent hike since 1991.

In charge of pruning the new title for Meredith was Douglas Jimerson, garden editor of *Better Homes & Gardens*, who told *The New York Times*, "As baby boomers put finishing touches on the inside of their houses, the logical place for them to turn their attention to is outside."

Home Garden is "for those who like gardening, but aren't out to recreate Versailles," says publisher Cathy Westerberg.

Meredith positioned *Home Garden* as a major start-up, promising a 400,000 rate base for the first issue and telling advertisers that it expected circulation to grow quickly. Westerberg adds: "Meredith wants us to be the dominant gardening magazine and that means a certain level of circulation. We hope to hit 800,000 to one million."

"*Home Garden* represents Meredith's largest circulation launch in five years," added *Inside Media*. "The company initiated a two-million piece, direct-mail effort in December [1994], and will do another in March [1995]."

Initial circulation shot up faster than the execs had planned. "*Home Garden* is flying off of New York City newsstands," *Crain's New York Business* reported soon after the first issue came out. "It sold out three times in Grand Central terminal alone and Meredith upped its print order by 150,000 copies to keep up with demand."

Rapid sales were more than just a testimony to flower power. *USA Today* applauded the new magazine's content, saying, "the features are lively and informative." Articles spanned straightforward pieces like "Practical Roses for Hard Places" to peeks into idyllic private gardens like "An Anglophile's Eden," the handiwork of a California homeowner who went "bloomin' mad for the lushness and artistry of the English cottage look."

READERSHIP PROFILE: *78% female; median age 43; 68% married; 74% attended and/or graduated from college; median household income $52,500; 32% employed in professional/managerial positions.*

EDITORIAL CONCEPT: *Celebrates the rewards of a garden and offers practical ideas for those with a passion for gardening and outdoor living.*

Infobahn

PUBLISHED BY: Postmodern Communications

985 E. Hillsdale Blvd., Suite 88

Foster City, CA 94404

TEL: n/a **FAX:** n/a

FREQUENCY: Bimonthly

COVER PRICE: $4.95

SUBSCRIPTION PRICE: $24.95

TOTAL NUMBER OF PAGES: 90

TOTAL NUMBER OF AD PAGES: 26

PUBLISHER: Michael C. Berch

EDITOR: Michael C. Berch

Infobahn purports to be "the magazine of Internet culture," thereby distinguishing itself from the many clones among other new computer and Internet titles. "We're perfectly happy to leave the lists of Cool Web Sites and newsgroups and other resources to other magazines and Internet guidebooks," says editor and publisher Michael C. Berch in his letter to readers of the premiere issue. "Same for 'how-to' articles and instructions on how to use basic Internet software.

"There are no sacred cows at *Infobahn* and no unchallengeable assumptions," he adds. "This means that practically every article will manage to offend someone."

In fact, the only thing that could be considered offensive in its pages is the preachiness the magazine sometimes employs when stating the obvious as brilliant insight. In the lofty treatise "The Geopolitics of Cyberspace," the writer warns against being drawn into the Net by evil forces: "The problem lies not in the propaganda that is obviously propaganda but in the propaganda that is not." The whole point of an article titled "The Internet As Igloo" is summed up in its final sentence meant to be bone-chilling: "We are all in the same igloo."

The magazine starts being fun when it stops taking itself so seriously and decides to eavesdrop on skinheads over on the alt.skinheads web site in order to find out what they're up to. The surprising answer: they're trading shaving tips.

Infobahn's most probing article is its profile of a man whose life is devoted to outwitting such cybersnooping. Paul Zimmerman created a new program to encode e-mail in order to fend off unwelcome eyes, but instead he ended up having to fend off patent lawyers wanting to sue him and federal investigators wanting to toss him in jail. Zimmerman fights on, he says, because "for government to take cryptography away is for government to take away the right to private conversation."

Infobahn also includes book reviews, far-out fiction and essays that ponder how today's info superhighway compares to America's old Route 66 ("instead of dreaming West, we are nudged to dream out into yet another final frontier, cyberspace," it gushes). This magazine is at its best, though, when it takes a mischievous turn. One of its most enjoyable articles reports on skirmishes between two newsgroups: when members of alt.bigfoot retaliated for a raid from alt.suicide.holiday, they bombarded the latter web site with "exaggerated poems on depression and sadness."

READERSHIP PROFILE: *N/A*

EDITORIAL CONCEPT: *"The magazine of Internet culture."*

InQuest

PUBLISHED BY: Gareb Shamus Enterprises Inc./

Wizard Press

151 Wells Avenue

Congers, NY 10920-2064

TEL: (914) 268-3594

DATE: May

FREQUENCY: Monthly

COVER PRICE: $3.50

SUBSCRIPTION PRICE: $24.95

TOTAL NUMBER OF PAGES: 84

TOTAL NUMBER OF AD PAGES: 19

PUBLISHER: Gareb S. Shamus

EDITOR: Pat McCallum

So whatever happened to those kids in high school who stayed home on Saturday nights to play *Dungeons & Dragons*? Some of them have conjured up *InQuest*, a new full-color magazine exploring the world of fantasy card games.

Evidently, *Dungeons & Dragons* has been overpowered by a new sensation *Magic: The Gathering*, which editor Pat McCallum says "breathed new life into [the gaming] industry" when it cast its spell over a huge number of buyers. The rest of the *InQuest* staff seems to be just as bewitched by it since the game dominates the editorial content of the magazine. A column on "Stumpers" answers reader questions about guidelines for playing the game; 24 pages of the 30-page pricing guide lists how much people are paying for it (the Alpha Set alone, with 295 cards, costs $2,750); and *Magic* triumphs over all others in "Ultimate Chaos!," a feature that finds the *InQuest* editors pitted in an all-out war to determine the best fantasy card game (*Dixie* and *Star Trek* are the first to be shot down).

What makes this magazine about games fun is its often comical spirit. A chart comparing the popularity of vampires places Count Chocula neck and neck with Vampira and Blacula. (In the "Confirmed Kills" category, Blacula scores "none, but some detective found a bloody glove.") An actual game called *Vampire: The Masquerade* casts light on the night stalker's origin and history. Readers' attention will likely be drained, however, by a long and dry interview with the production manager behind (what else?) *Magic: The Gathering*.

Rules for contests announced in the magazine appear under the heading "Legal Lingo" and restrict "employees of *Wizard Press*, their immediate families, and anybody who offs people with the Channel/Fireball combination." And the letters page, dubbed "Inquisition," begins by asking "How the hell do we have a letters page when this is our first issue?" It responds jokingly: "Good question. The answer — We made 'em up."

Anyone who doesn't know the difference between a Kudzu and the Ring of Ma'ruf will be lost in *InQuest*, but the "News & Notes" column alone, which demystifies the new products and developments in the industry, may be enough to lure fantasy fans inside.

READERSHIP PROFILE: *90% male; median age in the low 20s; average of $110 spent per month on collectible card games.*

EDITORIAL CONCEPT: *Devoted to the world of collectible card games.*

the journal of eatin' drinkin' & screwin' round

JUiCE

brews·booze·food & fun

Juice

PUBLISHED BY: Loco Lobos

P.O. Box 9068

Berkeley, CA 94709

TEL: (510) 548-0697

DATE: 1995

FREQUENCY: Bimonthly

COVER PRICE: $4.95

SUBSCRIPTION PRICE: $24.00

DISCOUNT SUBSCRIPTION PRICE: $19.95

TOTAL NUMBER OF PAGES: 64

TOTAL NUMBER OF AD PAGES: 20

PUBLISHER: Chick Wolf

EDITOR: Fred Dodsworth

Canned from his job as editor and art director of *Beer: The Magazine*, Fred Dodsworth decided to squeeze out a new magazine from his garage. He explains the philosophy of *Juice,* the self-proclaimed "journal of eatin', drinkin' & screwin' 'round," in his introductory column: "Life is very simple. *Sex* is nature's consolation prize for the big green weenie of death. *Food* is the consolation prize for not getting enough sex. And alcohol, it should be fairly obvious, is the mechanism (in moderation) by which we override our other operating systems so we can get more sex or food."

There's nothing moderate about the first issue, with articles like "Irish Whiskey True," which pores over the politics of whiskey-drinking, and "Brewpub Luv," which broods over the "sexual strategy of the beer joint." But some of what *Juice* serves is flat: "Neo (Drinkin') Women," an article with women sharing their memories of beer-drinking experiences is filled with drivel like "Beer is my friend. Suckin' down beer with your pals just can't be beat" and "I knew at that moment we'd be friends. And that's what beer's all about."

Dodsworth knows how to make a splash with the press. *Juice*'s arrival at the newsstands was covered by dailies like *The Chicago Tribune* ("It's about the gestalt of things we put into our mouths .... It's heavy on ads and freewheeling text about the liquid aspects of life") and *The L.A. Times* ("It likes to do what most food magazines don't: run features that use the word 'ain't' a lot, eschew the use of those funny French phrases, and remind their readers often that the pretty '93 Voignier the other guys wax rhapsodic about exist mostly to get you ripped."). *Inside Media* called *Juice* "a hedonist's guide to the galaxy of brews, booze, food and fun. Its editorial, thin on recipe, is stuffed with funky fonts and saucy opinion pieces."

Other new Epicurean magazines like *Coffee Journal* and *Gambero Rosso* won't need to worry about competing with *Juice* for ad dollars: Heineken and Samuel Adams, not gourmet coffees or Italian wines, make up most of the 20 pages of ads in the first issue.

READERSHIP PROFILE: *N/A*

EDITORIAL CONCEPT: *"The journal of eatin', drinkin', and screwin' 'round."*

LottoWorld

PUBLISHED BY: Lotto World Inc.

2150 Googlette Rd., Suite 200

Naples, FL 33940-4811

TEL: (941) 643-1677 **FAX:** (941) 263-0809

DATE: May

FREQUENCY: Biweekly

COVER PRICE: $1.75

SUBSCRIPTION PRICE: $29.97

DISCOUNT SUBSCRIPTION PRICE: n/a

TOTAL NUMBER OF PAGES: 82

TOTAL NUMBER OF AD PAGES: 30

PUBLISHER: Dennis B. Schroeder

EDITOR: Rich Holman

All magazine start-ups may be considered a gamble, but the backers of *LottoWorld* really anteed up. Investors chipped in $7 million to prove that America's first lottery magazine could hit the publishing jackpot.

LottoWorld was originally tested on the newsstands in 1993 and then rolled out nationally in June, 1995, targeted to the 30 million Americans who spend $30 billion a year on lotteries in 37 states and the District of Columbia. The digest-sized biweekly hoped to reach a circulation of 1 million by year's end and 3 million by 1997.

"Seventy-one percent of the adult population plays the lottery," notes editor Richard Holman. "Until now, they had no magazine. We want this to be the *TV Guide* of the lotto-playing public."

Holman and his partner, publisher Dennis Schroeder, had worked together at USF&G but were laid off during a staff squeeze in 1991. They tested the idea for their new business venture, *LottoWorld*, in 1993 by raising $350,000 in seed money from 16 private investors. What was it like to switch from the insurance game to publishing where everyone plays without a net? "Businesses all have the same components," Holman says. "Advertising, sales, personnel and distribution."

The magazine appears in 23 state editions sold at supermarket and convenience-store checkout newsstands where it competes with the gossip tabloids by using such sassy cover lines as "Wynonna Judd's Winning Numbers Revealed" and "Capital Cop Cashes In: Badge, Cruise Numbers Hit for $100,000 Jackpot."

LottoWorld gives readers practical advice on picking winning numbers plus offers more whimsical ways, too, such as using favorite celebrities' birthdays, ages and other vital star stats that it publishes. "We want to help readers learn techniques that will improve their chances," Holman says. "A lot don't understand this is possible." The magazine also advises winners on how to spend their newfound wealth. There are listings of state gambling hotlines, and even the horoscope is lottery specific. Sagittarians are told to "pick an aunt's birthday." Pisces players are warned to heed "the loudmouth at work who grates on your nerves. She does have excellent lotto tips."

Most dubious is the advice doled out by stars in the magazine's feature articles. TV's Robin Leach may be an expert on the lifestyles of the rich and famous, but not necessarily on how they got that way. "I have the lucky numbers 29 and 8 and 41 that I always punch in," he says. "Did I win? No, but I still believe that I can."

READERSHIP PROFILE: *52 percent male; 39 percent white collar; 42, average age; $45,000 average household income.*

EDITORIAL CONCEPT: *"America's lottery magazine." Featuring editorials and articles on how to play the lottery plus testimonies from winners.*

Modern America

PUBLISHED BY: Modern America Publishing Inc.

1075 NW Murray Rd., Suite 196

Portland, OR 97229-5501

TEL: (800) 220-8541

DATE: Summer

FREQUENCY: Quarterly

COVER PRICE: $3.00

SUBSCRIPTION PRICE: $10.00

TOTAL NUMBER OF PAGES: 78

TOTAL NUMBER OF AD PAGES: 8

PUBLISHER: David W. Edwards

EDITOR: David W. Edwards

Modern America poses the question "What does America stand for?" and adds, provocatively, "Our answers may surprise you."

But the responses are often less than shocking and usually are phrased like academic discourses on the state of contemporary times. The magazine's editorial premise has an equally high-minded, academic tone: "*Modern America* offers a journalism of ideas. It explores the frontiers of politics, art and culture from varied and often irreverent perspectives — perspectives routinely neglected by the usual newsweeklies and partisan journals. It's about fulfilling that pioneer longing for the joy of discovery."

Behind this magazine's scholarly voice are the many academics who speak up in its pages. One of them, New York University art professor Robert Rosenblum, believes that it's a pioneer longing that's missing from today's art scene. "The idea of a cutting edge has been blunted," he says, maintaining that the art world has finally seen the end of the avant garde.

Such brainy musings continue on a literary level in a Q&A interview with Yale critic Harold Bloom, who bemoans the modern decline in book reading: "I wonder about the long-range hope for a society that can no longer develop the kind of intellect, the kind of human sensitivity that comes out of being a solitary reader."

Modern America has a very nonmodern design in spots that uses woodcut illustrations and antique typefaces. In some cases the Old World look is appropriate, as in a reprint of an 1804 diatribe against Thomas Jefferson that attacks him for his "grievous violations of right principle," including his adulterous affair with the Monticello slave girl Sally. The discussion of Jefferson continues, much more reverentially, in an article elsewhere in the premiere issue that's entitled "A Country Without Citizens?" in which *Modern America*'s editor David W. Edwards declares that if the philandering founding father were alive today to see the immoral state of the nation, he'd be "appalled."

What's so appalling? An article titled "Storm Warning" sounds an alarm about the wave of violence seen in terrorist attacks against abortion clinics. There's also a discourse on American punk music spanning the Velvet Underground's heyday in the 1970s to Nirvana and Green Day today: "Punk rock, animated by a naive passion to change the world by destroying it, fulfills the role of Hate in the cycle of popular music."

Up front is a potpourri section called "Panopticon, A Gazette of American Civilization, Both Trivial and Profound." Under the heading "Signs of Decline," it bemoans the O.J. Simpson mania that swept America in 1995 and decries "the routine supernatural enhancement of female comic book characters." One example: Lady Death, whose "breasts defy not only Earth's gravity, but Jupiter's, too."

READERSHIP PROFILE: *N/A*

EDITORIAL CONCEPT: *American politics, art & culture.*

modern FERRET™

THE FERRET LIFESTYLE MAGAZINE™

PREMIER ISSUE!

For me?

Be My Valentine

MICHIGAN FERRETS LEGAL!

Volume #1, Issue #1
January/February 1995
$4.95

Modern Ferret

PUBLISHED BY: Crunchy Concepts Inc.

P.O. Box 338

Massapequa Park, NY 11762

TEL: (516) 799-1364 **FAX:** (516) 797-4021

DATE: January/February

FREQUENCY: Bimonthly

COVER PRICE: $4.95

SUBSCRIPTION PRICE: $24.95

DISCOUNT SUBSCRIPTION PRICE: n/a

TOTAL NUMBER OF PAGES: 32

TOTAL NUMBER OF AD PAGES: 6

PUBLISHER: Crunchy Concepts Inc.

EDITOR: Mary Shefferman

According to its masthead and media kit, *Modern Ferret* is published by two people — the husband-and-wife team of Eric & Mary Shefferman — and four ferrets: Sabrina, Ralph, Marshmellow & Knuks (pronounced "Nukes"). The bimonthly purports to be "the *Rolling Stone* of pet magazines" and is devoted exclusively to what its publishers maintain is the third largest companion mammal after cats and dogs.

The New York Times describes the new title as the "niche magazine about an animal that loves niches" and notes that *Modern Ferret* has "probing features, in-depth profiles and revealing centerfold shots providing the kind of worshipful attention that has long been denied the ferret by the mainstream pet media."

The twentysomething Sheffermans produce the magazine out of their Long Island home in between attempts by their furry fellow editors to run off with the computer mouse. What fuels their effort is the same affection that causes people to pay the going rate of $100 to $150 to acquire a ferret. Ownership may be considered hip these days, but it's illegal in some states like Massachusetts, California and Hawaii. The Sheffermans are out to change those state laws. Ferrets, they say, are often misclassified as wild animals when in fact they're innocent mischief makers who are cousins of the weasel and not, despite that steely look in their eyes, members of the rodent family.

"*Modern Ferret*'s goal is to help educate and entertain owners of domestic ferrets, something which is sorely needed," the Sheffermans say. "We seek to dispel many of the myths about these companion animals and to help owners, as well as veterinarians, learn more about the proper care of ferrets to improve their quality of life. This is all accomplished in the spirit of the ferret — fun-loving, playful, off-beat, and clever."

The premiere issue includes an interview with a ferret-rights' activist, photography tips from a former *National Geographic* staffer, new product reviews, nutrition pointers, veterinary medicine pieces, an events calendar and ferret fiction.

The magazine also contains photos catching ferrets at their mischief: "Mr. Bugatti" is seen toilet-papering his owner's house; Felix looks unrepentant after toppling a neat row of books; Smokey pokes his head out of an unzipped pair of blue jeans just above a caption that reads "I wish you'd use fabric softener!"

Upon seeing the first issue, a *USA Today* columnist wrote, "I love the fact that this is modern ferret. Will there be a *Traditional Ferret* magazine? *Victorian Ferret*? *Romantic Ferret Times*?"

READERSHIP PROFILE: N/A

EDITORIAL CONCEPT: *"The ferret lifestyle magazine" for the owners and lovers of those fuzzy little critters.*

Mountain Living

PUBLISHED BY: Wiesner Publishing

7009 S. Potomac

Englewood, CO 80112-9892

TEL: (303) 397-7600 **FAX:** (303) 397-7619

DATE: Winter

FREQUENCY: Quarterly

COVER PRICE: $2.95

SUBSCRIPTION PRICE: $9.99

TOTAL NUMBER OF PAGES: 116

TOTAL NUMBER OF AD PAGES: 36

PUBLISHER: Pat Cooley

EDITOR: Laurel Lund

All shelter magazines may believe they showcase the peak domestic experience, but *Mountain Living* goes to great heights to top them.

This new magazine, which debuted with 25,000 copies on the newsstand, celebrates the charm, beauty and tranquillity of living, vacationing or dreaming of a lofty life. It was designed for "Lone Eagles" — or independent professionals who are flying the big-city coop and flocking to a simpler, more satisfying lifestyle. The editorial terrain it covers en route spans idyllic remote locales, luxury homes and new ideas on interior design, food, sports, travel and more. The magazine's main mission is to belie the notion that rustic sky-high living is synonymous with roughing it.

In fact, it's a whole new world in the mountains these days as Robbie and Hope Levin's new "log cabin" attests in the article "A New Attitude" in the premiere issue. The residence's home office rivals any commercial high rise. The master bath incorporates Russian granite imported soon after the Iron Curtain fell. ("We were some of the first people in this country to get it," Hope says proudly.) There's a Swedish sauna, too, and full-service gym with high-tech touches. The 8,500-square-foot house is also appointed with such touches as a juniper-log cocktail table topped by a slab of glass sandblasted to mirror the outer shape of the log. Having made their mountain-home dream a reality after moving from L.A. to Park City, Utah, Robbie says, "This is a lifestyle that's a lot more suited to us."

Another article, "Instant Getaway," features a 1,600-foot second home located at the base of Snow King ski area in Jackson , Wyoming. Its owner is an interior designer who hired a Santa Fe artist to create textured wall surfaces that "look like brown-paper bags." Furnishings include a coffee table made of an old oxen yoke and a chair constructed of cattle horns.

The handiwork of another interior designer is featured in "Log Cabin Cozy," which recounts the revival of a 70-year-old mountain home in Estates Park, Colorado. The main house is infused with sprightly colored draperies, quilts and rugs. There are elk antlers on the wall and deer-motif candlesticks on the fireplace mantle. Bright patterns cover the sofa and mix well with pillows sporting plaid and Native American-styled designs. What's framed in the nearby windows, however, is what is most prized by this homeowner: inspirational views of Long's Peak from the heady height of 9,500 feet.

Editor Karen Coe notes: "In the pages of *Mountain Living*, our readers meet others who have carved out a little piece of high-country heaven — people who've fashioned a way of life from the best the mountains have to offer."

READERSHIP PROFILE: *79% female; 98% attended college; 52% own a mountain home; 58% plan to purchase a mountain home in the next 5 years.*

EDITORIAL CONCEPT: *"The most unique homes and lifestyles in some very different mountain communities."*

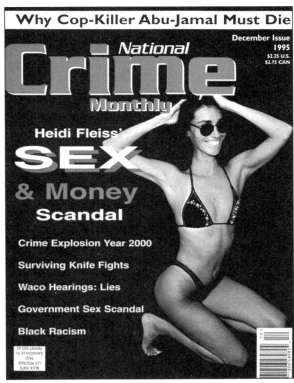

National Crime Monthly

PUBLISHED BY: Gentry Publications

P.O. Box 90328

Gainsville, FL 32607

TEL: (904) 371-1800 **FAX:** (904) 371-0802

DATE: 1995

FREQUENCY: Monthly

COVER PRICE: $2.25

SUBSCRIPTION PRICE: $16.95

TOTAL NUMBER OF PAGES: 64

TOTAL NUMBER OF AD PAGES: 18

PUBLISHER: Dave Gentry

EDITOR: Benjamin Gross

Trying to make crime pay, after all, one new magazine takes on steamy editorial in tabloid style for a readership comprised mostly of police officers, detectives and bounty hunters.

"Farmer Shoots Suspected Goat Molester," cries one article's headline in *National Crime Monthly.* Another: "Minnesota Man Accused of Sex With Cow!" Other articles reveal a Maryland mayor arrested for exposing himself in public for a third time and a Utah man swindled out of $40,000 by his "wife" of three years only to learn from police that she was really a he. "I feel pretty stupid," the Utah man told reporters.

National Crime Montly reports on some of the nation's most grisly crimes in graphic detail and sometimes a tongue-in-cheek voice. One article titled "Cracked Farmer Eats Sister-in-Law's Leg" is accompanied by a photo of the woman's dismembered body found in a shallow grave. Its caption reads: "When the killer invited his sister-in-law over for dinner, she didn't know she'd be the main course."

The magazine's attitude might be considered less than funny by the "faggots" and "bleeding-heart liberals" it takes pot shots at shamelessly. It also freely takes aim at Attorney General Janet Reno as "The Witch of Waco" and Hollywood madam Heidi Fleiss who tried "to screw the IRS."

"We tell it like it is!" roars the magazine's promotional material, bragging that it is "pro-American, pro-cop, pro-gun ... and proud of it!" It insists that its "editorial stance is favored by the majority of Americans."

National Crime Montly was launched by former high-school teacher and failed Republican Congressional candidate Dave Gentry of Gainesville, Florida, who told *The Gainesville Sun:* "Is it lurid? Good question. For some people, it's probably a little too far out there, but we are trying to serve the public interest. We're sill in the experimental stage and we are trying to find the right combination.

"It has a tabloid effect, but it also is a compendium of crime. We're trying to transcend that *True Detective* market. We're trying to be something more than that."

The magazine's 150,000 copies were targeted to law enforcement officers, military personnel and other gun owners and "citizens concerned about crime." *The Gainesville Sun* noted, however, that local "police officers who were shown the magazine said they either had never seen it before or had seen it but not read it. The officers said they deal with crime at work and don't want to read about it when they go home. None of them said they read crime magazines."

READERSHIP PROFILE: *72.9 % male; 43% married; 83% own fire arms, 61% belong to the NRA; $30,000, median household income.*

EDITORIAL CONCEPT: *"America's #1 crime awareness magazine."*

The Net

PUBLISHED BY: Imagine Publishing Inc

1350 Old Bayshore Highway, Suite 210

Burlington, CA 94010.

TEL: (415) 696-1688 **FAX:** (425) 696-1678

DATE: June

FREQUENCY: Monthly

COVER PRICE: $3.95 (premiere issue)

SUBSCRIPTION PRICE: $29.95

TOTAL NUMBER OF PAGES: 100

TOTAL NUMBER OF AD PAGES: 18

ASSOCIATE PUBLISHER: Karen "Hop" Tarrant

EDITOR: Mary Ellis

T wo hundred thousand copies of *The Net* were cast over America's news-stands in June aiming to draw in newbies by addressing their most basic cyberconcerns.

The Net looks a lot like a sober *Wired* in its design, but it's targeted more to neophytes, offering to serve as their guide during their first trip down that confounding info superhighway. A short article titled "All That Technical Stuff ..." explains basic computer operating systems. There's also coaching on appropriate etiquette — or "netiquette" — with the warning "A newbie can get mercilessly flamed for ignoring or flouting the Internet's social customs!"

En route elsewhere through the premiere issue, the editors take a turn at dispelling "myths" perpetrated by certain septagenarian U.S. Senators. "In fact, you have to hunt pretty far and wide to find sites from which porno-graphic pictures can be downloaded," one writer confesses without a sigh. Other myths are bolstered. *The Net* offers proof at last that cyberspace, as always suspected, is secretly ruled by Trekkers. An article explaining com-mon on-line launguage notes that the symbol \\/ means just what Spock's hand greeting does, which it mimics: "Live long and prosper."

Trips down the Internet, in the end, are meant to be fun, the editors remind readers throughout. To drive the point home, they use humor on their end page by quot-ing some of the more silly cyberchatter they've caught while eavesdropping lately. "We are from Microsoft. You will be assimilated," said one wry posting that suggested that com-puter nerds might have a sense of humor after all. Further proof: "When I die, I want to go like my grandfather did — quietly, peacefully, in his sleep. Not like his passengers."

The Net was launched by Imagine, also publishers of *CD-ROM Today*, *Game Players* and *PC Gamer*. Buyers of the company's newest title get a bonus catch in their *Net*: each issue comes with a CD-ROM full of free software courtesy of the magazine's advertisers.

READERSHIP PROFILE: *N/A*

EDITORIAL CONCEPT: *"A stylish, step-by-step guide to the Internet."*

One World

PUBLISHED BY: One World Magazine Inc.

352 Fulton Ave.

Hempstead, NY 11550

TEL: (516) 485-8681   **FAX:** (516) 485-8684

DATE: Spring

FREQUENCY: Quarterly

COVER PRICE: $3.95

SUBSCRIPTION PRICE: $15.00

TOTAL NUMBER OF PAGES: 68

TOTAL NUMBER OF AD PAGES: 10

PUBLISHERS: John N. Pasmore, Eddison Bramble

EDITOR: John N. Pasmore

"**W**elcome to *OneWorld*," invites this magazine's publisher in his introductory letter to readers — and, amazingly, we all fit.

OneWorld promises to fill its pages with people and ideas without prejudice and it manages to get just about everyone in: black, white, straight, gay, avant-garde Chinese film directors and at least one rap singer with a missing gold tooth and an attitude problem. It may sound a bit too politically correct to invite everyone into *OneWorld*, but only the politically correct really need apply. *OneWorld* is about being hip.

In *OneWorld*, the whole world is downtown. Visual artists profiled include Verna Hart, who chronicles the New York jazz scene in angry, soul-quivering brushstrokes. In the tradition of old *Interview*-style interviews, gritty social leaders are probed by superficial fashion models, in this case Kara Young, who takes on hip-hop mogul Russell Simmons with such stinging inqueries as "When I met you, you told me you wanted to open a modeling agency. Were you just trying to pick me up?"

Officially, the content of the magazine is designed to "pull the veneer off the carefully packaged world of fashion, music, and art." But when the veneer comes off, the magazine often comes up with only more veneer below. In an interview with designer Tommy Hilfiger, for example, the best that model Beverly Peele seems to dig up is the fact that the trendy designer owns a house on Mustique not far from David Bowie and Iman.

Still, the magazine is notable because of the many chances it takes and because of the occasional nugget it does unearth. One quite good article, "One Nation Under a Groove," gives readers a five-beer tour of the underground London music scene while "Chabela La Novela," a Latin soap opera told in photos, lets you know in the captions that the clothing these scantily clad models are clawing off each other include Anna Sui blouses and Calvin Klein underwear.

To the more attentive, it quickly becomes obvious that the magazine is targeted to the Gen X group with its "attempts to create a new sensibility that will serve to define the Nineties" and to dispel rumors that "the MTV generation has no attention span."

How it plans to change negative generational stereotypes, however, by printing a feature titled "Diary of a Mad Socialite — He's Hot, He's Young, He's So Popular" and photos of blue-lipped models with nose rings is anyone's guess.

READERSHIP PROFILE: *63% female; 24.5 median age; $49,200 household income; $24,400 average personal income; 74% single or divorced; 73% graduated college.*

EDITORIAL CONCEPT: *A global perspective on the worlds of art, fashion and music.*

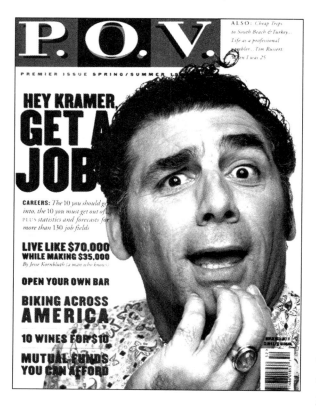

P.O.V.

PUBLISHED BY: B.Y.O.B. Ventures, Inc.

575 Lexington Ave., 25th Floor

New York, NY 10022

TEL: (212) 421-8676 **FAX:** (212) 421-7434

DATE: Spring/Summer

FREQUENCY: Bimonthly

COVER PRICE: $3.00

SUBSCRIPTION PRICE: $10.00/6 issues

DISCOUNT SUBSCRIPTION PRICE: n/a

TOTAL NUMBER OF PAGES: 98

TOTAL NUMBER OF AD PAGES: 26

PUBLISHER: Drew C. Massey

EDITOR: Randall Lane

One year ago the notable startups geared to the twentysomething crowd like *Swing* and *Might* focused on pop culture. If 1995 launches like *P.O.V.* and *Your Future* are new market indicators, Generation X is now more interested in taking stock of the business world than swinging with the fashion scene.

"Contrary to most magazines," assert the editors, "we at *P.O.V.* believe that a majority of our peers couldn't care less about the latest body-piercings, underground mosh clubs, or urban hip-hop fashion statements." *P.O.V.* believes that twentysomethings need their own business publication: "We don't have the time or money to rifle through dozens of business, personal finance, and active lifestyle magazines geared to an older and much more affluent audience."

Although his magazine aspires to be "the bible for young professionals," founder Drew C. Massey won't preach against accepting help from the over-30 crowd. To insure *P.O.V.* would make it to the newsstands, he banked on getting the more mature point of view and assistance of publisher Randy Jones, whose *Worth* was a notable business-magazine launch of recent years.

The result? Not only was *P.O.V.* eventually launched, it may finally prove that Generation X is really the TV Generation. Michael Richards ("Kramer" from *Seinfeld*), not Donald Trump, graces the cover of the premiere issue. An article entitled "Designing Women" profiles partners whose business took off when their knapsack creations became accessories for the actors on *Models, Inc.*

CNN called the first issue's cover story "an interesting study of the best careers for the next century." Almost half of the 10 jobs listed were directly related to the Internet and new media, but the list also included such positions as management consultant ("the cash is sweet and where else can a 27-year-old punk tell major companies how to behave?") and funeral director ("the job prospects are really very good [because] the baby-boom generation is going to terminate around the turn of the century"). Funeral director may be buried below the other nine on the coolness factor chart (it scores a "1," while multimedia software designer and Internet surfer top the list with "10s"), but with a "burnout factor" of "4," at least it's less stressful than industrial environmentalist ("burnout factor: 9").

P.O.V.'s own coolness factor is highest in the features and columns that offer practical advice, such as in "The Cult of One Good Thing," which advises how to "live like a $70,000-a-year trust fund baby" when you only make half of that, and articles on choosing cheap mutual funds and negotiating credit card fees. The burnout factor rises in numerous profiles on entrepreneurs (you, too, can be a success if you know someone who works for Aaron Spelling) and the Michael Richards' interview (revealing such shockers as the fact that the *Seinfeld* actor prefers paying bills over mountain biking with his interviewers).

READERSHIP PROFILE: *70 percent male; 85 percent have attended or graduated from college; 95 percent are between the ages 18-34; 85 percent are single; median household income $45,000.*

EDITORIAL CONCEPT: *"The business bible for the young professionals."*

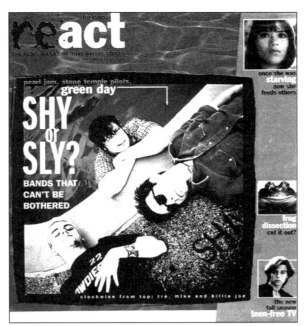

react

PUBLISHED BY: Advance Magazine Publications

711 Third Ave.

New York, NY 10017

TEL: 212-450-7000 **FAX:** 212-450-0975

DATE: September

FREQUENCY: Weekly

COVER PRICE: Free

SUBSCRIPTION PRICE: n/a

TOTAL NUMBER OF PAGES: 16

TOTAL NUMBER OF AD PAGES: 7

PUBLISHER: Carlo Vittorini

EDITOR: Lee Kravitz

Designed for maximum reaction, a press release trumpeted the introduction of *react* into 75 newspapers across the U.S. with the headline "Largest Magazine Launch In History Is Also First Simultaneous Launch In Cyberspace."

Four million copies of the new news and entertainment magazine reached kids aged 12 to 15 on Monday, September 11, while it also ventured into cyberspace where readers could participate in weekly polls, have access to news, games, jokes, readers' letters and ads plus sound off with their own opinions. *react* (with an initial lowercase "r") promised to be "the news magazine that raises voices in such a way that its readers feel empowered."

Created by the publishers of *Parade* and the former editorial director of *Scholastic* magazines, *react* was designed to be a reader call to action. (The word "act" is set off in the logo by a contrasting color.) "Free the frogs!" cries a line in the premiere issue decrying school science-class dissections, adding, "Do they deserve to croak?" The alternative? Readers are told to "take a stab at the virtual frog" in cyberspace at http://george.lbl.gov/vfrog.

But, like kids themselves, their magazine also takes seriously the showbiz world — where frogs aren't getting much more respect these days than they are in schools. Rock singer Daniel Jacobs, 16, of Silverchair talked to *react* so he could tell the press that he's sick and tired of talking to the press about his chart leaper *frogstomp*.

Other musicians are much less timid about their work. Take Yankee Jack McDowell, who uses his deft pitching hand at home, and sometimes on stage or in a recording studio, to pluck a 12-string electric guitar. "He is a rock musician — a serious singer, songwriter and guitarist," insists *react*. The ball player sometimes known spookily as "Black Jack" told the magazine, "In music, I can reveal myself."

At its best, *react* bubbles with typical teen angst, exuberance and hormones. An advice columnist called Manners Man lends an adult's understanding ear when one reader whines: "My mom lets my brother get away with MURDER!" Kids are on their own with other problems, but still seem to do OK. One article relates the tale of a 15-year-old girl who got fed up with being teased for her Attention Deficiency Disorder. Solution: she took up karate. "They don't tease me anymore," she says.

Sometimes *react*'s hip social conscience can seem a bit too flip or cheeky. Consumers are told, for example, "Now you can wear your care for the environment on your butt. Ecolojeans by Lee are 80% cotton and 20% recycled plastic soda pop bottles."

"If our magazine gets read by kids, if they find things in it they really want to read and, as a result, they start to read the rest of the newspaper, well, that's why we're here," says editor Lee Kravitz.

READERSHIP PROFILE: *12- to 15-year-old boys and girls.*

EDITORIAL CONCEPT: *A newspaper supplement aiming to be "the interactive news magazine for America's youth, offering young people a place to have their say."*

Risqué

PUBLISHED BY: Risqué Publications

564 Mission St., Box 345

San Francisco, CA 94105-2918

TEL: (800) 323-6481

DATE: June

FREQUENCY: Bimonthly

COVER PRICE: $5.95

SUBSCRIPTION PRICE: $25.00

TOTAL NUMBER OF PAGES: 158

TOTAL NUMBER OF AD PAGES: 60

PUBLISHER: R.C. Thompson

EDITOR: Chris Dotson

Since sex is back as the leading category for magazine startups, at least one skin title had to make the list of the 50 most notable.

And the choice is quite *Risqué* because it stands out for many reasons — most notably, its bulging breasts, erect male members and its acrobatic photographic ability to reveal a woman's inner secrets.

"Although *Risqué* is new to America, it is not a virgin publication," says a letter from the publisher in the premiere issue. "*Risqué* has been successfully distributed throughout Canada and Europe."

To ensure the success of its American introduction, the publisher promises "each issue will be stuffed to overflowing with seven pictorial layouts exposing classic covergirls, aspiring new models and the latest hardcore video queens. In addition, each issue will offer a hot two-girl spread that will be sure to turn you on. A sexy European model who has previously graced the pages of our European *Risqué* will provide American men with an exotic foreign flair."

The first issue also grabs men's interest with an American horror story — John Wayne Bobbitt talks about his encounter with a carving knife the night his wife Lorena got mad. The interview includes outtakes of his debut porno flick *John Wayne Bobbitt Unzipped* with photos showing that not only has the unkindest cut of all finally healed, but he's fully back in action, virtually unscarred. The accompanying article dares to add "Finding Ms. Right has proven a challenging task for the 27-year-old." Bobbitt himself beams: "This is the best thing that's ever happened to me!"

Risqué also features porn fiction and articles exploring "The Art of Oral Sex" as well as the future of cybersex. In the sex advice column "Ask Andrea," Andrea, pictured as a smirking porn star, soothes a 33-year-old-man suffering from impotency with the advice "Keep a stiff upper lip!"

Otherwise, the magazine is short on text and heavy on heavy-breathing photos that fall just short of depicting intercourse.

This skin magazine's chief come-on is a unique marketing trick: readers who call any of the many phone sex ads inside get their first five minutes for free. The ads scream and pant: "Try Tina!," "Spank Me!," "I'm Barely Legal," "I'm Candy ... Eat My Sweet Stuff" and "Asian Delights ... You Like Spicy?"

READERSHIP PROFILE: *N/A*

EDITORIAL CONCEPT: *Porn magazine offering readers five free minutes of phone sex.*

Scenario

PUBLISHED BY: RC Publications, Inc.

104 Fifth Ave.

New York, NY 10011

TEL: (212) 463-0600 **FAX:** (212) 989-9891

DATE: Winter

FREQUENCY: Quarterly

COVER PRICE: $20.00

SUBSCRIPTION PRICE: $59.95

TOTAL NUMBER OF PAGES: 210

TOTAL NUMBER OF AD PAGES: 3 1/2

PUBLISHER: Howard Cadel

EDITOR: Tod Lippy

Scenario maintains that screenplays are more than just the wordy part of films. The magazine's editors agree with Raymond Chandler, who once said, "The basic art of motion pictures is the screenplay. It is fundamental. Without it, there is nothing."

Rather than a how-to or behind-the-scenes magazine, however, *Scenario* is a collection of screenplays. Each issue offers four scripts ranging from box office blockbusters to those still on the page. The premiere issue offers a quadruple bill: *Four Weddings and a Funeral* (including parts on the cutting room floor); *Bernard and Huey* (all of which wound up on the shelf after a shuffle in management at Showtime); a revised draft of Robert Altman's *Nashville* (noteworthy for its unusual length of 180 pages); and the fourth and final draft of Oscar Best Picture *Silence of the Lambs*.

Screenwriters also serve up good, hot dish about their films: Gene Hackman was originally tapped to direct and star in *Silence of the Lambs* and even considered penning the screenplay; *Lambs* director Jonathan Demme favored Michelle Pfeiffer for the role of Clarice, which won Jodie Foster an Oscar; Ted Tally, who adapted *Lambs* for the screen, was initially unhappy with the choice of Demme for director ("I thought that was a horrible idea."). *Four Weddings and a Funeral* was almost titled *The Best Man* because there was a feeling that male filmgoers don't like weddings and no one likes funerals. The title suggested a film that everyone would want to miss.

Readers looking for photos of Anthony Hopkins, Hugh Grant and Andie McDowell will be disappointed when they open *Scenario*. The scripts are illustrated by artists "whose visions complement the authors' voices, resulting in interpretations that highlight each screenwriter's sensibility." Cartoons created by screenwriter Jules Feiffer to accompany his *Bernard and Huey* script give way to dark and eerie drawings by artist Marshall Arisman to illustrate *Silence of the Lambs*.

The $20 cover price and $59.95 subscription price may seem expensive, but as Pat Blanquies of *Script* magazine points out, "At four issues per year, four screenplays per issue, that's 16 scripts. Three places in southern California selling scripts charge $15-$20 for one feature-length script."

And at $20, *Scenario* is still cheaper than going to see three movies.

READERSHIP PROFILE: *N/A*

EDITORIAL CONCEPT: *The magazine of screenwriting art.*

Science Spectra

PUBLISHED BY: The Gordon and Breach

Publishing Group

Two Gateway Centre

Newark, NJ 07102-0301

TEL: (201) 643-7500 **FAX:** (201) 643-7676

FREQUENCY: Quarterly

COVER PRICE: $9.50

SUBSCRIPTION PRICE: $38.00

TOTAL NUMBER OF PAGES: 76

TOTAL NUMBER OF AD PAGES: 9

PUBLISHER: Ashley Crawford

EDITOR: Dr. Gerhart Friedlander

Hoping to make a big bang in the scientific community is the new quarterly *Science Spectra*, which explores the entire spectrum of scientific specialties with articles on important "discoveries, advances and ideas."

Editor-in-Chief Gerhart Friedlander, a chemist, explains the catalyst for the magazine: "In an earlier era, before extreme specialization became the order of the day in science, there were generalists and renaissance people: men and women with a broad sweep of knowledge spanning astronomy, physics, chemistry, biology, and more. Such scope is hardly possible at the end of the 20th century, as scientists have had to become more and more focused on the minutiae of their fields."

Along with a wide range of subject matter, the magazine also offers an international spectrum of contributors. The nine staff editors include experts from Russia and China. The premiere issue carries articles by scientists from Australia, the U.K., Japan, Germany and Argentina.

Subjects explored span the role of natural selection in evolution, detection of gravitational wave vibrations produced by black holes and the link between sex hormones, auxiliary organs and olfactory desensitization. If you can't decipher the previous sentence, good luck making it through most of the features in *Science Spectra*. Although Friedlander promises that the magazine will be free of "specialized jargon," readers who haven't spent time in the laboratory since high school will likely be lost in a theoretical, logical abyss.

A couple of the features are easier to understand and somewhat entertaining. In "The Scent of a Man," zoologist Mike Stoddart presents his theory on why smell is the least popular of the senses. In "The Big Crunch," Paul Davis, a professor of natural philosophy, asserts that the universe is subject to the second law of thermodynamics: "Chaos will always triumph over order." You can almost imagine *Star Trek*'s Mr. Spock uttering the words Davis uses to describe the end of the world: "During the last three minutes, everything would be pulverized, all physical structures destroyed. Even atomic nuclei would be smashed as the searing heat decomposed matter into its most primitive constituents."

But the evidence that the writers of this magazine are clearly not targeting their messages to the masses comes in one sentence by Professor David Blair: "To be able to listen to the birth of the universe itself, and to the final death of stars as they disappear from the visible universe, should be sufficient justification for spending millions of dollars of the taxpayers' money."

READERSHIP PROFILE: *N/A*

EDITORIAL CONCEPT: *A journal covering the spectrum of emerging scientific thought.*

Sí

PUBLISHED BY: Sí Magazine L.P.

6464 Odin St.

Los Angeles, CA 90068

TEL: (213) 465-6904 **FAX:** (213) 957-1114

DATE: September

FREQUENCY: Bimonthly

COVER PRICE: $2.95

SUBSCRIPTION PRICE: $8.95

TOTAL NUMBER OF PAGES: 98

TOTAL NUMBER OF AD PAGES: 17

PUBLISHER: Joie Davidow

EDITOR: Michael Lassell

"**S**í reads like a slick general-interest consumer book — including fiction, fashion and a horoscope — that just happens to have all Latino subjects," noted *MediaWeek*. In fact, *Sí* is part of a new trend that was evidenced by the introduction in 1993 of *A. Magazine* for Asian-Americans. General interest publications have been given an ethnic twist.

"Sí, an English-language, upscale lifestyle magazine, is attempting to seize upon the opportunities offered by affluent Hispanics," *Inside Media* added. "The oversized, glossy title is targeted to English-speaking people with roots in a Spanish-speaking culture."

The cover of the premiere issue poses the question "What's a Latino Anyway?" and attempts to answer it with soul-searching, essay-styled articles like "Speaking Latina," which struggles with the paradox of being both "Latin" and an assimilated American. As Esmeralda Santiago, author of *When I Was Puerto Rican*, says: "I can't even explain why there's no consensus on whether we're Hispanics or Latinos." Then there's the case of Julia Alvarez, a Dominican-born author, who explains in "Latin-o-rama" how she was told by the staff of a college library she wasn't "Latin enough."

In other articles, boxer Oscar de la Hoya plays fashion model showcasing the designs of Armani and Richard Tyler while MTV VJ Daisy Fuentes dishes with readers about the restaurant she co-owns and her exercise video. "A Tale of Two Women" explores both the pros and cons of affirmative action through interviews with Latin women while "The Hispanic Caucus" covers the members of the U.S. Congress who are either Latin (House of Representatives: 18, Senate: 0) or represent highly Latin constituencies. "Self-Portrait (With Price Tag)" documents "a stampede to Latin American art" by tracking the rise in prices that paintings by late Mexican artist Frida Kahlo have fetched at auction: from $44,000 in 1979 to $3.2 million in 1995. "Jimmy Smits in East Los Angeles" and "Angela Lanza" cover the entertainment world from each artist's viewpoint.

READERSHIP PROFILE: *N/A*

EDITORIAL CONCEPT: *"For Latinos, Latin lovers, and lovers of Latinos."*

Speak

PUBLISHED BY: Speak Magazine, Inc.

5150 El Camino Real, Suite B-24

Los Altos, CA 94022

TEL: (414) 428-0150 **FAX:** (414) 428-0153

DATE: February

FREQUENCY: Bimonthly

COVER PRICE: $3.95

SUBSCRIPTION PRICE: $15.95

TOTAL NUMBER OF PAGES: 76

TOTAL NUMBER OF AD PAGES: 11

PUBLISHER: Dan Rolleri

EDITOR: Scott Marion

Speak wants to be the voice of the twentysomething generation, sounding off on fashion and lifestyle ("*Speak* knows that fashion is about attitude, not hemlines and lapel widths," says its promotional material) plus whatever deserves to be talked about in entertainment, technology and the arts. The magazine "spotlights what's about to break rather than what's overhyped" in its attempt to be "a survival guide for a generation on the brink of a new era."

The magazine's outlook is best voiced in its graphics by *Ray Gun* art director David Carson. The text proves that it's scrappy by not conforming to traditional column widths and the headlines look like ransom notes from a drunken kidnapper — they're run upside down, sideways and chopped up. In fact, the wild art direction goes completely to pieces in this slim magazine's three fashion sections, which are photographed artfully in black and white and set in a diner, a bowling alley and other urban gutters. The problem: Few of the models are shown in poses so that readers can actually see the clothes, others are cut off at the waist and so many of the outfits are black that their details are lost in the heavy inks these magazine pages soaked up at the printing plant.

Speak is much more informative, and hip, in its extensive music coverage, including reviews of the latest works by the Boo Radleys, the San Francisco jazz funk trio Broun Fellinis and the sixtysomething jazz/funk/r&b artist Jimmy Smith. Also included is a profile of rap-radio disk-jockey Red Alert: "He's been the first radio DJ to play dozens of hip-hop records that went on to become national hits — tapes of his shows circulate on the street for as much as $25."

Speak dares to give fiction a voice, too, but the piece "Paris in the Rain" in the premiere issue is really more of a reflective personal essay than a traditional short story. New artistic styles have also taken over in an article that visits the Chelsea Hotel, the New York literary landmark that was once home to Dylan Thomas, Arthur Miller and Andy Warhol. This magazine now finds its rooms filled with a whole new crop of struggling *artistes*: an abstract painter, a producer of documentary films, and two drag queens ("they prefer to be called performance artists") who share their studio room with "mannequin heads, fabric scraps, mirrors, wigs and two sewing machines."

READERSHIP PROFILE: *48 % men; 25.5 median age; $41,000 median household income.*

EDITORIAL CONCEPT: *Fashion and modern culture for the twenty-something generation.*

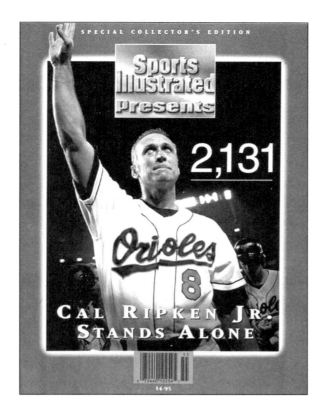

Sports Illustrated Presents College Football

Sports Illustrated Presents NFL '95

Sports Illustrated Presents Pro Basketball '95-'96

Sports Illustrated Presents College Basketball

PUBLISHED BY: Time Inc.

1271 Sixth Ave., N.Y., N.Y. 10020

TEL: (212) 522-1212 **FAX:** (212) 522-0102

DATE: August (pro and college football), October (pro basketball), November (college basketball).

FREQUENCY: Annually

COVER PRICE: $4.95

TOTAL NUMBER OF PAGES: 196

TOTAL NUMBER OF AD PAGES: 30 (NFL), 26 (college football), 20 (pro basketball), 24 (college basketball).

PUBLISHER: David L. Long   **EDITOR:** David Bauer

Sports coverage caused some vigorous competition between publishing titans when Time Inc. announced special *Sports Illustrated* preview issues to the pro and college sporting seasons that matched the editorial game plans Hearst had to test the strength of its ESPN brand in print. The media kit for S.I.'s special issues gave this official publishing rationale, though: "As the leagues continue to expand and college sports grow in popularity, we found that we simply needed more space to cover individual teams in detail. Though the weekly edition does a thorough job of previewing upcoming seasons, the annuals will allow S.I. to delve deeper into each team."

The editors promised that "a fresh look and cutting edge attitude will separate [these previews] from other newsstand issues."

Each edition contained team-by-team sneak peaks, scouting reports, profiles of star coaches and players plus pundit predictions of who would prevail at season's end. Just like the new *ESPN* title, S.I. kicked off with 500,000 newsstand copies of an NFL issue. It featured an eight-page tribute to future Hall of Famer Joe Montana, an attack by Dallas coach Jimmy Johnson on Giants coach Dan Reeves for his "poor" tutoring of QB Dave Brown from the previous season and an uncannily correct prophesy that Dallas would end up lapping up the Super Bowl. (ESPN's team of eight experts all got it wrong, splitting between San Francisco and Pittsburgh.)

S.I.'s prognostication skills were less astute in the college preview issue. Editors noted that Nebraska had "a solid chance of repeating" its national championship of the previous year, but yet ranked the Cornhuskers only #4 in the magazine's season forecast. USC, it asserted, would be #1. In fact, S.I. should have paid more attention to history, since Nebraska ended up coming through just as it had in 1971 after its reign in 1970.

The college preview issue did pay some attention to other pertinent sports history, however, by revisiting the old rivalry between coaches Frank Broyles of Arkansas and Darrell Royal of Texas. ("Were you picking up our signals from the bench at Little Rock in 1971?" Royal confronts Broyles in the article. Answer: a sheepish "I was.") The magazine also targeted some of the more recently forged rivalries like Notre Dame/Boston College and Penn State/Michigan.

Editor David Bauer says, "The appetite for information is enormous when a season begins and with these annual previews we have a new place to satisfy it. The great thing about these magazines is that they're really dense with data, but the design makes it all easy to get to."

READERSHIP PROFILE: *Mostly male; 35, median age; $41,701, median income; 83% college educated.*

EDITORIAL CONCEPT: *In-depth previews to the pro and college sporting seasons.*

The Stable Companion

PUBLISHED BY: Houyhnhnm Press

P.O. Box 6485

Lafayette, IN 47903

TEL: n/a

DATE: July

FREQUENCY: Quarterly

COVER PRICE: $7.00

SUBSCRIPTION PRICE: $24.00

TOTAL NUMBER OF PAGES: 60

TOTAL NUMBER OF AD PAGES: 0

EDITOR AND PUBLISHER: Susanna Brandon

The title of *The Stable Companion* has a double meaning. Not only is this magazine reader-friendly toward those favorite companion animals who warm up a stable — horses — but it also promises to be a stable companion to readers who share that love.

This is the first literary magazine for horse aficionados and it takes readers on a breezy ride through stories and poems full of sagebrush, wildflowers, strawberries, scrub oaks and the palominos and pintos who trot through them on gloriously sunny days. In "Desert Dust & Sadie," a woman recalls "a golden summer" she spent in Nevada when she was 24 and rode Sadie, a "fiesty, frosty" mule who frightened easily at the sight of wild horses, which inevitably appear in the story. In "Granny," a 90-year-old matriarch leaves her rest home to make a trip to her granddaughter's farm to see her seven ponies and horses, which are presented to the older woman one by one as she sits on the porch. "None of them hesitated," her granddaugher writes about her own stable companions as they approached the feeble figure in a wheelchair. "It was as if they knew they were receiving a blessing."

All of the writing in this magazine has the same kind of reverence for all things equestrian and everything seems to have a horsey touch. In one poem, "white clouds trail off like a mustang's mane." A headline making a plea to readers to take out gift subscriptions in order to help build circulation reads like the editor is trying to climb into the saddle: "Can You Give Us A Leg Up?"

The editor and publisher puts out *The Stable Companion* by night and Indiana's *Lafayette Journal & Courier* by day, where she is the deputy features editor.

"I did all of the editing, design, layout and production work on a Mac," says Susanna Brandon about the premiere issue, "and, no, I didn't learn any of this in j-school!"

READERSHIP PROFILE: *N/A*

EDITORIAL CONCEPT: *"For those who appreciate good horses and fine literature."*

Talk About Pets

PUBLISHED BY: Reiman Publications, L.P.

1 Pet Place

Greendale, WI 53129

TEL: (414) 423-0100 **FAX:** n/a

DATE: February

FREQUENCY: Bimonthly

COVER PRICE: $2.95

SUBSCRIPTION PRICE: $16.98

DISCOUNT SUBSCRIPTION PRICE: $10.98

TOTAL NUMBER OF PAGES: 68

TOTAL NUMBER OF AD PAGES: 0

PUBLISHER: Roy Reiman

EDITOR: Kathy Pohl

"**G**et people talking about their pets and you can't stop them! It's 'Wait till you hear what our dog did last week' or 'My cat does the funniest things' and off they go," notes the welcome letter to readers in the first issue of *Talk About Pets*. "Now there's a place for us to 'chat' with other pet owners who fully understand where we're coming from."

Pets joins *Birds & Blooms*, also among the 50 Most Notable Launches of 1995, as the latest new magazine from Reiman Publications, which specializes in giving readers private forums to share material on favorite pet subjects such as farm life and, in this case, kittens named Twinkle and an orphaned raccoon named Annie. Readers write most of the articles and provide the lion's share of photos. To keep things chummy and noncommercial, Reiman bans avertising.

Readers swap infomation such as how to build "bunny condos" and relate stories about tricks they've taught their pets. One Wisconsin couple shares a photo of their new puppy Charlie, who is shown next to the bell he's been taught to ring when he wants to go outside. A professional veterinarian answers reader questions such as "How often should a dog be bathed?"

More in-depth articles run no longer than a page or two. One profiles a canine bakery in Kansas City that specializes in making doggie delicacies such as pumpkin-flavored biscuits for Thanksgiving and reindeer-shaped snacks for Christmas. Another article introduces Mobile, Alabama's Do Dah Parade in which pet owners dress their critters up in costumes. "Each October since 1989," notes the text, "cats in spats, gussied-up pups and the like have trotted alongside their masters at the event, winning giggles and chuckles from appreciative onlookers. 'You can't help but laugh when you see the things people dream up for their pets!' relates organizer Hannah Deason."

Adding a dash of drama are stories of animal heroics such as the tale of a blue Amazon parrot named Elliott who woke up his owners when he sensed a gas leak. Adding a more light touch are sections like "Animal Crackers," which is devoted to crazy comments from kids. One example reveals what a boy said when he answered his grandmother's phone and heard that she'd just won an afghan in a raffle: "I'm sorry, but we can't accept it. My grandmother doesn't want a large dog."

Cuteness is what *Talk About Pets* is really all about, as evidenced by its many photos of kids getting licked and slurped by dogs, calves and ponies. In a section called "Kids and Critters," a photo shows a Missouri boy riding "high on the hog" as he receives a real piggyback ride from a porker named Floppy. Particularly touching is a section called "Pets from the Past" that recalls trusty old friends like the farm dog "Shep" who faithfully brought his master his lunch pails out in the fields during the Depression.

READERSHIP PROFILE: N/A

EDITORIAL CONCEPT: *"For people who love all kinds of pets."*

This Old House

PUBLISHED BY: Time Publishing Ventures Inc.

20 West 43rd St.

New York, NY 10036

TEL: (212) 522-9465

DATE: May/June

FREQUENCY: Bimonthly

COVER PRICE: $3.50

SUBSCRIPTION PRICE: $18.00

DISCOUNT SUBSCRIPTION PRICE: n/a

TOTAL NUMBER OF PAGES: 152

TOTAL NUMBER OF AD PAGES: 50

PUBLISHER: Eric G. Thorkilsen

EDITOR: Isolde Motley

The most popular series in the history of public television, *This Old House*, built this new magazine for its 10 million weekly viewers when Time Inc. licensed the title from WGBH of Boston, producer of the show for 16 years.

The response? "We have a new favorite magazine!" roared *The Detroit Free Press*. "It's aimed at people who want to install their own garden lighting, lay a floor or build their own barbecue — or at least fantasize about doing it. The preview issue has the first really good explanation we've seen on how to paint the outside of your house. We're eager to try the directions on soldering a copper lattice and building a stone barbecue."

Sensing that the magazine might be a hit-in-the-making, Time Inc. rolled out with 500,000 copies of an initial test issue in May. And just as if they knew that they'd be so warmly received by readers, the cover of the first issue shows TV host Steve Thomas and his sidekick carpenter buddy Norm Abrams wearing big smiles along with big toolbelts.

Inside, *New York Newsday* noted that the magazine had "the airy design and high-tone beauty of *Martha Stewart Living*," no small coincidence since *House* was created by the same editor who launched *Living* — Isolde Motley. Motley described *House*'s appeal thus: "When you fix up old homes, you're making something that will last a great deal longer than you. Everything else we do is pretty ephemeral. There's something extremely comforting about the concrete."

"Ever on the lookout for the next hot trend, the magazine industry is listening happily to the sweet sound of hammering resounding through the land," *The New York Times* wrote about the recent build-up of new home-improvement titles such as *This Old House* and and Meredith's *Traditional Home Renovation Style*. As explanation, the paper added: "Sometime around the year 2000, for the first time in American history, more money will be spent on home renovation and remodeling than on new construction."

The Columbus Dispatch applauded *This Old House*: "It falls somewhere between the handyman magazines that show you all the wonderful things you could build if you had all the time in the world and the shelter magazines, which show you all the wonderful things you could have built if you had all the money in the world."

READERSHIP PROFILE: *68% male; 67% married; 49% age 25-44; 77% attended/graduated college; 32% household income above $75,000.*

EDITORIAL CONCEPT: *The magazine version of the PBS television show.*

Time Out
New York

PUBLISHED BY: Time Out New York Partners

627 Broadway, 7th Floor

New York, NY 10012

TEL: (212) 539-4444 **FAX:** (212) 673-8382

DATE: September

FREQUENCY: Weekly

COVER PRICE: $1.95

SUBSCRIPTION PRICE: $39.95

TOTAL NUMBER OF PAGES: 130

TOTAL NUMBER OF AD PAGES: 39

PUBLISHER: Tony Elliott

EDITOR: Cyndi Stivers

London's sassy going-out guide *Time Out* has had successful offshoots in Amsterdam and Paris. The idea of bringing it to New York has always been met with skepticism, though, because of the hefty existing competition from *New York, New Yorker, New York Press* and *The Village Voice.* Using *The New York Times* as a megaphone, *Voice* pubisher David Schneiderman even shouted a public warning to *Time Out* owner Tony Elliott to stay out of the market, insisting that it was already "saturated." Part of the reason was his fault: two weeks before *Time Out* was finally due to arrive in New York, the *Voice* introduced its own new listings guide — *New York Listings,* just as exhaustive and free.

The $1.95-per-issue *Time Out New York* came prepared with a war chest of $10 million, one million of which was used to launch the magazine with a high-profile media campaign that echoed the irreverent voice of the parent London publication and the notorious arrogance of New Yorkers. One subway poster read: "Welcome to New York. Now get out." Another promised that the editors would list "all the clubs you'll never get into."

Helming the project was Cyndi Stivers, who was lured away from her job as deputy editor of *Premiere.* Her new job: to offer readers tiny-type listings of the trendiest clubs, hottest eateries and all the latest theater, film, art, sports and music goings-on. Also featured: TV listings and, on the funkier side of life in the Big Apple, best thrift shops, karaoke bars, poetry readings, what's happening in the gay and lesbian scene — and even where to find a lawyer at 3 a.m.

"There is no reason to be bored in New York," Stivers adds. There's also no reason to be bored with her magazine. *Time Out* doesn't merely dislike Bobby Short's legendary show at the Cafe Carlyle, it gives him a public flogging: "Would it be sacrilegious to say that there are some who find the vibrato-wracked voice grating and the puppy-dog personality cloying?"

Can such a bawdy, new, weekly listings magazine survive? Some don't think so, including *New York* editor Kurt Andersen: "The question is whether there is a business to be built on this premise."

Others cheered the publication on. New York University professor Ed Diamond told *The New York Post:* "Finally, we'll have a magazine that tells you where to get the best egg cream without some 10,000 word essay by Pete Hamill pining for the glory days of egg creams. I think people are looking for just the facts."

READERSHIP PROFILE: *Socially active, mostly single Manhattan residents aged 18 to 45; $50,000-plus household income.*

EDITORIAL CONCEPT: *The weekly magazine about where to go and what to do in New York City.*

Touring & Tasting

PUBLISHED BY: Vintage Communications

123 W. Padre, Suite B

Santa Barbara, CA 93105

TEL: (805) 563-7585 **FAX:** (805) 563-9985

DATE: June

FREQUENCY: Semi-annually

COVER PRICE: $6.95

SUBSCRIPTION PRICE: $12.00

TOTAL NUMBER OF PAGES: 100

TOTAL NUMBER OF AD PAGES: 4

PUBLISHER: Donald V. Fritzen

EDITOR: Joana Cook

This wine magazine promises not to be snooty since it's less about blue bloods arguing over the merits of amusing, off-year cabarnets than it is about the fun that everyone can have exploring the California coast where they're produced.

A letter from the publisher reminds readers how vast the area is: "From Mendocina Country north of San Francisco to Teecula in Riverside County, there are close to 350,000 acres planted with premium wine grapes in countryside ranging from verdant valleys to high, arid plateaus, from steep, rocky mountainsides to golden, undulating hills dotted with gnarled oak trees. Row upon row of precisely spaced vines run for miles across flatlands, beside sparkling rivers, up and over rounded peaks, and down to the sea."

Throughout this magazine's pages, readers are taken "from rustic barns to majestic, million-dollar French-style chateaux" that are inhabited by runaways from the real world who decided to set up their own little kingdoms in California wine country: former opthamologists, heart surgeons, Broadway dancers, a computer research scientist from Silicon Valley and even the actor Fess Parker, who once portrayed Davey Crockett on TV and now owns his own winery in Santa Barbara. Many of the larger, name establishments are also featured: Domaine Chandon, for example, is here insisting that it doesn't merely make wines, it sculpts them.

Each winery profiled offers info on its best vintages plus historic background such as the fact that the Santa Ynez Winery was originally planted by Catholic priests interested in cultivating altar wine. Also included are maps and descriptive directions on how to reach each winery by car plus details on tours, festivals, open houses and other special events.

So that *Touring & Tasting* doesn't end up seeming like the magazine for driving and drinking, hotels, resorts and country inns are recommended and there's information on helicopter and balloon tours.

What's not mentioned is the fact that this magazine's editorial pages are really advertising. Vintners pay about $2,000 per page to have articles on them featured in the 30,000 copies printed twice a year, one issue at the height of the tourist season in June and the other in January soon after the grape harvest.

Not only should this magazine be read with the kind of wink and a nod you'd expect from the town drunk as you passed him on Main Street, it can be read with a sigh, too. This magazine's tour of wine country makes no stops at some premiere wineries since they didn't advertise, so it skips over Mondavi and other top labels.

READERSHIP PROFILE: *49% aged 45 to 65; 60% attended graduate school; $75,000 average household income.*

EDITORIAL CONCEPT: *"A wine country guide" for the grape-growing people of the nation.*

Traditional Home Renovation Style

PUBLISHED BY: Meredith Corporation

1716 Locust St.

Des Moines, IA 50309-3023

TEL: (800) 513-2935 **FAX:** (800) 513-2935

DATE: September

FREQUENCY: Special

COVER PRICE: $4.95

TOTAL NUMBER OF PAGES: 132

TOTAL NUMBER OF AD PAGES: 29

PUBLISHER: Deborah Jones Barrow

EDITOR: Karol DeWulf

With designs on building upon the success of *Traditional Home* (circulation 775,000), Meredith tested a spin-off title on the newsstands in September meant to be a "building and renovation magazine that breaks new ground."

Whereas the new magazine is targeted to "people whose pulses naturally quicken at the sight of a 'handyman special,'" *Traditional Home's* editor John Riha said, "*Renovation Style* is not necessarily about historic preservation or restoration. It is about redoing a 1960s ranch as much as it is about fixing up a turn-of-the century Victorian. Above all, it is about the place we call home."

Quite a few nonmodest-styled residences were featured in the premiere issue. There's a Tudor Revival home revived by a St. Louis couple who discovered an "old newspaper and a dried boutonniere hidden behind a dining-room wall." The finished renovation was grand enough for a Tudor king to call home. Another feature showed how a Bucks County, Pennsylvania, couple relandscaped the 30 acres of their 1800 farmstead so it bloomed with phlox, delphinium and Japanese iris.

Less lavish but equally ambitious is what a pair of Wisconsin antique dealers did to transform an 1875 schoolhouse into a weekend dream house. A Mill Valley, California, couple revealed their recipe to revive their country-style kitchen.

Renovation Style makes no mention of what the overhauls cost homeowners whose handiwork is shown in the feature articles. Some columns are much more practical, such as an advice piece on adding crown molding (the leaf motif costs $3.50 per linear foot). Other advice-driven columns discuss how to get the proper building permits and how to reupholster old chairs.

"By the year 2000, the average American home will be 32 years old, and homeowners are increasingly engaged in the satisfying work of recondition and furnishing," editor Riha added. "*Renovation Style* differentiates itself from other building magazines by focusing on older homes and by taking a design approach to renovation — without the strictly historical perspective of the restoration publications. The magazine's mission is to help readers contemporize and individualize older structures to fit the way they live today."

Renovation Style was produced by *Traditional Home's* edit and art staffs and plans to go quarterly in 1996.

READERSHIP PROFILE: *N/A*

EDITORIAL CONCEPT: *For "people whose pulses naturally quicken at the sight of a 'handyman special.'"*

71

21-C: Scanning The Future

PUBLISHED BY: Gordon and Breach

Science Publishers S.A.

P.O. Box 200029, Riverfront Plaza Station

Newark, NJ 07102-0301

TEL: (201) 643-7500   **FAX:** (201) 643-7676

DATE: March

FREQUENCY: Quarterly

COVER PRICE: $6.95

SUBSCRIPTION PRICE: $21.00

TOTAL NUMBER OF PAGES: 86

TOTAL NUMBER OF AD PAGES: 10

PUBLISHER: Ashley Crawford

EDITOR: Ray Edgar

The far-sighted aim of *21-C: Scanning The Future* is to explore key issues in science, culture and technology that confront humanity as it heads into a new millennium.

 21-C was founded by the Australian government's Commission for the Future. Recently acquired by the international publishing group Gordon and Breach, *21-C: Scanning The Future* now has more of an international focus as it premieres on American newsstands offering "essays and interviews from scientific and cultural luminaries that delve deep into the psychological, philosophical, scientific and cultural issues," according to the magazine's promotional material.

 Proving that *21-C* is on "the cutting edge of ideas affecting the future," one article looks at what was recently put on the Internet by the *National Library of Medicine*: photo images of the finely dissected body of convicted murderer Joseph Paul Jernigan who signed an organ donor card before he was executed by the state of Texas in 1993. Now he exists in 1,871 pieces in cyberspace after his body was carved into one millimeter slices so that medical students could download his anatomy for study. The photos look like peeks into a cannibal's butcher shop, but their captions note: "The 3-D data set allow Jernigan to be taken apart and put back together. Organs can be isolated, dissected, orbited; sheets of muscle and layers of fat and skin can lift away; and bone structures can offer landmarks for a new kind of leisurely touring."

 21-C also tours cities of tomorrow. In "Future Noir," an urban theorist foresees Los Angeles as Hollywood once imagined the whole world — in *Blade Runner* where gangs and government soldiers rule and violence reigns. "Yen Zero" foresees Tokyo devastated by earthquakes with casualties running from 10,000 (a city government estimate) to 152,000 (Japanese National Land Agency study). A sizable quake "could represent Year Zero for Japan's financial might," the article says, adding, "The shockwaves would hit every stock market in the world."

 Other articles envision a more promising future, including one that foresees immortality for man. "Physicist and self-proclaimed heretic Frank Tipler claims that the defeat of death — Revelations-style — will be achieved by super intelligent machines in the far future," an article notes. "He says he has the mathematics to prove it." Scientists and theologians offer "violent opposition," however, including one Anglican priest who dismisses the theory as "a very ingenious piece of science fiction" and very bad math.

READERSHIP PROFILE: *N/A*

EDITORIAL CONCEPT: *A forward look at culture, technology and science.*

Virtual City

PUBLISHED BY: Virtual Communications Inc.

444 Madison Ave.

New York, N.Y. 10022

TEL (212) 593-1593

DATE: September

TOTAL NUMBER OF PAGES: 92

TOTAL NUMBER OF AD PAGES: 33

FREQUENCY: Quarterly

COVER PRICE: $2.95

SUBSCRIPTION PRICE: $7.99

PUBLISHER AND EDITORIAL DIRECTOR: Jonathan Sacks

EDITOR: Lewis D'Vorkin

Ask *Newsweek* and its newest publishing partners where cyberspace is and you'll learn that they believe it's not really a vast unchartered frontier in your computer, after all. It's a city, spectacular as Vegas and varied as New York, and, if the cyberpundits are right, soon it will be everyone's home town.

Virtual City bills itself as the first "city magazine of cyberspace" offering information and advice to newcomers on what to do and where to find it. "To my delight, *Virtual City* is written and packaged for mere mortals, not just techies," says *Newsweek* editor Richard Smith.

Newsweek partnered the new publication with Virtual Communications of San Francisco, which is headed by two former editors of computer publisher Ziff-Davis, Jonathan Sacks and Lewis D'Vorkin. One million *Newsweek* readers received a brief tour of their cybercity guide when a condensed version was included inside the Sept. 25 issue. Three hundred thousand full copies then hit the newsstands with a bizarre grouping of live and dead celebs on the cover under the heading "It's Your Party" — libertines Andy Warhol and Courtney Love alongside conservative iconoclast and veteran party pooper Newt Gingrich. Inside, the cover article noted: "Almost overnight, it seems, the online world has transformed itself from a private, closed domain to a new dynamic community of millions, a *Virtual City* — wide-open, market-driven."

"The premiere issue guides readers to computer sites aplenty," noted *Newsday*, "such as where to call up digitized mug shots from the Tulsa County sheriff's office, or fresh information about Paris restaurants or the latest game stats of basketball star Michael Jordan."

The premiere issue lists more than 500 web sites in all plus offers interviews with "Real People" who are fearless and proud citizens of *Virtual City* such as Dr. Joyce Brothers who gives readers her best professional advice on how to overcome technophobia ("just have fun with technology!"). When magic debunkers Penn & Teller are interviewed, the quiet one, Teller, at last speaks up and does so to address his love of going on line: "If this is addiction — well, viva addiction!" For readers who don't know if they've yet reached the point of being so overly dependent, the editors offer a quiz. It notes: "You know you're addicted when the only way your dog can get you to take him out for a walk is if he sets up his own home page."

Newsday declared *Virtual City* "a fresh and readable guide to cyberculture aimed at the masses who want to use the Internet in their daily lives and care little about the techno-wizardry that makes interactive media work."

READERSHIP PROFILE: *Professional adults who earn more than $50,000 per year and spend $2,000 per year or more on their computers.*

EDITORIAL CONCEPT: *"City magazine of cyberspace."*

Having spent $3 million to launch *The Weekly Standard* with great fanfare, media baron Rupert Murdoch seemed poised to swoop down on Washington, D.C., with his new conservative thinksheet much like the magazine's cover sketch showed Newt Gingrich landing on the Capitol building looking like Rambo.

The New Yorker commented: "*The Standard*'s chances of success are extraordinarily high. Not only does it have the funds — Murdoch appears ready to invest the many millions it will take to establish his D.C. beachhead — but it also has talent, an obvious niche, exquisite timing and a distinct idea of itself."

Editor and publisher William Kristol had formerly served as a first aide to Education Secretary William Bennett and Vice President Dan Quayle. His father, Irving, had been a founding editor of *Public Interest*. Kristol's partner also came from solid conservative journalistic stock: John Podhoretz is the son of *Commentary* editor-in-chief Norman Podhoretz, who chose to announce his retirement at the same time his son's star rose over Washington D.C. with *The Weekly Standard*. Fred Barnes defected from *The New Republic* to become executive editor.

Kristol insisted that the magazine would not be a predictable mouthpiece for the Republican party. "If we don't make the Republicans unhappy with some regularity, we won't be doing our job well," he said. The premiere issue carried four articles on Newt Gingrich. "One chastises the Speaker for timidity," noted *The New York Times*, "while another gives a resoundingly negative review to the Speaker's recent book and, more significantly, to the political philosophy it implies."

Another article went after the competition, "Dem Crazy Dems," while a piece by Kristol pressed General Colin Powell to announce a bid for the presidency. On the cultural front, the magazine took aim at novelist John Grisham for banging out suspense novels "without any suspense." It also went after *Sports Illustrated* with the same sledgehammer force that Rupert Murdoch hoped to wield with *The Score*, the sportsweekly competitor he had planned to launch but killed just a few months before *The Standard* unfurled.

But Kristol insisted that his new magazine was not a secret mouthpiece for Murdoch either. Kristol claimed to have complete editorial control and said that his benefactor didn't even know what was printed in the first issue until he held it in his hands.

Kristol also insisted that, unlike *The Score*, Murdoch was fully committed to *The Standard*, which would need a further investment spanning $10 million to $20 million. Fred Barnes added his optimism, telling *Newsweek,* "New magazines usually fail because they're undercapitalized. Well, we're not going to have *that* problem."

The Weekly Standard

PUBLISHED BY: News America Publishing Inc.

1150 17th St. NW, 5th floor

Washington, D.C. 20036

TEL: (202) 293-4900

FAX: (202) 293-4901

DATE: September

FREQUENCY: Weekly

COVER PRICE: $2.95

SUBSCRIPTION PRICE: $79.96

DISCOUNT SUBSCRIPTION PRICE: $29.00

TOTAL NUMBER OF PAGES: 76

TOTAL NUMBER OF AD PAGES: 30

PUBLISHER: William Kristol

EDITOR: William Kristol

READERSHIP PROFILE: N/A

EDITORIAL CONCEPT: *"The nation's only weekly journal of conservative opinion."*

Women's Sports Traveler

PUBLISHED BY: Sports Traveler

167 Madison Avenue, Suite 405

New York, NY 10016

TEL: (212) 759-1357 **FAX:** (212) 759-1282

DATE: September

FREQUENCY: Bimonthly

COVER PRICE: $2.95

SUBSCRIPTION PRICE: $9.97

TOTAL NUMBER OF PAGES: 114

TOTAL NUMBER OF AD PAGES: 32

PUBLISHER: Polly Perkins

EDITOR: Karen Walden

Women's *Sports Traveler* staked out an editorial course that had only been lightly traveled in the past. It seemed similar to *Women's Sports & Fitness*, but was a bit more worldly and also offered an adventurous new dose of fashion. *MediaWeek* called *Traveler* "a slightly more mainstream version of the formula that has worked so well for *Women's Sports & Fitness*."

Other media-watchers ventured different comparisons. *USA Today* called it "a macho-free *Men's Journal* with fashion tips." *Traveler*'s publisher described it as "*Outside* with *Elle* graphics."

Traveler was launched by Polly Perkins, former publisher of *Bon Appetit* and *Elle Decor*, who teamed up with former *New Woman* editor Karen Walden. They introduced *Traveler* by dropping 250,000 copies of a premiere test issue on the newsstands in September.

"Men and women think differently about sports," Perkins told *MediaWeek*. "Men are interested in competition, strategy and the newest technology and toys. Women are more experiential. They tend to think about who they do sports with and where they do them."

Typical articles included a roundup of family resorts in Florida, St. Lucia and Honduras as well as a listing of the top tennis and golf resorts in Arizona. But it's the magazine's fashion sense that gave it added editorial flair. An article on joining a vigorous bike tour along Maryland's eastern shore was followed by a fashion spread showing "free-wheeling" sports gear, including quilted vests, spandex unitards and metalic t-shirts. A feature on a six-day hiking trip through Utah's national parks was accompanied by a section showcasing Adidas windbreakers, cotton sweatpants by Adrienne Vittadini and Danskin socks.

After dressing up the body, the magazine went after what women are really traveling for: a discovery of their inner selves. In one essay article, a "true virgin-fisher-woman" "gets hooked" when she tackles fly fishing in some of Ireland's 9,000 rivers teeming with trout and salmon. After four days, she finds that "the real joy is in the journey — wading in the water and savoring the sights and sounds of nature. I also had begun to learn how to get inside the mind of a fish while getting inside my own."

READERSHIP PROFILE: *34, median age, 33% hold a professional or managerial position, 60% married; 72% attended college; $48,600 median household income.*

EDITORIAL CONCEPT: *The sporting lifestyle for today's fitness-oriented women.*

Your Future

PUBLISHED BY: Time Inc.

1271 Ave. of the Americas

New York, NY 10020-1393

TEL: (212) 522-1212

DATE: Spring

FREQUENCY: Bimonthly

COVER PRICE: $2.50

SUBSCRIPTION PRICE: $15.00

TOTAL NUMBER OF PAGES: 114

TOTAL NUMBER OF AD PAGES: 38

EDITOR: Caroline Donnelly

PUBLISHER: Geoffrey Dodge

"*Y*our Future isn't your father's personal-finance magazine," promises this new publication aimed at youthful, affluent, college-educated types who crave essential investment information but scorn the more mature financial titles such as Money. There's a curious irony here, however: it's published by the editors of Money.

"Those who are very interested in investing know they have to start young, but realize their formal education hasn't prepared them to do so," notes editor Caroline Donnelly as the reason Money decided that a spin-off publication was a good idea for young professionals.

Your Future addresses today's Gen Xers' unique financial concerns and positions with such articles as "Escape From Debt Hell" and "The Best Places to be Young" (Fort Collins, Colorado, tops the list — "a spirited small city that's a terrific place to raise a family, get a job or start a business"). It also addresses such issues as "Investing on the Cheap," which covers getting into mutual funds without having to plunk down $3,000 to $5,000. "Investing Basics for the Financially Challenged" assures readers that they needn't be a seasoned broker to make money on Wall Street and offers layman's advice on stocks, mutual funds and diversified portfolios in language that's easy to understand and clearly geared to neophytes. The magazine's approach to finance is so elementary, in fact, that it risks insulting sophisticated readers with simplistic sidebars explaining what stocks and mutual funds are. Readers could also be put off by the magazine's overall voice, which is clearly not theirs, beginning with the title. "*Your Future*" struck some readers as if it were being uttered by a scornful parent warning them to save their pennies.

The premiere issue did adopt its readers' voice when it embraced an irreverent spirit. The article "The Tax Bonehead" ends with a Top-10 list of what to do with a tax refund. Number one: "Take a trip to Belize." Number three: "See a therapist about the meaningless encounter you had in Belize."

"*Your Future* is dedicated to helping its readers — many of whom are just starting to manage their money — get what they want out of life," says editor Donnelly. "We don't believe in information overload. We think you should get a grip on your finances and then forget about them. Life is short."

READERSHIP PROFILE: *32, median age; 58% under the age of 35; 58%, male; 56% married; 59% graduated college; $45,880 median household income.*

EDITORIAL CONCEPT: *A new personal finance publication for young adults from the editors of* **Money**.

SAMIR HUSNI'S GUIDE TO
NEW CONSUMER
MAGAZINES

1996 Edition

Create

PUBLISHED BY: Create Magazine

751 Laurel Street #335

San Carlos, CA 94070

TEL: (415) 508-9526

DATE: Summer

FREQUENCY: Quarterly

COVER PRICE: $4.95

SUBSCRIPTION PRICE: n/a

TOTAL NUMBER OF PAGES: 100

TOTAL NUMBER OF AD PAGES: 35

PUBLISHERS: Roger Strukhoff, John A. Barry, Dee Cravens, Chip Woerner

EDITORIAL DIRECTOR: John A. Barry

EDITORIAL CONCEPT: *"The resource for integrating digital technology and design."*

Serif

PUBLISHED BY: Quixote Digital Typography

555 Guilford Ave.

Claremont, CA 91711-5439

TEL: (909) 621-1291 **FAX:** (909) 625-1342

FREQUENCY: Quarterly

COVER PRICE: $7.95

SUBSCRIPTION PRICE: $28.00

TOTAL NUMBER OF PAGES: 66

TOTAL NUMBER OF AD PAGES: 4

EDITOR: D.A. Hosek

EDITORIAL CONCEPT: *"The magazine of type and typography."*

Iké Udé's aRUDE

PUBLISHED BY: aRUDE Publications

P.O. Box 172, Mid-Town Station

New York, NY 10018

TEL: (212) 268-4086

DATE: Spring

FREQUENCY: Quarterly

COVER PRICE: $6.00

SUBSCRIPTION PRICE: $20.00

TOTAL NUMBER OF PAGES: 84

TOTAL NUMBER OF AD PAGES: 13

PUBLISHER: Iké Udé

EDITOR: Iké Udé

EDITORIAL CONCEPT: *"Style, art, culture, scenes and beyond."* Focuses on the art scene with a look at new artists and their works.

Watercolor '95

PUBLISHED BY: BPI Communications

1515 Broadway

New York, NY 10036

TEL: (212) 764-7300

DATE: Winter

FREQUENCY: Quarterly

COVER PRICE: $5.95

SUBSCRIPTION PRICE: $19.95

TOTAL NUMBER OF PAGES: 132

TOTAL NUMBER OF AD PAGES: 12

PUBLISHER: Don Frost

EDITOR: M. Stephen Doherty

EDITORIAL CONCEPT: *Articles about portraits, French mats and marketing ideas, published exclusively for watercolor painters.*

Juxtapoz

PUBLISHED BY: High Speed Productions

1303 Underwood Ave.

San Francisco, CA 94124

TEL: (415) 822-3083 **FAX:** (415) 822-8359

DATE: Spring

FREQUENCY: Quarterly

COVER PRICE: $3.95

SUBSCRIPTION PRICE: n/a

TOTAL NUMBER OF PAGES: 84

TOTAL NUMBER OF AD PAGES: 10

PUBLISHER: Kevin J. Thatcher

EDITOR: Kevin J. Thatcher

EDITORIAL CONCEPT: *A "low-brow art d'elegance" magazine featuring art and art criticism.*

ANNUAL, SPECIAL OR FREQUENCY UNKNOWN

Artnews For Students

PUBLISHED BY: Artnews

48 W. 38th St.

New York, NY 10018

TEL: (212) 398-1690

FREQUENCY: Special

COVER PRICE: Free

SUBSCRIPTION PRICE: n/a

TOTAL NUMBER OF PAGES: 16

TOTAL NUMBER OF AD PAGES: 0

PUBLISHER: Milton Esterow

EDITOR: Milton Esterow

EDITORIAL CONCEPT: *A complimentary preview issue of the upcoming student edition of Artnews magazine, for students in grades 6-10.*

Learning From Today's Art Masters

PUBLISHED BY: BPI Communications

1515 Broadway

New York, NY 10036

TEL: (212) 764-7300

FREQUENCY: Special

COVER PRICE: $3.95

SUBSCRIPTION PRICE: n/a

TOTAL NUMBER OF PAGES: 92

TOTAL NUMBER OF AD PAGES: 11

PUBLISHER: Don Frost

EDITOR: Bonne Iris

EDITORIAL CONCEPT: American Artist *magazine presents this special publication of award-winning artists offering "their own ways of looking at art."*

Oil Highlights I: Landscapes

PUBLISHED BY: BPI Communications

1515 Broadway

New York, NY 10036

TEL: (212) 764-7300

FREQUENCY: Special

COVER PRICE: $6.95

SUBSCRIPTION PRICE: n/a

TOTAL NUMBER OF PAGES: 164

TOTAL NUMBER OF AD PAGES: 9

PUBLISHER: Don Frost

EDITOR: M. Stephen Doherty

EDITORIAL CONCEPT: *A collection of American Artist's best articles from 1987 to 1994 on landscape painting in oil.*

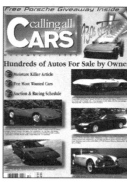

Calling All Cars

PUBLISHED BY: Calling All Cars

10824 Old Mill Rd., Suite 2

Omaha, NE 68154

TEL: (402) 333-6191 **FAX:** (800) 546-8459

FREQUENCY: Bimonthly

COVER PRICE: $2.95

SUBSCRIPTION PRICE: n/a

TOTAL NUMBER OF PAGES: 82

TOTAL NUMBER OF AD PAGES: 18

PUBLISHER: David Haggart

EDITOR: Andrew Haggart

EDITORIAL CONCEPT: *A colorful registry of fine and classic automobiles.*

Exotic Cars

PUBLISHED BY: Ashley Communications

P.O. Box 1053

Malibu, CA 90265

TEL: (818) 885-6800

FREQUENCY: Semiannually

COVER PRICE: $4.95

SUBSCRIPTION PRICE: n/a

TOTAL NUMBER OF PAGES: 48

TOTAL NUMBER OF AD PAGES: 2

EDITOR: David Fetherstone

EDITORIAL CONCEPT: *Features some of the fastest and rarest sports cars in the world.*

Chevy Truck

PUBLISHED BY: Dobbs Publishing Group

3816 Industrial Blvd.

Lakeland, FL 33811

TEL: (941) 644-0449

DATE: November

FREQUENCY: Bimonthly

COVER PRICE: $3.95

SUBSCRIPTION PRICE: n/a

TOTAL NUMBER OF PAGES: 112

TOTAL NUMBER OF AD PAGES: 44

PUBLISHER: Larry Dobbs

EDITOR: Lisa M. Ludy

EDITORIAL CONCEPT: *"The all-Chevrolet truck magazine."*

Ford High Performance

PUBLISHED BY: McMullen & Yee

774 S. Placentia Ave.

Placentia, CA 92670

TEL: (714) 572-2255 **FAX:** (714) 572-1864

DATE: April

FREQUENCY: Bimonthly

COVER PRICE: $3.50

SUBSCRIPTION PRICE: n/a

TOTAL NUMBER OF PAGES: 88

TOTAL NUMBER OF AD PAGES: 23.66

EDITOR: Tom Vogele

EDITORIAL CONCEPT: *The editors of* Mustang Illustrated *bring you an entire magazine dedicated to high-performance Fords, with features on race cars and customs.*

Corvette Review

PUBLISHED BY: Thomas & Taylor

P.O. Box 3236

Shreveport, LA 71133

TEL: (318) 459-2475

DATE: November

FREQUENCY: Monthly

COVER PRICE: $3.99

SUBSCRIPTION PRICE: n/a

TOTAL NUMBER OF PAGES: 76

TOTAL NUMBER OF AD PAGES: 13

EDITOR: K.R. Taylor

EDITORIAL CONCEPT: *"Articles and photographs of America's favorite car."*

4x4 Mechanix

PUBLISHED BY: CSK Publishing Co. Inc.

299 Market St.

Saddle Brook, NJ 07663

TEL: (201) 712-9300 **FAX:** (201) 712-9899

FREQUENCY: Bimonthly

COVER PRICE: $3.25

SUBSCRIPTION PRICE: $16.00

TOTAL NUMBER OF PAGES: 76

TOTAL NUMBER OF AD PAGES: 13

PUBLISHER: Ralph Monti

EDITOR: Brian C. Brennan

EDITORIAL CONCEPT: *A magazine for those who are interested in modifying their 4x4s for off-road use; includes sections on engine modification.*

GM Collector's Guide

PUBLISHED BY: MCG Publishing Inc.

10067 El Camino Ave.

Baton Rouge, LA 70815

TEL: (504) 926-6954

DATE: March

FREQUENCY: Monthly

COVER PRICE: $3.50

EDITORIAL CONCEPT: *Features General Motors vehicles and a classified section.*

SUBSCRIPTION PRICE: $25.00

TOTAL NUMBER OF PAGES: 64

TOTAL NUMBER OF AD PAGES: 30

PUBLISHER: John D. Ellis Sr.

EDITOR: Randy Holden

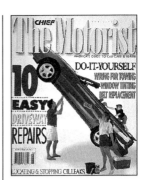

The Motorist

PUBLISHED BY: Magnolia Media Group

1227 W. Magnolia, Garden Level Suite

Ft. Worth, TX 76104

TEL: (817) 921-9300

DATE: June

FREQUENCY: Bimonthly

COVER PRICE: $2.95

EDITORIAL CONCEPT: *America's guide to car care and repair.*

SUBSCRIPTION PRICE: n/a

TOTAL NUMBER OF PAGES: 82

TOTAL NUMBER OF AD PAGES: 37

PUBLISHER: Mark Hulme

EDITOR: Peter Hubbard

High-Tech Performance

PUBLISHED BY: CSK Publishing Co. Inc.

299 Market St.

Saddle Brook, NJ 07663

TEL: (201) 712-9300

DATE: December

FREQUENCY: Bimonthly

COVER PRICE: $3.75

EDITORIAL CONCEPT: *Features fuel-injected cars and related electronics.*

SUBSCRIPTION PRICE: n/a

TOTAL NUMBER OF PAGES: 76

TOTAL NUMBER OF AD PAGES: 18

PUBLISHER: Stephen Schneider

EDITOR: John Hunkins

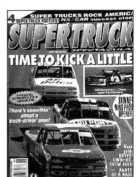

NASCAR Super Truck Racing Magazine

PUBLISHED BY: McMullen & Yee Publishing

774 S. Placentia Ave.

Placentia, CA 92670

TEL: (714) 572-2255 **FAX:** (714) 572-1864

DATE: March

FREQUENCY: Bimonthly

COVER PRICE: $3.00

EDITORIAL CONCEPT: *Profiles on drivers and tracks for Super Truck racing enthusiasts, from the editors of Truckin' magazine.*

SUBSCRIPTION PRICE: $18.00

TOTAL NUMBER OF PAGES: 96

TOTAL NUMBER OF AD PAGES: 20

EDITOR: Steve Stillwell

Inside Racing

PUBLISHED BY: Petersen Publishing Co.

6420 Wilshire Blvd.

Los Angeles, CA 90048-5515

TEL: (213) 782-2000

DATE: March

FREQUENCY: Monthly

COVER PRICE: $3.50

EDITORIAL CONCEPT: *"See and experience the full panorama of the whirlwind life of stock car racing."*

SUBSCRIPTION PRICE: n/a

TOTAL NUMBER OF PAGES: 80

TOTAL NUMBER OF AD PAGES: 13

PUBLISHER: John Dianna

EDITOR: Stephanie Coles Torres

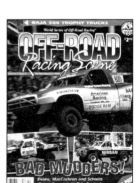

Off-Road Racing Scene

PUBLISHED BY: R.J. Conlin Inc.

6111 Jackson Rd.

Ann Arbor, MI 48103

TEL: (313) 662-1828

DATE: July

FREQUENCY: Bimonthly

COVER PRICE: $2.95

EDITORIAL CONCEPT: *Focuses on the World Series of Off-Road Racing with articles like "Bad Mudders!" and "Baja 500 Trophy Trucks."*

SUBSCRIPTION PRICE: n/a

TOTAL NUMBER OF PAGES: 40

TOTAL NUMBER OF AD PAGES: 6

PUBLISHER: Bob Conlin

EDITOR: Theresa Gralinski

Road & Track Presents Open Road

PUBLISHED BY: Hachette Filipacchi

1633 Broadway

New York, NY 10019

TEL: (212) 767-6779

DATE: Fall/Winter

FREQUENCY: 3/year

COVER PRICE: $3.95

SUBSCRIPTION PRICE: n/a

TOTAL NUMBER OF PAGES: 140

TOTAL NUMBER OF AD PAGES: 32

PUBLISHER: William Jeanes

EDITOR: Ron Sessions

EDITORIAL CONCEPT: *"The four-wheel drive adventure magazine."*

Sportsman's Journal Off-The-Road

PUBLISHED BY: Thicket Publishing Inc.

2100 Riverchase Ctr., Suite 118

Birmingham, AL 35244

TEL: (205) 987-6007

FREQUENCY: Quarterly

COVER PRICE: $3.50

SUBSCRIPTION PRICE: $8.00

TOTAL NUMBER OF PAGES: 92

TOTAL NUMBER OF AD PAGES: 24

PUBLISHER: Brock Ray

EDITOR: Don Kirk

EDITORIAL CONCEPT: *"Your complete source for light-truck parts and accessories."*

Rod & Customs Pictorial

PUBLISHED BY: McMullen & Yee Publications

774 S. Placentia Ave.

Placentia, CA 92670

TEL: (714) 572-2255 **FAX:** (714) 572-1864

DATE: Spring

FREQUENCY: Quarterly

COVER PRICE: $3.95

SUBSCRIPTION PRICE: n/a

TOTAL NUMBER OF PAGES: 134

TOTAL NUMBER OF AD PAGES: 23

EDITOR: Tom Vogele

EDITORIAL CONCEPT: *A pictorial look at some of the finest custom cars from the people of Street Rodder magazine.*

Stock Car Superstars

PUBLISHED BY: Starlog Entertainment Inc.

475 Park Ave. S.

New York, NY 10016

TEL: (212) 689-2830 **FAX:** (212) 889-7983

DATE: March

FREQUENCY: Quarterly

COVER PRICE: $3.99

SUBSCRIPTION PRICE: n/a

TOTAL NUMBER OF PAGES: 72

TOTAL NUMBER OF AD PAGES: 6

PUBLISHER: Norman Jacobs

EDITOR: Michael Benson

EDITORIAL CONCEPT: *"Complete NASCAR coverage."*

Speedway Pit Pass Magazine

PUBLISHED BY: Pit Pass Magazine Inc.

7030 Osteen Rd.

New Port Richey, FL 34653

TEL: (813) 847-4190 **FAX:** (813) 843-8474

FREQUENCY: Monthly

COVER PRICE: $3.50

SUBSCRIPTION PRICE: $16.95

TOTAL NUMBER OF PAGES: 50

TOTAL NUMBER OF AD PAGES: 11

PUBLISHER: J.W. Murray

EDITOR: James D. Lipsey

EDITORIAL CONCEPT: *The "racer's monthly almanac" of stock-car racing.*

Super Truck Spectacular

PUBLISHED BY: Starlog Group Inc.

475 Park Ave. S.

New York, NY 10016

TEL: (212) 689-2830 **FAX:** (212) 889-7983

DATE: June

FREQUENCY: Quarterly

COVER PRICE: $3.99

SUBSCRIPTION PRICE: n/a

TOTAL NUMBER OF PAGES: 68

TOTAL NUMBER OF AD PAGES: 5

PUBLISHER: Norman Jacobs

EDITOR: Michael Benson

EDITORIAL CONCEPT: *Features articles such as "Anatomy of a NASCAR Super Truck!"*

Z Car Magazine

PUBLISHED BY: Seacoast Publishing Inc.

1565-A Lakeside Dr.

Felton, CA 95018

TEL: (408) 335-7550

DATE: March/April

FREQUENCY: Bimonthly

COVER PRICE: $3.95

SUBSCRIPTION PRICE: $20.00

TOTAL NUMBER OF PAGES: 48

TOTAL NUMBER OF AD PAGES: 13

PUBLISHER: Don Hazen

EDITOR: Don Hazen

EDITORIAL CONCEPT: *The magazine for fans of Nissan's Z-car.*

The Best Of Low Rider Magazine

PUBLISHED BY: Park Avenue Publishing

106 Exchange Pl.

Pomona, CA 91768

TEL: (909) 598-2300

FREQUENCY: Special

COVER PRICE: $4.95

SUBSCRIPTION PRICE: n/a

TOTAL NUMBER OF PAGES: 84

TOTAL NUMBER OF AD PAGES: 12

PUBLISHER: Alberto Lopez

EDITOR: Dick DeLoach

EDITORIAL CONCEPT: *A look at the best low-rider cars and trucks featured in prior issues of the magazine.*

ANNUAL, SPECIAL OR FREQUENCY UNKNOWN

Automobile Buying & Leasing '95

PUBLISHED BY: K-III Magazine Corp.

888 Seventh Ave.

New York, NY 10106

TEL: (212) 745-0100

FREQUENCY: Special

COVER PRICE: $4.95

SUBSCRIPTION PRICE: n/a

TOTAL NUMBER OF PAGES: 202

TOTAL NUMBER OF AD PAGES: 47

PUBLISHER: David E. Davis Jr.

EDITOR: Michael Jordas

EDITORIAL CONCEPT: *"Coupes, sedans, pickups, sport-utilities and vans; plus straight talk about leasing."*

Chrysler Engines Etc.

PUBLISHED BY: RHO Publications

1580 Hampton Rd.

Bensalem, PA 19020-4610

TEL: (215) 639-4456

FREQUENCY: Special

COVER PRICE: $3.95

SUBSCRIPTION PRICE: n/a

TOTAL NUMBER OF PAGES: 82

TOTAL NUMBER OF AD PAGES: 15

EDITOR: Robert Oskiera

EDITORIAL CONCEPT: *"Hot horsepower, tech power special for the Chrysler car enthusiast."*

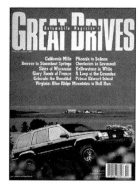

Automobile Magazine's Great Drives

PUBLISHED BY: K-III Magazine Corp.

888 Seventh Ave.

New York, NY 10106

TEL: (212) 745-0100

FREQUENCY: Special

COVER PRICE: $3.95

SUBSCRIPTION PRICE: n/a

TOTAL NUMBER OF PAGES: 124

TOTAL NUMBER OF AD PAGES: 21

EDITOR: Jean Lindamood

EDITORIAL CONCEPT: *"The editors of* Automobile Magazine *have taken the road less traveled, and we'd like to share our adventures with you."*

Dune Buggies & Hot VWs *Presents* Sand Sports Collector's Edition

PUBLISHED BY: Wright Publishing Co. Inc.

P.O. Box 2260

Costa Mesa, CA 92628

TEL: (714) 979-2561

DATE: Fall

FREQUENCY: Special

COVER PRICE: $5.95

SUBSCRIPTION PRICE: n/a

TOTAL NUMBER OF PAGES: 116

TOTAL NUMBER OF AD PAGES: 11

PUBLISHER: Judy Wright

EDITOR: Tom Chambers

EDITORIAL CONCEPT: *Includes articles like "Hopped-Up Honda," "Where to Ride Duning U.S.A.," "How-To Budget Engine" and "Fabricating Basics."*

Dune Buggies & Hot VWs *Presents*
The California Look And How To Get It!

PUBLISHED BY: Wright Publishing Co. Inc.

P.O. Box 2260, Costa Mesa, CA 92628

TEL: (714) 979-2560

DATE: Summer

FREQUENCY: Special

COVER PRICE: $5.95

SUBSCRIPTION PRICE: n/a

TOTAL NUMBER OF PAGES: 128

TOTAL NUMBER OF AD PAGES: 17

PUBLISHER: Judy Wright

EDITOR: Tom Chambers

EDITORIAL CONCEPT: *Features VWs altered to have "the old Cal look" characteristics of lowered, dechromed nerf bars, big engines and very subtle paint and interiors.*

Hemi Muscle

PUBLISHED BY: CSK Publishing Co. Inc.

299 Market St.

Saddle Brook, NJ 07663

TEL: (201) 712-9300

FREQUENCY: Special

COVER PRICE: $4.50

SUBSCRIPTION PRICE: n/a

TOTAL NUMBER OF PAGES: 100

TOTAL NUMBER OF AD PAGES: 11

PUBLISHER: Ralph Monti

EDITOR: Jeff Bauer

EDITORIAL CONCEPT: *A magazine dedicated to the Hemi V8 engine.*

5.0 Mustang Hop-Ups

PUBLISHED BY: Petersen Publishing Co.

6420 Wilshire Blvd.

Los Angeles, CA 90048

TEL: (213) 782-2000

FREQUENCY: Special

COVER PRICE: $3.95

SUBSCRIPTION PRICE: n/a

TOTAL NUMBER OF PAGES: 100

TOTAL NUMBER OF AD PAGES: 14

PUBLISHER: John Dianna

EDITOR: Tara Baulkus Mello

EDITORIAL CONCEPT: *"Great techniques that can help you turn your project vehicle into a powerful, performing pony car."*

Hot Shoebox Chevys

PUBLISHED BY: Petersen Publishing Co.

6420 Wilshire Blvd.

Los Angeles, CA 90048-5515

TEL: (213) 782-2000

FREQUENCY: Special

COVER PRICE: $4.95

SUBSCRIPTION PRICE: n/a

TOTAL NUMBER OF PAGES: 164

TOTAL NUMBER OF AD PAGES: 12

PUBLISHER: Jim Adolph

EDITOR: Tara Baukus Mello

EDITORIAL CONCEPT: *Articles include "250-Plus Truck Parts and Tools."*

Ford Truckin'

PUBLISHED BY: McMullen & Yee Publishing

774 S. Placentia Ave.

Placentia, CA 92670-6846

TEL: (714) 572-2255 **FAX:** (714) 572-1864

DATE: Winter

FREQUENCY: Special

COVER PRICE: $4.95

SUBSCRIPTION PRICE: 3

TOTAL NUMBER OF PAGES: 164

TOTAL NUMBER OF AD PAGES: 22

PUBLISHER: Tom McMullen

EDITOR: Steve Stillwell

EDITORIAL CONCEPT: *The editors of Truckin' magazine present this special edition for Ford lovers. It includes solid technical material and a look at Ford's current crop of workhorse trucks.*

Motor Trend Performance Cars

PUBLISHED BY: Petersen Publishing Co.

6420 Wilshire Blvd.

Los Angeles, CA 90048

TEL: (213) 282-2000

FREQUENCY: Special

COVER PRICE: $4.95

SUBSCRIPTION PRICE: n/a

TOTAL NUMBER OF PAGES: 154

TOTAL NUMBER OF AD PAGES: 24

PUBLISHER: Lee Kelley

EDITOR: Robert MacLeod

EDITORIAL CONCEPT: *The complete 1995 buyer's guide to over 100 models, including full specifications and pricing.*

Mustang Classics

PUBLISHED BY: Starlog Entertainment Inc.

475 Park Ave. S.

New York, NY 10016

TEL: (212) 689-2830   **FAX:** (212) 889-7983

FREQUENCY: Special

COVER PRICE: $6.99

SUBSCRIPTION PRICE: n/a

TOTAL NUMBER OF PAGES: 84

TOTAL NUMBER OF AD PAGES: 7

PUBLISHER: Norman Jacobs

EDITOR: Michael Benson

EDITORIAL CONCEPT: *Four decades of Mustangs presented in richly photographed form.*

Street Machine Special: Super Coupes

PUBLISHED BY: Challenge Publications Inc.

7950 Deering Ave.

Canoga Park, CA 91304

TEL: (818) 887-0550   **FAX:** (818) 884-1343

FREQUENCY: Special

COVER PRICE: $4.95

SUBSCRIPTION PRICE: n/a

TOTAL NUMBER OF PAGES: 80

TOTAL NUMBER OF AD PAGES: 5

PUBLISHER: Edwin A. Schnepf

EDITOR: Rex Reese

EDITORIAL CONCEPT: *"Covers the spectrum of coupedom. Resto rods, nostalgia, traditional rods, glass bodies and showtime favorites are profiled here."*

Slammer

PUBLISHED BY: Four Wheeler Publishing Ltd.

277 Park Ave.

New York, NY 10172

TEL: (212) 496-6100

FREQUENCY: n/a

COVER PRICE: $3.25

SUBSCRIPTION PRICE: n/a

TOTAL NUMBER OF PAGES: 132

TOTAL NUMBER OF AD PAGES: 51

PUBLISHER: Bob Guccione

EDITOR: Hoyt Vandenberg

EDITORIAL CONCEPT: *Features "extreme" trucks, with a look inside America's truck shows.*

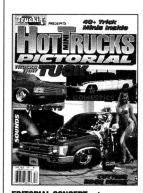

Truckin' Presents Hot Mini-Trucks Pictorial

PUBLISHED BY: McMullen & Yee Publishing

774 S. Placentia Ave.

Placentia, CA 92670

TEL: (714) 572-2255   **FAX:** (714) 572-1864

FREQUENCY: n/a

COVER PRICE: $4.95

SUBSCRIPTION PRICE: n/a

TOTAL NUMBER OF PAGES: 164

TOTAL NUMBER OF AD PAGES: 14

PUBLISHER: Chris C. Yee

EDITOR: Steve Stillwell

EDITORIAL CONCEPT: *A magazine devoted to custom truck builders.*

Sport Truck Annual '95

PUBLISHED BY: Peterson Publishing Co.

6420 Wilshire Blvd.

Los Angeles, CA 90048-5515

TEL: (213) 782-2000

FREQUENCY: n/a

COVER PRICE: $4.95

SUBSCRIPTION PRICE: n/a

TOTAL NUMBER OF PAGES: 132

TOTAL NUMBER OF AD PAGES: 10

PUBLISHER: John Dianna

EDITOR: Glenn Grissom

EDITORIAL CONCEPT: *"Stuffed full of pages of easy-to-use buyer's guides, tech tips and 100+ best bolt-ons."*

Aviation Art Showcase

PUBLISHED BY: Vector Publishing Group

P.O. Box 1320

Summerland, CA 93067

TEL: (805) 565-4782 **FAX:** (805) 565-5590

DATE: Fall

FREQUENCY: Quarterly

COVER PRICE: $4.95

SUBSCRIPTION PRICE: n/a

TOTAL NUMBER OF PAGES: 84

TOTAL NUMBER OF AD PAGES: 21

PUBLISHER: Jim Bender

EDITOR: Jim Bender

EDITORIAL CONCEPT: *A showcase for aviation art and artists.*

Military Surplus Warplanes

PUBLISHED BY: Challenge Publications Inc.

7950 Deering Ave.

Canoga Park, CA 91304

TEL: (818) 887-0550 **FAX:** (818) 884-1343

FREQUENCY: Quarterly

COVER PRICE: $5.95

SUBSCRIPTION PRICE: n/a

TOTAL NUMBER OF PAGES: 88

TOTAL NUMBER OF AD PAGES: 5

PUBLISHER: Edwin A. Schnepf

EDITOR: Michael O'Leary

EDITORIAL CONCEPT: *A magazine which looks at the destruction as well as the whereabouts of vintage military aircraft.*

High Performance Kitbuilts

PUBLISHED BY: Challenge Publications Inc.

7950 Deering Ave.

Canoga Park, CA 91304

TEL: (818) 887-0550 **FAX:** (818) 884-1343

FREQUENCY: Quarterly

COVER PRICE: $5.95

SUBSCRIPTION PRICE: n/a

TOTAL NUMBER OF PAGES: 88

TOTAL NUMBER OF AD PAGES: 8

PUBLISHER: Edwin A. Schnepf

EDITOR: Norm Goyer

EDITORIALCONCEPT: *"Affordable flying special," which features some of the best high performance kit planes you can build at home.*

Mountain Pilot

PUBLISHED BY: Wiesner Publishing

7009 S. Potomac St.

Englewood, CO 80112

TEL: (303) 397-7600

DATE: October

FREQUENCY: Monthly

COVER PRICE: $2.95

SUBSCRIPTION PRICE: n/a

TOTAL NUMBER OF PAGES: 48

TOTAL NUMBER OF AD PAGES: 24

PUBLISHER: Edward D. Huber

EDITOR: Edward D. Huber

EDITORIAL CONCEPT: *Formerly titled Wings West, this magazine provides useful information for flying in the mountains.*

Jet Classics

PUBLISHED BY: Challenge Publications Inc.

7950 Deering Ave.

Canoga Park, CA 91304

TEL: (818) 887-0550 **FAX:** (818) 884-1343

DATE: Spring

FREQUENCY: Quarterly

COVER PRICE: $4.50

SUBSCRIPTION PRICE: n/a

TOTAL NUMBER OF PAGES: 72

TOTAL NUMBER OF AD PAGES: 5

PUBLISHER: Edwin A. Schnepf

EDITOR: Michael O'Leary

EDITORIAL CONCEPT: *A magazine devoted to the great jets of the past, featuring articles on the history and evolution of jet fighters.*

Ultralights

PUBLISHED BY: Challenge Publications Inc.

7950 Deering Ave.

Canoga Park, CA 91304

TEL: (818) 887-0550 **FAX:** (818) 884-1343

DATE: Spring

FREQUENCY: Quarterly

COVER PRICE: $3.95

SUBSCRIPTION PRICE: n/a

TOTAL NUMBER OF PAGES: 80

TOTAL NUMBER OF AD PAGES: 5

PUBLISHER: Edwin A. Schnepf

EDITOR: Robert M. Goyer

EDITORIAL CONCEPT *Articles for ultralight enthusiasts, plus a directory of ultralight clubs, flight parks and instructors.*

Learn to Fly

PUBLISHED BY: Challenge Publications Inc.

7950 Deering Ave.

Canoga Park, CA 91304

TEL: (818) 887-0550   **FAX:** (818) 884-1343

FREQUENCY: Special

COVER PRICE: $5.95

SUBSCRIPTION PRICE: n/a

TOTAL NUMBER OF PAGES: 96

TOTAL NUMBER OF AD PAGES: 8

PUBLISHER: Edwin A. Schnepf

EDITOR: Norm Goyer

EDITORIAL CONCEPT: *Instructions from articles such as "How to Take-Off and Land" show aspiring pilots how to fulfill their dreams.*

Warbird

PUBLISHED BY: Challenge Publications Inc.

7950 Deering Ave.

Canoga Park, CA 91304

TEL: (818) 887-0550   **FAX:** (818) 884-1343

FREQUENCY: Special

COVER PRICE: $5.95

SUBSCRIPTION PRICE: n/a

TOTAL NUMBER OF PAGES: 88

TOTAL NUMBER OF AD PAGES: 3

PUBLISHER: Edwin A. Schnepf

EDITOR: Michael O'Leary

EDITORIAL CONCEPT: *"A magazine dedicated to the history of great warplanes from past wars."*

American Baby: *Baby Fair Special*

EDITORIAL CONCEPT: *A special issue for expectant and new parents emphasizing the enjoyable aspects of the new parent experience.*

PUBLISHED BY: Cahners Publishing Co.

249 W. 17th St.

New York, NY 10011

TEL: (212) 645-0067

FREQUENCY: Special

COVER PRICE: Free

SUBSCRIPTION PRICE: n/a

TOTAL NUMBER OF PAGES: 52

TOTAL NUMBER OF AD PAGES: 18

PUBLISHER: Judith Princz

EDITOR: Judith Nolte

Baby Names

EDITORIAL CONCEPT: *"Guidance through the myths, mysteries and meanings of hundreds of boys' and girls' names."*

PUBLISHED BY: Four Star Publications Inc.

P.O. Box 23368

Shawnee Mission, KS 66223

TEL: n/a

FREQUENCY: Special

COVER PRICE: $2.95

SUBSCRIPTION PRICE: n/a

TOTAL NUMBER OF PAGES: 100

TOTAL NUMBER OF AD PAGES: 1

EDITOR: n/a

Black Child

PUBLISHED BY: Interrace Publications Inc.

2870 Peachtree Rd., Suite 264

Atlanta, GA 30305

TEL: (404) 364-9195

FREQUENCY: Bimonthly

COVER PRICE: $2.50

SUBSCRIPTION PRICE: $12.00

TOTAL NUMBER OF PAGES: 40

TOTAL NUMBER OF AD PAGES: 3

PUBLISHER: Candy Mills

EDITOR: Candy Mills

EDITORIAL CONCEPT: *A new magazine for African-American parents, featuring articles on encouraging children to read, healthy soul cuisine and breast-feeding.*

Black Professional

PUBLISHED BY: Career Communications

729 E. Pratt St., Suite 504

Baltimore, MD 21202

TEL: (410) 244-7101

FAX: (410) 752-1837

DATE: Spring/Summer

FREQUENCY: Quarterly

COVER PRICE: $5.00

SUBSCRIPTION PRICE: $15.00

TOTAL NUMBER OF PAGES: 44

TOTAL NUMBER OF AD PAGES: 22

PUBLISHER: Hayward Henderson

EDITOR: Garland Thompson

EDITORIAL CONCEPT: *"The insider's guide to career savvy" offers features like "America's Hottest Growth Industries."*

Black College Magazine

PUBLISHED BY: Black College Magazine

P.O. Box 44095

Kennesaw, GA 30144

TEL: (770) 424-3797

FREQUENCY: Semiannually

COVER PRICE: $3.95

SUBSCRIPTION PRICE: $7.43

TOTAL NUMBER OF PAGES: 76

TOTAL NUMBER OF AD PAGES: 24

PUBLISHER: Robert K. Settle

EDITOR: Spaulding Settle

EDITORIAL CONCEPT: *A magazine devoted to African-American parents and students, designed to help ease the burden of research in preparation for higher learning.*

Blackriders

PUBLISHED BY: Blackriders Magazine Inc.

4320 Hamilton St.

Hyattsville, MD 20781

TEL: (301) 927-6686

DATE: Fall

FREQUENCY: Quarterly

COVER PRICE: $3.95

SUBSCRIPTION PRICE: $12.00

TOTAL NUMBER OF PAGES: 66

TOTAL NUMBER OF AD PAGES: 8

PUBLISHER: N.H. Lacy

EDITOR: n/a

EDITORIAL CONCEPT: *"The motorcycle magazine for today's black riders," featuring editorials and reviews directed toward America's black cyclists.*

Black Elegance Presents Belle

PUBLISHED BY: Starlog Entertainment Inc.

475 Park Ave. S.

New York, NY 10016

TEL: (212) 689-2830

DATE: Fall

FREQUENCY: Quarterly

COVER PRICE: $3.99

SUBSCRIPTION PRICE: $12.97

TOTAL NUMBER OF PAGES: 84

TOTAL NUMBER OF AD PAGES: 17

PUBLISHER: Robert Taylor, William Tramell

EDITOR: Sonia Alleyne

EDITORIAL CONCEPT: *This magazine for full-figured women "celebrates the lifestyles of real women" while also addressing the issues and concerns they face living in a "thin-is-in" society.*

Bovanti

PUBLISHED BY: Bovanti Communications

4820 Old National Hwy.

Atlanta, GA 30337

TEL: (404) 209-0909

DATE: Spring

FREQUENCY: Quarterly

COVER PRICE: $1.95

SUBSCRIPTION PRICE: $7.00

TOTAL NUMBER OF PAGES: 40

TOTAL NUMBER OF AD PAGES: 13

PUBLISHER: Michael J. Bohannon

EDITOR: Anita H. Bohannon

EDITORIAL CONCEPT: *A fashion magazine for African-Americans including features about Shaka King, "Your Scentsual ID" and "Authentic African Patterns."*

IBA Magazine

PUBLISHED BY: IBA Publications Inc.

P.O. Box 470401

Los Angeles, CA 90047

TEL: (213) 569-3439

FREQUENCY: Bimonthly

COVER PRICE: $2.00

SUBSCRIPTION PRICE: n/a

TOTAL NUMBER OF PAGES: 68

TOTAL NUMBER OF AD PAGES: 20

PUBLISHER: Bernard Garrett

EDITOR: Willie Garrett-Kemp

EDITORIAL CONCEPT: *Focuses on Issues in Black America with articles about health care reform, high-risk pregnancy, the Urban Minister's Alliance and real estate.*

African-American History Magazine

PUBLISHED BY: Cowles History Group Inc.

741 Miller Dr. SE, Suite D-2

Leesburg, VA 22075

TEL: (703) 771-9400 **FAX:** (703) 779-8345

DATE: Spring

FREQUENCY: Special

COVER PRICE: $3.95

SUBSCRIPTION PRICE: n/a

TOTAL NUMBER OF PAGES: 92

TOTAL NUMBER OF AD PAGES: 24

PUBLISHER: Timothy L. Jenkins

EDITOR: Joanne Harrii

EDITORIAL CONCEPT: *This collector's issue celebrating Black History Month features "The Untold Story of Blacks in the White House."*

American Woman
Bridal Hair Guide

EDITORIAL CONCEPT: *"Choose your perfect bridal style from photos. Plus, ideas for the groom, bridesmaids and mother of the bride."*

PUBLISHED BY: GCR Publishing Group Inc.

1700 Broadway

New York, NY 10019

TEL: (212) 541-7100

FREQUENCY: Annually

COVER PRICE: $3.95

SUBSCRIPTION PRICE: n/a

TOTAL NUMBER OF PAGES: 84

TOTAL NUMBER OF AD PAGES: 0

PUBLISHER: Charles Goodman

EDITOR: Stephanie Pedersen

Victorian Bride

EDITORIAL CONCEPT: *A magazine dedicated to celebrating Victorian-style weddings.*

PUBLISHED BY: GCR Publishing Group Inc.

1700 Broadway

New York, NY 10019

TEL: (212) 541-7100

FREQUENCY: Annually

COVER PRICE: $3.95

SUBSCRIPTION PRICE: n/a

TOTAL NUMBER OF PAGES: 84

TOTAL NUMBER OF AD PAGES: 5

PUBLISHER: Charles Goodman

EDITOR: Mary Arrigo

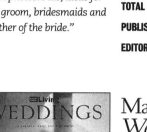

Martha Stewart Living
Weddings

EDITORIAL CONCEPT: *"A special issue for the bride."*

PUBLISHED BY: Time Inc. Ventures

20 W. 43rd St.

New York, NY 10036

TEL: (212) 522-7800

FREQUENCY: Special

COVER PRICE: $5.50

SUBSCRIPTION PRICE: n/a

TOTAL NUMBER OF PAGES: 276

TOTAL NUMBER OF AD PAGES: 154

PUBLISHER: Eric C. Thorkilsen

EDITOR: Martha Stewart

Consultants Report

PUBLISHED BY: Future Learning Press

P.O. Box 1902

Lake Oswego, OR 97035

TEL: (503) 635-4107 **FAX:** (503) 635-8728

DATE: August/September

FREQUENCY: Bimonthly

COVER PRICE: $3.95

SUBSCRIPTION PRICE: n/a

TOTAL NUMBER OF PAGES: 48

TOTAL NUMBER OF AD PAGES: 9

PUBLISHER: Elizabeth Korsmo-Severin

EDITOR: C. Sherman Severin

EDITORIAL CONCEPT: *"The authoritative source of new ideas for executives, consultants, businesses and communities."*

The National Home Business Directory Magazine

PUBLISHED BY: United Marketing & Research

P.O. Box 2712

Huntington Beach, CA 92647

TEL: (714) 843-8223 **FAX:** (714) 962-7722

DATE: Summer

FREQUENCY: Bimonthly

COVER PRICE: $3.95

SUBSCRIPTION PRICE: n/a

TOTAL NUMBER OF PAGES: 84

TOTAL NUMBER OF AD PAGES: 39

EDITOR: Stacy and Richard Henderson

EDITORIAL CONCEPT: *"The magazine of profitable home-based business opportunities."*

Fast Company

PUBLISHED BY: Fast Company Inc.

745 Boylston St.

Boston, MA 02116

TEL: (617) 927-2240

FREQUENCY: Bimonthly

COVER PRICE: $3.95

SUBSCRIPTION PRICE: n/a

TOTAL NUMBER OF PAGES: 178

TOTAL NUMBER OF AD PAGES: 94

PUBLISHER: Thomas R. Evans

EDITOR: Bill Breen

EDITORIAL CONCEPT: *"The new rules of business"* for fast-paced business people.

Opportunist

PUBLISHED BY: American Small Business & Investors Association

375 Douglas Ave., Suite 1012

Altamonte Springs, FL 32714

TEL: (407) 788-0123 **FAX:** (407) 788-3933

DATE: Winter

FREQUENCY: Quarterly

COVER PRICE: $4.95

SUBSCRIPTION PRICE: $10.00

TOTAL NUMBER OF PAGES: 110

TOTAL NUMBER OF AD PAGES: 55

PUBLISHER: Roy Meadows

EDITOR: Roy Meadows

EDITORIAL CONCEPT: *The first newsstand issue of the ASBIA's magazine includes articles like "Donald Trump: Alive and Well" and "Electronic Superhighway."*

Individual Investor

PUBLISHED BY: Individual Investor Group

333 Seventh Ave.

New York, NY 10001

TEL: (212) 843-2777 **FAX:** (212) 843-2789

DATE: July

FREQUENCY: Monthly

COVER PRICE: $2.95

SUBSCRIPTION PRICE: $22.95

TOTAL NUMBER OF PAGES: 140

TOTAL NUMBER OF AD PAGES: 50

EDITOR: Jonathan Steinberg

EDITORIAL CONCEPT: *The redesigned magazine promises readers "a huge volume of great investment ideas."*

Outlook Americas

PUBLISHED BY: Afiniti Communications

1 Metro Square Building

2695 Villa Creek Dr., Suite 107

Dallas, TX 95234

TEL: (800) 632-9332

DATE: Fall

FREQUENCY: Quarterly

COVER PRICE: $4.95

SUBSCRIPTION PRICE: $12.00

TOTAL NUMBER OF PAGES: 68

TOTAL NUMBER OF AD PAGES: 16

PUBLISHER: Eric Kleinsorge

EDITOR: Eric Kleinsorge

EDITORIAL CONCEPT: *"The magazine for America's corporate leaders."*

P.O.V.

PUBLISHED BY: B.Y.O.B. Ventures Inc.

575 Lexington Ave., 25th Floor

New York, NY 10022

TEL: (212) 421-8676 **FAX:** (212) 421-7434

DATE: Spring/Summer

FREQUENCY: 5/year

COVER PRICE: $3.00

SUBSCRIPTION PRICE: $10.00

TOTAL NUMBER OF PAGES: 98

TOTAL NUMBER OF AD PAGES: 26

PUBLISHER: Drew C. Massey

EDITOR: Randall Lane

EDITORIAL CONCEPT: *A magazine from the "Be Your Own Boss" company designed "to help each of us take better control of our professional, financial and personal lives."*

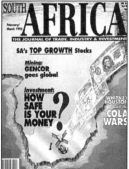

South Africa: The Journal Of Trade, Industry & Investment

PUBLISHED BY: South Africa Journal

100 Ave. of the Americas

New York, NY 10013-1699

TEL: (212) 297-6118 **FAX:** (212) 679-6915

DATE: February/March

FREQUENCY: Bimonthly

COVER PRICE: $3.95

SUBSCRIPTION PRICE: $10.00

TOTAL NUMBER OF PAGES: 100

PUBLISHER: David Altman

EDITOR: Martin Schneider

EDITORIAL CONCEPT: *"The journal of trade, industry and investment for the business person who needs to know about the changing face of business in South Africa."*

Winning Strategies

PUBLISHED BY: Harris Media Inc.

77 W. Huron, Suite 2002

Chicago, IL 60610

TEL: (312) 664-2100 **FAX:** (312) 915-4051

FREQUENCY: Bimonthly

COVER PRICE: $4.95

SUBSCRIPTION PRICE: $25.00

TOTAL NUMBER OF PAGES: 52

TOTAL NUMBER OF AD PAGES: 9

PUBLISHER: Alexandra Harris

EDITOR: Alexandra Harris

EDITORIAL CONCEPT: *"Real-life stories and advice from ordinary women doing extraordinary things." Topics deal with finance, business, education, investments, health and travel.*

Working At Home

PUBLISHED BY: Success Multimedia

Enterprises

230 Park Ave.

New York, NY 10169

TEL: (212) 551-9414

DATE: Winter

FREQUENCY: Quarterly

COVER PRICE: $3.95

SUBSCRIPTION PRICE: n/a

TOTAL NUMBER OF PAGES: 130

TOTAL NUMBER OF AD PAGES: 22

PUBLISHER: Scott DeGarmo

EDITOR: Scott DeGarmo

EDITORIAL CONCEPT: *A guide to doing what you want, where you want.*

World Business: The Global Perspective

PUBLISHED BY: KPMG Peat Marwick L.L.P.

767 Fifth Ave.

New York, NY 10153

TEL: (212) 909-5242 **FAX:** (212) 909-5087

FREQUENCY: Quarterly

COVER PRICE: $7.00

SUBSCRIPTION PRICE: $20.00

TOTAL NUMBER OF PAGES: 52

TOTAL NUMBER OF AD PAGES: 11

PUBLISHER: Pamela Middleton

EDITOR: John Van Doorn

EDITORIAL CONCEPT: *"To help ease readers through the '90s and into the 21st century on the inevitable voyage to globalization."*

Your Future

PUBLISHED BY: Time Inc.

1271 Ave. of the Americas

Rockefeller Center

New York, NY 10020-1393

TEL: (212) 522-1212

DATE: Spring

FREQUENCY: Bimonthly

COVER PRICE: $2.50

SUBSCRIPTION PRICE: $15.00

TOTAL NUMBER OF PAGES: 114

TOTAL NUMBER OF AD PAGES: 38

EDITOR: Caroline Donnelly

EDITORIAL CONCEPT: *The editors of Money magazine present this new kind of personal finance publication for young adults.*

Inc. *Special Issue: The State Of Small Business*

PUBLISHED BY: Inc. Magazine

38 Commercial Wharf

Boston, MA 02110

TEL: (617) 248-8000 **FAX:** (617) 248-8090

FREQUENCY: Special

COVER PRICE: $3.00

SUBSCRIPTION PRICE: n/a

TOTAL NUMBER OF PAGES: 128

TOTAL NUMBER OF AD PAGES: 48

PUBLISHER: James J. Spanfeller

EDITOR: Michael S. Hopskin

EDITORIAL CONCEPT: *A special issue of Inc. Magazine focusing on the important issues for small business owners.*

Income Plus *Presents Success Secrets*

PUBLISHED BY: Opportunity Associates

73 Spring St., Suite 303

New York, NY 10012

TEL: (212) 925-3180 **FAX:** (212) 925-3612

DATE: Spring

FREQUENCY: Special

COVER PRICE: $2.50

SUBSCRIPTION PRICE: n/a

TOTAL NUMBER OF PAGES: 52

TOTAL NUMBER OF AD PAGES: 39

PUBLISHER: Shirrel Rhoades

EDITOR: Frances Marshall

EDITORIAL CONCEPT: *Success stories to get you started on the road to a secure financial future.*

Outdoor Action Magazine

PUBLISHED BY: McMullen & Yee Publishing

774 S. Placentia Ave.

Placentia, CA 92670

TEL: (714) 572-2255

DATE: June

FREQUENCY: Bimonthly

COVER PRICE: $3.00

SUBSCRIPTION PRICE: n/a

TOTAL NUMBER OF PAGES: 96

TOTAL NUMBER OF AD PAGES: 12

EDITOR: Daniel Sanchez

EDITORIAL CONCEPT: *Articles for beginner, intermediate and advanced outdoor activity enthusiasts.*

Great Outdoors: 1995 Annual Guide

PUBLISHED BY: Adirondack Life Inc.

P.O. Box 97

Jay, NY 12941-0097

TEL: (518) 946-2191

FREQUENCY: Annually

COVER PRICE: $3.95

SUBSCRIPTION PRICE: n/a

TOTAL NUMBER OF PAGES: 108

TOTAL NUMBER OF AD PAGES: 46

PUBLISHER: Tom Hughes

EDITOR: Elizabeth Folwell

EDITORIAL CONCEPT: *Adirondack Life magazine's 1995 guide to the New York mountain range.*

Outdoor Gear

PUBLISHED BY: Harris Publications Inc.

1115 Broadway

New York, NY 10010

TEL: (212) 807-7100   **FAX:** (212) 627-4678

FREQUENCY: Quarterly

COVER PRICE: $3.95

SUBSCRIPTION PRICE: n/a

TOTAL NUMBER OF PAGES: 100

TOTAL NUMBER OF AD PAGES: 31

PUBLISHER: Stanley R. Harris

EDITOR: Jane Ryan Beck

EDITORIAL CONCEPT: *"The buyer's guide to the hottest new products."*

Outside Buyer's Guide 1995

PUBLISHED BY: Mariah Media Inc.

420 Lexington Ave., Suite 440

New York, NY 10170

TEL: n/a

FREQUENCY: Special

COVER PRICE: $3.95

SUBSCRIPTION PRICE: n/a

TOTAL NUMBER OF PAGES: 202

TOTAL NUMBER OF AD PAGES: 67

PUBLISHER: Lawrence J. Burke

EDITOR: Lawrence J. Burke

EDITORIAL CONCEPT: *A guide to great values and smart choices in bikes, running shoes, in-line skates, electronics, hiking boots, clothing, tents, cameras and much more.*

ANNUAL, SPECIAL OR FREQUENCY UNKNOWN

Rodale's Guide To Family Camping

PUBLISHED BY: Rodale Press Inc.

33 E. Minor St.

Emmaus, PA 18098

TEL: (610) 967-5171   **FAX:** (610) 967-8181

DATE: Spring

FREQUENCY: Special

COVER PRICE: $3.95

SUBSCRIPTION PRICE: $16.93

TOTAL NUMBER OF PAGES: 130

TOTAL NUMBER OF AD PAGES: 54

EDITOR: Tom Shealey

EDITORIAL CONCEPT: *"Within these pages you'll find all the practical information you'll need to undertake memorable family camping adventures that everyone will enjoy."*

Children's Book Review Magazine

PUBLISHED BY: Grove Publishing

1204 New York Dr.

Altadena, CA 91001-3146

TEL: (818) 791-5595 **FAX:** (818) 791-2905

DATE: Fall/Holiday

FREQUENCY: Quarterly

COVER PRICE: $3.95

SUBSCRIPTION PRICE: n/a

TOTAL NUMBER OF PAGES: 72

TOTAL NUMBER OF AD PAGES: 16

PUBLISHER: Greg Grove

EDITOR: Anita Sorenson

EDITORIAL CONCEPT: *"Devoted entirely to finding and presenting each season's most exceptional books for children of all ages."*

Time For Kids

PUBLISHED BY: Time Inc.

Time and Life Building

1271 Ave. of the Americas

New York, NY 10020-1393

TEL: (800) 777-8600

DATE: November

FREQUENCY: Weekly

COVER PRICE: n/a

SUBSCRIPTION PRICE: $3.95

TOTAL NUMBER OF PAGES: 8

TOTAL NUMBER OF AD PAGES: 0

EDITOR: Claudia Wallis

EDITORIAL CONCEPT: *Time covers world events in a way that young kids can understand.*

PopSci

PUBLISHED BY: PopSci for Kids

2 Park Ave.

New York, NY 10016

TEL: (212) 779-5081

FREQUENCY: Bimonthly

COVER PRICE: $2.50

SUBSCRIPTION PRICE: $9.97

TOTAL NUMBER OF PAGES: 36

TOTAL NUMBER OF AD PAGES: 5

EDITOR: Carol Hoidra

EDITORIAL CONCEPT: *A scientific magazine for kids "about how all the neat things in the world work."*

Zigzag

PUBLISHED BY: B&P Publishing Co. Inc.

575 Boylston St.

Boston, MA 02116

TEL: (617) 536-5536

FREQUENCY: Bimonthly

COVER PRICE: $1.95

SUBSCRIPTION PRICE: $17.97

DISCOUNT SUBSCRIPTION PRICE: $14.97

TOTAL NUMBER OF PAGES: 48

TOTAL NUMBER OF AD PAGES: 7

PUBLISHER: Alan Segal

EDITOR: R. Wayne Schmittberger

EDITORIAL CONCEPT: *"The amusement park you can take home" is full of puzzles, contests, magic tricks and even a new board game.*

Spiderman Magazine

PUBLISHED BY: Marvel Family Publishing

387 Park Ave. S.

New York, NY 10016

TEL: (212) 696-0808

DATE: Fall

FREQUENCY: 5/year

COVER PRICE: $2.50

SUBSCRIPTION PRICE: $12.50

TOTAL NUMBER OF PAGES: 36

TOTAL NUMBER OF AD PAGES: 10

EDITOR: Katy Dobbs

EDITORIAL CONCEPT: *A Spiderman comic book aimed at children includes a collectible poster and articles on the animated TV show.*

ANNUAL, SPECIAL OR FREQUENCY UNKNOWN

Disney's Big Time

PUBLISHED BY: Disney Magazine Publishing Inc.

114 Fifth Ave.

New York, NY 10011

TEL: (212) 633-4400 **FAX:** (212) 633-4817

DATE: May

FREQUENCY: n/a

COVER PRICE: Supplement

SUBSCRIPTION PRICE: n/a

TOTAL NUMBER OF PAGES: 64

TOTAL NUMBER OF AD PAGES: 23

PUBLISHER: Dorian Adams

EDITOR: Phyllis Ehrlich

EDITORIAL CONCEPT: *This magazine for kids covers the world of entertainment and points out "what's hot, what's not and what you gotta see and do."*

Animerica: Anime & Manga Monthly

PUBLISHED BY: VIZ Communications Inc.

P.O. Box 77010

San Francisco, CA 94107

TEL: (415) 546-7073

FREQUENCY: Monthly

COVER PRICE: $4.95

SUBSCRIPTION PRICE: n/a

TOTAL NUMBER OF PAGES: 74

TOTAL NUMBER OF AD PAGES: 14

PUBLISHER: Keizo Inoue

EDITOR: Seiji Horibuchi

EDITORIAL CONCEPT: *This Anime and Manga monthly promises "news, reviews, video games, music and more."*

Comics Lit Magazine

PUBLISHED BY: NBM Publishing Inc.

185 Madison Ave., Suite 1504

New York, NY 10016

TEL: (800) 886-1223

FREQUENCY: Monthly

COVER PRICE: $2.95

SUBSCRIPTION PRICE: $34.00

TOTAL NUMBER OF PAGES: 36

TOTAL NUMBER OF AD PAGES: 3

EDITOR: Terry Nantier

EDITORIAL CONCEPT: *Illustrated fiction from around the world.*

Big Guy And Rusty The Boy Robot

PUBLISHED BY: Dark Horse Comics Inc.

10956 SE Main St.

Milwaukie, OR 97222

TEL: (503) 652-8815   **FAX:** (503) 654-9440

DATE: July

FREQUENCY: Monthly

COVER PRICE: $4.95

SUBSCRIPTION PRICE: n/a

TOTAL NUMBER OF PAGES: 34

TOTAL NUMBER OF AD PAGES: 0

PUBLISHER: Mike Richardson

EDITOR: Bob Schreck

EDITORIAL CONCEPT: *A traditional comic style magazine packed with action, adventure and an oversized superhero.*

Conan The Savage

PUBLISHED BY: Marvel Comics

387 Park Ave. S.

New York, NY 10016

TEL: (212) 696-0808

FREQUENCY: Monthly

COVER PRICE: $2.95

SUBSCRIPTION PRICE: $35.40

TOTAL NUMBER OF PAGES: 52

TOTAL NUMBER OF AD PAGES: 2

PUBLISHER: Stan Lee

EDITOR: Carl Potts

EDITORIAL CONCEPT: *"Beginning a new era of barbarian action," presented in comic book style and richly illustrated.*

Comic Relief Presents Funny Stuff

PUBLISHED BY: Page One Publishers

2834 F St.

Eureka, CA 95502-6606

TEL: (707) 443-2820

FREQUENCY: Monthly

COVER PRICE: $3.95

SUBSCRIPTION PRICE: $28.00

TOTAL NUMBER OF PAGES: 84

TOTAL NUMBER OF AD PAGES: 4

PUBLISHER: Michael A. Kunz

EDITOR: Michael A. Kunz

EDITORIAL CONCEPT: *A monthly collection of the best comic strips from around the nation.*

Just The Write Touch

PUBLISHED BY: DiFonzo Enterprises Inc.

16 Conant Rd.

Nashua, NH 03062

TEL: (603) 598-9141   **FAX:** (603) 598-9141

DATE: December

FREQUENCY: Bimonthly

COVER PRICE: $5.00

SUBSCRIPTION PRICE: $25.00

TOTAL NUMBER OF PAGES: 28

TOTAL NUMBER OF AD PAGES: 0

PUBLISHER: Doris P. DiFonzo

EDITOR: Autumn-Rose Clarke

EDITORIAL CONCEPT: *Dedicated to the "cartoon character in you," this magazine offers interviews and articles on animation art and comic drawings.*

The Mighty I

PUBLISHED BY: Image Fan Club

P.O. Box 25468

Anaheim, CA 92825

TEL: (714) 634-4644

DATE: May/June

FREQUENCY: Bimonthly

COVER PRICE: $1.25

SUBSCRIPTION PRICE: $20.00 (2 years)

TOTAL NUMBER OF PAGES: 50

TOTAL NUMBER OF AD PAGES: 4

PUBLISHER: Tony Lobito

EDITOR: Kelly Van Landingham

EDITORIAL CONCEPT: *The comprehensive "map" to Image Comics and all of their related activities.*

Penthouse Men's Adventure Comix

PUBLISHED BY: Penthouse International

1965 Broadway

New York, NY 10023-5965

TEL: (212) 496-6100

FREQUENCY: Bimonthly

COVER PRICE: $4.95

SUBSCRIPTION PRICE: $32.00 (2 years)

TOTAL NUMBER OF PAGES: 98

TOTAL NUMBER OF AD PAGES: 21

PUBLISHER: Bob Guccione

EDITOR: George Caragonne

EDITORIAL CONCEPT: *"The illustrated pulp magazine for men."*

Spider-Man: The Lost Years

PUBLISHED BY: Marvel Comics

387 Park Ave. S.

New York, NY 10016

TEL: (212) 696-0808

FREQUENCY: Monthly

COVER PRICE: $2.95

SUBSCRIPTION PRICE: n/a

TOTAL NUMBER OF PAGES: 36

TOTAL NUMBER OF AD PAGES: 0

PUBLISHER: Stan Lee

EDITOR: Bob Budiansky

EDITORIAL CONCEPT: *"The story of how Ben Reilly, in his quest to find peace and happiness, crosses paths with the mysterious, murderous Kaine, a man dedicated to Reilly's destruction."*

Vantage Comic & Card Picks

PUBLISHED BY: Vantage-Golub Comm.

1300 W. Blue Mound Rd., Suite 110

Elm Grove, WI 53122

TEL: (414) 797-8221   **FAX:** (414) 797-7960

DATE: May

FREQUENCY: Monthly

COVER PRICE: $2.95

SUBSCRIPTION PRICE: $34.95

TOTAL NUMBER OF PAGES: 52

TOTAL NUMBER OF AD PAGES: 6

PUBLISHER: Rob Golub

EDITOR: Rob Golub

EDITORIAL CONCEPT: *Inside information for comic dealers and collectors.*

ANNUAL, SPECIAL OR FREQUENCY UNKNOWN

Disney's Pocohontas

PUBLISHED BY: Marvel Comics

387 Park Ave. S.

New York, NY 10016

TEL: (212) 696-0808

FREQUENCY: Special

COVER PRICE: $2.50

SUBSCRIPTION PRICE: n/a

TOTAL NUMBER OF PAGES: 52

TOTAL NUMBER OF AD PAGES: 3

PUBLISHER: Stan Lee

EDITOR: Hildy Mesnik, Karen Rosenfield

EDITORIAL CONCEPT: *The blockbuster animated feature of the year in comic book form.*

Heavy Metal Overdrive

PUBLISHED BY: Heavy Metal Magazine

584 Broadway, Suite 608

New York, NY 10012

TEL: (212) 274-8462   **FAX:** (212) 274-8696

FREQUENCY: Special

COVER PRICE: $4.50

SUBSCRIPTION PRICE: n/a

TOTAL NUMBER OF PAGES: 118

TOTAL NUMBER OF AD PAGES: 19

PUBLISHER: Kevin Eastman

EDITOR: Kevin Eastman

EDITORIAL CONCEPT: *A heavy metal comic book.*

Big Bad Mad

PUBLISHED BY: E.C. Publications Inc.

1700 Broadway

New York, NY 10019

TEL: (212) 636-5400

FREQUENCY: Special

COVER PRICE: $3.99

SUBSCRIPTION PRICE: n/a

TOTAL NUMBER OF PAGES: 100

TOTAL NUMBER OF AD PAGES: 1

PUBLISHER: Paul Levitz

EDITOR: Nick Meglin, John Ficarra

EDITORIAL CONCEPT: Mad Magazine's *usual brand of humor.*

Omni Comix

PUBLISHED BY: Omni Publications International Ltd.

277 Park Ave.

New York, NY 10172

TEL: (800) 289-6664

FREQUENCY: Special

COVER PRICE: $3.95

SUBSCRIPTION PRICE: n/a

TOTAL NUMBER OF PAGES: 138

TOTAL NUMBER OF AD PAGES: 51

PUBLISHER: Bob Guccione

EDITOR: Bob Guccione

EDITORIAL CONCEPT: *The creators of* Omni *present a science fiction comic.*

Mad TV

PUBLISHED BY: E.C. Publications Inc.

1700 Broadway

New York, NY 10019

TEL: (800) 462-3624

FREQUENCY: Special

COVER PRICE: $2.99

SUBSCRIPTION PRICE: n/a

TOTAL NUMBER OF PAGES: 50

TOTAL NUMBER OF AD PAGES: 1

PUBLISHER: Paul Levitz

EDITOR: Jenette Kahn

EDITORIAL CONCEPT: *"A special 'telezine' companion to the new Fox late night show"* featuring the comedic cartoon style of Mad Magazine.

Adobe Magazine

PUBLISHED BY: Adobe Systems Inc.

411 First Ave. S.

Seattle, WA 98104-2871

TEL: (206) 628-2321

FREQUENCY: 7/year

COVER PRICE: $5.00

SUBSCRIPTION PRICE: $35.00

TOTAL NUMBER OF PAGES: 108

TOTAL NUMBER OF AD PAGES: 54

PUBLISHER: Carla Noble

EDITOR: Nicholas H. Allison

EDITORIAL CONCEPT: *"Publishing, design, and digital media." A guide to Adobe products with the latest releases in techniques for graphic design.*

BackOffice Magazine

PUBLISHED BY: Affinity Publishing

100 W. Harrison, N. Tower

Suite 225

Seattle, WA 98119

TEL: (206) 281-0089

FREQUENCY: Quarterly

COVER PRICE: $4.95

SUBSCRIPTION PRICE: $17.95

TOTAL NUMBER OF PAGES: 60

TOTAL NUMBER OF AD PAGES: 16

EDITOR: Jeffrey Sloman

EDITORIAL CONCEPT: *A magazine dedicated to providing features and articles on Microsoft's BackOffice systems.*

Adult PC Guide

PUBLISHED BY: Dugent Publishing Corp.

2600 Douglas Rd., Suite 600

Coral Gables, FL 33134

TEL: (305) 557-0071

DATE: December

FREQUENCY: Bimonthly

COVER PRICE: $4.99

SUBSCRIPTION PRICE: n/a

TOTAL NUMBER OF PAGES: 84

TOTAL NUMBER OF AD PAGES: 12

EDITOR: Ward Mullens

EDITORIAL CONCEPT: *"The guide to X-rated cyberspace."*

Blaster

PUBLISHED BY: Blast Publishing Inc.

2223 Shattuck Ave.

Berkeley, CA 94704

TEL: n/a

DATE: January

FREQUENCY: Monthly

COVER PRICE: $3.95

SUBSCRIPTION PRICE: $19.95

TOTAL NUMBER OF PAGES: 80

TOTAL NUMBER OF AD PAGES: 29

PUBLISHER: Craig Lagron

EDITOR: Jon Phillips

EDITORIAL CONCEPT: *A magazine for digital technology enthusiasts, with articles on the newest products to hit the market.*

AutoCAD Tech Journal

PUBLISHED BY: Miller Freeman Inc.

600 Harrison St.

San Francisco, CA 94107

TEL: (415) 905-2200

FREQUENCY: Quarterly

COVER PRICE: $14.95

SUBSCRIPTION PRICE: $49.95

TOTAL NUMBER OF PAGES: 76

TOTAL NUMBER OF AD PAGES: 12

PUBLISHER: Michele Maguire

EDITOR: George Walsh

EDITORIAL CONCEPT: *"Your road map and guide for understanding and working with the many changes to come in AutoCAD."*

CD-ROM Advisor

PUBLISHED BY: Universal Media

801 Second Ave.

New York, NY 10017

TEL: (212) 986-5100

FREQUENCY: Quarterly

COVER PRICE: $5.99

SUBSCRIPTION PRICE: $11.97

TOTAL NUMBER OF PAGES: 234

TOTAL NUMBER OF AD PAGES: 22

PUBLISHER: Steven Rosenfield

EDITOR: Michael D. Espindle

EDITORIAL CONCEPT: *Reviews of over 1,000 CD-ROMs with ratings.*

CD-ROM Power

PUBLISHED BY: HG Publications Inc.

9171 Wilshire Blvd., Suite 300

Beverly Hills, CA 90210

TEL: n/a

DATE: February

FREQUENCY: Bimonthly

COVER PRICE: $3.99

SUBSCRIPTION PRICE: $21.95

TOTAL NUMBER OF PAGES: 100

TOTAL NUMBER OF AD PAGES: 5

PUBLISHER: Larry Flynt

EDITOR: Chris Gore

EDITORIAL CONCEPT: *"Your guide to the interactive world covers the latest CD's for your personal computer and video systems."*

Digit

PUBLISHED BY: Digital Education Cooperative

P.O. Box 488

Andover, NJ 07821

TEL: (201) 729-4315

FREQUENCY: Bimonthly

COVER PRICE: $2.95

SUBSCRIPTION PRICE: n/a

TOTAL NUMBER OF PAGES: 44

TOTAL NUMBER OF AD PAGES: 17

PUBLISHER: P.C. Carullo

EDITOR: Marcia Nehemiah

EDITORIAL CONCEPT: *"It's about the PEOPLE... not the machines!"*

Cyber Sports

PUBLISHED BY: Sendai Publishing Group

1920 Highland Ave., 2nd Floor

Lombard, IL 60148

TEL: (708) 916-7222   **FAX:** (708) 916-7227

DATE: Fall

FREQUENCY: Quarterly

COVER PRICE: $4.99

SUBSCRIPTION PRICE: $14.95

TOTAL NUMBER OF PAGES: 84

TOTAL NUMBER OF AD PAGES: 14

PUBLISHER: Steve Harris

EDITOR: Todd Mowatt

EDITORIAL CONCEPT: *"The magazine for sports video gaming enthusiasts"* contains articles on some of the best games to hit the market.

Fusion

PUBLISHED BY: Decker Publications Inc.

1920 Highland Ave., Suite 222

Lombard, IL 60148

TEL: (708) 916-7222   **FAX:** (708) 916-7227

DATE: August

FREQUENCY: Monthly

COVER PRICE: $3.99

SUBSCRIPTION PRICE: $23.95

TOTAL NUMBER OF PAGES: 116

TOTAL NUMBER OF AD PAGES: 27

PUBLISHER: Steve Harris

EDITOR: Bill Kunkel

EDITORIAL CONCEPT: *"The magazine of interactive entertainment."*

Delphi Informant

PUBLISHED BY: Informant Communications

10519 E. Stockton Blvd., Suite 142

Elk Grove, CA 95624-9704

TEL: (916) 686-6610   **FAX:** (916) 686-8497

FREQUENCY: Monthly

COVER PRICE: $4.95

SUBSCRIPTION PRICE: $49.95

TOTAL NUMBER OF PAGES: 68

TOTAL NUMBER OF AD PAGES: 13.5

PUBLISHER: Mitchell Koulouris

EDITOR: Jerry Coffey

EDITORIAL CONCEPT: *"The complete monthly guide to Delphi development."*

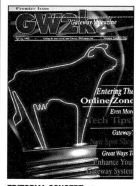

GW2K: Gateway Magazine

PUBLISHED BY: Gateway 2000 Inc.

610 Gateway Dr.

North Sioux City, SD 57049

TEL: (800) 846-2000   **FAX:** (605) 232-2023

FREQUENCY: Quarterly

COVER PRICE: Free

SUBSCRIPTION PRICE: n/a

TOTAL NUMBER OF PAGES: 36

TOTAL NUMBER OF AD PAGES: 7

EDITOR: Ann Vander Wiel

EDITORIAL CONCEPT: A magazine for owners of Gateway 2000 PCs, with articles on new equipment and tech tips.

Infobahn

PUBLISHED BY: Postmodern
Communications Inc.

985 E. Hillsdale Blvd., Suite 88

Foster City, CA 94404

TEL: (415) 638-2191

FREQUENCY: Bimonthly

COVER PRICE: $4.95

SUBSCRIPTION PRICE: $24.95

TOTAL NUMBER OF PAGES: 90

TOTAL NUMBER OF AD PAGES: 26

PUBLISHER: Michael C. Berch

EDITOR: Michael C. Berch

EDITORIAL CONCEPT: *A colorful trip down the information superhighway with well-written editorials as your road map.*

Maximize

PUBLISHED BY: Business Computer
Publishing Inc.

86 Elm St.

Peterborough, NH 03458

TEL: (603) 924-7271   **FAX:** (603) 924-6972

DATE: April

FREQUENCY: Bimonthly

COVER PRICE: $4.95

SUBSCRIPTION PRICE: $15.95

TOTAL NUMBER OF PAGES: 100

TOTAL NUMBER OF AD PAGES: 35.5

PUBLISHER: Stephen Robbins

EDITOR: Michael J. Comendul

EDITORIAL CONCEPT: *"The practical guide to Windows."*

Internet Underground

PUBLISHED BY: Sendai Media Group Inc.

1920 HIghland Ave., Suite 222

Lombard, IL 60148

TEL: (818) 712-9400

DATE: December

FREQUENCY: Monthly

COVER PRICE: $4.99

SUBSCRIPTION PRICE: $23.95

TOTAL NUMBER OF PAGES: 100

TOTAL NUMBER OF AD PAGES: 20

PUBLISHER: Steve Harris

EDITOR: Joe Funk

EDITORIAL CONCEPT: *Miscellaneous articles on the ins and outs of the Internet, including reviews of new technology and roadmaps to the superhighway.*

Multimedia Producer

PUBLISHED BY: Knowledge Industry
Publications Inc.

701 Westchester Ave.

White Plains, NY 10604

TEL: (914) 328-9157   **FAX:** (914) 328-9093

FREQUENCY: Bimonthly

COVER PRICE: $5.00

SUBSCRIPTION PRICE: $40.00

TOTAL NUMBER OF PAGES: 62

TOTAL NUMBER OF AD PAGES: 24.25

PUBLISHER: Andrew Mintz

EDITOR: Shonan Noronha

EDITORIAL CONCEPT: *"For creators and developers of interactive multimedia."*

Lotus Notes Advisor

PUBLISHED BY: Advisor Publications Inc.

4010 Morena Blvd.

San Diego, CA 92117

TEL: (619) 483-6400   **FAX:** (619) 483-9851

FREQUENCY: Bimonthly

COVER PRICE: $6.95

SUBSCRIPTION PRICE: $45.00

DISCOUNT SUBSCRIPTION PRICE: $39.00

TOTAL NUMBER OF PAGES: 60

TOTAL NUMBER OF AD PAGES: 19.25

PUBLISHER: William T. Ota

EDITOR: John L. Hawkins

EDITORIAL CONCEPT: *"A useful, insightful tool for those developing value-added solutions for Lotus Notes."*

Music & Computers

PUBLISHED BY: Miller Freeman Inc.

600 Harrison St.

San Francisco, CA 94107

TEL: (415) 905-2200   **FAX:** (415) 905-2233

FREQUENCY: Quarterly

COVER PRICE: $4.95

SUBSCRIPTION PRICE: n/a

TOTAL NUMBER OF PAGES: 82

TOTAL NUMBER OF AD PAGES: 17.2

PUBLISHER: Pat Cameron

EDITOR: Tom Darter

EDITORIAL CONCEPT: *A magazine for musicians of the computer age.*

The Net

PUBLISHED BY: Imagine Publishing Inc.

1350 Old Bayshore Hwy., Suite 210

Burlingame, CA 94010

TEL: (415) 696-1661

DATE: June

FREQUENCY: Monthly

COVER PRICE: $3.95

SUBSCRIPTION PRICE: $29.95

TOTAL NUMBER OF PAGES: 98

TOTAL NUMBER OF AD PAGES: 20.5

EDITOR: Mary Ellis

EDITORIAL CONCEPT: *A publication dedicated to helping readers get on the Internet.*

PC Sims Buyer's Guide

PUBLISHED BY: Challenge Publications Inc.

7950 Deering Ave.

Canoga Park, CA 91304

TEL: (818) 887-0550 **FAX:** (818) 884-1343

DATE: Summer

FREQUENCY: Quarterly

COVER PRICE: $4.95

SUBSCRIPTION PRICE: n/a

TOTAL NUMBER OF PAGES: 72

TOTAL NUMBER OF AD PAGES: 16.5

PUBLISHER: Edwin A. Schnepf

EDITOR: Jim Bender

EDITORIAL CONCEPT: *A look at some of the hottest games for your PC and some of the new games hitting the market.*

Next Generation

PUBLISHED BY: Imagine Publishing Inc.

1350 Old Bayshore Hwy, Suite 210

Burlingame, CA 94010

TEL: (415) 696-1688 **FAX:** (415) 696-1678

DATE: January

FREQUENCY: Monthly

COVER PRICE: $4.99

SUBSCRIPTION PRICE: $29.00

TOTAL NUMBER OF PAGES: 120

TOTAL NUMBER OF AD PAGES: 39

PUBLISHER: Jonathan Simpson-Bint

EDITOR: Neil West

EDITORIAL CONCEPT: *The essential guide to video games focuses on the future of interactive entertainment.*

Power Programmer Magazine

PUBLISHED BY: Sys-Con Publications

46 Holly St.

Jersey City, NJ 07305

TEL: (201) 332-1515 **FAX:** (201) 333-7361

DATE: February/March

FREQUENCY: Bimonthly

COVER PRICE: $6.95

SUBSCRIPTION PRICE: $41.00

TOTAL NUMBER OF PAGES: 52

TOTAL NUMBER OF AD PAGES: 20.5

PUBLISHER: Fuat A. Kircaali

EDITOR: Michael MacDonald

EDITORIAL CONCEPT: *A magazine devoted to high-end computer programming used in business and graphics.*

Online User

PUBLISHED BY: Online Inc.

462 Danbury Rd.

Wilton, CT 06897

TEL: (203) 761-1466

DATE: October/November

FREQUENCY: Bimonthly

COVER PRICE: $3.95

SUBSCRIPTION PRICE: n/a

TOTAL NUMBER OF PAGES: 68

TOTAL NUMBER OF AD PAGES: 14

PUBLISHER: Jefferey K. Pemberton

EDITOR: Paula Hane, Nancy Garman

EDITORIAL CONCEPT: *"Practical, how-to articles for professionals aimed at maximizing online effectiveness."*

Signal

PUBLISHED BY: Armed Forces Communications and Electronics Assn.

4400 Fair Lakes Ct.

Fairfax, VA 22033-3899

TEL: (703) 631-6100

DATE: June

FREQUENCY: Monthly

COVER PRICE: $5.00

SUBSCRIPTION PRICE: $44.00

TOTAL NUMBER OF PAGES: 108

TOTAL NUMBER OF AD PAGES: 34

PUBLISHER: Adm. James B. Busey IV

EDITOR: Clarence A. Robinson Jr.

EDITORIAL CONCEPT: *AFCEA's international journal brings readers the latest on the world of technology and military.*

Smart Computer & Software Retailing

PUBLISHED BY: Cahners Publishing Co.

275 Washington St.

Newton, MA 02158-1630

TEL: (910) 605-1136

FREQUENCY: 21/year

COVER PRICE: $3.95

SUBSCRIPTION PRICE: $79.94

TOTAL NUMBER OF PAGES: 64

TOTAL NUMBER OF AD PAGES: 26

PUBLISHER: George Lee Hundly Jr.

EDITOR: David English

EDITORIAL CONCEPT: *Provides information to help computer and software retailers make more profitable business decisions.*

Virtual City

PUBLISHED BY: Newsweek Inc. & Virtual Communications

444 Madison Ave.

New York, NY 10022

TEL: (212) 593-1541

DATE: Fall

FREQUENCY: Quarterly

COVER PRICE: $2.95

SUBSCRIPTION PRICE: $7.99

TOTAL NUMBER OF PAGES: 92

TOTAL NUMBER OF AD PAGES: 33

PUBLISHER: Jonathan Sacks

EDITOR: Lewis D'Vorkin

EDITORIAL CONCEPT: *Bringing you the latest information on the social scenes taking place on the Internet. Includes articles on celebrities who surf the Net and Web sites to see.*

3D Design

PUBLISHED BY: Miller Freeman Inc.

600 Harrison St.

San Francisco, CA 94107

TEL: (415) 905-2200

FREQUENCY: Monthly

COVER PRICE: $3.95

SUBSCRIPTION PRICE: $29.95

TOTAL NUMBER OF PAGES: 100

TOTAL NUMBER OF AD PAGES: 33

PUBLISHER: Johanna Kleppe

EDITOR: Kelly Dove

EDITORIAL CONCEPT: *A magazine designed to help the reader "control the many phases of 3-D design with hands-on tips, techniques and solutions."*

Visual Objects Advisor

PUBLISHED BY: Advisor Publications Inc.

4010 Morena Blvd.

San Diego, CA 92117

TEL: (619) 483-6400

FREQUENCY: Bimonthly

COVER PRICE: $5.95

SUBSCRIPTION PRICE: $39.00

TOTAL NUMBER OF PAGES: 52

TOTAL NUMBER OF AD PAGES: 12

PUBLISHER: William T. Ota

EDITOR: John L. Hawkins

EDITORIAL CONCEPT: *"The magazine for using Computer Associates' Visual Objects."*

VB Tech Journal

PUBLISHED BY: Oakley Publishing Co.

150 N. 4th St.

Springfield, OR 97477

TEL: (800) 234-0386   **FAX:** (503) 746-0071

FREQUENCY: Monthly

COVER PRICE: $3.50

SUBSCRIPTION PRICE: $24.95

TOTAL NUMBER OF PAGES: 82

TOTAL NUMBER OF AD PAGES: 28

PUBLISHER: Bobbi Sinyard

EDITOR: J.D. Hildebrand

EDITORIAL CONCEPT: *"Your visual basic resource offers tips and features on the latest techniques for visual presentations."*

VR World

PUBLISHED BY: Mecklermedia Corp.

20 Ketchum St.

Westport, CT 06880

TEL: (203) 226-6967

DATE: January/February

FREQUENCY: Bimonthly

COVER PRICE: $4.95

SUBSCRIPTION PRICE: $29.00

TOTAL NUMBER OF PAGES: 68

TOTAL NUMBER OF AD PAGES: 13

PUBLISHER: Alan M. Meckler

EDITOR: Sandra Kay Helsel

EDITORIAL CONCEPT: *"The magazine for virtual reality development and utilization."*

Windows NT Magazine

PUBLISHED BY: Duke Communications

P.O. Box 447

Loveland, CO 80539-0447

TEL: (800) 621-1544 **FAX:** (970) 663-4700

FREQUENCY: Monthly

COVER PRICE: $3.95

SUBSCRIPTION PRICE: $39.95

TOTAL NUMBER OF PAGES: 92

TOTAL NUMBER OF AD PAGES: 27

PUBLISHER: Mark Smith

EDITOR: Jane Morrill

EDITORIAL CONCEPT: *"Solutions for the next wave of enterprise computing."*

WWWiz

PUBLISHED BY: WWWiz Corp.

17971 Sky Park Cir., Building 33B

Irvine, CA 92714

http://wwwiz.com

TEL: (714) 474-0554 **FAX:** (714) 474-0668

DATE: November

FREQUENCY: Monthly

COVER PRICE: Free

SUBSCRIPTION PRICE: n/a

TOTAL NUMBER OF PAGES: 42

TOTAL NUMBER OF AD PAGES: 9

EDITOR: Don Hamilton

EDITORIAL CONCEPT: *"Putting the Web to work for you."* The guide to business on the Internet.

ZD Internet Life

PUBLISHED BY: Ziff-Davis Publishing Co.

10 Presidents Landing

Medford, MA 02155

TEL: (617) 393-3531

DATE: Winter

FREQUENCY: Quarterly

COVER PRICE: $7.95

SUBSCRIPTION PRICE: n/a

TOTAL NUMBER OF PAGES: 118

TOTAL NUMBER OF AD PAGES: 23

PUBLISHER: Bill Machrone

EDITOR: Eric Hippeau

EDITORIAL CONCEPT: *From the people that brought you* Computer Life *comes this exploration of what's hot on the Net.*

The America Online Guide To Multimedia Online

PUBLISHED BY: Redgate Communications

660 Beachland Blvd.

Vero Beach, FL 32963

TEL: (407) 231-6904

FREQUENCY: Special

COVER PRICE: $9.95

SUBSCRIPTION PRICE: n/a

TOTAL NUMBER OF PAGES: 132

TOTAL NUMBER OF AD PAGES: 43

EDITOR: n/a

EDITORIAL CONCEPT: *Provides America Online members with information about the emerging world of online multimedia and new media.*

Computer Shopper
Holiday Issue Buying Guide

PUBLISHED BY: Ziff-Davis Publishing Co.

1 Park Ave.

New York, NY 10016

TEL: (303) 665-8930 **FAX:** (303) 604-7455

DATE: November/December

FREQUENCY: Special

COVER PRICE: $4.95

SUBSCRIPTION PRICE: n/a

TOTAL NUMBER OF PAGES: 400

TOTAL NUMBER OF AD PAGES: 282

PUBLISHER: Al DiGuido

EDITOR: John Blackford

EDITORIAL CONCEPT: *A compilation of "super values," including computers and peripherals, presented with all of the ads of a typical* Computer Shopper *issue.*

Consumer Review: Power Windows 1996

PUBLISHED BY: Harris Publications Inc.

1115 Broadway

New York, NY 10010

TEL: (212) 807-7100 **FAX:** (212) 627-4678

FREQUENCY: Annually

COVER PRICE: $4.95

SUBSCRIPTION PRICE: n/a

TOTAL NUMBER OF PAGES: 100

TOTAL NUMBER OF AD PAGES: 3

PUBLISHER: Stanley R. Harris

EDITOR: Dave Elrich

EDITORIAL CONCEPT: *A consumer review of* Power Windows *featuring laptop computer comparison charts, information on how to buy a desktop PC and hands-on reviews of computer equipment.*

Dr. Dobb's Sourcebook: Games Programming

PUBLISHED BY: Miller Freeman Inc.

600 Harrison St.

San Francisco, CA 94107

TEL: (415) 358-9500

FREQUENCY: Special

COVER PRICE: $4.95

SUBSCRIPTION PRICE: n/a

TOTAL NUMBER OF PAGES: 66

TOTAL NUMBER OF AD PAGES: 20

PUBLISHER: Graham J.S. Wilson

EDITOR: Jonathan Erickson

EDITORIAL CONCEPT: *Computer games are the focus of this magazine about software for the professional programmer.*

Game Sport

PUBLISHED BY: Harris Publications Inc.

1115 Broadway

New York, NY 10010

TEL: (212) 807-7100 **FAX:** (212) 627-4678

FREQUENCY: n/a

COVER PRICE: $4.95

SUBSCRIPTION PRICE: n/a

TOTAL NUMBER OF PAGES: 108

TOTAL NUMBER OF AD PAGES: 21

PUBLISHER: Dennis S. Page

EDITOR: Tony Gervino

EDITORIAL CONCEPT: *"The first all-sports video game magazine with reviews and tips for playing the games."*

Dr. Dobb's Sourcebook: Internet And World Wide Web Development

PUBLISHED BY: Miller Freeman Inc.

600 Harrison St.

San Francisco, CA 94107

TEL: (415) 905-2200

DATE: November/December

FREQUENCY: Special

COVER PRICE: $9.95

TOTAL NUMBER OF PAGES: 66

TOTAL NUMBER OF AD PAGES: 20

PUBLISHER: Peter Hutchinson

EDITOR: Jonathan Erickson

EDITORIAL CONCEPT: *A guide for Internet users with articles on setting up Web sites and surfing the Net.*

Inc. On Technology

PUBLISHED BY: Inc. Magazine

38 Commercial Wharf

Boston, MA 02110-3883

TEL: (617) 248-8000

DATE: Summer

FREQUENCY: Special

COVER PRICE: $3.00

SUBSCRIPTION PRICE: n/a

TOTAL NUMBER OF PAGES: 120

TOTAL NUMBER OF AD PAGES: 52

PUBLISHER: James J. Spanfeller

EDITOR: David H. Freeman

EDITORIAL CONCEPT: *"The publishers of* Inc. Magazine *show you how new information systems can take your company to the next level."*

Dr. Dobb's The Interoperable Objects Special Report

PUBLISHED BY: Miller Freeman Inc.

411 Borel Ave.

San Mateo, CA 94402-3522

TEL: (415) 358-9500

DATE: Winter

FREQUENCY: Special

COVER PRICE: $4.95

SUBSCRIPTION PRICE: n/a

TOTAL NUMBER OF PAGES: 76

TOTAL NUMBER OF AD PAGES: 14

PUBLISHER: Peter Hutchinson

EDITOR: Jonathan Erickson

EDITORIAL CONCEPT: *Software tools for the computer programmer.*

I-Way: Your Guide To The Information Superhighway

PUBLISHED BY: Business Computer Publishing

86 Elm St.

Peterborough, NH 03458

TEL: (603) 924-7271 **FAX:** (603) 924-6972

FREQUENCY: Special

COVER PRICE: $5.95

SUBSCRIPTION PRICE: n/a

TOTAL NUMBER OF PAGES: 98

TOTAL NUMBER OF AD PAGES: 14.25

PUBLISHER: Stephen Robbins

EDITOR: George Bond

EDITORIAL CONCEPT: *The Internet user's guide to "where to go, what to see and how to get there."*

Mobile Computing

PUBLISHED BY: Cowles Business Media

470 Park Ave. S., 14th Floor

North Tower

New York, NY 10016

TEL: (212) 683-3540

DATE: October

FREQUENCY: Special

COVER PRICE: $3.95

SUBSCRIPTION PRICE: n/a

TOTAL NUMBER OF PAGES: 152

TOTAL NUMBER OF AD PAGES: 71

EDITOR: Rich Malloy

EDITORIAL CONCEPT: *A buyer's guide to the 17 lightest notebooks.*

Personal Database

PUBLISHED BY: Miller Freeman Inc.

411 Borel Ave., Suite 100

San Mateo, CA 94402

TEL: (415) 358-0950 **FAX:** (415) 905-2233

DATE: Fall

FREQUENCY: n/a

COVER PRICE: $4.95

SUBSCRIPTION PRICE: n/a

TOTAL NUMBER OF PAGES: 66

TOTAL NUMBER OF AD PAGES: 9

PUBLISHER: Philip Chapnick

EDITOR: David M. Kalman

EDITORIAL CONCEPT: *"The ultimate user's guide to database software."*

PC Magic

PUBLISHED BY: Connell Communications

86 Elm St.

Peterborough, NH 03458

TEL: (603) 924-7271

DATE: Summer

FREQUENCY: Special

COVER PRICE: $5.95

SUBSCRIPTION PRICE: n/a

TOTAL NUMBER OF PAGES: 98

TOTAL NUMBER OF AD PAGES: 10

EDITOR: Marilyn McMaster

EDITORIAL CONCEPT: *A computer magazine with tips for running Windows and DOS.*

Scenarios: Special Wired Edition

PUBLISHED BY: Wired Ventures Ltd.

520 Third St., 4th Floor

San Francisco, CA 94107

TEL: (415) 222-6200 **FAX:** (415) 222-6209

FREQUENCY: Special

COVER PRICE: $5.95

SUBSCRIPTION PRICE: n/a

TOTAL NUMBER OF PAGES: 174

TOTAL NUMBER OF AD PAGES: 88

PUBLISHER: Louis Rossetto

EDITOR: Louis Rossetto

EDITORIAL CONCEPT: *A special edition of Wired magazine offering a glimpse into the future of the world of computers.*

PC Novice Guide To Going Online

PUBLISHED BY: Peed Corp.

120 W. Harvest Dr.

P.O. Box 85380

Lincoln, NE 68521

TEL: (800) 544-1264 **FAX:** (402) 479-2104

FREQUENCY: Special

COVER PRICE: $4.95

SUBSCRIPTION PRICE: n/a

TOTAL NUMBER OF PAGES: 180

TOTAL NUMBER OF AD PAGES: 14

PUBLISHER: Ronald D. Kobler

EDITOR: Ronald D. Kobler

EDITORIAL CONCEPT: *A beginner's guide to every aspect of online service.*

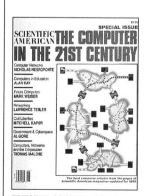

Scientific American: The Computer In The 21st Century

PUBLISHED BY: Scientific American Inc.

415 Madison Ave.

New York, NY 10017-1111

TEL: (212) 754-0350

FREQUENCY: Special

COVER PRICE: $3.95

SUBSCRIPTION PRICE: n/a

TOTAL NUMBER OF PAGES: 200

TOTAL NUMBER OF AD PAGES: 23

PUBLISHER: Richard Sasso

EDITOR: John Rennie

EDITORIAL CONCEPT: *"The best computer articles from the pages of* Scientific American *magazine — updated for 1995."*

All Number Fill-It-Ins Special

PUBLISHED BY: Official Publications Inc.

7002 W. Butler Pike

Ambler, PA 19002

TEL: (215) 628-0924

DATE: November

FREQUENCY: Bimonthly

COVER PRICE: $1.99

SUBSCRIPTION PRICE: $10.00

TOTAL NUMBER OF PAGES: 92

TOTAL NUMBER OF AD PAGES: 9

EDITOR: Bethany Lawler

EDITORIAL CONCEPT: *90 fill-it-in puzzles guaranteed to please number buffs of all ages.*

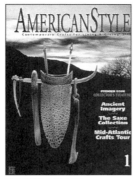

American Style

PUBLISHED BY: The Rosen Group Inc.

3000 Chesnut Ave., Suite 300

Baltimore, MD 21211

TEL: (410) 889-2933

DATE: Winter

FREQUENCY: Quarterly

COVER PRICE: $7.00

SUBSCRIPTION PRICE: $19.57

TOTAL NUMBER OF PAGES: 68

TOTAL NUMBER OF AD PAGES: 16

PUBLISHER: Wendy Rosen

EDITOR: Laura W. Rosen

EDITORIAL CONCEPT: *A great resource for what's happening in the world of studio art, featuring "contemporary crafts for living and giving."*

The Best Of Logic Puzzles

PUBLISHED BY: Dell Magazines Inc.

1540 Broadway

New York, NY 10036

TEL: (212) 782-8532

FREQUENCY: Bimonthly

COVER PRICE: $3.25

SUBSCRIPTION PRICE: n/a

TOTAL NUMBER OF PAGES: 74

TOTAL NUMBER OF AD PAGES: 10

PUBLISHER: Carla Graubard

EDITOR: Nancy Schuster

EDITORIAL CONCEPT: *53 brainteasers to solve with common sense and deduction.*

Better Homes And Gardens Crafts Showcase

PUBLISHED BY: Meredith Corp.

1716 Locust St., Des Moines, IA 50309

TEL: (515) 284-3439 **FAX:** (515) 284-3343

FREQUENCY: Quarterly

COVER PRICE: $4.95

SUBSCRIPTION PRICE: $19.97

DISCOUNT SUBSCRIPTION PRICE: $15.97

TOTAL NUMBER OF PAGES: 212

TOTAL NUMBER OF AD PAGES: 4

PUBLISHER: William R. Reed

EDITOR: Beverly Rivers

EDITORIAL CONCEPT: *"American handcrafts for the home shopper."*

Bizarre

PUBLISHED BY: Sister Moon Press

P.O. Box 40371

Phoenix, AZ 85067-0371

TEL: (602) 407-2632

FREQUENCY: Quarterly

COVER PRICE: $5.00

SUBSCRIPTION PRICE: $18.00

TOTAL NUMBER OF PAGES: 56

TOTAL NUMBER OF AD PAGES: 6.5

PUBLISHER: Amy M. Bowling

EDITOR: Amy M. Bowling, Shad J. Kvetko

EDITORIAL CONCEPT: *A magazine specializing in the strange and unusual, with art and editorials from the edge.*

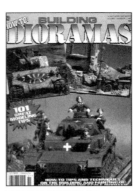

Building Dioramas

PUBLISHED BY: Challenge Publications Inc.

7950 Deering Ave.

Canoga Park, CA 91304

TEL: (818) 887-0550

FAX: (818) 884-1343

FREQUENCY: Quarterly

COVER PRICE: $6.95

SUBSCRIPTION PRICE: n/a

TOTAL NUMBER OF PAGES: 96

TOTAL NUMBER OF AD PAGES: 6

PUBLISHER: Edwin A. Schnepf

EDITOR: Sydney P. Chivers

EDITORIAL CONCEPT: *"How-to tips and techniques on the building and painting of dioramas for the scale modeler."*

Car Toys Magazine

PUBLISHED BY:

Full-Throttle Enterprises

6043 Tampa Ave., Suite 203

Tarzana, CA 91356

TEL: (818) 881-4768 **FAX:** (818) 881-4956

DATE: November

FREQUENCY: Bimonthly

COVER PRICE: $4.50

SUBSCRIPTION PRICE: $15.00

TOTAL NUMBER OF PAGES: 40

TOTAL NUMBER OF AD PAGES: 14

PUBLISHER: Sue Elliot

EDITOR: Sue Elliot

EDITORIAL CONCEPT: *"The collectibles magazine for car lovers," featuring editorials on the latest offerings from the world of car toys.*

Country Crafts

PUBLISHED BY: PJS Publications

News Plaza, P.O. Box 1790

Peoria, IL 61656

TEL: (309) 682-6626

DATE: March

FREQUENCY: Monthly

COVER PRICE: $3.95

SUBSCRIPTION PRICE: $35.40

DISCOUNT SUBSCRIPTION PRICE: $16.98

TOTAL NUMBER OF PAGES: 100

TOTAL NUMBER OF AD PAGES: 5

PUBLISHER: Del Rusher

EDITOR: Judith Brossarth

EDITORIAL CONCEPT: *Over 100 crafts that say "welcome, warmth, comfort, relaxation, security, a retreat, handmade, timeliness and love."*

Collecting

PUBLISHED BY: Odyssey Publications Inc.

510-A S. Corona Mall

Corona, CA 91719-1420

TEL: (909) 734-9636 **FAX:** (909) 371-7139

DATE: April

FREQUENCY: Monthly

COVER PRICE: $2.95

SUBSCRIPTION PRICE: $25.00

TOTAL NUMBER OF PAGES: 48

TOTAL NUMBER OF AD PAGES: 23

PUBLISHER: Kevin Sherman

EDITOR: Kevin Sherman

EDITORIAL CONCEPT: *A magazine for those who collect movie and celebrity memorabilia.*

Crafting Traditions

PUBLISHED BY: Reiman Publications L.P.

5400 S. 60th St.

Greendale, WI 53129

TEL: (414) 423-0100 **FAX:** (414) 423-1143

DATE: August

FREQUENCY: Bimonthly

COVER PRICE: $2.95

SUBSCRIPTION PRICE: $16.98

TOTAL NUMBER OF PAGES: 68

TOTAL NUMBER OF AD PAGES: 0

EDITOR: Kathleen Zimmer

EDITORIAL CONCEPT: *"Stitchery, wood, crochet and more."*

The Collectors' Bulletin

PUBLISHED BY: Rosie Wells Enterprises Inc.

R.R. #1

Canton, IL 61520

TEL: (309) 668-2211 **FAX:** (309) 668-2795

DATE: April/May

FREQUENCY: Bimonthly

COVER PRICE: $3.95

SUBSCRIPTION PRICE: $21.95

TOTAL NUMBER OF PAGES: 42

TOTAL NUMBER OF AD PAGES: 12

PUBLISHER: Rosie Wells

EDITOR: Rosie Wells

EDITORIAL CONCEPT: *Editorials and news about collectibles.*

Deluxe Variety Puzzles

PUBLISHED BY: Official Publications Inc.

7002 W. Butler Pike

Ambler, PA 19002

TEL: (215) 628-0924

DATE: December

FREQUENCY: Bimonthly

COVER PRICE: $1.99

SUBSCRIPTION PRICE: $10.00

TOTAL NUMBER OF PAGES: 84

TOTAL NUMBER OF AD PAGES: 8

EDITOR: Judy Weightman

EDITORIAL CONCEPT: *"Acrostics, code crosswords, crypto-clans, cryptograms and much more!"*

Dimension PS•X

PUBLISHED BY: Dimension Publishing Inc.

1175 Chess Dr., Suite E

Foster City, CA 94404

TEL: (415) 372-0942

FREQUENCY: Monthly

COVER PRICE: $3.99

SUBSCRIPTION PRICE: n/a

TOTAL NUMBER OF PAGES: 64

TOTAL NUMBER OF AD PAGES: 13

PUBLISHER: Tim Lindquist

EDITOR: David Jon Winding

EDITORIAL CONCEPT: *"The player's monthly guide to the Sony Playstation," featuring editorials and reviews of the hottest new game titles.*

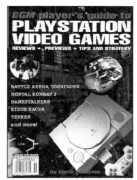

EGM *Player's Guide To Playstation Video Games*

PUBLISHED BY: Sendai Publishing Group

1920 Highland Ave., 2nd Floor

Lombard, IL 60148

TEL: (708) 916-7222   **FAX:** (708) 916-7227

FREQUENCY: Quarterly

COVER PRICE: $9.99

SUBSCRIPTION PRICE: n/a

TOTAL NUMBER OF PAGES: 100

TOTAL NUMBER OF AD PAGES: 3

PUBLISHER: Steve Harris

EDITOR: Joe Funk

EDITORIAL CONCEPT: *A magazine of reviews, previews, tips and strategies for Sony Playstation video games.*

Dimension 3

PUBLISHED BY: Dimension Publishing Inc.

567 Edna St.

San Francisco, CA 94112

TEL: (415) 372-0942

FREQUENCY: Monthly

COVER PRICE: $4.95

SUBSCRIPTION PRICE: n/a

TOTAL NUMBER OF PAGES: 84

TOTAL NUMBER OF AD PAGES: 3

PUBLISHER: David Jon Winding

EDITOR: David Jon Winding

EDITORIAL CONCEPT: *Covers the next dimension in electronic gaming, with hints, tips, reviews and editorials.*

EGM *Player's Guide To Sega Saturn Video Games*

PUBLISHED BY: Sendai Publishing Group

1920 Highland Ave., 2nd Floor

Lombard, IL 60148

TEL: (708) 916-7222   **FAX:** (708) 916-7227

FREQUENCY: Quarterly

COVER PRICE: $9.99

SUBSCRIPTION PRICE: n/a

TOTAL NUMBER OF PAGES: 100

TOTAL NUMBER OF AD PAGES: 3

PUBLISHER: Steve Harris

EDITOR: Mike Forassiepi

EDITORIAL CONCEPT: *Reviews, previews, tips and strategies for Sega's Saturn video games.*

Easy Wood

PUBLISHED BY: MSC Publishing Inc.

243 Newton-Sparta Rd.

Newton, NJ 07860

TEL: (201) 383-8080

DATE: Spring

FREQUENCY: Quarterly

COVER PRICE: $4.50

SUBSCRIPTION PRICE: n/a

TOTAL NUMBER OF PAGES: 48

TOTAL NUMBER OF AD PAGES: 1

PUBLISHER: Jerry Cohen

EDITOR: Robert A. Becker

EDITORIAL CONCEPT: *Features for the hobbyist ranging from woodcrafts and painting on wood to scroll-sawing and general woodworking.*

Figurines & Collectibles

PUBLISHED BY: Cowles Magazines

6405 Flank Dr.

Harrisburg, PA 17112

TEL: (717) 657-9555   **FAX:** (717) 540-6728

DATE: Spring

FREQUENCY: Bimonthly

COVER PRICE: $3.95

SUBSCRIPTION PRICE: $23.70

TOTAL NUMBER OF PAGES: 100

TOTAL NUMBER OF AD PAGES: 28

PUBLISHER: David L. Miller

EDITOR: David L. Miller

EDITORIAL CONCEPT: *"The first magazine devoted exclusively to the world of figurine collectors."*

Inquest

PUBLISHED BY: Gareb Shamus Enterprises

151 Wells Ave.

Congers, NY 10920-2064

TEL: (914) 268-3594

DATE: May

FREQUENCY: Monthly

COVER PRICE: $3.50

SUBSCRIPTION PRICE: $24.95

TOTAL NUMBER OF PAGES: 84

TOTAL NUMBER OF AD PAGES: 19

PUBLISHER: Gareb S. Shamus

EDITOR: Pat McCallum

EDITORIAL CONCEPT: *Devoted to the world of collectible card games.*

Miniature Quilt Ideas

PUBLISHED BY: Harris Publications Inc.

1115 Broadway

New York, NY 10010

TEL: (212) 807-7100

FREQUENCY: Semiannually

COVER PRICE: $3.95

SUBSCRIPTION PRICE: n/a

TOTAL NUMBER OF PAGES: 100

TOTAL NUMBER OF AD PAGES: 5

PUBLISHER: Stanley Harris

EDITOR: Jean Ann Eitel

EDITORIAL CONCEPT: *"23 sensational small quilt projects."*

Large Fill-Ins Special!

PUBLISHED BY: Ebb Publishing Co.

7002 W. Butler Pike

Ambler, PA 19002

TEL: (215) 628-0924

DATE: October

FREQUENCY: Bimonthly

COVER PRICE: $1.99

SUBSCRIPTION PRICE: $10.00

TOTAL NUMBER OF PAGES: 92

TOTAL NUMBER OF AD PAGES: 9

EDITOR: n/a

EDITORIAL CONCEPT: *Full-page, easy-to-read, fill-in puzzles.*

Money Card Collector

PUBLISHED BY: Amos Press Inc.

911 Vandemark Rd.

Sidney, OH 45365

TEL: (800) 645-7456   **FAX:** (513) 498-0876

DATE: June

FREQUENCY: Monthly

COVER PRICE: $4.95

SUBSCRIPTION PRICE: $19.95

TOTAL NUMBER OF PAGES: 52

TOTAL NUMBER OF AD PAGES: 25

PUBLISHER: Murray Church

EDITOR: Randy Moser

EDITORIAL CONCEPT: *Articles and a monthly card price guide for card collecting enthusiasts.*

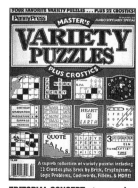

Master's Variety Puzzles Plus Crostics

PUBLISHED BY: Penny Press Inc.

6 Prowitt St.

Norwalk, CT 06855-1220

TEL: (203) 866-6688

FREQUENCY: Quarterly

COVER PRICE: $2.99

SUBSCRIPTION PRICE: $11.67

TOTAL NUMBER OF PAGES: 116

TOTAL NUMBER OF AD PAGES: 5.5

EDITOR: Fran Danon

EDITORIAL CONCEPT: *A superb collection of variety puzzles, including 22 crostics, brick-by-bricks, cryptograms, logic problems, codewords, fill-ins and more.*

Official's Logic Problems

PUBLISHED BY: Official Publications Inc.

7002 W. Butler Pike

Ambler, PA 19002

TEL: (215) 628-0924

DATE: October

FREQUENCY: Bimonthly

COVER PRICE: $2.50

SUBSCRIPTION PRICE: $13.50

TOTAL NUMBER OF PAGES: 68

TOTAL NUMBER OF AD PAGES: 6

EDITOR: Bethany Lawler

EDITORIAL CONCEPT: *Logic puzzles.*

Official's Varieties And Crosswords

PUBLISHED BY: Official Publications Inc.

7002 W. Butler Pike

Ambler, PA 19002

TEL: (215) 628-0924

DATE: November

FREQUENCY: Bimonthly

COVER PRICE: $1.99

SUBSCRIPTION PRICE: $10.75

TOTAL NUMBER OF PAGES: 84

TOTAL NUMBER OF AD PAGES: 7

EDITOR: Janis Weiner

EDITORIAL CONCEPT: 30 crosswords, plus acrostics, code crosswords, crypto-clans, cryptograms, droplines, logic problems, word divisions and more.

Precious Collectibles

PUBLISHED BY: Rosie Wells Enterprises Inc.

R.R. #1

Canton, IL 61520

TEL: (309) 668-2565

FAX: (309) 668-2795

DATE: Spring (first newsstand issue)

FREQUENCY: Quarterly

COVER PRICE: $3.95

SUBSCRIPTION PRICE: $21.95

TOTAL NUMBER OF PAGES: 44

TOTAL NUMBER OF AD PAGES: 8

PUBLISHER: Rosie Wells

EDITOR: Rosie Wells

EDITORIAL CONCEPT: This 12-year-old magazine for figurine collectors is now available at newsstands.

The Ornament Collector

PUBLISHED BY: Rosie Wells Enterprises Inc.

R.R. #1

Canton, IL 61520

TEL: (309) 668-2565   **FAX:** (309) 668-2795

DATE: Summer

FREQUENCY: Quarterly

COVER PRICE: $3.95

SUBSCRIPTION PRICE: $21.95

TOTAL NUMBER OF PAGES: 42

TOTAL NUMBER OF AD PAGES: 12

PUBLISHER: Rosie Wells

EDITOR: Rosie Wells

EDITORIAL CONCEPT: Celebrating the variety and beauty of ornament collecting.

Premium Crosswords

PUBLISHED BY: Hachette Filipacchi Magazines Inc.

1633 Broadway

New York, NY 10019

TEL: (800) 825-2866

FREQUENCY: Monthly

COVER PRICE: $1.75

SUBSCRIPTION PRICE: $21.00

TOTAL NUMBER OF PAGES: 100

TOTAL NUMBER OF AD PAGES: 8

PUBLISHER: Michael McCarthy

EDITOR: Florence Bierman

EDITORIAL CONCEPT: "A magazine full of challenging crosswords."

Picture Word-Finds

PUBLISHED BY: Ebb Publishing Co.

7002 W. Butler Pike

Ambler, PA 19002

TEL: (215) 628-0924

FREQUENCY: Semiannually

COVER PRICE: $2.95

SUBSCRIPTION PRICE: n/a

TOTAL NUMBER OF PAGES: 132

TOTAL NUMBER OF AD PAGES: 5

EDITOR: Bethany Lawler

EDITORIAL CONCEPT: "A new kind of puzzle fun!"

P.S.X. Playstation Experience

PUBLISHED BY: Sendai Publishing Group

1920 Highland Ave., 2nd Floor

Lombard, IL 60148

TEL: (708) 916-7222   **FAX:** (708) 916-7227

DATE: Fall

FREQUENCY: Quarterly

COVER PRICE: $3.99

SUBSCRIPTION PRICE: $14.95

TOTAL NUMBER OF PAGES: 68

TOTAL NUMBER OF AD PAGES: 5

PUBLISHER: Steve Harris

EDITOR: Al Manuel

EDITORIAL CONCEPT: "The unofficial publication of Playstation maniacs" offers reviews and tips for Sony's new mega game machine.

Quick & Easy Painting

PUBLISHED BY: All American Crafts Inc.

243 Newton-Sparta Rd.

Newton, NJ 07860

TEL: (201) 383-1215

DATE: Fall

FREQUENCY: Quarterly

COVER PRICE: $4.95

EDITORIAL CONCEPT: *The new decorative painting magazine from the publishers of Paintworks.*

SUBSCRIPTION PRICE: $19.80

DISCOUNT SUBSCRIPTION PRICE: $11.95

TOTAL NUMBER OF PAGES: 64

TOTAL NUMBER OF AD PAGES: 6

PUBLISHER: Jerry Cohen

EDITOR: Linda R. Heller

Special! Superb Word-Find

PUBLISHED BY: Official Publications Inc.

7002 W. Butler Pike, #100

Ambler, PA 19002

TEL: (215) 628-0924

FREQUENCY: Bimonthly

COVER PRICE: $1.99

EDITORIAL CONCEPT: *A magazine dedicated solely to word- and number-find puzzles.*

SUBSCRIPTION PRICE: $10.00

TOTAL NUMBER OF PAGES: 100

TOTAL NUMBER OF AD PAGES: 10

EDITOR: Bethany Lawler

Ragtyme Sports

PUBLISHED BY: Waupaca Publishing Co.

717 10th St.

Waupaca, WI 54981-9990

TEL: (715) 258-5546

FREQUENCY: Monthly

COVER PRICE: $3.95

EDITORIAL CONCEPT: *"The monthly magazine that caters to the vintage sports collector."*

SUBSCRIPTION PRICE: $24.95

TOTAL NUMBER OF PAGES: 100

TOTAL NUMBER OF AD PAGES: 32

PUBLISHER: Rick Hines

EDITOR: Rick Hines

Special! Variety Word-Find Puzzles

PUBLISHED BY: Official Publications Inc.

7002 W. Butler Pike, #100

Ambler, PA 19002

TEL: (215) 628-0924

DATE: December

FREQUENCY: Bimonthly

COVER PRICE: $1.99

EDITORIAL CONCEPT: *An entire magazine filled with crossword puzzles in the large page format.*

SUBSCRIPTION PRICE: $10.00

TOTAL NUMBER OF PAGES: 100

TOTAL NUMBER OF AD PAGES: 10

EDITOR: Mary Lon Tobias

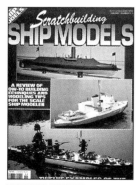

Scratchbuilding Ship Models

PUBLISHED BY: Challenger Publications

7950 Deering Ave.

Canoga Park, CA 91304

TEL: (818) 887-0550   **FAX:** (818) 884-1343

FREQUENCY: Quarterly

COVER PRICE: $5.95

EDITORIAL CONCEPT: *A magazine for those who enjoy building model ships from scratch.*

SUBSCRIPTION PRICE: n/a

TOTAL NUMBER OF PAGES: 96

TOTAL NUMBER OF AD PAGES: 12

PUBLISHER: Edwin A. Schnepf

EDITOR: Sydney P. Chivers

Style: 1900

PUBLISHED BY: Style: 1900

9 S. Main St.

Lambertville, NJ 08530

TEL: (609) 397-4104   **FAX:** (609) 397-9377

FREQUENCY: Quarterly

COVER PRICE: $4.95

SUBSCRIPTION PRICE: $25.00

EDITORIAL CONCEPT: *Formerly Arts & Crafts Quarterly Magazine, it is the only publication devoted solely to the works and thoughts of the arts and crafts movement.*

DISCOUNT SUBSCRIPTION PRICE: $43.00 (2 years)

TOTAL NUMBER OF PAGES: 62

TOTAL NUMBER OF AD PAGES: 18

PUBLISHER: Steven Becker

EDITOR: David Rago

Superb Crosswords And Varieties

PUBLISHED BY: Official Publications Inc.

7002 W. Butler Pike, #100

Ambler, PA 19002

TEL: (215) 628-0924

FREQUENCY: Bimonthly

COVER PRICE: $1.50

SUBSCRIPTION PRICE: $8.00

TOTAL NUMBER OF PAGES: 100

TOTAL NUMBER OF AD PAGES: 10

PUBLISHER: Despina McNulty

EDITOR: Judy Weightman

EDITORIAL CONCEPT: *"Official Publications, recognized as a leader in puzzle magazines for more than 40 years, offers this new bimonthly collection of crosswords."*

White's Guide To Collecting Figures

PUBLISHED BY: Collecting Concepts Inc.

8100 Three Chopt Rd., Suite 226

Richmond, VA 23229

TEL: (804) 285-0994

DATE: November

FREQUENCY: Monthly

COVER PRICE: $4.95

SUBSCRIPTION PRICE: $34.95

TOTAL NUMBER OF PAGES: 116

PUBLISHER: Ernie White

EDITOR: Rick Hall

EDITORIAL CONCEPT: *A guide for the collectors of action and collectible figures, including price guides and articles on finding collectibles.*

Ultimate Gamer

PUBLISHED BY: L.F.P. Inc.

9171 Wilshire Blvd., Suite 300

Beverly Hills, CA 90210

TEL: (213) 651-5400

DATE: July

FREQUENCY: Monthly

COVER PRICE: $4.99

SUBSCRIPTION PRICE: $19.95

TOTAL NUMBER OF PAGES: 100

TOTAL NUMBER OF AD PAGES: 14

PUBLISHER: Larry Flynt

EDITOR: Chris Gore

EDITORIAL CONCEPT: *A magazine for high-end gamers with reviews on new equipment as well as soon-to-be released video games.*

ANNUAL, SPECIAL OR FREQUENCY UNKNOWN

Adventures Of Sword & Sorcery

PUBLISHED BY: Double Star Press

P.O. Box 285

Xenia, OH 45385

TEL: n/a

FREQUENCY: n/a

COVER PRICE: $4.50

SUBSCRIPTION PRICE: $15.95

TOTAL NUMBER OF PAGES: 92

TOTAL NUMBER OF AD PAGES: 4

PUBLISHER: Camila Lin

EDITOR: Randy Dannenfelser

EDITORIAL CONCEPT: *"Full of the best sword and sorcery fiction and art available anywhere."*

Ventura

PUBLISHED BY: Warrior Publications Inc.

1920 Highland Ave., Suite 222

Lombardo, IL 60148

TEL: (708) 268-2498

DATE: August

FREQUENCY: Bimonthly

COVER PRICE: $3.99

SUBSCRIPTION PRICE: $14.95

TOTAL NUMBER OF PAGES: 100

TOTAL NUMBER OF AD PAGES: 23

PUBLISHER: Steve Horris

EDITOR: Don Butler

EDITORIAL CONCEPT: *"The ultimate guide to collectible card games."*

All Number-Finds

PUBLISHED BY: Official Publications Inc.

7002 W. Butler Pike, #100

Ambler, PA 19002

TEL: (215) 628-0924

DATE: April

FREQUENCY: Special

COVER PRICE: $1.25

SUBSCRIPTION PRICE: n/a

TOTAL NUMBER OF PAGES: 100

TOTAL NUMBER OF AD PAGES: 7

EDITOR: Bethany Lawler

EDITORIAL CONCEPT: *"From America's best-selling word-find publisher, an exciting new magazine!"*

Amazing Figure Modeler

PUBLISHED BY: Amazing Publications & Communications Inc.

P.O. Box 30885

Columbus, OH 43230

TEL: (614) 882-2125   **FAX:** (614) 882-6012

FREQUENCY: n/a

COVER PRICE: $6.00

SUBSCRIPTION PRICE: $28.00

TOTAL NUMBER OF PAGES: 76

TOTAL NUMBER OF AD PAGES: 19

PUBLISHER: Terry J. Webb

EDITOR: Terry J. Webb

EDITORIAL CONCEPT: *A magazine for kit builders, profiling the latest kits available and the people who design them.*

Country Accents' White Christmas Crafts

PUBLISHED BY: GCR Publishing Group Inc.

1700 Broadway

New York, NY 10019

TEL: (212) 541-7100

FREQUENCY: Annually

COVER PRICE: $4.50

SUBSCRIPTION PRICE: n/a

TOTAL NUMBER OF PAGES: 84

TOTAL NUMBER OF AD PAGES: 6

PUBLISHER: Charles Goodman

EDITOR: Eleanor Levie

EDITORIAL CONCEPT: *"75 fabulous gifts to make," from the publishers of Country Accents Magazine.*

Ben Franklin Crafts Magazine

PUBLISHED BY: Sampler Publications

707 Kautz Rd.

St. Charles, IL 60174

TEL: (708) 377-8000   **FAX:** (708) 377-8194

DATE: October

FREQUENCY: Special

COVER PRICE: $2.95

SUBSCRIPTION PRICE: $15.97

TOTAL NUMBER OF PAGES: 66

TOTAL NUMBER OF AD PAGES: 20

PUBLISHER: Steve Slack

EDITOR: Lynn M. Shanley

EDITORIAL CONCEPT: *Rediscover the splendor of fall; rejuvenate the celebration of crafting; and alleviate daily stress with autumn.*

Crafting: Plastic Canvas

PUBLISHED BY: MSC Publishing Inc.

243 Newton-Sparta Rd.

Newton, NJ 07860

TEL: (201) 383-8080

DATE: Summer

FREQUENCY: Special

COVER PRICE: $4.95

SUBSCRIPTION PRICE: n/a

TOTAL NUMBER OF PAGES: 68

TOTAL NUMBER OF AD PAGES: 0

PUBLISHER: Jerry Cohen

EDITOR: Deborah McGowan

EDITORIAL CONCEPT: *Over 30 innovative designs, projects for beginners and experts, and home decor ideas for the kitchen, bathroom and bedroom!*

Collector's World Of Racing

PUBLISHED BY: Na-Tex Publishing Inc.

5700 Hwy. 29 S.

Harrisburg, NC 28075

TEL: (704) 455-1702

DATE: January

FREQUENCY: Special

COVER PRICE: $3.95

SUBSCRIPTION PRICE: n/a

TOTAL NUMBER OF PAGES: 68

TOTAL NUMBER OF AD PAGES: 19

EDITOR: n/a

EDITORIAL CONCEPT: *The collector's guide to values and prices of racing collectibles, including articles and illustrations.*

Crafting Today: Christmas Ornaments

PUBLISHED BY: MSC Publishing Inc.

243 Newton-Sparta Rd.

Newton, NJ 07860

TEL: (201) 383-8080

DATE: Winter

FREQUENCY: Annually

COVER PRICE: $4.95

SUBSCRIPTION PRICE: n/a

TOTAL NUMBER OF PAGES: 68

TOTAL NUMBER OF AD PAGES: 5

PUBLISHER: Jerry Cohen

EDITOR: Marion Bucieri

EDITORIAL CONCEPT: *"A treasury of heirloom designs" for Christmas ornaments.*

1995 Video Game Buyer's Guide

PUBLISHED BY: Sendai Publishing Group

1920 Highland Ave., Suite 222

Lombard, IL 60148

TEL: (708) 916-7222 **FAX:** (708) 916-7227

FREQUENCY: Annually

COVER PRICE: $5.99

SUBSCRIPTION PRICE: n/a

TOTAL NUMBER OF PAGES: 148

TOTAL NUMBER OF AD PAGES: 23

PUBLISHER: Steve Harris

EDITOR: Ed Semrad

EDITORIAL CONCEPT: *Over 900 reviews and reports on the best video games of 1995.*

Puppetry International

PUBLISHED BY: UNIMA U.S.A. Inc.

1404 Spring St. NW

Atlanta, GA 30309-2820

TEL: (404) 873-3089 **FAX:** (404) 873-9907

FREQUENCY: n/a

COVER PRICE: $5.00

SUBSCRIPTION PRICE: n/a

TOTAL NUMBER OF PAGES: 44

TOTAL NUMBER OF AD PAGES: 0

EDITOR: Andrew Periale

EDITORIAL CONCEPT: *Editorials and illustrations on the puppet in contemporary theatre, film and media.*

Sports Cards Presents The Comprehensive Guide To Fleer Trading Cards

PUBLISHED BY: Krause Publications Inc.

700 E. State St.

Iola, WI 54990-0001

TEL: (715) 445-2214

DATE: March

FREQUENCY: Special

COVER PRICE: $3.50

SUBSCRIPTION PRICE: n/a

TOTAL NUMBER OF PAGES: 84

TOTAL NUMBER OF AD PAGES: 19

PUBLISHER: Hugh McAloon

EDITOR: Greg Ambrosius

EDITORIAL CONCEPT: *A comprehensive guide to Fleer trading cards, featuring articles on Fleer's new offerings and the history and future of the Fleer Company.*

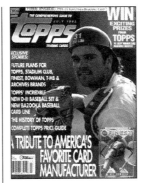

Sports Cards Presents The Comprehensive Guide To Topps Trading Cards

PUBLISHED BY: Krause Publications Inc.

700 E. State St., Iola, WI 54990-0001

TEL: (715) 445-2214

DATE: July

FREQUENCY: Special

COVER PRICE: $3.50

SUBSCRIPTION PRICE: n/a

TOTAL NUMBER OF PAGES: 100

TOTAL NUMBER OF AD PAGES: 23

PUBLISHER: Hugh McAloon

EDITOR: Greg Ambrosius

EDITORIAL CONCEPT: *In honor of the "founding father of the modern card collecting hobby," this magazine is the definitive resource of Topps Cards.*

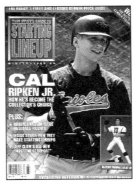

Super Mario World 2: Yoshi's Island

PUBLISHED BY: Nintendo of America Inc.

4820 150th Ave. NE

Redmond, WA 98052

TEL: (206) 882-2040

FREQUENCY: Special

COVER PRICE: $11.00

SUBSCRIPTION PRICE: n/a

TOTAL NUMBER OF PAGES: 132

TOTAL NUMBER OF AD PAGES: 1

PUBLISHER: M. Arakawa

EDITOR: Gail Tilden

EDITORIAL CONCEPT: *A player's guide to help you through the video game Super Mario World 2: Yoshi's Island.*

Tuff Stuff's Guide To Starting Lineup

PUBLISHED BY: Tuff Stuff Publications

P.O. Box 1637

Glen Allen, VA 23060

TEL: (800) 899-8833

DATE: Winter

FREQUENCY: n/a

COVER PRICE: $4.95

SUBSCRIPTION PRICE: n/a

TOTAL NUMBER OF PAGES: 52

TOTAL NUMBER OF AD PAGES: 12

PUBLISHER: Randy Burton

EDITOR: Larry Canale

EDITORIAL CONCEPT: *The first and leading Kenner price guide for sports figurine collectors.*

Woman's Day Weekend Crafts

EDITORIAL CONCEPT: *A publication for hobbyists who enjoy crafts, filled with 173 fast, fun projects.*

PUBLISHED BY: Hachette Filipacchi Magazines Inc.

1633 Broadway

New York, NY 10019

TEL: (212) 767-5924

FREQUENCY: Special

COVER PRICE: $3.50

SUBSCRIPTION PRICE: n/a

TOTAL NUMBER OF PAGES: 116

TOTAL NUMBER OF AD PAGES: 20

PUBLISHER: Sharri R. Jarmain

EDITOR: Yvonne Beecher

Wood Magazine's Best Woodworking Tips

EDITORIAL CONCEPT: *Offers more than 200 shop-tested ideas.*

PUBLISHED BY: Meredith Corp.

1716 Locust St.

Des Moines, IA 50336

TEL: (515) 284-3000

FREQUENCY: Special

COVER PRICE: $4.95

SUBSCRIPTION PRICE: n/a

TOTAL NUMBER OF PAGES: 68

TOTAL NUMBER OF AD PAGES: 3

PUBLISHER: William R. Reed

EDITOR: Larry Clayton

Modern Ferret

PUBLISHED BY: Crunchy Concepts Inc.

P.O. Box 338

Massapegua Park, NY 11762

TEL: (516) 799-1364

DATE: January/February

FREQUENCY: Bimonthly

COVER PRICE: $4.95

SUBSCRIPTION PRICE: $24.95

TOTAL NUMBER OF PAGES: 32

TOTAL NUMBER OF AD PAGES: 6

EDITOR: Mary Shefferman

EDITORIAL CONCEPT: *"The ferret lifestyle magazine" for the owners and lovers of those fuzzy little critters.*

Wolf Clan

PUBLISHED BY: Wolf Clan Publications Inc.

3952 N. Southport Ave., Suite 122

Chicago, IL 60613

TEL: (312) 935-1000   **FAX:** (312) 935-1083

DATE: June/July

FREQUENCY: Bimonthly

COVER PRICE: $3.50

SUBSCRIPTION PRICE: $18.00

TOTAL NUMBER OF PAGES: 38

TOTAL NUMBER OF AD PAGES: 14

PUBLISHER: Carin A. Segal

EDITOR: Laura Wallingford

EDITORIAL CONCEPT: *"A guardian's guide to holistic health for dogs."*

Talk About Pets

PUBLISHED BY: Reiman Publications L.P.

5400 S. 60th St.

Greendale, WI 53129

TEL: (414) 423-0100   **FAX:** (414) 423-1143

DATE: February/March

FREQUENCY: Bimonthly

COVER PRICE: $2.95

SUBSCRIPTION PRICE: $16.98

DISCOUNT SUBSCRIPTION PRICE: $10.98

TOTAL NUMBER OF PAGES: 68

TOTAL NUMBER OF AD PAGES: 0

PUBLISHER: Roy Reiman

EDITOR: Kathy Pohl

EDITORIAL CONCEPT: *For people who love all kinds of pets, with articles such as "Fantastic Pet Feats," "Appealing Pet Portraits," "Pet Peeves," "Pet Treats" and "Pet Fun!"*

The Stitchery Magazine

PUBLISHED BY: Stitchworld Inc.

P.O. Box 2507

Norcross, GA 30091-2507

TEL: (404) 825-0303

DATE: November

FREQUENCY: Monthly

COVER PRICE: $4.50

SUBSCRIPTION PRICE: $22.00

TOTAL NUMBER OF PAGES: 68

TOTAL NUMBER OF AD PAGES: 11

PUBLISHER: Carl Christenson

EDITOR: Kim D. Carvell

EDITORIAL CONCEPT: *"Your complete source for information on cross-stitch, needlepoint and embroidery."*

Easy Crochet

PUBLISHED BY: MSC Publishing Inc.

243 Newton-Sparta Rd.

Newton, NJ 07860

TEL: (201) 383-8080

DATE: Spring

FREQUENCY: Annually

COVER PRICE: $3.95

SUBSCRIPTION PRICE: n/a

TOTAL NUMBER OF PAGES: 52

TOTAL NUMBER OF AD PAGES: 3

PUBLISHER: Jerry Cohen

EDITOR: Karen Manthey

EDITORIAL CONCEPT: *"Dedicated to providing interesting, fashionable crochet projects using easy stitches."*

ANNUAL, SPECIAL OR FREQUENCY UNKNOWN

American Country Afghans

PUBLISHED BY: MSC Publications Inc.

243 Newton-Sparta Rd.

Newton, NJ 07860

TEL: (201) 383-8080

DATE: Spring/Summer

FREQUENCY: Annually

COVER PRICE: $3.95

SUBSCRIPTION PRICE: n/a

TOTAL NUMBER OF PAGES: 68

TOTAL NUMBER OF AD PAGES: 10

PUBLISHER: Jerry Cohen

EDITOR: Rita E. Greenfeder

EDITORIAL CONCEPT: *Directions on how to crochet over 20 afghans, plus tips on designing your own.*

Quick Knit & Crochet

PUBLISHED BY: MSC Publishing Inc.

243 Newton-Sparta Rd.

Newton, NJ 07860

TEL: (201) 383-8080

DATE: Summer

FREQUENCY: Special

COVER PRICE: $4.95

SUBSCRIPTION PRICE: $18.49

TOTAL NUMBER OF PAGES: 64

TOTAL NUMBER OF AD PAGES: 4

PUBLISHER: Jerry Cohen

EDITOR: Sally V. Klein

EDITORIAL CONCEPT: *"Quick knit and crochet" gift ideas for all ages.*

American Patchwork & Quilting: Quilt Sampler

PUBLISHED BY: Meredith Corp.

1716 Locust St.

Des Moines, IA 50309-3023

TEL: (512) 284-3785 **FAX:** (515) 284-3884

FREQUENCY: n/a

COVER PRICE: $4.95

SUBSCRIPTION PRICE: n/a

TOTAL NUMBER OF PAGES: 100

TOTAL NUMBER OF AD PAGES: 12

PUBLISHER: William R. Reed

EDITOR: Heidi Kaisand

EDITORIAL CONCEPT: *"Patchwork, appliqué, foundation piecing, ribbon embroidery and more."*

Quilter's Gallery

PUBLISHED BY: All American Crafts Inc.

243 Newton-Sparta Rd.

Newton, NJ 07860

TEL: (201) 383-8080

FREQUENCY: Special

COVER PRICE: $4.95

SUBSCRIPTION PRICE: n/a

TOTAL NUMBER OF PAGES: 52

TOTAL NUMBER OF AD PAGES: 11

PUBLISHER: Jerry Cohen

EDITOR: Matthew T. Jones

EDITORIAL CONCEPT: *Showcases the artistic expression of contemporary quilt artists.*

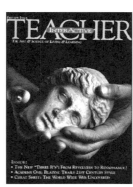

InterActive Teacher

PUBLISHED BY: Millennium Publishing/
Interactive Teacher L.C.

118 N. Monroe St., Suite 300

Tallahassee, FL 32301

TEL: (904) 425-1351   **FAX:** (904) 425-6390

FREQUENCY: Bimonthly

COVER PRICE: n/a

SUBSCRIPTION PRICE: n/a

TOTAL NUMBER OF PAGES: 42

TOTAL NUMBER OF AD PAGES: 21

PUBLISHER: Robert Bush

EDITOR: Lora N. Boehlke

EDITORIAL CONCEPT: *"The art and science of living and learning," for and by teachers.*

Cult Movies

PUBLISHED BY: Cult Movies

6201 Sunset Blvd., Suite 152

Hollywood, CA 90028

TEL: n/a

FREQUENCY: Quarterly

COVER PRICE: $4.95

SUBSCRIPTION PRICE: $18.00

TOTAL NUMBER OF PAGES: 124

TOTAL NUMBER OF AD PAGES: 16

PUBLISHER: Buddy Barnett

EDITOR: Michael Copner

EDITORIAL CONCEPT: *Features many of the cult flicks on the market today.*

script

PUBLISHED BY: Forum Inc.

P.O. Box 7

Long Green Pike

Baldwin, MD 21013

TEL: (410) 592-3466 **FAX:** (410) 592-8062

DATE: November/December

FREQUENCY: Bimonthly

COVER PRICE: $6.95

SUBSCRIPTION PRICE: $38.00

TOTAL NUMBER OF PAGES: 54

TOTAL NUMBER OF AD PAGES: 0

PUBLISHER: David Geatty

EDITOR: Shelly Geatty

EDITORIAL CONCEPT: *Interviews with movie writers, producers and directors.*

Films Of The Golden Age

PUBLISHED BY: Muscatine Journal

301 E. 3rd St.

Muscatine, IA 52761

TEL: (319) 263-2331 **FAX:** (319) 262-8042

DATE: Summer

FREQUENCY: Quarterly

COVER PRICE: $4.95

SUBSCRIPTION PRICE: $18.20

TOTAL NUMBER OF PAGES: 92

TOTAL NUMBER OF AD PAGES: 22

EDITOR: Bob King

EDITORIAL CONCEPT: *A look back at some of the great classics of the early 20th century.*

Star Trek Voyager

PUBLISHED BY: Starlog Group

475 Park Ave. S., 8th Floor

New York, NY 10016

TEL: (212) 689-2830 **FAX:** (212) 889-7933

DATE: April

FREQUENCY: Bimonthly

COVER PRICE: $5.99

SUBSCRIPTION PRICE: $30.00

TOTAL NUMBER OF PAGES: 76

TOTAL NUMBER OF AD PAGES: 23

PUBLISHER: Norman Jacobs

EDITOR: David McDonnell

EDITORIAL CONCEPT: *The official magazine of the spectacular new Star Trek adventure.*

John A. Russo's Making Movies

PUBLISHED BY: Market Square Productions

20 Market Sq.

Pittsburgh, PA 15222

TEL: (412) 471-1511

FREQUENCY: Bimonthly

COVER PRICE: $5.95

SUBSCRIPTION PRICE: $36.00

TOTAL NUMBER OF PAGES: 64

TOTAL NUMBER OF AD PAGES: 8

PUBLISHER: John A. Russo

EDITOR: John A. Russo

EDITORIAL CONCEPT: *"The film school in a magazine" offers tips on making your own feature movie on home video and goes behind the scenes of many film productions.*

Television Today

PUBLISHED BY: Palm Tree Publications

10061 Riverside Dr., #162

Toluca Lake, CA 91602

TEL: n/a

DATE: Spring

FREQUENCY: Quarterly

COVER PRICE: $ 2.95

SUBSCRIPTION PRICE: $15.00 (6 issues)

TOTAL NUMBER OF PAGES: 60

TOTAL NUMBER OF AD PAGES: 1

EDITOR: Michael Williamson

EDITORIAL CONCEPT: *The magazine for today's television viewer."*

Trauma

PUBLISHED BY: Draculina Publishing

P.O. Box 969

Centralia, IL 62801

TEL: n/a

FREQUENCY: Quarterly

COVER PRICE: $5.95

SUBSCRIPTION PRICE: n/a

TOTAL NUMBER OF PAGES: 52

TOTAL NUMBER OF AD PAGES: 14

EDITOR: Kristian P. Molgaard

EDITORIAL CONCEPT: *A splatter movie magazine with in-depth interviews, articles, reviews and free posters.*

Batman Forever *Official Movie Magazine*

PUBLISHED BY: Topps Publishing

1 Whitehall St.

New York, NY 10004

TEL: (212) 376-3000

DATE: June

FREQUENCY: Special

COVER PRICE: $4.95

SUBSCRIPTION PRICE: n/a

TOTAL NUMBER OF PAGES: 68

TOTAL NUMBER OF AD PAGES: 3

PUBLISHER: Ira Friedman

EDITOR: Kevin Fitzpatrick

EDITORIAL CONCEPT: *The official magazine for the Batman Forever motion picture, featuring articles on the actors and how the movie was made.*

Visions

PUBLISHED BY: Montike Publications Inc.

7240 W. Roosevelt Rd.

Forest Park, IL 60130

TEL: (708) 366-5566

FREQUENCY: Quarterly

COVER PRICE: $5.95

SUBSCRIPTION PRICE: $18.00

TOTAL NUMBER OF PAGES: 64

TOTAL NUMBER OF AD PAGES: 3.5

PUBLISHER: Frederick S. Clarke

EDITOR: Anthony P. Montesano

EDITORIAL CONCEPT: *"The magazine of fantasy TV, home video and new media."*

Batman Forever *Official Poster Magazine*

PUBLISHED BY: Topps Publishing

1 Whitehall St.

New York, NY 10004

TEL: (212) 376-3000

DATE: June

FREQUENCY: Special

COVER PRICE: $2.95

SUBSCRIPTION PRICE: n/a

TOTAL NUMBER OF PAGES: 24

TOTAL NUMBER OF AD PAGES: 0

PUBLISHER: Ira Friedman

EDITOR: Kevin Fitzpatrick

EDITORIAL CONCEPT: *The official poster magazine for the Batman Forever movie.*

ANNUAL, SPECIAL OR FREQUENCY UNKNOWN

Babylon 5

PUBLISHED BY: Sendai Licensing Inc.

1920 Highland Ave., Suite 222

Lombard, IL 60148

TEL: (708) 916-7222   **FAX:** (708) 916-7227

FREQUENCY: Special

COVER PRICE: $4.99

SUBSCRIPTION PRICE: n/a

TOTAL NUMBER OF PAGES: 68

TOTAL NUMBER OF AD PAGES: 5

PUBLISHER: Steve Harris

EDITOR: Mike Stokes

EDITORIAL CONCEPT: *"The official Babylon 5 collector's magazine."*

Cinescape's 1995 *Science Fiction Television Yearbook*

PUBLISHED BY: Cinescape Group Inc.

1920 Highland Ave, Suite 222

Lombard, IL 60148

TEL: (708) 268-2498

DATE: Fall

FREQUENCY: Annually

COVER PRICE: $4.99

SUBSCRIPTION PRICE: n/a

TOTAL NUMBER OF PAGES: 84

TOTAL NUMBER OF AD PAGES: 7

PUBLISHER: Steve Harris

EDITOR: Edward Gross, Douglas Perry

EDITORIAL CONCEPT: *Exclusive interviews, behind-the-scenes info and comprehensive episode guides.*

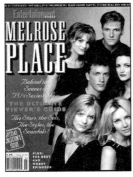

Entertainment Weekly: Melrose Place

PUBLISHED BY: Entertainment Weekly Inc.

1675 Broadway

New York, NY 10019

TEL: (212) 516-1212

DATE: Fall

FREQUENCY: Special

COVER PRICE: $3.95

SUBSCRIPTION PRICE: n/a

TOTAL NUMBER OF PAGES: 104

TOTAL NUMBER OF AD PAGES: 33

PUBLISHER: Michael J. Klingensmith

EDITOR: James W. Seymore, Jr.

EDITORIAL CONCEPT: *This special collector's issue for fans of TV's sexiest show is "the ultimate viewer's guide" to the stars, the sets, the styles and the scandals.*

Mortal Kombat

PUBLISHED BY: Starlog Group

475 Park Ave. S., 8th Floor

New York, NY 10016

TEL: (212) 689-2830 **FAX:** (212) 889-7933

FREQUENCY: Special

COVER PRICE: $6.99

SUBSCRIPTION PRICE: n/a

TOTAL NUMBER OF PAGES: 68

TOTAL NUMBER OF AD PAGES: 15

PUBLISHER: Norman Jacobs

EDITOR: David McDonnell

EDITORIAL CONCEPT: *"The official movie magazine."*

Martial Arts Movies

PUBLISHED BY: CFW Enterprises Inc.

4201 Vanowen Pl.

Burbank, CA 91505

TEL: (818) 845-2656 **FAX:** (818) 845-7761

DATE: November

FREQUENCY: Special

COVER PRICE: $3.00

SUBSCRIPTION PRICE: n/a

TOTAL NUMBER OF PAGES: 80

TOTAL NUMBER OF AD PAGES: 22

PUBLISHER: Mark Komuro

EDITOR: John Corcoran

EDITORIAL CONCEPT: *Articles and photographs about martial arts movies, including interviews with the leading men and women in the business.*

Nick At Night

PUBLISHED BY: Viacom International Inc.

1515 Broadway

New York, NY 10036

TEL: (212) 258-6000

DATE: Summer

FREQUENCY: Special

COVER PRICE: $3.95

SUBSCRIPTION PRICE: n/a

TOTAL NUMBER OF PAGES: 74

TOTAL NUMBER OF AD PAGES: 10

PUBLISHER: Lynn Lehmkuhl

EDITOR: Laura Galen

EDITORIAL CONCEPT: *"A celebration of classic TV on the printed page," featuring behind-the-scenes stories from the cable network's most popular shows.*

MK3 *Official Kollector's Book*

PUBLISHED BY: Sendai Licensing Inc.

1920 Highland Ave., Suite 222

Lombard, IL 60148

TEL: (708) 916-7222 **FAX:** (708) 916-7227

FREQUENCY: Special

COVER PRICE: $9.99

SUBSCRIPTION PRICE: n/a

TOTAL NUMBER OF PAGES: 100

TOTAL NUMBER OF AD PAGES: 4

PUBLISHER: Steve Harris

EDITOR: Joe Funk

EDITORIAL CONCEPT: *The inside story on Mortal Kombat 3, featuring interviews with the creators and profiles of all the MK3 clan.*

The *Official* Congo *Collector's Magazine*

PUBLISHED BY: Sendai Licensing Inc

1920 Highland Ave., Suite 222

Lombard, IL 60148

TEL: (708) 916-7222 **FAX:** (708) 916-7227

FREQUENCY: Special

COVER PRICE: $4.99

SUBSCRIPTION PRICE: n/a

TOTAL NUMBER OF PAGES: 68

TOTAL NUMBER OF AD PAGES: 5

EDITOR: n/a

EDITORIAL CONCEPT: *"An explorer's guide to the movie Congo, with behind-the-scenes shots and interviews with the stars.*

The Official Golden Eye Collector's Magazine

PUBLISHED BY: Sendai Licensing Inc.

1920 Highland Ave., Suite 222

Lombard, IL 60148

TEL: (708) 916-7222 **FAX:** (708) 916-7227

FREQUENCY: Special

COVER PRICE: $4.99

SUBSCRIPTION PRICE: n/a

TOTAL NUMBER OF PAGES: 68

TOTAL NUMBER OF AD PAGES: 6

EDITOR: n/a

EDITORIAL CONCEPT: *Bond is back on the silver screen in Golden Eye — and in this official magazine for the motion picture.*

Species

PUBLISHED BY: Starlog Group

475 Park Ave. S.

New York, NY 10016

TEL: (212) 689-2830 **FAX:** (212) 889-7933

FREQUENCY: Special

COVER PRICE: $5.99

SUBSCRIPTION PRICE: n/a

TOTAL NUMBER OF PAGES: 68

TOTAL NUMBER OF AD PAGES: 12

PUBLISHER: Norman Jacobs

EDITOR: Anthony Timpone

EDITORIAL CONCEPT: *"The official* Species *movie magazine."*

100 Years Of Moving Pictures

PUBLISHED BY: Faircount International Inc.

3816 W. Linebaugh Ave., Suite 401

Tampa, FL 33624

TEL: (813) 961-0006 **FAX:** (813) 264-4237

FREQUENCY: Special

COVER PRICE: $4.95

SUBSCRIPTION PRICE: n/a

TOTAL NUMBER OF PAGES: 188

TOTAL NUMBER OF AD PAGES: 39

PUBLISHER: Peter M. Antell

EDITOR: Robert L. Yehling

EDITORIAL CONCEPT: *Celebrating the 100th anniversary of the motion picture.*

Starbase

PUBLISHED BY: Sterling/Macfadden Partnership

233 Park Ave. S.

New York, NY 10003

TEL: (212) 979-4800 **FAX:** (212) 979-7342

FREQUENCY: Special

COVER PRICE: $3.95

SUBSCRIPTION PRICE: n/a

TOTAL NUMBER OF PAGES: 76

TOTAL NUMBER OF AD PAGES: 8

PUBLISHER: Allen Tuller

EDITOR: Susan M. Rasco

EDITORIAL CONCEPT: *"Sci-fi's #1 interview magazine."*

Sci-Fi TV Fall Preview

PUBLISHED BY: Sovereign Media Co. Inc.

441 Carlisle Dr.

Hendron, VA 22070

TEL: (703) 471-1556

DATE: October

FREQUENCY: Special

COVER PRICE: $4.95

SUBSCRIPTION PRICE: n/a

TOTAL NUMBER OF PAGES: 76

TOTAL NUMBER OF AD PAGES: 20

PUBLISHER: Mark Hintz

EDITOR: Dan Perez

EDITORIAL CONCEPT: *Behind the scenes of some of the hottest new sci-fi shows on television as well as a look back at the last fifty years of the genre.*

Starlog Platinum Edition

PUBLISHED BY: Starlog Group

475 Park Ave. S., 8th Floor

New York, NY 10016

TEL: (212) 689-2830 **FAX:** (212) 889-7933

DATE: April

FREQUENCY: Special

COVER PRICE: $4.99

SUBSCRIPTION PRICE: n/a

TOTAL NUMBER OF PAGES: 84

TOTAL NUMBER OF AD PAGES: 18

PUBLISHER: Norman Jacobs

EDITOR: David McDonnell

EDITORIAL CONCEPT: *A magazine for science-fiction entertainment enthusiasts.*

Super Summer Movie Heroes

PUBLISHED BY: Sovereign Media Co. Inc.

441 Carlisle Dr.

Herndon, VA 22070

TEL: (703) 471-1556

DATE: July

FREQUENCY: Special

COVER PRICE: $4.95

SUBSCRIPTION PRICE: n/a

TOTAL NUMBER OF PAGES: 76

TOTAL NUMBER OF AD PAGES: 19

PUBLISHER: Mark Hintz

EDITOR: Edward Flixman

EDITORIAL CONCEPT: *Behind-the-scenes interviews and color photographs from the best of the 1995 summer movie.*

Wes Craven's New Nightmare

PUBLISHED BY: Starlog Group

475 Park Ave. S.

New York, NY 10016

TEL: (212) 689-2830   **FAX:** (212) 889-7933

DATE: January

FREQUENCY: Special

COVER PRICE: $4.95

SUBSCRIPTION PRICE: n/a

TOTAL NUMBER OF PAGES: 68

TOTAL NUMBER OF AD PAGES: 9

PUBLISHER: Norman Jacobs

EDITOR: Anthony Timpone

EDITORIAL CONCEPT: *The official movie magazine saluting Freddy's 10th anniversary.*

TV Guide: *Star Trek*

PUBLISHED BY: News America Publications

100 Madsonford Rd.

Radner, PA 19088

TEL: (610) 293-8500

FREQUENCY: Special

COVER PRICE: $3.95

SUBSCRIPTION PRICE: n/a

TOTAL NUMBER OF PAGES: 132

TOTAL NUMBER OF AD PAGES: 25

PUBLISHER: Mary G. Berner

EDITOR: Anthea Disney

EDITORIAL CONCEPT: *"Delves into TV Guide's extensive archive of historical articles and never-published photographs to tell the tale of Trek from a unique perspective."*

The X-Files & Other Eerie TV

PUBLISHED BY: Starlog Group

475 Park Ave. S., 8th Floor

New York, NY 10016

TEL: (212) 689-2830

FREQUENCY: Annually

COVER PRICE: $5.99

SUBSCRIPTION PRICE: n/a

TOTAL NUMBER OF PAGES: 84

TOTAL NUMBER OF AD PAGES: 10

PUBLISHER: Norman Jacobs

EDITOR: David McDonnell

EDITORIAL CONCEPT: *"Inside The X-Files."*

American Cake Decorating

PUBLISHED BY: Sotano Publishing

P.O. Box 1385

Sterling, VA 20167-8440

TEL: (703) 430-2356

DATE: November/December

FREQUENCY: Bimonthly

COVER PRICE: $3.95

SUBSCRIPTION PRICE: $19.00

TOTAL NUMBER OF PAGES: 48

TOTAL NUMBER OF AD PAGES: 3

PUBLISHER: Robert W. Harte

EDITOR: Adlynn K. Harte

EDITORIAL CONCEPT: *All about cake making and decorating with methods for successful cakes.*

Country Folk Art's Quick 'n Easy Home Cooking

PUBLISHED BY: Long Publications Inc.

8393 E. Holly Rd., Holly, MI 48442-9978

TEL: (810) 634-8700

DATE: December

FREQUENCY: Bimonthly

COVER PRICE: $2.99

SUBSCRIPTION PRICE: $12.99

TOTAL NUMBER OF PAGES: 68

TOTAL NUMBER OF AD PAGES: 8

PUBLISHER: Betty Long

EDITOR: Cheryl Anderson

EDITORIAL CONCEPT: *"Recipes from the kitchens of home cooks just like you."*

Brew Your Own

PUBLISHED BY: Niche Publications

216 F St., Suite 160

Davis, CA 95616

TEL: (916) 758-4596   **FAX:** (916) 758-7477

FREQUENCY: Monthly

COVER PRICE: $3.95

SUBSCRIPTION PRICE: $44.95

DISCOUNT SUBSCRIPTION PRICE: $29.95

TOTAL NUMBER OF PAGES: 76

TOTAL NUMBER OF AD PAGES: 30

PUBLISHER: Carl B. Landau

EDITOR: Craig Bystrynski

EDITORIAL CONCEPT: *"To celebrate the art and science of brewing."*

Cups: The Cafe Culture Magazine

PUBLISHED BY: Cups: The Cafe Culture Magazine Inc.

1101 Clay St.

San Francisco, CA 94108

TEL: (415) 776-1412   **FAX:** (415) 441-9060

FREQUENCY: Monthly

COVER PRICE: $2.00

SUBSCRIPTION PRICE: n/a

TOTAL NUMBER OF PAGES: 64

TOTAL NUMBER OF AD PAGES: 21

PUBLISHER: Paul Millman

EDITOR: David Latimer

EDITORIAL CONCEPT: *The cafe culture magazine with music, books, film, poetry and culture.*

Coffee Journal

PUBLISHED BY: Tiger-Oak Publications Inc.

119 N. 4th St., Suite 211

Minneapolis, MN 55401

TEL: (612) 338-4125   **FAX:** (612) 338-0532

FREQUENCY: Quarterly

COVER PRICE: $3.95

SUBSCRIPTION PRICE: $12.97

DISCOUNT SUBSCRIPTION PRICE: $22.77 (2 years)

TOTAL NUMBER OF PAGES: 84

TOTAL NUMBER OF AD PAGES: 21.5

PUBLISHER: R. Craig Bednar

EDITOR: Susan Bonne

EDITORIAL CONCEPT: *A journal that focuses on the coffee and tea lifestyle.*

Gambero Rosso

PUBLISHED BY: Gambero Rosso Inc.

5 E. 22nd St.

New York, NY 10010

TEL: (212) 388-9449   **FAX:** (212) 388-9453

DATE: Winter

FREQUENCY: Quarterly

COVER PRICE: $4.95

SUBSCRIPTION PRICE: $15.85

TOTAL NUMBER OF PAGES: 100

TOTAL NUMBER OF AD PAGES: 14

PUBLISHER: Stefano Bonilla

EDITOR: Stefano Bonilla

EDITORIAL CONCEPT: *"Gambero rosso" literally means "red shrimp," a common name for restaurants and pizzerias all over Italy. The magazine features wine, travel and food.*

Good Taste

PUBLISHED BY: International Recipe Collection Inc.

4151 Knob Dr.

Egan, MN 55122

TEL: (612) 452-0571

FREQUENCY: Bimonthly

COVER PRICE: $3.25

SUBSCRIPTION PRICE: $12.95

TOTAL NUMBER OF PAGES: 100

TOTAL NUMBER OF AD PAGES: 8

PUBLISHER: Russ Moore

EDITOR: Carla Waldemar

EDITORIAL CONCEPT: *"Food with an attitude."*

Pastry Art & Design

PUBLISHED BY: Haymarket Group Ltd.

45 W. 34th St., Suite 600

New York, NY 10001

TEL: (815) 734-1109

FREQUENCY: Bimonthly

COVER PRICE: $5.95

SUBSCRIPTION PRICE: n/a

TOTAL NUMBER OF PAGES: 76

TOTAL NUMBER OF AD PAGES: 28

PUBLISHER: Michael Schneider

EDITOR: Michael Schneider

EDITORIAL CONCEPT: *A magazine for pastry professionals, emphasizing intricate techniques and special ingredients.*

Juice

PUBLISHED BY: Loco Lobos L.L.C.

P.O. Box 9068

Berkeley, CA 94709

TEL: (510) 548-0697

FREQUENCY: Bimonthly

COVER PRICE: $4.95

SUBSCRIPTION PRICE: $24.00

DISCOUNT SUBSCRIPTION PRICE: $19.95

TOTAL NUMBER OF PAGES: 64

TOTAL NUMBER OF AD PAGES: 20

EDITOR: Fred Dodsworth

EDITORIAL CONCEPT: *"The journal of eatin', drinkin', and screwin' round."*

Summer Cooking & Entertaining

PUBLISHED BY: Hachette Filipacchi

1633 Broadway

New York, NY 10019

TEL: (212) 767-5924

DATE: Summer

FREQUENCY: 5/year

COVER PRICE: $3.50

SUBSCRIPTION PRICE: n/a

TOTAL NUMBER OF PAGES: 116

TOTAL NUMBER OF AD PAGES: 13

PUBLISHER: Sharri R. Jurmain

EDITOR: Carolyn M. Gatto

EDITORIAL CONCEPT: *The people behind Woman's Day offer an assortment of new summer recipes, with articles on types of food to eat and how to prepare them.*

Pasta Press

PUBLISHED BY: Pasta Press

P.O. Box 3070

San Diego, CA 92163

TEL: (619) 295-3939 **FAX:** (619) 295-4141

FREQUENCY: Quarterly

COVER PRICE: $3.00

SUBSCRIPTION PRICE: $8.00

TOTAL NUMBER OF PAGES: 16

TOTAL NUMBER OF AD PAGES: 0

PUBLISHER: Chris and Mary Gluck

EDITOR: Chris and Mary Gluck

EDITORIAL CONCEPT: *"The newsletter for connoisseurs of flavored pasta — with a healthy twist!"*

Touring & Tasting

PUBLISHED BY: Vintage Communications

123 W. Padre, Suite B

Santa Barbara, CA 93105

TEL: (805) 563-7585

DATE: Summer

FREQUENCY: Semiannually

COVER PRICE: $6.95

SUBSCRIPTION PRICE: $12.00

DISCOUNT SUBSCRIPTION PRICE: $20.00 (2 years)

TOTAL NUMBER OF PAGES: 100

TOTAL NUMBER OF AD PAGES: 4

PUBLISHER: Donald V. Fritzen

EDITOR: Joanna Cook

EDITORIAL CONCEPT: *A wine country guide for the grape-growing people of the nation.*

Vegetarian Times' Low-Fat & Fast

PUBLISHED BY: Vegetarian Times Inc.

4 High Ridge Park

Stamford, CT 06905

TEL: (203) 322-2900 **FAX:** (203) 322-1966

DATE: Spring/Summer

FREQUENCY: Semiannually

COVER PRICE: $3.95

SUBSCRIPTION PRICE: n/a

TOTAL NUMBER OF PAGES: 100

TOTAL NUMBER OF AD PAGES: 28

PUBLISHER: Marianne Harkness

EDITOR: Toni Apgar

EDITORIAL CONCEPT: *71 meatless recipes.*

Wine & Spirits Guide To Understanding Wine

PUBLISHED BY: Wine & Spirits

818 Brannan St., San Francisco, CA 94103

TEL: (415) 255-7736 **FAX:** (415) 255-9659

DATE: Fall

FREQUENCY: 8/year

COVER PRICE: $3.95

SUBSCRIPTION PRICE: $22.00

TOTAL NUMBER OF PAGES: 116

TOTAL NUMBER OF AD PAGES: 24.5

PUBLISHER: Joshua Greene

EDITOR: Joshua Greene

EDITORIAL CONCEPT: *"A guide to understanding wine."*

ANNUAL, SPECIAL OR FREQUENCY UNKNOWN

Better Homes And Gardens' Prizewinning Recipes

PUBLISHED BY: Meredith Publishing

1912 Grand Ave.

Des Moines, IA 50309-3379

TEL: (515) 284-3433 **FAX:** (515) 284-3412

FREQUENCY: Special

COVER PRICE: $2.99

SUBSCRIPTION PRICE: n/a

TOTAL NUMBER OF PAGES: 100

TOTAL NUMBER OF AD PAGES: 10

EDITOR: n/a

EDITORIAL CONCEPT: *65 award-winning recipes from* Better Homes and Gardens *magazine.*

Betty Crocker's Cooking Today

PUBLISHED BY: General Mills Inc.

P.O. Box 1113-2BT

Minneapolis, MN 55440

TEL: (612) 540-2311

DATE: Fall

FREQUENCY: Special

COVER PRICE: $2.99

SUBSCRIPTION PRICE: n/a

TOTAL NUMBER OF PAGES: 100

TOTAL NUMBER OF AD PAGES: 2

PUBLISHER: Sheila Burke

EDITOR: Lois Tlusty

EDITORIAL CONCEPT: *Offers recipes, photos and short articles about cooking, healthy eating and casual entertaining.*

Celebrity Recipes

PUBLISHED BY: HIS Publishing Inc.

Box 213

Berne, IN 46711

TEL: (800) 786-4723

FREQUENCY: Special

COVER PRICE: $2.95

SUBSCRIPTION PRICE: n/a

TOTAL NUMBER OF PAGES: 68

TOTAL NUMBER OF AD PAGES: 1

PUBLISHER: Roger C. Muselman

EDITOR: Janice Tomano

EDITORIAL CONCEPT: *"Over 140 recipes from your favorite stars!"*

Cooking Light's Quick & Easy Weeknights

PUBLISHED BY: Southern Living Inc.

2100 Lakeshore Dr.

Birmingham, AL 35209

TEL: (205) 877-6000 **FAX:** (205) 877-6600

FREQUENCY: Special

COVER PRICE: $3.95

SUBSCRIPTION PRICE: n/a

TOTAL NUMBER OF PAGES: 124

TOTAL NUMBER OF AD PAGES: 50

PUBLISHER: Jeffrey C. Ward

EDITOR: Ellen Templeton Carroll

EDITORIAL CONCEPT: *A magazine aimed at simplifying suppertime with 40 recipes that each take under 20 minutes to prepare.*

Country Accents' Soups, Stews & Chili

PUBLISHED BY: GCR Publishing Group

1700 Broadway, 34th Floor

New York, NY 10019

TEL: (212) 541-7100   **FAX:** (212) 245-1241

FREQUENCY: Special

COVER PRICE: $2.95

SUBSCRIPTION PRICE: n/a

TOTAL NUMBER OF PAGES: 84

TOTAL NUMBER OF AD PAGES: 0

PUBLISHER: Charles Goodman

EDITOR: Devera Pine

EDITORIAL CONCEPT: *Country Accents serves up a collection of quick and easy stews, plus low-calorie, low-fat soups and chili.*

Fit, Fresh And Fast Flavors From Florida

PUBLISHED BY: Meredith Publishing

1912 Grand Ave.

Des Moines, IA 50309-3379

TEL: (515) 284-3433   **FAX:** (515) 284-3412

FREQUENCY: Special

COVER PRICE: $2.99

SUBSCRIPTION PRICE: n/a

TOTAL NUMBER OF PAGES: 96

TOTAL NUMBER OF AD PAGES: 4

EDITOR: n/a

EDITORIAL CONCEPT: *A collection of more than 80 "sun-sational citrus recipes" from the Florida Citrus Growers.*

Eating Right, Feeling Fit

PUBLISHED BY: Meredith Publishing

1912 Grand Ave.

Des Moines, IA 50309

TEL: (515) 284-3433   **FAX:** (515) 284-3412

FREQUENCY: Special

COVER PRICE: $2.99

SUBSCRIPTION PRICE: n/a

TOTAL NUMBER OF PAGES: 100

TOTAL NUMBER OF AD PAGES: 1

EDITOR: n/a

EDITORIAL CONCEPT: *Features 80 low-fat and low-calorie recipes tested in the kitchens of Better Homes and Gardens.*

Green Giant's Dinner Tonight

PUBLISHED BY: The Pillsbury Co.

200 S. 6th St.

Minneapolis, MN 55402

TEL: (612) 330-5452

DATE: February/March

FREQUENCY: Special

COVER PRICE: $2.95

SUBSCRIPTION PRICE: n/a

TOTAL NUMBER OF PAGES: 100

TOTAL NUMBER OF AD PAGES: 2

PUBLISHER: Sally Parks

EDITOR: Jackie Sheehan, Betsy Wray

EDITORIAL CONCEPT: *The magazine's menu includes main dishes, appetizers, soups, salads and more.*

Eating Well Holiday Recipes

PUBLISHED BY: EW Communications L.P.

Ferry Rd.,P.O. Box 1001

Charlotte, VT 05445-1001

TEL: (802) 425-3961

DATE: Winter

FREQUENCY: Special

COVER PRICE: $3.95

SUBSCRIPTION PRICE: n/a

TOTAL NUMBER OF PAGES: 116

TOTAL NUMBER OF AD PAGES: 28

PUBLISHER: Scott Mowbray

EDITOR: Scott Mowbray

EDITORIAL CONCEPT: *"125 recipes for Thanksgiving to New Year's."*

Hunt's Simple Meals

PUBLISHED BY: Meredith Publishing

1912 Grand Ave.

Des Moines, IA 50309-3379

TEL: (515) 284-3433   **FAX:** (515) 284-3412

FREQUENCY: Special

COVER PRICE: $2.99

SUBSCRIPTION PRICE: n/a

TOTAL NUMBER OF PAGES: 96

TOTAL NUMBER OF AD PAGES: 4

EDITOR: n/a

EDITORIAL CONCEPT: *"65 exciting recipes using Hunt Food Co.'s products that will fit into even the busiest of schedules."*

Kraft Holiday Homecoming

PUBLISHED BY: Meredith Publishing

1912 Grand Ave.

Des Moines, IA 50309-3379

TEL: (515) 284-3433　**FAX:** (515) 284-3412

FREQUENCY: Special

COVER PRICE: $2.99

SUBSCRIPTION PRICE: n/a

TOTAL NUMBER OF PAGES: 94

TOTAL NUMBER OF AD PAGES: 0

EDITOR: n/a

EDITORIAL CONCEPT:
"Dedicated to the holidays, and making each moment reflect a celebration of good food and warm hospitality."

New Body's Low-Fat, No-Fat Cookbook

PUBLISHED BY: GCR Publishing Group Inc.

1700 Broadway, 34th Floor

New York, NY 10019

TEL: (212) 541-7100　**FAX:** (212) 245-1241

FREQUENCY: Special

COVER PRICE: $3.50

SUBSCRIPTION PRICE: n/a

TOTAL NUMBER OF PAGES: 84

TOTAL NUMBER OF AD PAGES: 0

PUBLISHER: Charles Goodman

EDITOR: Devera Pine

EDITORIAL CONCEPT: *67 fast and healthy recipes.*

Light, Lively & Low-Fat

PUBLISHED BY: Prestige Publications Inc.

P.O. Box 23368

Overland Park, KS 66223

TEL: n/a

FREQUENCY: Special

COVER PRICE: $2.99

SUBSCRIPTION PRICE: n/a

TOTAL NUMBER OF PAGES: 100

TOTAL NUMBER OF AD PAGES: 1

EDITOR: n/a

EDITORIAL CONCEPT: *Over 50 low-fat, waist-trimming recipes, plus a fat and calorie counter.*

The Old Farmer's Almanac *Good Cook's Companion 1996*

PUBLISHED BY: Yankee Publishing Inc.

P.O. Box 520

Dublin, NH 03444

TEL: (603) 563-8111　**FAX:** (603) 563-8252

FREQUENCY: Annually

COVER PRICE: $2.99

SUBSCRIPTION PRICE: n/a

TOTAL NUMBER OF PAGES: 148

TOTAL NUMBER OF AD PAGES: 22

PUBLISHER: John Pierce

EDITOR: Georgia Orcutt

EDITORIAL CONCEPT: *A cooking guide with food tips and preparation techniques.*

Nestle Toll House Best-Loved Cookies

PUBLISHED BY: Meredith Publishing

1912 Grand Ave.

Des Moines, IA 50309-3397

TEL: (515) 284-3433

FREQUENCY: Special

COVER PRICE: $2.99

SUBSCRIPTION PRICE: n/a

TOTAL NUMBER OF PAGES: 94

TOTAL NUMBER OF AD PAGES: 0

EDITOR: n/a

EDITORIAL CONCEPT: *A collection of some of the best cookie recipes, brought to you by the people at Nestle.*

Simply Perfect Pasta

PUBLISHED BY: Better Homes and Gardens Special Interest Publications

1716 Locust St.

Des Moines, IA 50309-3023

TEL: (800) 678-2872

FREQUENCY: Special

COVER PRICE: $4.95

SUBSCRIPTION PRICE: n/a

TOTAL NUMBER OF PAGES: 131

TOTAL NUMBER OF AD PAGES: 8

PUBLISHER: Stephen B. Levinson

EDITOR: William T. Yates

EDITORIAL CONCEPT: *Offers many kinds of pasta recipes.*

Summertime Grilling

PUBLISHED BY: Meredith Publishing

1912 Grand Ave.

Des Moines, IA 50309-3379

TEL: (515) 284-3433   **FAX:** (515) 284-3412

FREQUENCY: Special

COVER PRICE: $2.99

SUBSCRIPTION PRICE: n/a

TOTAL NUMBER OF PAGES: 94

TOTAL NUMBER OF AD PAGES: 1

EDITOR: n/a

EDITORIAL CONCEPT: *A handy guide for those who want to try new things cooked on the grill.*

Vegetarian Gourmet Presents Low-Fat Special

PUBLISHED BY: Chariot Publishing Inc.

2 Public Ave.

Montrose, PA 18801-1220

TEL: (717) 278-1984

FREQUENCY: Special

COVER PRICE: $3.50

SUBSCRIPTION PRICE: n/a

TOTAL NUMBER OF PAGES: 52

TOTAL NUMBER OF AD PAGES: 1

PUBLISHER: Christiane Meunier

EDITOR: Jessica Dubey

EDITORIAL CONCEPT: *Features 76 "deliciously light" recipes.*

30 Easy Menu Ideas

PUBLISHED BY: Meredith Publishing

1912 Grand Ave.

Des Moines, IA 50309-3339

TEL: (515) 284-3433   **FAX:** (515) 284-3412

FREQUENCY: Special

COVER PRICE: $2.99

SUBSCRIPTION PRICE: n/a

TOTAL NUMBER OF PAGES: 100

TOTAL NUMBER OF AD PAGES: 0

EDITOR: n/a

EDITORIAL CONCEPT: *Features "easy, casual and seasonal" recipes for everyday meals, entertaining and celebrations.*

Carabella

PUBLISHED BY: Carabella Collection

1852 McGraw

Irvine, CA 92714

TEL: (714) 263-2300 **FAX:** (714) 263-2323

DATE: October/November

FREQUENCY: Bimonthly

COVER PRICE: $2.95

SUBSCRIPTION PRICE: $9.95

TOTAL NUMBER OF PAGES: 88

TOTAL NUMBER OF AD PAGES: 6

PUBLISHER: Houshang Jalili

EDITOR: Laura Bennett

EDITORIAL CONCEPT: *A catalog of women's fashions with editorials on health, fitness and romance.*

Swimsuit Illustrated

PUBLISHED BY: Swimsuit Illustrated Inc.

505 S. Beverly Dr., Suite 1200

Beverly Hills, CA 90212

TEL: (310) 289-6000

DATE: Summer

FREQUENCY: Quarterly

COVER PRICE: $2.95

SUBSCRIPTION PRICE: n/a

TOTAL NUMBER OF PAGES: 82

TOTAL NUMBER OF AD PAGES: 10

PUBLISHER: George Ede

EDITOR: Roy Hahn

EDITORIAL CONCEPT: *Richly illustrated guide to fashion activewear for both men and women.*

Niko

PUBLISHED BY: Modern Asian-Pacific American News Inc.

P.O. Box 19569

Austin, TX 78760

TEL: n/a

FREQUENCY: Monthly

COVER PRICE: $3.50

SUBSCRIPTION PRICE: $20.00

TOTAL NUMBER OF PAGES: 86

TOTAL NUMBER OF AD PAGES: 7

PUBLISHER: Richard A. Nguyen

EDITOR: Kim Ono

EDITORIAL CONCEPT: *"Insightful and in-depth articles about topics that are relevant to modern Asian-American women."*

Vary Magazine

PUBLISHED BY: Vary Inc.

7502 Greenville Ave., Suite 500

Dallas, TX 75231

TEL: (214) 747-8279 **FAX:** (214) 742-8279

DATE: November

FREQUENCY: Monthly

COVER PRICE: $3.95

SUBSCRIPTION PRICE: 24

TOTAL NUMBER OF PAGES: 162

TOTAL NUMBER OF AD PAGES: 19

PUBLISHER: Ceslie J. Armstrong

EDITOR: Ceslie J. Armstrong

EDITORIAL CONCEPT: *The name suggests it all — a plethora of information from fashion to fitness, for women and men.*

Season

PUBLISHED BY: Season Publishing Inc.

1234 Washington Ave., Suite 201

Miami Beach, FL 33139

TEL: (305) 534-4050 **FAX:** (305) 538-6772

FREQUENCY: Bimonthly

COVER PRICE: $2.95

SUBSCRIPTION PRICE: $26.00

TOTAL NUMBER OF PAGES: 84

TOTAL NUMBER OF AD PAGES: 26

PUBLISHER: Michael Micone

EDITOR: Tina Malave

EDITORIAL CONCEPT: *Articles about fashion, fashion accessories and beauty tips.*

ANNUAL, SPECIAL OR FREQUENCY UNKNOWN

Aveda

PUBLISHED BY: Hachtte Filipacchi

1633 Broadway

New York, NY 10019

TEL: (212) 767-5611

FREQUENCY: n/a

COVER PRICE: $3.95

SUBSCRIPTION PRICE: n/a

TOTAL NUMBER OF PAGES: 100

TOTAL NUMBER OF AD PAGES: 8

PUBLISHER: Beth-Ann Burzon

EDITOR: Corynne Corbett

EDITORIAL CONCEPT: *A new world of information that provides fresh, environmentally-sound concepts for every aspect of your life.*

The Complete Hair & Beauty Guide

EDITORIAL CONCEPT: *Dedicated to hair styles and hair and general beautification products.*

PUBLISHED BY: GCR Publishing Group Inc.

1700 Broadway

New York, NY 10019

TEL: (212) 541-7100

FREQUENCY: Special

COVER PRICE: $3.95

SUBSCRIPTION PRICE: n/a

TOTAL NUMBER OF PAGES: 84

TOTAL NUMBER OF AD PAGES: 14

PUBLISHER: Charles Goodman

EDITOR: Shelly Dawson-Davies

Madeleine

EDITORIAL CONCEPT: *Europe's premier fashion journal, featuring fashion with an elegant difference, yet with a clear focus on real life.*

PUBLISHED BY: Madeleine Fashions Inc.

1112 Seventh Ave.

Madison, WI 53566-9952

TEL: (800) 394-1994 **FAX:** (608) 324-6666

DATE: Fall/Winter

FREQUENCY: n/a

COVER PRICE: $3.95

SUBSCRIPTION PRICE: n/a

TOTAL NUMBER OF PAGES: 52

TOTAL NUMBER OF AD PAGES: 0

EDITOR: n/a

HotHair

EDITORIAL CONCEPT: *A magazine for women, featuring a guide to hair styles.*

PUBLISHED BY: Four Star Publications Inc.

Box 23368

Overland Park, KS 66223

TEL: n/a

FREQUENCY: Special

COVER PRICE: $2.99

SUBSCRIPTION PRICE: n/a

TOTAL NUMBER OF PAGES: 100

TOTAL NUMBER OF AD PAGES: 0

EDITOR: n/a

Aqua-Field World Of Hunting And Shooting

PUBLISHED BY: Aqua-Field Publishing Co.

66 W. Gilbert St.

Shrewsbury, NJ 07702

TEL: (908) 842-8300 **FAX:** (908) 842-0281

DATE: May

FREQUENCY: Bimonthly

COVER PRICE: $2.95

SUBSCRIPTION PRICE: $20.00

TOTAL NUMBER OF PAGES: 80

TOTAL NUMBER OF AD PAGES: 30

PUBLISHER: Steve Ferber

EDITOR: Steve Ferber

EDITORIAL CONCEPT: *Tips and techniques for hunting and shooting, with each issue focusing on different game.*

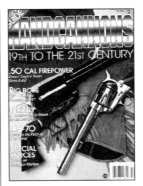

Handcannons

PUBLISHED BY: Challenge Publications Inc.

7950 Deering Ave.

Canoga Park, CA 91304

TEL: (818) 887-0550 **FAX:** (818) 884-1343

FREQUENCY: Quarterly

COVER PRICE: $5.95

SUBSCRIPTION PRICE: n/a

TOTAL NUMBER OF PAGES: 88

TOTAL NUMBER OF AD PAGES: 9

PUBLISHER: Edwin A. Schnepf

EDITOR: Joe Poyer

EDITORIAL CONCEPT: *Devoted entirely to big bore handguns from the 19th to the 21st centuries. Features up-close reviews on old and new models and an illustrated buyer's guide.*

Fly Tyer

PUBLISHED BY: Abenaki Publishers Inc.

126 North St., P.O. Box 4100

Bennington, VT 05201-4100

TEL: (802) 447-1518 **FAX:** (802) 447-2471

DATE: Autumn

FREQUENCY: Quarterly

COVER PRICE: $4.95

SUBSCRIPTION PRICE: $19.95

TOTAL NUMBER OF PAGES: 84

TOTAL NUMBER OF AD PAGES: 19

PUBLISHER: Joe Migliore

EDITOR: Art Scheck

EDITORIAL CONCEPT: *A magazine about fly-tying for anglers.*

Saltwater Fly Fishing

PUBLISHED BY: Abenaki Publishers Inc.

126 North St., P.O. Box 4100

Bennington, VT 05201-4100

TEL: (802) 447-1518 **FAX:** (802) 447-2471

DATE: Autumn

FREQUENCY: Quarterly

COVER PRICE: $3.95

SUBSCRIPTION PRICE: $17.95

TOTAL NUMBER OF PAGES: 82

TOTAL NUMBER OF AD PAGES: 18

PUBLISHER: Joe Migliore

EDITOR: Art Scheck

EDITORIAL CONCEPT: *A magazine for the sportsman interested in fly-fishing, fly-tying and fly-casting.*

Gun News Digest

PUBLISHED BY: Second Amendment Foundation

P.O. Box 488, Station C

Buffalo, NY 14209

TEL: (716) 885-6408 **FAX:** (716) 884-4471

DATE: Spring

FREQUENCY: Quarterly

COVER PRICE: $2.95

SUBSCRIPTION PRICE: n/a

TOTAL NUMBER OF PAGES: 68

TOTAL NUMBER OF AD PAGES: 10

PUBLISHER: Alan M. Gottlieb

EDITOR: Joseph P. Tartaro

EDITORIAL CONCEPT: *"To fill perceived gaps in the information resources available to American gun owners concerned by the ever-growing governmental threat to their firearm civil rights."*

Tactical Knives

PUBLISHED BY: Harris Publications Inc.

1115 Broadway

New York, NY 10010

TEL: (212) 807-7100 **FAX:** (212) 627-4678

DATE: Winter

FREQUENCY: Quarterly

COVER PRICE: $3.95

SUBSCRIPTION PRICE: n/a

TOTAL NUMBER OF PAGES: 92

TOTAL NUMBER OF AD PAGES: 21

PUBLISHER: Stanley R. Harris

EDITOR: Steven Dick

EDITORIAL CONCEPT: *"The cutting edge of survival."*

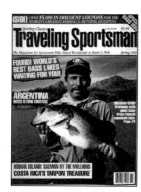

Traveling Sportsman

PUBLISHED BY: Live Oak Press Inc.

3031 Scotsman Rd.

Columbia, SC 29224

TEL: (803) 425-1003

DATE: Spring

FREQUENCY: Quarterly

COVER PRICE: $3.95

SUBSCRIPTION PRICE: $15.95

TOTAL NUMBER OF PAGES: 98

TOTAL NUMBER OF AD PAGES: 36

PUBLISHER: John Cornett

EDITOR: Art Carter

EDITORIAL CONCEPT: *"The magazine for sportsmen who travel worldwide to hunt and fish."*

Western Deer Hunting

PUBLISHED BY: Krause Publications

700 E. State St.

Iola, WI 54990

TEL: (715) 445-2214 **FAX:** (715) 445-4087

FREQUENCY: 8/year

COVER PRICE: $3.95

SUBSCRIPTION PRICE: $14.95

TOTAL NUMBER OF PAGES: 84

TOTAL NUMBER OF AD PAGES: 11

PUBLISHER: Debbie Khauer

EDITOR: Patrick Durkin

EDITORIAL CONCEPT: *A deer hunting magazine focusing on techniques and tips on how to hunt in the mountain regions of the West.*

Trophy Magazine

PUBLISHED BY: Trophy Magazine

5810 San Bernardo

Laredo, TX 78041

TEL: (210) 718-0789

DATE: October/November

FREQUENCY: Bimonthly

COVER PRICE: $2.95

SUBSCRIPTION PRICE: n/a

TOTAL NUMBER OF PAGES: 52

TOTAL NUMBER OF AD PAGES: 16

PUBLISHER: C.Y. Benquides, III

EDITOR: Linda Morris

EDITORIAL CONCEPT: *A magazine about deer hunting in South Texas.*

American Hunter's Guide

PUBLISHED BY: Aqua-Field Publishing Co.

66 W. Gilbert St.

Shrewsbury, NJ 07702

TEL: (908) 842-8300 **FAX:** (908) 842-0281

FREQUENCY: Special

COVER PRICE: $2.95

SUBSCRIPTION PRICE: n/a

TOTAL NUMBER OF PAGES: 64

TOTAL NUMBER OF AD PAGES: 11

PUBLISHER: Steve Ferber

EDITOR: Steve Ferber

EDITORIAL CONCEPT: *"The journal for serious hunters and exploring sportsmen."*

Varmit Masters Magazine

PUBLISHED BY: Thicket Publishing Inc.

2100 Riverchase Ctr., Suite 118

Birmingham, AL 35244

TEL: (205) 987-6007

FREQUENCY: Bimonthly

COVER PRICE: $2.95

SUBSCRIPTION PRICE: n/a

DISCOUNT SUBSCRIPTION PRICE: $15.00

TOTAL NUMBER OF PAGES: 92

TOTAL NUMBER OF AD PAGES: 47.5

PUBLISHER: Brock Ray

EDITOR: Don Kirk

EDITORIAL CONCEPT: *The official publication of the Varmit Masters Association.*

Deer Hunter

PUBLISHED BY: Harris Publications Inc.

1115 Broadway

New York, NY 10010

TEL: (212) 807-7100 **FAX:** (212) 807-1479

FREQUENCY: Annually

COVER PRICE: $4.95

SUBSCRIPTION PRICE: n/a

TOTAL NUMBER OF PAGES: 100

TOTAL NUMBER OF AD PAGES: 22

PUBLISHER: Stanley R. Harris

EDITOR: Gerald C. Bethge

EDITORIAL CONCEPT: *Deer-hunting tips and tactics.*

Glock Autopistols

PUBLISHED BY: Harris Publications Inc.

1115 Broadway

New York, NY 10010

TEL: (212) 807-7100   **FAX:** (212) 627-4678

FREQUENCY: Annually

COVER PRICE: $3.95

SUBSCRIPTION PRICE: n/a

TOTAL NUMBER OF PAGES: 100

TOTAL NUMBER OF AD PAGES: 15

PUBLISHER: Stanley R. Harris

EDITOR: Harry Kane

EDITORIAL CONCEPT: *The first magazine devoted entirely to Glock autopistols.*

Guns & Weapons For Self Defense

PUBLISHED BY: Harris Publications Inc.

1115 Broadway

New York, NY 10010

TEL: (212) 807-7100   **FAX:** (212) 627-4678

FREQUENCY: Annually

COVER PRICE: $5.50

SUBSCRIPTION PRICE: n/a

TOTAL NUMBER OF PAGES: 100

TOTAL NUMBER OF AD PAGES: 13

PUBLISHER: Stanley R. Harris

EDITOR: Harry Kane

EDITORIAL CONCEPT: *"An expert's guide to survival on the street and in the home."*

Guns & Ammo: Firearms For Law Enforcement

PUBLISHED BY: Petersen Publishing Co.

6420 Wilshire Blvd.

Los Angeles, CA 90048-5515

TEL: (213) 782-2160

FREQUENCY: Special

COVER PRICE: $3.95

SUBSCRIPTION PRICE: n/a

TOTAL NUMBER OF PAGES: 100

TOTAL NUMBER OF AD PAGES: 3

PUBLISHER: Doug Hamlin

EDITOR: Jerry Lee

EDITORIAL CONCEPT: *Focuses on firearms and tactics used in law enforcement.*

Lethal Force!

PUBLISHED BY: Challenge Publications Inc.

7950 Deering Ave.

Canoga Park, CA 91304

TEL: (818) 887-0550   **FAX:** (818) 884-1343

FREQUENCY: Special

COVER PRICE: $5.95

SUBSCRIPTION PRICE: n/a

TOTAL NUMBER OF PAGES: 96

TOTAL NUMBER OF AD PAGES: 4

PUBLISHER: Edwin A. Schnepf

EDITOR: Edwin A. Schnepf

EDITORIAL CONCEPT: *"How to stay alive in '95."*

Guns & Weapons For Law Enforcement

PUBLISHED BY: Harris Publications Inc.

1115 Broadway

New York, NY 10010

TEL: (212) 807-7100   **FAX:** (212) 627-4678

FREQUENCY: Annually

COVER PRICE: $4.95

SUBSCRIPTION PRICE: n/a

TOTAL NUMBER OF PAGES: 100

TOTAL NUMBER OF AD PAGES: 33

PUBLISHER: Stanley R. Harris

EDITOR: Harry Kane

EDITORIAL CONCEPT: *A law enforcement equipment guide.*

Monster Bow Bucks

PUBLISHED BY: Harris Publications Inc.

1115 Broadway

New York, NY 10010

TEL: (212) 807-7100   **FAX:** (212) 627-4678

FREQUENCY: Annually

COVER PRICE: $4.50

SUBSCRIPTION PRICE: n/a

TOTAL NUMBER OF PAGES: 100

TOTAL NUMBER OF AD PAGES: 21

PUBLISHER: Stanley R. Harris

EDITOR: Gerald C. Bethge

EDITORIAL CONCEPT: *A magazine for bow-hunt enthusiasts.*

Smith & Wesson Handguns '95

PUBLISHED BY: PJS Publications Inc.

News Plaza, Box 1790

Peoria, IL 61656

TEL: (309) 682-6626   **FAX:** (309) 682-7394

FREQUENCY: Special

COVER PRICE: Free

SUBSCRIPTION PRICE: n/a

TOTAL NUMBER OF PAGES: 100

TOTAL NUMBER OF AD PAGES: 14

EDITOR: Ken Jorgensen

EDITORIAL CONCEPT: *A complimentary handgun buyer's guide distributed with* Shooting Times *magazine, featuring over 40 models.*

Tactical Bowhunting

PUBLISHED BY: Harris Publications Inc.

1115 Broadway

New York, NY 10010

TEL: (212) 807-7100   **FAX:** (212) 627-4678

FREQUENCY: Annually

COVER PRICE: $5.50

SUBSCRIPTION PRICE: n/a

TOTAL NUMBER OF PAGES: 100

TOTAL NUMBER OF AD PAGES: 14

PUBLISHER: Stanley R. Harris

EDITOR: Gerald C. Bethge

EDITORIAL CONCEPT: *Tactical information to improve a hunter's bowhunting technique and knowledge of his prey.*

Fit

PUBLISHED BY: GCR Publishing Group Inc.

1700 Broadway

New York, NY 10019

TEL: (212) 541-7100   **FAX:** (212) 245-1241

DATE: June/July

FREQUENCY: Bimonthly

COVER PRICE: $1.95

SUBSCRIPTION PRICE: $19.97

DISCOUNT SUBSCRIPTION PRICE: $14.97

TOTAL NUMBER OF PAGES: 100

TOTAL NUMBER OF AD PAGES: 36

PUBLISHER: Charles Goodman

EDITOR: Nichole Dorsey

EDITORIAL CONCEPT: *"An exercise bible, a dieter's guide, a healing voice of reason and a fly on your lover's locker room wall."*

1001 Weight Loss Secrets

PUBLISHED BY: Harris Publications Inc.

1115 Broadway

New York, NY 10010

TEL: (212) 807-7100   **FAX:** (212) 627-4678

DATE: Summer

FREQUENCY: Quarterly

COVER PRICE: $3.25

SUBSCRIPTION PRICE: n/a

TOTAL NUMBER OF PAGES: 92

TOTAL NUMBER OF AD PAGES: 0

PUBLISHER: Stanley R. Harris

EDITOR: Phyllis Goldstein

EDITORIAL CONCEPT: *A beginner's guide to weight training that allows you to have fun as you work out.*

Personal Styles Fitness

PUBLISHED BY: International Recipe Collection Inc.

4151 Knob Dr.

Eagan, MN 55122

TEL: (612) 452-0571

FREQUENCY: Bimonthly

COVER PRICE: $3.25

SUBSCRIPTION PRICE: $12.95

DISCOUNT SUBSCRIPTION PRICE: $35.00 (3 years)

TOTAL NUMBER OF PAGES: 84

TOTAL NUMBER OF AD PAGES: 4.5

PUBLISHER: Russ Moore

EDITOR: Nicole Niemi

EDITORIAL CONCEPT: *Improving your life and enhancing your longevity through exercise and diet.*

Shape Presents Fit Pregnancy

PUBLISHED BY: Weider Publications Inc.

21100 Erwin St.

Woodland Hills, CA 91367

TEL: (818) 884-6800   **FAX:** (818) 704-5734

DATE: Spring

FREQUENCY: Semiannually

COVER PRICE: $2.95

SUBSCRIPTION PRICE: n/a

TOTAL NUMBER OF PAGES: 132

TOTAL NUMBER OF AD PAGES: 26

PUBLISHER: Joe Weider

EDITOR: Barbara S. Harris

EDITORIAL CONCEPT: *Shape magazine's guide to a fit pregnancy.*

Shaping Your Figure Through Health

PUBLISHED BY: Four Star Publications Inc.

P.O. Box 23368

Overland Park, KS 66223

TEL: n/a

DATE: August

FREQUENCY: 8/year

COVER PRICE: $2.99

SUBSCRIPTION PRICE: n/a

TOTAL NUMBER OF PAGES: 100

TOTAL NUMBER OF AD PAGES: 3

EDITOR: n/a

EDITORIAL CONCEPT: *Features articles about binge eating, shaping up and more.*

Total Fitness For Men

PUBLISHED BY: Crosstrainer Publications

505 Saddle River Rd., Suite H

Saddle Brook, NJ 07662

TEL: (201) 368-2140

DATE: February

FREQUENCY: Bimonthly

COVER PRICE: $3.95

SUBSCRIPTION PRICE: n/a

TOTAL NUMBER OF PAGES: 100

TOTAL NUMBER OF AD PAGES: 20

PUBLISHER: Alan Paul

EDITOR: Bob McCann

EDITORIAL CONCEPT: *The fitness magazine formerly known as Crosstrainer offers articles on all aspects of keeping fit, with tips on diet and exercise.*

Bodywise: Diet & Exercise

PUBLISHED BY: Four Star Publications Inc.

P.O. Box 23368

Overland Park, KS 66223

TEL: n/a

FREQUENCY: Special

COVER PRICE: $2.99

SUBSCRIPTION PRICE: n/a

TOTAL NUMBER OF PAGES: 84

TOTAL NUMBER OF AD PAGES: 2

EDITOR: n/a

EDITORIAL CONCEPT: *"Fat-cutting tips, diets and exercises to help you get the figure you're looking for."*

Sensuous Muscle: The Women Of Bodybuilding

PUBLISHED BY: I, Brute Enterprises Inc.

21100 Erwin St.

Woodland Hills, CA 91367

TEL: (800) 483-0648

DATE: Summer

FREQUENCY: Special

COVER PRICE: $4.95

SUBSCRIPTION PRICE: n/a

TOTAL NUMBER OF PAGES: 174

TOTAL NUMBER OF AD PAGES: 39

PUBLISHER: Joe Weider

EDITOR: Jerry Kindela

EDITORIAL CONCEPT: *The ultimate photo compilation of women and muscle*

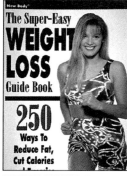

New Body: The Super-Easy Weight Loss Guide Book

PUBLISHED BY: GCR Publishing Group Inc.

1700 Broadway

New York, NY 10019

TEL: (212) 541-7100

FREQUENCY: Special

COVER PRICE: $2.95

SUBSCRIPTION PRICE: n/a

TOTAL NUMBER OF PAGES: 68

TOTAL NUMBER OF AD PAGES: 0

PUBLISHER: Charles Goodman

EDITOR: Sallie Batson

EDITORIAL CONCEPT: *"250 ways to reduce fat, cut calories and exercise without pain."*

Star Magazine Special: Star Diets

PUBLISHED BY: Star Division of American Media Operations Inc.

600 S. East Coast Ave.

Lantana, FL 33464

TEL: (407) 586-1111

DATE: Spring

FREQUENCY: Special

COVER PRICE: $2.50

SUBSCRIPTION PRICE: n/a

TOTAL NUMBER OF PAGES: 76

TOTAL NUMBER OF AD PAGES: 9

EDITOR: Lynne Dorsey

EDITORIAL CONCEPT: *"Safe, sure slimming secrets of Demi, Melanie, Oprah, Cybill, Whitney, Pam, Reba, etc.*

New Body's Firm Butt, Thin Thighs In 30 Days

PUBLISHED BY: GCR Publications Group Inc.

1700 Broadway

New York, NY 10019

TEL: (212) 541-7100 **FAX:** (212) 245-1241

FREQUENCY: Special

COVER PRICE: $2.95

SUBSCRIPTION PRICE: n/a

TOTAL NUMBER OF PAGES: 68

TOTAL NUMBER OF AD PAGES: 0

PUBLISHER: Charles Goodman

EDITOR: Lisa Klugman

EDITORIAL CONCEPT: *"Your personal training guide, with hundreds of diet and exercise tips."*

Stretching For Success

PUBLISHED BY: Chelo Publishing Inc.

350 Fifth Ave., Suite 3323

New York, NY 10118

TEL: (212) 947-4322 **FAX:** (212) 563-4774

FREQUENCY: Special

COVER PRICE: $4.95

SUBSCRIPTION PRICE: n/a

TOTAL NUMBER OF PAGES: 116

TOTAL NUMBER OF AD PAGES: 2

PUBLISHER: Cheh N. Low

EDITOR: John S. Bruel

EDITORIAL CONCEPT: *More than 30 different stretching exercises.*

30 Days To A Flatter Stomach

PUBLISHED BY: Prestige Publications Inc.

P.O. Box 23368

Shawnee Mission, KS 66223

TEL: n/a

FREQUENCY: n/a

COVER PRICE: $2.99

SUBSCRIPTION PRICE: n/a

TOTAL NUMBER OF PAGES: 100

TOTAL NUMBER OF AD PAGES: 0

EDITOR: Monica Mathed Humbard

EDITORIAL CONCEPT: *Over 35 pages of exercise and scrumptious recipes, plus a tummy-trimming, 8-day diet.*

Ultimate Body

PUBLISHED BY: Starlog Communications

International Inc.

475 Park Ave. S.

New York, NY 10016

TEL: (212) 689-2830

FREQUENCY: Special

COVER PRICE: $4.99

SUBSCRIPTION PRICE: n/a

TOTAL NUMBER OF PAGES: 72

TOTAL NUMBER OF AD PAGES: 5

PUBLISHER: Norman Jacobs

EDITOR: Julie Davis

EDITORIAL CONCEPT: *The fitness guide for women, with a focus on weight training.*

Lottery Winner's Weekly

PUBLISHED BY: Lottery Winner's Weekly

P.O. Box 4813

Winston-Salem, NC 27115-4813

TEL: n/a

DATE: March

FREQUENCY: Weekly

COVER PRICE: $1.50

SUBSCRIPTION PRICE: n/a

TOTAL NUMBER OF PAGES: 84

TOTAL NUMBER OF AD PAGES: 0

EDITOR: n/a

EDITORIAL CONCEPT: *The winning lottery numbers nationwide, with results from every game, in every state, every week.*

Buzz Daly's Players Guide To Las Vegas Sports Books: 1995 Football Edition

PUBLISHED BY:

14350 Addison St., Suite 208

Sherman Oaks, CA 91423

TEL: (818) 907-6261

FREQUENCY: Annually

COVER PRICE: $5.95

SUBSCRIPTION PRICE: $6.95

TOTAL NUMBER OF PAGES: 48

TOTAL NUMBER OF AD PAGES: 6

PUBLISHER: Buzz Daly

EDITOR: Buzz Daly

EDITORIAL CONCEPT: *Features the "exclusive inside dope."*

Lotto World

PUBLISHED BY: Lotto World Inc.

2150 Goodlette Rd., Suite 200

Naples, FL 33940-4811

TEL: (941) 643-1677 **FAX:** (941) 263-0809

DATE: May

FREQUENCY: Biweekly

COVER PRICE: $1.75

SUBSCRIPTION PRICE: $29.97

TOTAL NUMBER OF PAGES: 82

TOTAL NUMBER OF AD PAGES: 30

PUBLISHER: Dennis B. Schroeder

EDITOR: Rich Holman

EDITORIAL CONCEPT: *Lotto World becomes "America's lottery magazine" with its national launch. Features editorials and articles on how to play the lottery, plus testimonies from winners.*

Score: 1995 Betting Guide For College And NFL Football

PUBLISHED BY: Sportfolio Publications

304 Newbury St., Suite 504

Boston, MA 02115-2832

TEL: (800) 242-4464

FREQUENCY: Annually

COVER PRICE: $5.95

SUBSCRIPTION PRICE: n/a

TOTAL NUMBER OF PAGES: 148

TOTAL NUMBER OF AD PAGES: 24

EDITOR: n/a

EDITORIAL CONCEPT: *Reviews of and betting odds on all college and NFL teams.*

ANNUAL, SPECIAL OR FREQUENCY UNKNOWN

Anvil Magazine

PUBLISHED BY: Anvil Publications

P.O. Box 105

Folsom, PA 19033

TEL: (414) 763-9175

FREQUENCY: n/a

COVER PRICE: $1.95

SUBSCRIPTION PRICE: n/a

TOTAL NUMBER OF PAGES: 32

TOTAL NUMBER OF AD PAGES: 3

EDITOR: Joseph Goodman

EDITORIAL CONCEPT: *"The magazine of miniatures gaming."*

Winning Sports Gambling Illustrated

PUBLISHED BY: W.S.G.I.

TEL: n/a

DATE: Fall

FREQUENCY: Annually

COVER PRICE: $5.95

SUBSCRIPTION PRICE: n/a

TOTAL NUMBER OF PAGES: 148

TOTAL NUMBER OF AD PAGES: 39

EDITOR: n/a

EDITORIAL CONCEPT: *The 1995 annual college and pro football betting guide.*

Birds & Blooms: Beauty In Your Own Backyard

PUBLISHED BY: Reiman Publications L.P.

5400 S. 60th St.

Greendale, WI 53129

TEL: (414) 423-0100   **FAX:** (414) 423-1143

FREQUENCY: Bimonthly

COVER PRICE: $2.95

SUBSCRIPTION PRICE: $16.98

DISCOUNT SUBSCRIPTION PRICE: $10.98

TOTAL NUMBER OF PAGES: 68

TOTAL NUMBER OF AD PAGES: 0

PUBLISHER: Roy Reiman

EDITOR: Tom Curl

EDITORIAL CONCEPT: *Welcome to the world of new sounds, scents and scenes, right in your own backyard.*

Garden Gate

PUBLISHED BY: Woodsmith Corp.

2200 Grand Ave.

Des Moines, IA 50312

TEL: (800) 341-4769

DATE: February/March

FREQUENCY: Bimonthly

COVER PRICE: $3.95

SUBSCRIPTION PRICE: $19.95

TOTAL NUMBER OF PAGES: 32

TOTAL NUMBER OF AD PAGES: 0

PUBLISHER: Donald B. Peschke

EDITOR: Tom Crosgrove

EDITORIAL CONCEPT: *The illustrated guide to home gardening and design, with articles presenting step-by-step instructions, tips for gardening and plant profiles.*

Craftsman Practical Lawns & Gardens

PUBLISHED BY: Aqua-Field Publishing Co.

66 W. Gilbert St.

Shrewsbury, NJ 07702

TEL: (908) 842-8300   **FAX:** (908) 842-0281

FREQUENCY: Quarterly

COVER PRICE: $2.95

SUBSCRIPTION PRICE: n/a

TOTAL NUMBER OF PAGES: 84

TOTAL NUMBER OF AD PAGES: 21

PUBLISHER: Stephen Ferber

EDITOR: Stephen Ferber

EDITORIAL CONCEPT: *The source for all things green and beautiful.*

Greenthumb

PUBLISHED BY: Greenthumb Magazine

756 Ridge Lake Blvd., Suite 206

Memphis, TN 38120-9445

TEL: (901) 767-1446   **FAX:** (901) 767-1286

FREQUENCY: Bimonthly

COVER PRICE: $2.95

SUBSCRIPTION PRICE: $17.70

TOTAL NUMBER OF PAGES: 36

TOTAL NUMBER OF AD PAGES: 7

PUBLISHER: Pete Ceren

EDITOR: Jennifer Griffin, Janet Haire

EDITORIAL CONCEPT: *Gardening information for Memphis and the Mid-South.*

The Flowerlover

PUBLISHED BY: The Flowerlover

30 Hwy. 200

Heron, MT 59844

TEL: (406) 847-2482

FREQUENCY: Bimonthly

COVER PRICE: $5.50

SUBSCRIPTION PRICE: $26.00

TOTAL NUMBER OF PAGES: 68

TOTAL NUMBER OF AD PAGES: 5

PUBLISHER: Chris Griscom

EDITOR: Chris Griscom

EDITORIAL CONCEPT: *"Everything about flowers... in their world and ours." Articles cover different species of flowers and how to take care of them.*

Home Garden

PUBLISHED BY: Meredith Corp.

1716 Locust St.

Des Moines, IA 50309-3023

TEL: (515) 284-2335

DATE: March/April

FREQUENCY: Bimonthly

COVER PRICE: $3.99

SUBSCRIPTION PRICE: $19.97

TOTAL NUMBER OF PAGES: 140

TOTAL NUMBER OF AD PAGES: 38

PUBLISHER: Catherine Potkay Westberg

EDITOR: Douglas A. Jamerson

EDITORIAL CONCEPT: *Celebrates the rewards of a garden and offers practical ideas for those with a passion for gardening and outdoor living.*

Indoor & Patio Gardening

PUBLISHED BY: Family Digest Inc.

7002 W. Butler Pk.

Ambler, PA 19002

TEL: (215) 643-6385

FREQUENCY: Bimonthly

COVER PRICE: $3.50

SUBSCRIPTION PRICE: $17.85

TOTAL NUMBER OF PAGES: 84

TOTAL NUMBER OF AD PAGES: 2.2

PUBLISHER: Camille Pomaco

EDITOR: Camille Pomaco

EDITORIAL CONCEPT: *Articles on choosing and caring for smaller house plants.*

Flower Gardening

PUBLISHED BY: Meredith Corp.

1716 Locust St.

Des Moines, IA 50309-3023

TEL: (800) 678-2872

FREQUENCY: Special

COVER PRICE: $3.99

SUBSCRIPTION PRICE: n/a

TOTAL NUMBER OF PAGES: 114

TOTAL NUMBER OF AD PAGES: 17

PUBLISHER: Stephen B. Levinson

EDITOR: William J. Yates

EDITORIAL CONCEPT: *Everything you need to know to grow beautiful flowers.*

ANNUAL, SPECIAL OR FREQUENCY UNKNOWN

Fall Garden Planner

PUBLISHED BY: Hachette Filipacchi

1633 Broadway

New York, NY 10019

TEL: (212) 767-6000 **FAX:** (212) 767-5612

FREQUENCY: Special

COVER PRICE: $3.99

SUBSCRIPTION PRICE: n/a

TOTAL NUMBER OF PAGES: 116

TOTAL NUMBER OF AD PAGES: 19

PUBLISHER: Sharri R. Jurmain

EDITOR: Eleanore Lewis

EDITORIAL CONCEPT: *This* Woman's Day *gardening special features the 28 longest-blooming perennials and landscape fix-ups.*

Gardens, Decks & Patios

PUBLISHED BY: Harris Publications Inc.

1115 Broadway

New York, NY 10010

TEL: (212) 807-7100 **FAX:** (212) 627-4678

FREQUENCY: Annually

COVER PRICE: $4.50

SUBSCRIPTION PRICE: n/a

TOTAL NUMBER OF PAGES: 84

TOTAL NUMBER OF AD PAGES: 9

PUBLISHER: Stanley R. Harris

EDITOR: Barbara Mayer

EDITORIAL CONCEPT: *"Chock-full of tips, ideas and step-by-step projects for making an outdoor space more livable."*

EDITORIAL CONCEPT: *For lesbian and gay parents and their friends.*

The Family Next Door

PUBLISHED BY: Next Door Publishing Ltd.

P.O. Box 21580

Oakland, CA 94620

TEL: (510) 482-5778   **FAX:** (510) 482-5778

FREQUENCY: Bimonthly

COVER PRICE: $3.00

SUBSCRIPTION PRICE: $40.00 (3 years)

TOTAL NUMBER OF PAGES: 32

TOTAL NUMBER OF AD PAGES: 4

PUBLISHER: Lisa Orta, Keren Rust

EDITOR: Lisa Orta

EDITORIAL CONCEPT: *"The elements shared by the artists of Provocateur are a rebellious soul and an un-tamable spirit."*

Provocateur

PUBLISHED BY: Alluvial Publishing

8599 Santa Monica Blvd.

West Hollywood, CA 90069

TEL: (310) 659-6654   **FAX:** (310) 659-6634

DATE: October

FREQUENCY: Bimonthly

COVER PRICE: $11.95

SUBSCRIPTION PRICE: $43.00

TOTAL NUMBER OF PAGES: 84

TOTAL NUMBER OF AD PAGES: 11

PUBLISHER: Robert Madden

EDITOR: Ryan Brookhart

EDITORIAL CONCEPT: *"Introducing cutting-edge gay and lesbian talent."*

50•50 Magazine

PUBLISHED BY: 50•50 Magazine

2336 Market St., #20

San Francisco, CA 94114

TEL: (415) 789-8493

FREQUENCY: Bimonthly

COVER PRICE: $4.95

SUBSCRIPTION PRICE: $25.00

TOTAL NUMBER OF PAGES: 48

TOTAL NUMBER OF AD PAGES: 17

PUBLISHER: Wendy Jill York

EDITOR: Lisa Roth

EDITORIAL CONCEPT: *The national gay and lesbian entrepreneur magazine.*

Victory!

PUBLISHED BY: Intercultural Science Group

2261 Market St., Suite 296

San Francisco, CA 94114

TEL: (510) 215-1780   **FAX:** (510) 215-0812

FREQUENCY: Bimonthly

COVER PRICE: $3.95

SUBSCRIPTION PRICE: $20.00

TOTAL NUMBER OF PAGES: 36

TOTAL NUMBER OF AD PAGES: 11

PUBLISHER: M.J. McKean-Reich

EDITOR: Thomas A. McKean-Reich

EDITORIAL CONCEPT: *A magazine that covers real-life issues for gay men.*

Men's Style

PUBLISHED BY: Baio & Co.

P.O. Box 993

Edison, NJ 08818-0993

TEL: (800) 568-2246   **FAX:** (908) 287-4210

FREQUENCY: Bimonthly

COVER PRICE: $3.95

SUBSCRIPTION PRICE: $23.70

TOTAL NUMBER OF PAGES: 116

TOTAL NUMBER OF AD PAGES: 20

PUBLISHER: Louis T. Baio, Sr.

EDITOR: Marvin Bevans

EDITORIAL CONCEPT: *"Covering men from head to toe": a sex and lifestyle magazine for gay men.*

Wilde

PUBLISHED BY: PDA Press Inc.

530 Howard St., #400

San Francisco, CA 94105

TEL: (415) 243-3232

DATE: May/June

FREQUENCY: Bimonthly

COVER PRICE: $5.95

SUBSCRIPTION PRICE: $31.50

TOTAL NUMBER OF PAGES: 92

TOTAL NUMBER OF AD PAGES: 27

EDITOR: John Fall

Heroes Of The Heartland

PUBLISHED BY: Globe International Inc.

5401 NW Broken Sound Blvd.

Boca Raton, FL 33487

TEL: (800) 749-7733

FREQUENCY: Special

COVER PRICE: $2.50

SUBSCRIPTION PRICE: n/a

TOTAL NUMBER OF PAGES: 48

TOTAL NUMBER OF AD PAGES: 3

EDITOR: Mike Irish

EDITORIAL CONCEPT: *A pictorial look at the men and women who risked their lives in the wake of the Oklahoma federal building bombing.*

Prevention's Guide: Personal Safety

PUBLISHED BY: Rodale Press Inc.

33 E. Minor St.

Emmaus, PA 18098

TEL: (610) 967-5171

FREQUENCY: Special

COVER PRICE: $2.95

SUBSCRIPTION PRICE: n/a

TOTAL NUMBER OF PAGES: 100

TOTAL NUMBER OF AD PAGES: 7

PUBLISHER: Richard Alleger

EDITOR: Catherine M. Cassidy

EDITORIAL CONCEPT: *"Your guide to crime and accident prevention."*

Alternative Medicine Digest

PUBLISHED BY: Future Medicine Publishing Inc.

5009 Pacific Hwy. E., Suite 6

Fife, WA 98424

TEL: (206) 922-9550

FREQUENCY: Bimonthly

COVER PRICE: $3.00

SUBSCRIPTION PRICE: $18.00

TOTAL NUMBER OF PAGES: 52

TOTAL NUMBER OF AD PAGES: 10

EDITOR: Richard Leviton

EDITORIAL CONCEPT: *"The voice of alternative medicine."*

Life Extension

PUBLISHED BY: Life Extension Foundation

P.O. Box 229120

Hollywood, FL 33022

TEL: (954) 966-4886

DATE: September

FREQUENCY: 17/year

COVER PRICE: $4.95

SUBSCRIPTION PRICE: n/a

TOTAL NUMBER OF PAGES: 68

TOTAL NUMBER OF AD PAGES: 15

PUBLISHER: William Faloon

EDITOR: Saul Kent

EDITORIAL CONCEPT: *"The ultimate source for health and medical breakthroughs from around the world."*

Health Digest

PUBLISHED BY: Schulhof, Lind, Walsh & Associates

Mequon, Wisconsin

TEL: (414) 238-1070

DATE: Spring/Summer

FREQUENCY: Semiannually

COVER PRICE: Supplement

SUBSCRIPTION PRICE: n/a

TOTAL NUMBER OF PAGES: 36

TOTAL NUMBER OF AD PAGES: 0

PUBLISHER: Stephen A. Geppi

EDITOR: Ramsey Flynn

EDITORIAL CONCEPT: *"Vital health information every family should have."*

The Natural Way

PUBLISHED BY: Natural Way Publications

566 Westchester Ave.

Rye Brook, NY 10573

TEL: (914) 939-2111

DATE: March

FREQUENCY: Bimonthly

COVER PRICE: $2.95

SUBSCRIPTION PRICE: n/a

TOTAL NUMBER OF PAGES: 84

TOTAL NUMBER OF AD PAGES: 9

PUBLISHER: Jack Tabatch

EDITOR: Randy Blaur

EDITORIAL CONCEPT: *The best of alternative health news and views.*

Healthy & Natural Journal

PUBLISHED BY: Measurements & Data Corp.

100 Wallace Ave., Suite 100

Sarasota, FL 34237

TEL: (941) 366-1153

FREQUENCY: Bimonthly

COVER PRICE: $4.50

SUBSCRIPTION PRICE: n/a

TOTAL NUMBER OF PAGES: 180

TOTAL NUMBER OF AD PAGES: 57

PUBLISHER: Robert S. Aronson

EDITOR: Michael L. Keenan

EDITORIAL CONCEPT: *A complete health guide with an environmental perspective.*

Joe Weider's Prime Fitness & Health

PUBLISHED BY: I, Brute Enterprises Inc.

21100 Erwin St.

Woodland Hills, CA 91367

TEL: (800) 998-0731

DATE: Spring

FREQUENCY: Bimonthly

COVER PRICE: $2.95

SUBSCRIPTION PRICE: $12.97

TOTAL NUMBER OF PAGES: 130

TOTAL NUMBER OF AD PAGES: 44

PUBLISHER: Joe Weider

EDITOR: Mary Ann Mucica

EDITORIAL CONCEPT: *"A guide to total well-being for the man over 35."*

The Medizine Guidebook To Women's Medications

PUBLISHED BY: Medizine Inc.

230 Park Ave., 7th Floor

New York, NY 10169

TEL: (212) 551-9738

FREQUENCY: Special

COVER PRICE: Free

SUBSCRIPTION PRICE: n/a

TOTAL NUMBER OF PAGES: 68

TOTAL NUMBER OF AD PAGES: 0

PUBLISHER: J. Traver Hutchins

EDITOR: Katherine Callan

EDITORIAL CONCEPT: "A practical guide to taking your medicine correctly."

Sexual Health, New Body Health

PUBLISHED BY: GCR Publishing Group Inc.

1700 Broadway

New York, NY 10019

TEL: (212) 541-7100   **FAX:** (212) 245-1241

FREQUENCY: Special

COVER PRICE: $2.95

SUBSCRIPTION PRICE: n/a

TOTAL NUMBER OF PAGES: 68

TOTAL NUMBER OF AD PAGES: 0

PUBLISHER: Charles Goodman

EDITOR: Lisa Klugman

EDITORIAL CONCEPT: A magazine featuring articles on sexuality and sexual health.

New Body's Quick & Easy Diet & Exercise Guide

PUBLISHED BY: GCR Publishing Group Inc.

1700 Broadway

New York, NY 10019

TEL: (212) 541-7100   **FAX:** (212) 245-1241

FREQUENCY: n/a

COVER PRICE: $2.95

SUBSCRIPTION PRICE: n/a

TOTAL NUMBER OF PAGES: 68

TOTAL NUMBER OF AD PAGES: 3

PUBLISHER: Charles Goodman

EDITOR: Lisa Klugman

EDITORIAL CONCEPT: "Improve health and reduce stress levels all in the same program."

All-American Home Plans

PUBLISHED BY: Meredith Corp.

1716 Locust St.

Des Moines, IA 50309-3023

TEL: (800) 678-2872

DATE: Winter

FREQUENCY: Quarterly

COVER PRICE: $3.99

SUBSCRIPTION PRICE: n/a

TOTAL NUMBER OF PAGES: 196

TOTAL NUMBER OF AD PAGES: 16

EDITOR: William J. Yates

EDITORIAL CONCEPT: "More than 160 innovative designs to suit any budget, any dream."

Building Ideas For Your New Home

PUBLISHED BY: Special Interest Publications

Meredith Corp.

1716 Locust St.

Des Moines, IA 50309-3023

TEL: (800) 678-2872

DATE: Winter

FREQUENCY: Quarterly

COVER PRICE: $3.99

SUBSCRIPTION PRICE: n/a

TOTAL NUMBER OF PAGES: 124

TOTAL NUMBER OF AD PAGES: 26

EDITOR: William J. Yates

EDITORIAL CONCEPT: Creative ideas for the person building a new home.

America's Favorite Home Plans

PUBLISHED BY: Hanley-Wood Inc.

1 Thomas Cir. NW, Suite 600

Washington, DC 20005

TEL: (202) 452-0800

DATE: Spring

FREQUENCY: Quarterly

COVER PRICE: $4.95

SUBSCRIPTION PRICE: n/a

TOTAL NUMBER OF PAGES: 322

TOTAL NUMBER OF AD PAGES: 17

EDITOR: n/a

EDITORIAL CONCEPT: "The best-loved plans in the U.S.A."

Christie's Great Estates

PUBLISHED BY: Christie's Great Estates

4 Camino Pequeno

Santa Fe, NM 87501

TEL: (505) 983-8733   **FAX:** (505) 982-0348

DATE: Fall/Winter

FREQUENCY: 3/year

COVER PRICE: $7.00

SUBSCRIPTION PRICE: $21.00

TOTAL NUMBER OF PAGES: 130

TOTAL NUMBER OF AD PAGES: 2

PUBLISHER: Kay Coughlin

EDITORIAL CONCEPT: "The international showcase for distinctive properties."

Architect: Home Plans

PUBLISHED BY: HIS Publishing Inc.

P.O. Box 213

Berne, IN 46711

TEL: (219) 589-2145

FREQUENCY: Quarterly

COVER PRICE: $5.95

SUBSCRIPTION PRICE: n/a

TOTAL NUMBER OF PAGES: 290

TOTAL NUMBER OF AD PAGES: 7

PUBLISHER: Wendy Schroeder

EDITOR: Pamela Robertson

EDITORIAL CONCEPT: Over 275 plans of homes for sale.

Coastal Home

PUBLISHED BY: Thomasson Publishing Corp.

203 Lookout Pl., Suite C

Maitland, FL 32751

TEL: (407) 740-6199

FREQUENCY: Bimonthly

COVER PRICE: $3.00

SUBSCRIPTION PRICE: $24.00

TOTAL NUMBER OF PAGES: 138

TOTAL NUMBER OF AD PAGES: 31

PUBLISHER: Jack Thomasson

EDITOR: Sharon Cobb

EDITORIAL CONCEPT: Features articles on "stylish interiors, extraordinary architecture, inspirational gardening, irresistible coastal cuisine, tantalizing travel and gracious living."

Country Accents' Today's Home

PUBLISHED BY: GCR Publishing Group Inc.

1700 Broadway

New York, NY 10019

TEL: (212) 541-7100

DATE: Spring

FREQUENCY: Quarterly

COVER PRICE: $3.50

SUBSCRIPTION PRICE: n/a

TOTAL NUMBER OF PAGES: 84

TOTAL NUMBER OF AD PAGES: 10

PUBLISHER: Charles Goodman

EDITOR: Deborah Harding

EDITORIAL CONCEPT: *Problem-solving decorating ideas.*

Craftsman At Home: Decks And Outdoor Living

PUBLISHED BY: Aqua-Field Publications

66 W. Gilbert St.,Shrewsbury, NJ 07702

TEL: (908) 842-8300   **FAX:** (908) 842-0281

DATE: Summer

FREQUENCY: Quarterly

COVER PRICE: $2.95

SUBSCRIPTION PRICE: n/a

TOTAL NUMBER OF PAGES: 84

TOTAL NUMBER OF AD PAGES: 11

PUBLISHER: Stephen Ferber

EDITOR: Stephen Ferber

EDITORIAL CONCEPT: *A magazine with helpful hints on designing and building decks and patios, as well as landscaping and maintenance.*

Country Collections

PUBLISHED BY: Magnolia Media Group

1227 W. Magnolia

Fort Worth, TX 76104

TEL: (817) 921-9300

DATE: Winter

FREQUENCY: Quarterly

COVER PRICE: $4.95

SUBSCRIPTION PRICE: $12.00

TOTAL NUMBER OF PAGES: 84

TOTAL NUMBER OF AD PAGES: 1

PUBLISHER: Mark Hulme

EDITOR: Terri Talbert

EDITORIAL CONCEPT: *"America's source for direct-order home furnishings."*

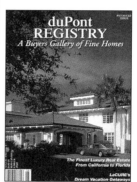

duPont Registry: A Buyer's Gallery Of Fine Homes

PUBLISHED BY: duPont Publishing

P.O. Box 25237

Tampa, FL 33622

TEL: (800) 233-1731   **FAX:** (813) 572-5523

DATE: August

FREQUENCY: Bimonthly

COVER PRICE: $4.95

SUBSCRIPTION PRICE: $29.92

DISCOUNT SUBSCRIPTION PRICE: $24.97

TOTAL NUMBER OF PAGES: 180

PUBLISHER: Thomas L. duPont

EDITOR: Eric V. Kennedy

EDITORIAL CONCEPT: *A high-end real-estate magazine focusing homes for sale.*

Country Sampler's Romantic Homes

PUBLISHED BY: Sampler Publications Inc.

707 Kautz Rd.

St. Charles, IL 60174

TEL: (708) 377-8000   **FAX:** (708) 377-8194

DATE: May

FREQUENCY: Bimonthly

COVER PRICE: $3.95

SUBSCRIPTION PRICE: $23.97

TOTAL NUMBER OF PAGES: 82

TOTAL NUMBER OF AD PAGES: 18

PUBLISHER: Mark A. Nickel

EDITOR: Carol Schalla

EDITORIAL CONCEPT: *"Bring a little romance into your home and save; authentic country decorating ideas, original furnishings and delightful folk art."*

Metropolitan Home Plans

PUBLISHED BY: Hachette Filipacchi

1633 Broadway

New York, NY 10019

TEL: (212) 767-6000

FREQUENCY: Bimonthly

COVER PRICE: $3.95

SUBSCRIPTION PRICE: n/a

TOTAL NUMBER OF PAGES: 188

TOTAL NUMBER OF AD PAGES: 7

PUBLISHER: John J. Miller, III

EDITOR: Sherise Dorf

EDITORIAL CONCEPT: *Plans for 200 great home designs like "The Ecohouse of Your Dreams" and "The Best Little 2-Bedroom House in America."*

Minnesota Fabrics: Home Expressions

PUBLISHED BY: Harvest Media Inc.

820 N. Main St.

Forth Worth, TX 76106

TEL: (817) 335-4864

DATE: Holiday

FREQUENCY: Quarterly

COVER PRICE: $4.50

SUBSCRIPTION PRICE: $11.25

TOTAL NUMBER OF PAGES: 116

TOTAL NUMBER OF AD PAGES: 24

PUBLISHER: Daniel Collins

EDITOR: Gina Bertagni

EDITORIAL CONCEPT: *"A magazine featuring craft projects, holiday decorating how-to's and quick and easy tips."*

This Old House

PUBLISHED BY: Time Publishing Ventures

20 W. 43rd St.

New York, NY 10036

TEL: (212) 522-9465

DATE: May/June

FREQUENCY: Bimonthly

COVER PRICE: $3.50

SUBSCRIPTION PRICE: $18.00

TOTAL NUMBER OF PAGES: 152

TOTAL NUMBER OF AD PAGES: 50

PUBLISHER: Eric G. Thorkilsen

EDITOR: Isolde Motley

EDITORIAL CONCEPT: *The magazine version of the PBS television show.*

Mountain Living

PUBLISHED BY: Wiesner Publishing

7009 S. Potomac St.

Englewood, CO 80112-9892

TEL: (303) 397-7600   **FAX:** (303) 397-7619

DATE: Winter

FREQUENCY: Quarterly

COVER PRICE: $2.95

SUBSCRIPTION PRICE: $9.99

TOTAL NUMBER OF PAGES: 116

TOTAL NUMBER OF AD PAGES: 36

PUBLISHER: Pat Cooley

EDITOR: Laurel Lund

EDITORIAL CONCEPT: *A look at the most unique homes and lifestyles in some very different mountain communities.*

Traditional Home: Renovation Style

PUBLISHED BY: Meredith Corp.

1716 Locust St.

Des Moines, IA 50309

TEL: (515) 284-2335

DATE: Fall

FREQUENCY: Quarterly

COVER PRICE: $4.95

SUBSCRIPTION PRICE: $12.00

TOTAL NUMBER OF PAGES: 132

TOTAL NUMBER OF AD PAGES: 37

PUBLISHER: Deborah Jones Barrow

EDITOR: Karol DeWulf Nickell

EDITORIAL CONCEPT: *The editors of Traditional Home offer this new magazine with articles on renovating homes, furniture and yards.*

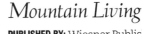

Su Casa

PUBLISHED BY: Sierra Publishing Group

P.O. Box 30550

Albuquerque, NM 87190

TEL: n/a

DATE: Autumn

FREQUENCY: Quarterly

COVER PRICE: $3.50

SUBSCRIPTION PRICE: $16.50

TOTAL NUMBER OF PAGES: 104

TOTAL NUMBER OF AD PAGES: 35

PUBLISHER: Myra Cochnar

EDITOR: Robert J. Cochnar

EDITORIAL CONCEPT: *The New Mexico homes magazine featuring articles on gaining and owning your own home.*

Victorian Homes & Gardens

PUBLISHED BY: GCR Publishing Group Inc.

1700 Broadway

New York, NY 10019

TEL: (212) 541-7100

DATE: Fall

FREQUENCY: Quarterly

COVER PRICE: $3.95

SUBSCRIPTION PRICE: $16.00

TOTAL NUMBER OF PAGES: 84

TOTAL NUMBER OF AD PAGES: 13.3

EDITOR: Deborah Harding

EDITORIAL CONCEPT: *A magazine dedicated to bringing its readers the latest products and ideas for decorating homes in the Victorian style.*

Additions & Decks

PUBLISHED BY: Hachette Filipacchi

1633 Broadway

New York, NY 10019

TEL: (212) 767-6000 **FAX:** (212) 489-4577

FREQUENCY: Special

COVER PRICE: $3.50

SUBSCRIPTION PRICE: n/a

TOTAL NUMBER OF PAGES: 130

TOTAL NUMBER OF AD PAGES: 24

PUBLISHER: Sharri R. Johnson

EDITOR: Liz Wagner

EDITORIAL CONCEPT: *40 space-stretching ideas for decks, porches, sunrooms, baths, family rooms and bedrooms.*

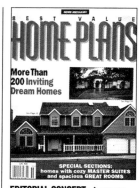

Best Value Home Plans

PUBLISHED BY: Times-Mirror

2 Park Ave.

New York, NY 10016

TEL: (212) 779-5000

FREQUENCY: n/a

COVER PRICE: $5.95

SUBSCRIPTION PRICE: n/a

TOTAL NUMBER OF PAGES: 212

TOTAL NUMBER OF AD PAGES: 3

PUBLISHER: John W. Young

EDITOR: Paul Spring

EDITORIAL CONCEPT: *A magazine featuring the blueprints for 200 different home.*

The Best Of Decks And Backyard Projects

PUBLISHED BY: Aqua-Field Publishing Co.

66 W. Gilbert St.

Shrewsbury, NJ 07702

TEL: (908) 842-8300 **FAX:** (908) 842-0281

FREQUENCY: Special

COVER PRICE: $2.95

SUBSCRIPTION PRICE: n/a

TOTAL NUMBER OF PAGES: 62

TOTAL NUMBER OF AD PAGES: 9

PUBLISHER: Stephen Ferber

EDITOR: Edward Montague

EDITORIAL CONCEPT: *Designed to satisfy the needs of every potential deck builder.*

Better Homes And Gardens' *Home Buyer's Guide*

PUBLISHED BY: Meredith Corp.

1716 Locust St.

Des Moines, IA 50309-3023

TEL: (515) 284-3000 **FAX:** (515) 284-2877

FREQUENCY: Special

COVER PRICE: $3.99

SUBSCRIPTION PRICE: n/a

TOTAL NUMBER OF PAGES: 116

TOTAL NUMBER OF AD PAGES: 8

PUBLISHER: Stephen B. Levinson

EDITOR: Kathy Barnes

EDITORIAL CONCEPT: *Better Homes and Gardens' guide to buying or sell ing your home.*

The Best Of Things

PUBLISHED BY: Fairchild Publications

7 W. 34 St.

New York, NY 10001

TEL: (212) 630-4000

DATE: October

FREQUENCY: n/a

COVER PRICE: $1.00

SUBSCRIPTION PRICE: n/a

TOTAL NUMBER OF PAGES: 60

TOTAL NUMBER OF AD PAGES: 25

PUBLISHER: Geri Brin

EDITOR: Laurie Sohng

EDITORIAL CONCEPT: *"An exclusive magazine" for customers of Linens 'n Things, offering decorating ideas for sprucing up the house.*

Country Accents: *Decks And Gardening Ideas*

PUBLISHED BY: GCR Publishing Group

1700 Broadway

New York, NY 10019

TEL: (212) 541-7100

FREQUENCY: Annually

COVER PRICE: $4.50

SUBSCRIPTION PRICE: n/a

TOTAL NUMBER OF PAGES: 84

TOTAL NUMBER OF AD PAGES: 7.5

PUBLISHER: Charles Goodman

EDITOR: Ron Renulli

EDITORIAL CONCEPT: *A magazine offering great tips on the design, building and upkeep of your lawn, garden and deck.*

Country Home: Holidays At Home

PUBLISHED BY: Meredith Corp.

1716 Locust St.

Des Moines, IA 50309-3023

TEL: (515) 284-3000 **FAX:** (515) 284-3343

FREQUENCY: Special

COVER PRICE: $3.95

SUBSCRIPTION PRICE: $13.97

TOTAL NUMBER OF PAGES: 130

TOTAL NUMBER OF AD PAGES: 52

PUBLISHER: Joseph Lagani

EDITOR: Molly Culbertson

EDITORIAL CONCEPT: *Festive recipes, fantasy trees and handmade gifts with a country touch for the holidays.*

Home Improvement

PUBLISHED BY: Popular Mechanics

224 W. 57 St.

New York, NY 10019

TEL: (212) 649-2000

DATE: Spring

FREQUENCY: Special

COVER PRICE: $3.50

SUBSCRIPTION PRICE: n/a

TOTAL NUMBER OF PAGES: 124

TOTAL NUMBER OF AD PAGES: 26

EDITOR: Joe Oldham

EDITORIAL CONCEPT: *This Popular Mechanics special issue is devoted entirely to home improvements, with articles on everything from laying brick to hanging wallpaper.*

Country Kitchens

PUBLISHED BY: GCR Publishing Group Inc.

1700 Broadway

New York, NY 10019

TEL: (212) 541-7100

FREQUENCY: Annually

COVER PRICE: $3.50

SUBSCRIPTION PRICE: n/a

TOTAL NUMBER OF PAGES: 84

TOTAL NUMBER OF AD PAGES: 7

PUBLISHER: Charles Goodman

EDITOR: Deborah Harding

EDITORIAL CONCEPT: *A look at new designs and simple fix-up ideas for your kitchen.*

Home Plans *Presents Country & Farmhouse Designs*

PUBLISHED BY: Archway Press Inc.

19 W. 44th St.

New York, NY 10036

TEL: (212) 757-5580

FREQUENCY: Special

COVER PRICE: $.95

SUBSCRIPTION PRICE: n/a

TOTAL NUMBER OF PAGES: 68

TOTAL NUMBER OF AD PAGES: 2

EDITOR: n/a

EDITORIAL CONCEPT: *"60 pages of contemporary plans with traditional looks."*

Craftsman At Home: *Painting & Decorating*

PUBLISHED BY: Aqua-Field Publications

66 W. Gilbert St.

Shrewsbury, NJ 07702

TEL: (908) 842-8300 **FAX:** (908) 842-0281

DATE: Fall

FREQUENCY: Special

COVER PRICE: $2.95

SUBSCRIPTION PRICE: n/a

TOTAL NUMBER OF PAGES: 84

TOTAL NUMBER OF AD PAGES: 21

PUBLISHER: Stephen Ferber

EDITOR: Stephen Ferber

EDITORIAL CONCEPT: *"The source for beautiful ,do-it-yourself interiors to put heart into your home."*

Homes From the Heartland

PUBLISHED BY: Meredith Corp.

1716 Locust St.

Des Moines, IA 50309-3023

TEL: (800) 678-2872

FREQUENCY: Special

COVER PRICE: $3.99

SUBSCRIPTION PRICE: n/a

TOTAL NUMBER OF PAGES: 196

TOTAL NUMBER OF AD PAGES: 11

PUBLISHER: Stephen B. Levinson

EDITOR: William J. Yates

EDITORIAL CONCEPT: *A special magazine by Better Homes and Gardens featuring 162 floor plans.*

Kitchen Planning Guide

PUBLISHED BY: Special Interest Publications

Meredith Corp.

1716 Locust St.

Des Moines, IA 50309-3023

TEL: (800) 678-2872

FREQUENCY: Special

COVER PRICE: $3.99

SUBSCRIPTION PRICE: n/a

TOTAL NUMBER OF PAGES: 132

TOTAL NUMBER OF AD PAGES: 19

PUBLISHER: Stephen B. Levinson

EDITOR: William Yates

EDITORIAL CONCEPT: *The people of* Better Homes and Gardens *bring you a special edition devoted entirely to kitchens.*

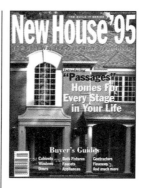

New House '95

PUBLISHED BY: Gruner & Jahr USA

110 Fifth Ave.

New York, NY 10011

TEL: (212) 878-8700 **FAX:** (212) 286-0935

DATE: Spring

FREQUENCY: Special

COVER PRICE: $4.95

SUBSCRIPTION PRICE: n/a

TOTAL NUMBER OF PAGES: 132

TOTAL NUMBER OF AD PAGES: 24

PUBLISHER: George C. Fields

EDITOR: n/a

EDITORIAL CONCEPT: *A magazine designed to help you plan your very own dream house.*

Log Home Lifestyle

PUBLISHED BY: Wilderness Log Homes Inc.

P.O. Box 902

Plymouth, WI 53073

TEL: (414) 893-8416

DATE: Winter

FREQUENCY: Annually

COVER PRICE: $4.95

SUBSCRIPTION PRICE: n/a

TOTAL NUMBER OF PAGES: 136

TOTAL NUMBER OF AD PAGES: 2

PUBLISHER: Paul Maxon

EDITOR: Kim E. Lacina

EDITORIAL CONCEPT: *"A complete guide to buying and building your log home."*

The Old Farmers Almanac *Home Owners Companion*

PUBLISHED BY: Yankee Publishing Inc.

Main St.

Dublin, NH 03444

TEL: (603) 563-8111 **FAX:** (603) 563-8282

FREQUENCY: Annually

COVER PRICE: $2.99

SUBSCRIPTION PRICE: n/a

TOTAL NUMBER OF PAGES: 164

TOTAL NUMBER OF AD PAGES: 26.5

PUBLISHER: John Pierce

EDITOR: Georgia Orcutt

EDITORIAL CONCEPT: *A do-it-yourself guide to small home repairs and fix-up ideas.*

Low-Budget Weekend Decorating Ideas

PUBLISHED BY: GCR Publishing Group Inc.

1700 Broadway

New York, NY 10019

TEL: (212) 541-7100

FREQUENCY: Special

COVER PRICE: $3.95

SUBSCRIPTION PRICE: n/a

TOTAL NUMBER OF PAGES: 84

TOTAL NUMBER OF AD PAGES: 9

PUBLISHER: Charles Goodman

EDITOR: Ron Renzulli

EDITORIAL CONCEPT: *Features articles such as "A Fresh New Look for Any Room" and "100 Small Touches That Make Big Improvements."*

Sunsational Home Plans

PUBLISHED BY: Special Interest Publications

Meredith Corp.

1716 Locust St.

Des Moines, IA 50309-3023

TEL: (800) 678-2872

FREQUENCY: Special

COVER PRICE: $3.99

SUBSCRIPTION PRICE: n/a

TOTAL NUMBER OF PAGES: 196

TOTAL NUMBER OF AD PAGES: 8

PUBLISHER: Stephen B. Levinson

EDITOR: William J. Yates

EDITORIAL CONCEPT: *A magazine dedicated to some of the best home plans on the market today, with over 100 different styles to choose from.*

Weekend

PUBLISHED BY: Meredith Publishing

1912 Grand Ave.

Des Moines, IA 50309

TEL: (515) 284-3000   **FAX:** (515) 284-2877

FREQUENCY: n/a

COVER PRICE: $3.25

SUBSCRIPTION PRICE: n/a

TOTAL NUMBER OF PAGES: 100

TOTAL NUMBER OF AD PAGES: 12

PUBLISHER: Kevin Ford

EDITOR: Greg Cook

EDITORIAL CONCEPT: *Ideas for "do-it-yourself" home improvement projects.*

Woman's Day: *Weekend Projects*

PUBLISHED BY: Hachette Filipacchi

1633 Broadway

New York, NY 10019

TEL: (212) 767-6296

FREQUENCY: Special

COVER PRICE: $3.50

SUBSCRIPTION PRICE: n/a

TOTAL NUMBER OF PAGES: 132

TOTAL NUMBER OF AD PAGES: 17

PUBLISHER: Sharri R. Jurmain

EDITOR: Julie Sinclair

EDITORIAL CONCEPT: *85 summer-fresh looks for your home.*

The Horse

PUBLISHED BY: Modern Horse Breeding Inc.

P.O. Box 4680

Lexington, KY 40544-4680

TEL: n/a

DATE: March

FREQUENCY: Monthly

COVER PRICE: $2.95

SUBSCRIPTION PRICE: $35.40

DISCOUNT SUBSCRIPTION PRICE: $29.00

TOTAL NUMBER OF PAGES: 48

TOTAL NUMBER OF AD PAGES: 17

PUBLISHER: Stacy V. Bearse

EDITOR: Kimberly S. Herbert

EDITORIAL CONCEPT : *Formerly Modern Horse Breeding, the magazine guarantees readers "a commitment to the total health and well-being of your horses."*

The Stable Companion

PUBLISHED BY: Houyhnhnm Press

P.O. Box 6485

Lafayette, IN 47903

TEL: (317) 477-0710

DATE: Summer/Fall

FREQUENCY: Quarterly

COVER PRICE: $6.50

SUBSCRIPTION PRICE: $24.00

TOTAL NUMBER OF PAGES: 60

TOTAL NUMBER OF AD PAGES: 2

PUBLISHER: Susanna Brandon

EDITOR: Susanna Brandon

EDITORIAL CONCEPT: *"The best in equine fiction, poetry, true stories and art."*

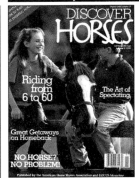

Discover Horses

PUBLISHED BY: Fleet Street Publishing Co.

220 E. 42nd St.

New York, NY 10017

TEL: (212) 972-2472

FREQUENCY: Special

COVER PRICE: $3.95

SUBSCRIPTION PRICE: n/a

TOTAL NUMBER OF PAGES: 100

TOTAL NUMBER OF AD PAGES: 23

PUBLISHER: FSPC, AHSA

EDITOR: Roberta Jo Lieberman

EDITORIAL CONCEPT: *"Complete guide to riding and enjoying horses," featuring editorials and colorful photographs.*

The Baffler

PUBLISHED BY: Thomas Frank & Matt Weiland

P.O. Box 378293

Chicago, IL 60637

TEL: n/a

FREQUENCY: Quarterly

COVER PRICE: $5.00

SUBSCRIPTION PRICE: $16.00

TOTAL NUMBER OF PAGES: 130

TOTAL NUMBER OF AD PAGES: 11

EDITOR: Thomas Frank

EDITORIAL CONCEPT: *"The journal that blunts the cutting edge," filled with short stories and satires on the new world society.*

Bookforum

PUBLISHED BY: Artforum

65 Bleecker St.

New York, NY 10012

TEL: (212) 475-4000

DATE: Fall/Winter

FREQUENCY: Semiannually

COVER PRICE: $1.50

SUBSCRIPTION PRICE: n/a

TOTAL NUMBER OF PAGES: 36

TOTAL NUMBER OF AD PAGES: 18

EDITOR: n/a

EDITORIAL CONCEPT: *"The book for art and culture."*

Bizára

PUBLISHED BY: The Slow X Press

P.O. Box 3118

Albany, NY 12203-0118

TEL: n/a

FREQUENCY: Semiannually

COVER PRICE: $3.00

SUBSCRIPTION PRICE: $6.00

TOTAL NUMBER OF PAGES: 46

TOTAL NUMBER OF AD PAGES: 1

PUBLISHER: Ted Kusio

EDITOR: Ted Kusio

EDITORIAL CONCEPT: *Short stories, poetry and editorials are presented here in a dark, somewhat "bizarre" fashion.*

Century

PUBLISHED BY: Century Publishing Inc.

P.O. Box 150510

Brooklyn, NY 11215-0510

TEL: (608) 251-2225 **FAX:** (608) 251-5222

FREQUENCY: Bimonthly

COVER PRICE: $5.95

SUBSCRIPTION PRICE: $27.00

TOTAL NUMBER OF PAGES: 148

TOTAL NUMBER OF AD PAGES: 1

PUBLISHER: Meg Hamel

EDITOR: Robert K.J. Killheffer

EDITORIAL CONCEPT: *A magazine composed of short-story fiction, described as "a literary neighborhood where dark coexists with light... a neighborhood with lots to do and see, where many different sorts of story find home."*

Bookcase

PUBLISHED BY: Tumbleweed Productions

1447 Campus Rd.

Los Angeles, CA 90042

TEL: (213) 257-9269 **FAX:** (213) 256-1600

DATE: March

FREQUENCY: Monthly

COVER PRICE: $3.50

SUBSCRIPTION PRICE: $40.00

TOTAL NUMBER OF PAGES: 24

TOTAL NUMBER OF AD PAGES: 4

PUBLISHER: Angela Maria Ortiz

EDITOR: Kathleen Lawrence

EDITORIAL CONCEPT: *A magazine dedicated to "the joy of reading and collecting."*

Forkroads

PUBLISHED BY: Forkroads Press

P.O. Box 150

Spencertown, NY 12165

TEL: (518) 392-9607 **FAX:** (518) 392-3295

DATE: Fall

FREQUENCY: Quarterly

COVER PRICE: $6.00

SUBSCRIPTION PRICE: $20.00

TOTAL NUMBER OF PAGES: 104

TOTAL NUMBER OF AD PAGES: 2

EDITOR: David Kherdian

EDITORIAL CONCEPT: *This journal of ethnic American literature is a "celebration of our sameness and our difference."*

I'll Take Romance Magazine

PUBLISHED BY: I.T.R. America Corp.

P.O. Box 22-0380

Brooklyn, NY 11222-0380

TEL: (718) 375-7015

DATE: Fall

FREQUENCY: Quarterly

COVER PRICE: $3.25

SUBSCRIPTION PRICE: $15.00

TOTAL NUMBER OF PAGES: 98

TOTAL NUMBER OF AD PAGES: 16

EDITOR: Charlene Keel

EDITORIAL CONCEPT: *A magazine that focuses on romance novels, with articles and monthly "themes."*

Two Girls Review

PUBLISHED BY: Two Girls Review

341 Adams

Eugene, OR 97402

TEL: (503) 484-2446 **FAX:** (503) 344-2955

FREQUENCY: Semiannually

COVER PRICE: $6.00

SUBSCRIPTION PRICE: $12.00

TOTAL NUMBER OF PAGES: 132

TOTAL NUMBER OF AD PAGES: 3

EDITOR: Lidia Yukman

EDITORIAL CONCEPT: *A magazine for the modern arts, including poetry, short stories, non-fiction, paintings and drawings.*

Many Mountains Moving

PUBLISHED BY: Denver Women's Press Club

1325 Logan St.

Denver, CO 80203

TEL: (303) 839-1519

FREQUENCY: 3/year

COVER PRICE: $6.50

SUBSCRIPTION PRICE: $18.00

TOTAL NUMBER OF PAGES: 180

TOTAL NUMBER OF AD PAGES: 6

EDITOR: Naomi Harii

EDITORIAL CONCEPT: *"A literary journal of diverse contemporary voices."*

Vignette

PUBLISHED BY: Vignette Press

4150-G Riverside Dr.

Toluca Lake, CA 91505

TEL: (818) 955-5368 **FAX:** (818) 848-0585

DATE: Fall

FREQUENCY: Quarterly

COVER PRICE: $9.95

SUBSCRIPTION PRICE: $29.00

TOTAL NUMBER OF PAGES: 108

TOTAL NUMBER OF AD PAGES: 2

EDITOR: Dawn Baillie

EDITORIAL CONCEPT: *A collection of lyrical short stories.*

Scenario: The Magazine Of Screenwriting Art

PUBLISHED BY: RC Publications Inc.

104 Fifth Ave.

New York, NY 10011

TEL: (212) 463-0600 **FAX:** (212) 989-9891

DATE: Winter

FREQUENCY: Quarterly

COVER PRICE: $20.00

SUBSCRIPTION PRICE: $59.95

TOTAL NUMBER OF PAGES: 210

TOTAL NUMBER OF AD PAGES: 3.5

PUBLISHER: Howard Cadel

EDITOR: Tod Lippy

EDITORIAL CONCEPT: *"The inauguration of a new forum for screenwriting, in which the screenwriter is no longer considered an 'assistant picturemaker' but, instead, the creator of some of the most influential dramatic art of our time."*

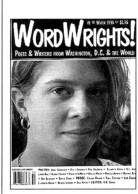

Word Wrights!

PUBLISHED BY: Argonne Hotel Press

1620 Argonne Pl. NW

Washington, DC 20009

TEL: (202) 328-9769

DATE: Winter

FREQUENCY: Quarterly

COVER PRICE: $3.95

SUBSCRIPTION PRICE: $10.00

TOTAL NUMBER OF PAGES: 36

TOTAL NUMBER OF AD PAGES: 2

PUBLISHER: R.D. Baker

EDITOR: R.D. Baker

EDITORIAL CONCEPT: *A magazine offering poetry and stories from authors in the Washington, D.C., area.*

ANNUAL, SPECIAL OR FREQUENCY UNKNOWN

High Adventure

PUBLISHED BY: Adventure House

914 Laredo Rd.

Silver Spring, MD 20901

TEL: (301) 754-1533

FREQUENCY: n/a

COVER PRICE: $6.00

SUBSCRIPTION PRICE: n/a

EDITORIAL CONCEPT: *A magazine devoted to pulp fiction stories.*

TOTAL NUMBER OF PAGES: 100

TOTAL NUMBER OF AD PAGES: 0

EDITOR: John P. Gunnison

I Have Seen The Mermaids Singing

PUBLISHED BY: New Thought Journal Press

P.O. Box 700754

Tulsa, OK 74170

TEL: (918) 299-7330

FREQUENCY: Special

COVER PRICE: $2.95

SUBSCRIPTION PRICE: n/a

EDITORIAL CONCEPT: *A compilation of poems by Jean Jones.*

TOTAL NUMBER OF PAGES: 40

TOTAL NUMBER OF AD PAGES: 1

EDITOR: Edward Wincentsen

EDITORIAL CONCEPT: *A magazine covering the lifestyles of senior citizens.*

GrandParenting And Other Great Adventures

PUBLISHED BY: Royal Magazine Group Inc.

404 BNA Dr., Suite 508

Building 200

Nashville, TN 37217

TEL: n/a

FREQUENCY: Bimonthly

COVER PRICE: $2.99

SUBSCRIPTION PRICE: n/a

TOTAL NUMBER OF PAGES: 68

TOTAL NUMBER OF AD PAGES: 16

PUBLISHER: Timothy L. Gilmour

EDITOR: Vicki Huffman

Baywatch

PUBLISHED BY: Starlog Entertainment Inc.

475 Park Ave. S.

New York, NY 10016

TEL: (212) 689-2830   **FAX:** (212) 889-7933

DATE: September

FREQUENCY: 3/year

COVER PRICE: $4.99

SUBSCRIPTION PRICE: n/a

TOTAL NUMBER OF PAGES: 76

TOTAL NUMBER OF AD PAGES: 9

PUBLISHER: Norman Jacobs

EDITOR: Len Canter

EDITORIAL CONCEPT: *The official magazine for lovers of the Baywatch television series.*

B.B. King : The Best Of Guitar Player

PUBLISHED BY: Miller Freeman Inc.

600 Harris St.,San Francisco, CA 94107

TEL: (415) 905-2200   **FAX:** (415) 905-2233

DATE: February

FREQUENCY: 10/year

COVER PRICE: $4.95

SUBSCRIPTION PRICE: $29.95

DISCOUNT SUBSCRIPTION PRICE: $18.00

TOTAL NUMBER OF PAGES: 82

TOTAL NUMBER OF AD PAGES: 19

PUBLISHER: Pat Cameron

EDITOR: Dominic Milano

EDITORIAL CONCEPT: *B.B.'s story, told by him to his friends, along with his music.*

Bop's BB

PUBLISHED BY: Laufer Publishing Co.

12711 Ventura Blvd., Suite 220

Studio City, CA 91604

TEL: (818) 508-2010

DATE: October

FREQUENCY: Monthly

COVER PRICE: $3.50

SUBSCRIPTION PRICE: $22.00

TOTAL NUMBER OF PAGES: 48

TOTAL NUMBER OF AD PAGES: 4

EDITOR: Rick Rodgers

EDITORIAL CONCEPT: *A poster book of teen idols, "plus stories, gossip and cool stuff."*

Countrybeat Presents Exclusive Interviews With Country's Top Stars!

PUBLISHED BY: Glendi Publications Inc.

7002 W. Butler Pike

Ambler, PA 19002

TEL: (215) 628-0924

DATE: Winter

FREQUENCY: Quarterly

COVER PRICE: $4.95

SUBSCRIPTION PRICE: $15.85

TOTAL NUMBER OF PAGES: 68

PUBLISHER: Camille Pomaco

EDITOR: Craig Peters

EDITORIAL CONCEPT: *Exclusive interviews with country's top stars.*

Soap Opera Stars

PUBLISHED BY: Laufer Publishing Co.

12711 Ventura Blvd., Suite 22

Studio City, CA 91604

TEL: (818) 508-2010

DATE: October

FREQUENCY: Monthly

COVER PRICE: $3.50

SUBSCRIPTION PRICE: $22.00

TOTAL NUMBER OF PAGES: 48

TOTAL NUMBER OF AD PAGES: 4

EDITOR: Rick Rodgers

EDITORIAL CONCEPT: *A revamped look and attitude that includes more pictures, interviews, features and gossip about your favorite soap stars.*

ANNUAL, SPECIAL OR FREQUENCY UNKNOWN

Action Heroes '95

PUBLISHED BY: Jacobs Publications

475 Park Ave. S., 8th Floor

New York, NY 10016

TEL: (212) 689-2830

DATE: May

FREQUENCY: Annually

COVER PRICE: $4.99

SUBSCRIPTION PRICE: n/a

TOTAL NUMBER OF PAGES: 68

TOTAL NUMBER OF AD PAGES: 8

PUBLISHER: Marc Bernardin

EDITOR: David McDonnell

EDITORIAL CONCEPT: *A look at some of the year's best action movies and the people who made them possible.*

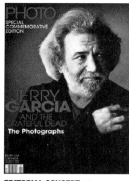

American Photo: Jerry Garcia And The Grateful Dead

PUBLISHED BY: Hachette Filipacchi

1633 Broadway

New York, NY 10019

TEL: (212) 767-6000 **FAX:** (212) 489-4577

FREQUENCY: Special

COVER PRICE: $5.00

SUBSCRIPTION PRICE: n/a

TOTAL NUMBER OF PAGES: 98

TOTAL NUMBER OF AD PAGES: 26

EDITOR: n/a

EDITORIAL CONCEPT: *A commemorative issue of American Photo, filled with photographs of Garcia and the Grateful Dead, presented as a gift for all who loved the man and his music.*

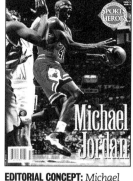

Beckett Sports Heroes: Michael Jordan

PUBLISHED BY: Beckett Publications

15850 Dallas Pkwy.

Dallas, TX 75248

TEL: (214) 448-9157 **FAX:** (214) 991-8930

FREQUENCY: Special

COVER PRICE: $9.95

SUBSCRIPTION PRICE: n/a

TOTAL NUMBER OF PAGES: 138

TOTAL NUMBER OF AD PAGES: 9

PUBLISHER: Dr. James Beckett

EDITOR: Dr. James Beckett

EDITORIAL CONCEPT: *Michael Jordan's return allows his legions of admirers to become unconditional fans once again.*

Batman And Other Dark Heroes

PUBLISHED BY: Starlog Group Inc.

475 Park Ave. S.

New York, NY 10016

TEL: (212) 689-2830 **FAX:** (212) 889-7933

FREQUENCY: Annually

COVER PRICE: $5.99

SUBSCRIPTION PRICE: n/a

TOTAL NUMBER OF PAGES: 84

TOTAL NUMBER OF AD PAGES: 12

PUBLISHER: Norman Jacobs

EDITOR: David McDonnell

EDITORIAL CONCEPT: *Features reviews of the movies* Batman Forever *and* Judge Dredd.

Celebrity Posters Magazine

PUBLISHED BY: n/a

TEL: n/a

FREQUENCY: Special

COVER PRICE: $4.95

SUBSCRIPTION PRICE: n/a

TOTAL NUMBER OF PAGES: 36

TOTAL NUMBER OF AD PAGES: 0

EDITOR: n/a

EDITORIAL CONCEPT: *Incredible pull-out posters of Jonathan Taylor Thomas and other teen idols.*

The Beatles Forever

PUBLISHED BY: Starlog Group Inc.

475 Park Ave. S.

New York, NY 10016

TEL: (212) 689-2830 **FAX:** (212) 889-7933

FREQUENCY: Special

COVER PRICE: $4.99

SUBSCRIPTION PRICE: n/a

TOTAL NUMBER OF PAGES: 76

TOTAL NUMBER OF AD PAGES: 4

PUBLISHER: Norman Jacobs

EDITOR: Milburn Smith

EDITORIAL CONCEPT: *The Beatles' complete history, including behind-the-scenes interviews and photographs.*

Death Of A Model: Linda Sobek

PUBLISHED BY: Ashley Communications

P.O. Box 1053

Malibu, CA 90265

TEL: (818) 885-6800

DATE: December

FREQUENCY: Special

COVER PRICE: $3.99

SUBSCRIPTION PRICE: n/a

TOTAL NUMBER OF PAGES: 48

TOTAL NUMBER OF AD PAGES: 1

PUBLISHER: Brian Ashley

EDITOR: Doreen Lioy

EDITORIAL CONCEPT: *"A loving tribute to Linda in the way in which she will always be remembered — as a breathtakingly beautiful, vibrant young woman."*

Dennis!

PUBLISHED BY: H&S Media Inc.

3400 Dundee Rd.

Northbrook, IL 60062

TEL: n/a

FREQUENCY: Special

COVER PRICE: $5.99

SUBSCRIPTION PRICE: n/a

TOTAL NUMBER OF PAGES: 84

TOTAL NUMBER OF AD PAGES: 0

PUBLISHER: Michael M. Meyers

EDITOR: Chuck Carlson

EDITORIAL CONCEPT: *Dennis Rodman makes the move to a new uniform... that of the Chicago Bulls.*

Garcia : Reflections

PUBLISHED BY: CSK Publishing Co. Inc.

299 Market St.

Saddle Brook, NJ 07663

TEL: (201) 712-9300

FREQUENCY: Special

COVER PRICE: $4.99

SUBSCRIPTION PRICE: n/a

TOTAL NUMBER OF PAGES: 74

TOTAL NUMBER OF AD PAGES: 10

PUBLISHER: Ralph Monti

EDITOR: Jeff Bauer

EDITORIAL CONCEPT: *"A 'Deadhead' tribute and poster memorial celebrating the life of Jerry Garcia."*

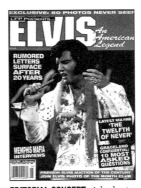

Elvis : An American Legend

PUBLISHED BY: L.F.P. Inc.

9171 Wilshire Blvd., Suite 300

Beverly Hills, CA 90210

TEL: (213) 651-5400

DATE: Summer

FREQUENCY: Special

COVER PRICE: $3.95

SUBSCRIPTION PRICE: n/a

TOTAL NUMBER OF PAGES: 88

TOTAL NUMBER OF AD PAGES: 10.33

PUBLISHER: Larry Flynt

EDITOR: Chris Davidson

EDITORIAL CONCEPT: *A look at the life of "The King," Elvis Presley. The focus is on Elvis during the '70s, with his gold lamé jumpsuits and muttonchop sideburns*

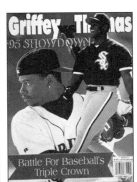

Griffey vs. Thomas '95 Showdown

PUBLISHED BY: H&S Media Inc.

3400 Dundee Rd.

Northbrook, IL 60062

TEL: (708) 291-1135   **FAX:** (708) 498-1190

FREQUENCY: Special

COVER PRICE: $4.99

SUBSCRIPTION PRICE: n/a

TOTAL NUMBER OF PAGES: 96

TOTAL NUMBER OF AD PAGES: 0

PUBLISHER: Jim Mohr

EDITOR: n/a

EDITORIAL CONCEPT: *A pictorial and statistical look at major league baseball's two most likely candidates to win the Triple Crown (most home runs, most stolen bases and highest batting average in a seas on).*

Forever Beatles

PUBLISHED BY: n/a

TEL: n/a

FREQUENCY: Special

COVER PRICE: $6.95

SUBSCRIPTION PRICE: n/a

TOTAL NUMBER OF PAGES: 66

TOTAL NUMBER OF AD PAGES: 0

EDITOR: n/a

EDITORIAL CONCEPT: *A photo history of the Beatles with character profiles of each of the four superstars.*

Immature

PUBLISHED BY: Sterling/Macfadden Partnership

35 Wilbur St.

Lynbrook, NY 11563

TEL: (212) 780-3500

DATE: May

FREQUENCY: Special

COVER PRICE: $3.50

SUBSCRIPTION PRICE: n/a

TOTAL NUMBER OF PAGES: 100

TOTAL NUMBER OF AD PAGES: 15

EDITOR: Cynthia Marie Horner

EDITORIAL CONCEPT: *The editors of Sisters in Style present this special issue of articles on the groups of little kids who make up the singing group Immature.*

Jerry Garcia

PUBLISHED BY: Hit Parader Publications

TEL: n/a

FREQUENCY: Special

COVER PRICE: $3.99

SUBSCRIPTION PRICE: n/a

TOTAL NUMBER OF PAGES: 16

TOTAL NUMBER OF AD PAGES: 0

EDITOR: n/a

EDITORIAL CONCEPT: *Memorial magazine and poster of the lead man for the Grateful Dead, Jerry Garcia.*

JTT's Scrapbook

PUBLISHED BY: Starline Publications Inc.

210 Rt. 4 E., Suite 210

Paramus, NJ 07652

TEL: (201) 843-4004

FREQUENCY: Special

COVER PRICE: $3.99

SUBSCRIPTION PRICE: n/a

TOTAL NUMBER OF PAGES: 80

TOTAL NUMBER OF AD PAGES: 8

EDITOR: Anne M. Raso

EDITORIAL CONCEPT: *Features Home Improvement's Jonathan Taylor Thomas and other young celebrities.*

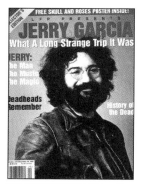

Jerry Garcia: What A Long Strange Trip It Was

PUBLISHED BY: L.F.P. Inc.

8484 Wilshire Blvd., Suite 900

Beverly Hills, CA 90211

TEL: (213) 651-5400

FREQUENCY: Special

COVER PRICE: $4.99

SUBSCRIPTION PRICE: n/a

TOTAL NUMBER OF PAGES: 80

TOTAL NUMBER OF AD PAGES: 0

PUBLISHER: Larry Flynt

EDITOR: Michael Goldstein

EDITORIAL CONCEPT: *This tribute to Jerry Garcia includes photographs, a poster and articles about the history of the Grateful Dead.*

LFP Presents An Inside Look At Melrose Place

PUBLISHED BY: L.F.P. Inc.

9171 Wilshire Blvd., Suite 300

Beverly Hills, CA 90210

TEL: (213) 651-5400

FREQUENCY: Special

COVER PRICE: $3.95

SUBSCRIPTION PRICE: n/a

TOTAL NUMBER OF PAGES: 96

TOTAL NUMBER OF AD PAGES: 4

PUBLISHER: Larry Flynt

EDITOR: Katherine Turman

EDITORIAL CONCEPT: *Page after page of fabulous full-color photos of the cast of Melrose Place.*

Jordan, The Sequel

PUBLISHED BY: Sports Media Inc.

Manhattan Tower

101 E. 52nd St., 9th Floor

New York, NY 10022

TEL: n/a

FREQUENCY: Special

COVER PRICE: $9.95

SUBSCRIPTION PRICE: n/a

TOTAL NUMBER OF PAGES: 116

TOTAL NUMBER OF AD PAGES: 3

EDITOR: Frank Ciffey

EDITORIAL CONCEPT: *A look at Michael Jordan's short baseball career, his return to basketball and the fans who love to watch him play.*

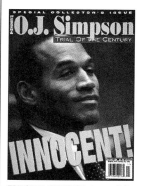

LFP Presents O.J. Simpson: Trial Of The Century

PUBLISHED BY: L.F.P. Inc.

8484 Wilshire Blvd., Suite 900

Beverly Hills, CA 90211

TEL: (213) 651-5400

FREQUENCY: Special

COVER PRICE: $4.99

SUBSCRIPTION PRICE: n/a

TOTAL NUMBER OF PAGES: 80

TOTAL NUMBER OF AD PAGES: 0

PUBLISHER: Larry Flynt

EDITOR: Steve Ryan

EDITORIAL CONCEPT: *A special collector's issue focusing on the last couple of months of the trial. Including a full rundown of the proceedings.*

Martial Arts Legends Presents Steven Seagal: Master Of Harmony

PUBLISHED BY: CFW Enterprises Inc.

4201 W. Vanowen Pl.

Burbank, CA 91505

TEL: (818) 845-7761 **FAX:** (818) 845-2656

FREQUENCY: Special

COVER PRICE: $4.95

SUBSCRIPTION PRICE: n/a

TOTAL NUMBER OF PAGES: 116

TOTAL NUMBER OF AD PAGES: 21

EDITOR: John Steven Soet

EDITORIAL CONCEPT: *Features martial arts techniques and Steven Seagal.*

Michael Jordan: Pro Basketball Illustrated

PUBLISHED BY: Sterling/Macfadden Partnership

233 Park Ave. S.

New York, NY 10003

TEL: (212) 780-3500

DATE: Spring

FREQUENCY: Annually

COVER PRICE: $3.95

SUBSCRIPTION PRICE: n/a

TOTAL NUMBER OF PAGES: 100

TOTAL NUMBER OF AD PAGES: 4

EDITOR: Stephen Ciacciarelli

EDITORIAL CONCEPT: *"Michael in action! 18 color pinups, plus 4 giant pullout posters!"*

Michael!

PUBLISHED BY: Time Inc.

Time-Life Building, Rockerfeller Center

New York, NY 10020-1393

TEL: (212) 552-3034 **FAX:** (212) 765-2699

FREQUENCY: Special

COVER PRICE: $3.95

SUBSCRIPTION PRICE: n/a

TOTAL NUMBER OF PAGES: 76

TOTAL NUMBER OF AD PAGES: 7

PUBLISHER: David L. Long

EDITOR: Norman Pearlstine

EDITORIAL CONCEPT: *A "special kids edition" of* Sports Illustrated *featuring photos and editorials recounting the career of Michael Jordan.*

Michael Jordan Returns

PUBLISHED BY: H&S Media Inc.

3400 Dundee Rd.

Northbrook, IL 60062

TEL: (708) 291-1135 **FAX:** (708) 498-1190

FREQUENCY: Special

COVER PRICE: $4.95

SUBSCRIPTION PRICE: n/a

TOTAL NUMBER OF PAGES: 96

TOTAL NUMBER OF AD PAGES: 0

EDITOR: n/a

EDITORIAL CONCEPT: *This collector's edition features "96 pages of the airborne marvel."*

Michael Jackson: His Life In Pictures

PUBLISHED BY: H&S Media Inc.

3400 Dundee Rd.

Northbrook, IL 60062

TEL: (708) 498-5014

FREQUENCY: Special

COVER PRICE: $4.99

SUBSCRIPTION PRICE: n/a

TOTAL NUMBER OF PAGES: 68

TOTAL NUMBER OF AD PAGES: 1

EDITOR: Jim Mohr

EDITORIAL CONCEPT: *A pictorial look at the long and sometimes controversial career of Michael Jackson.*

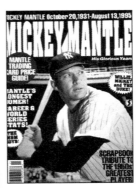

Mickey Mantle: His Glorious Years

PUBLISHED BY: Starlog Entertainment Inc.

475 Park Ave. S.

New York, NY 10016

TEL: (212) 689-2830

FREQUENCY: Special

COVER PRICE: $3.99

SUBSCRIPTION PRICE: n/a

TOTAL NUMBER OF PAGES: 32

TOTAL NUMBER OF AD PAGES: 0

PUBLISHER: Norman Jacobs

EDITOR: Michael Benson

EDITORIAL CONCEPT: *"Scrapbook tribute to the 1950s' greatest baseball player."*

More Michael Jordan Returns

PUBLISHED BY: H&S Media Inc.

3400 Dundee Rd.

Northbrook, IL 60062

TEL: (708) 291-1135 **FAX:** (708) 498-1190

FREQUENCY: Special

COVER PRICE: $4.95

SUBSCRIPTION PRICE: n/a

TOTAL NUMBER OF PAGES: 96

TOTAL NUMBER OF AD PAGES: 0

PUBLISHER: Jim Mohr

EDITOR: n/a

EDITORIAL CONCEPT: *A pictorial look at the return of basketball's greatest player, Michael Jordan.*

Princess Di: A Look At The Royal Woman

PUBLISHED BY: H&S Media Inc.

3400 Dundee Rd.

Northbrook, IL 60062

TEL: (708) 291-1135

FAX: (708) 498-1190

DATE: Summer/Fall

FREQUENCY: Special

COVER PRICE: $5.99

SUBSCRIPTION PRICE: n/a

TOTAL NUMBER OF PAGES: 100

TOTAL NUMBER OF AD PAGES: 0

EDITOR: Martin Jones

EDITORIAL CONCEPT: *A pictorial look at the life of Princess Di.*

The National O.J.

PUBLISHED BY: n/a

TEL: n/a

FREQUENCY: Special

COVER PRICE: $3.95

SUBSCRIPTION PRICE: n/a

TOTAL NUMBER OF PAGES: 20

TOTAL NUMBER OF AD PAGES: 0

EDITOR: n/a

EDITORIAL CONCEPT: *A parody of supermarket tabloids' coverage of the Simpson trial.*

RAD!

PUBLISHED BY: Ashley Communications

P.O. Box 1053

Malibu, CA 90265

TEL: (818) 885-6800

DATE: July

FREQUENCY: Special

COVER PRICE: $3.99

SUBSCRIPTION PRICE: n/a

TOTAL NUMBER OF PAGES: 64

TOTAL NUMBER OF AD PAGES: 2

PUBLISHER: Brian Ashley

EDITOR: Doreen Liov

EDITORIAL CONCEPT: *Interviews and profiles of pre-teen and teenage television stars.*

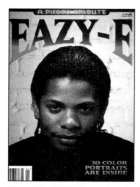

A Photo Tribute To Eazy-E

PUBLISHED BY: n/a

TEL: n/a

FREQUENCY: Special

COVER PRICE: $4.95

SUBSCRIPTION PRICE: n/a

TOTAL NUMBER OF PAGES: 48

TOTAL NUMBER OF AD PAGES: 0

EDITOR: n/a

EDITORIAL CONCEPT: *A pictorial look at the life of rapper Eazy-E.*

Return Of The Beatles

PUBLISHED BY: H & S Media Inc.

3400 Dundee Rd.

Northbrook, IL 60062

TEL: (708) 291-1135   **FAX:** (708) 291-0612

FREQUENCY: Special

COVER PRICE: $6.95

SUBSCRIPTION PRICE: n/a

TOTAL NUMBER OF PAGES: 90

TOTAL NUMBER OF AD PAGES: 0

PUBLISHER: Michael M. Myers

EDITOR: Jennifer Winquist

EDITORIAL CONCEPT: *140 collectible photos of the "Fab Four."*

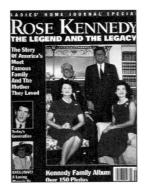

Rose Kennedy: The Legend And The Legacy

EDITORIAL CONCEPT: *Features over 150 photographs and several stories about Rose Kennedy and her family.*

PUBLISHED BY: Meredith Publishing

1912 Grand Ave.

Des Moines, IA 50309

TEL: (515) 284-3433

FREQUENCY: Special

COVER PRICE: $3.95

SUBSCRIPTION PRICE: n/a

TOTAL NUMBER OF PAGES: 100

TOTAL NUMBER OF AD PAGES: 13

PUBLISHER: Donna Galotti

EDITOR: Carolyn Noyes

Starflash Poster Magazine

EDITORIAL CONCEPT: *8 giant pullout posters, including 4 of Home Improvement's Jonathan Taylor Thomas.*

PUBLISHED BY: n/a

TEL: n/a

FREQUENCY: n/a

COVER PRICE: $4.95

SUBSCRIPTION PRICE: n/a

TOTAL NUMBER OF PAGES: 34

TOTAL NUMBER OF AD PAGES: 0

EDITOR: n/a

Shaq: The Magic Strikes

EDITORIAL CONCEPT: *A look at the career of Shaquille O'Neal from his early days to NBA stardom.*

PUBLISHED BY: TD Media Inc.

Manhattan Tower

101 E. 52nd St., 9th Floor

New York, NY 10021

TEL: n/a

FREQUENCY: Special

COVER PRICE: $9.95

SUBSCRIPTION PRICE: n/a

TOTAL NUMBER OF PAGES: 116

TOTAL NUMBER OF AD PAGES: 3

PUBLISHER: John P. Holms

EDITOR: Frank Coffey

Starz!

EDITORIAL CONCEPT: *A magazine for teenagers, focusing on the young actors and actresses on TV and in the movies.*

PUBLISHED BY: Ashley Communications

P.O. Box 1053

Malibu, CA 90269

TEL: (818) 885-6800

DATE: May

FREQUENCY: Special

COVER PRICE: $4.99

SUBSCRIPTION PRICE: n/a

TOTAL NUMBER OF PAGES: 48

TOTAL NUMBER OF AD PAGES: 0

EDITOR: Meg Howard

Soap Opera Spectacular

EDITORIAL CONCEPT: *Photographs of soap stars and articles such as "Who's Who From All the Shows!" and "Backstage With All Your Favorite Stars and Stories."*

PUBLISHED BY: K-III Magazine Corp.

45 W. 25th St.

New York, NY 10010

TEL: (212) 229-8400

DATE: Summer

FREQUENCY: Special

COVER PRICE: $2.50

SUBSCRIPTION PRICE: n/a

TOTAL NUMBER OF PAGES: 68

TOTAL NUMBER OF AD PAGES: 7

PUBLISHER: Linda Vaughan

EDITOR: Stephanie Sloan

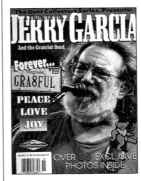

A Tribute To Jerry Garcia

EDITORIAL CONCEPT: *This tribute includes over 85 exclusive photos of Garcia and the Grateful Dead.*

PUBLISHED BY: H&S Media Inc.

3400 Dundee Rd.

Northbrook, IL 60062

TEL: (708) 291-1135   **FAX:** (708) 291-0612

FREQUENCY: Special

COVER PRICE: $5.99

SUBSCRIPTION PRICE: n/a

TOTAL NUMBER OF PAGES: 68

TOTAL NUMBER OF AD PAGES: 0

PUBLISHER: Michael M. Meyers

EDITOR: Michelle Benton

EDITORIAL CONCEPT: *A tribute to Mickey Mantle's life and baseball career.*

A Tribute To Mickey Mantle

PUBLISHED BY: L.F.P. Inc.

8484 Wilshire Blvd., Suite 900

Beverly Hills, CA 90211

TEL: (213) 651-5400

FREQUENCY: Special

COVER PRICE: $4.99

SUBSCRIPTION PRICE: n/a

TOTAL NUMBER OF PAGES: 80

TOTAL NUMBER OF AD PAGES: 10

PUBLISHER: Larry Flynt

EDITOR: Steve Ryan

Men's Perspective

PUBLISHED BY: Metropolis Publications

5670 Wilshire Blvd., Suite 1240

Los Angeles, CA 90036

TEL: (213) 980-9800

FREQUENCY: 10/year

COVER PRICE: $3.00

SUBSCRIPTION PRICE: $24.95

TOTAL NUMBER OF PAGES: 146

TOTAL NUMBER OF AD PAGES: 36

PUBLISHER: John Thomas

EDITOR: Trevor Miller

EDITORIAL CONCEPT: *"The American men's magazine" covers issues which are relevant to a man's life.*

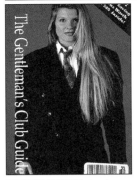

The Gentleman's Club Guide

PUBLISHED BY: G.C.G. Inc.

17 Maywood Dr.

Marlboro, NJ 07746

TEL: n/a

FREQUENCY: n/a

COVER PRICE: $14.95

SUBSCRIPTION PRICE: n/a

TOTAL NUMBER OF PAGES: 194

TOTAL NUMBER OF AD PAGES: 40

EDITOR: Tom Michael

EDITORIAL CONCEPT: *A colorful, pocket-sized book designed to provide the reader with all information needed to find the perfect evening of exotic dance entertainment.*

Swimsuit Photo Edition

PUBLISHED BY: Ashley Communications

P.O. Box 1053

Malibu, CA 90265

TEL: n/a

DATE: February

FREQUENCY: Semiannually

COVER PRICE: $4.95

SUBSCRIPTION PRICE: n/a

TOTAL NUMBER OF PAGES: 48

TOTAL NUMBER OF AD PAGES: 2

EDITOR: n/a

EDITORIAL CONCEPT: *28 color portraits and short biographies of young women in bathing suits.*

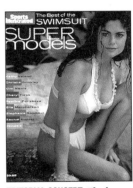

Sports Illustrated: The Best Of The Swimsuit Supermodels

PUBLISHED BY: Time Inc.

1271 Ave. of the Americas

Rockefeller Center

New York, NY 10020

TEL: (212) 522-1212

FREQUENCY: Special

COVER PRICE: $9.95

SUBSCRIPTION PRICE: n/a

TOTAL NUMBER OF PAGES: 140

TOTAL NUMBER OF AD PAGES: 0

EDITOR: n/a

EDITORIAL CONCEPT: *The best of Sports Illustrated's swimsuit editions.*

Alabama Teen Sports Magazine

PUBLISHED BY: Alabama Teen Sports

P.O. Box 660

Addison, AL 35540-0660

TEL: (205) 747-6977 **FAX:** (205) 737-4559

DATE: February

FREQUENCY: Monthly

COVER PRICE: $2.95

SUBSCRIPTION PRICE: $19.95

TOTAL NUMBER OF PAGES: 52

TOTAL NUMBER OF AD PAGES: 9

PUBLISHER: Dan Cobb

EDITOR: Dan Cobb

EDITORIAL CONCEPT: *Photographs, profiles and predictions about various Alabama youth sports teams.*

Architecture South

PUBLISHED BY: Point Communications Inc.

1111 Battlewood St.

Franklin, TN 30764

TEL: n/a

DATE: Spring

FREQUENCY: Quarterly

COVER PRICE: $7.50

SUBSCRIPTION PRICE: $25.00

TOTAL NUMBER OF PAGES: 20

TOTAL NUMBER OF AD PAGES: 1

PUBLISHER: Richard Dreves, Aldie Beard

EDITOR: Robert A. Ivy, Jr.

EDITORIAL CONCEPT: *The official journal of the Gulf States Regional Council of the American Institute of Architects features some of the latest trends in and classic styles of southern architecture.*

Arizona Style

PUBLISHED BY: Vision 2000 Inc.

49 E. Thomas Rd., Suite 103

Phoenix, AZ 85012

TEL: (602) 234-0990

DATE: Fall

FREQUENCY: Quarterly

COVER PRICE: $2.95

SUBSCRIPTION PRICE: $10.00

TOTAL NUMBER OF PAGES: 64

TOTAL NUMBER OF AD PAGES: 7

PUBLISHER: Leo Simon

EDITOR: Brad Melton

EDITORIAL CONCEPT: *Featuring the beauty, fashion, lifestyle and entertainment of Arizona.*

Bay Style

PUBLISHED BY: Designers Illustrated Publications

4410 El Camino Real

Los Altos, CA 94022

TEL: (415) 568-9500

FREQUENCY: Quarterly

COVER PRICE: n/a

SUBSCRIPTION PRICE: $16.95

TOTAL NUMBER OF PAGES: 38

TOTAL NUMBER OF AD PAGES: 13

PUBLISHER: Sherry Shields

EDITOR: Kristine Carber

EDITORIAL CONCEPT: *San Francisco Bay area beauty, health and fitness resources.*

Book Of Lists

PUBLISHED BY: The Nautilus Group

P.O. Box 2178

Oxford, MS 38655

TEL: (601) 234-5082

DATE: Summer

FREQUENCY: Quarterly

COVER PRICE: Free

SUBSCRIPTION PRICE: n/a

TOTAL NUMBER OF PAGES: 32

TOTAL NUMBER OF AD PAGES: 14

PUBLISHER: Neil W. White, III

EDITOR: Neil W. White, III

EDITORIAL CONCEPT: *A quarterly business reference publication for Oxford, Mississippi, and the surrounding area.*

Branson Living

PUBLISHED BY: Branson Living Magazine

P.O. Box 7194

Branson, MO 65615

TEL: (800) 746-8625

DATE: June/July/August

FREQUENCY: Bimonthly

COVER PRICE: $2.95

SUBSCRIPTION PRICE: $15.98

DISCOUNT SUBSCRIPTION PRICE: $12.98

TOTAL NUMBER OF PAGES: 58

TOTAL NUMBER OF AD PAGES: 33

PUBLISHER: Gaye Lisby

EDITOR: Carol S. Harris

EDITORIAL CONCEPT: *Celebrating life in the Ozark region with articles on people and places to go.*

Brooklyn Bridge

PUBLISHED BY: The Brooklyn Bridge Inc.

388 Atlantic Ave.

Brooklyn, NY 11217

TEL: (718) 596-7400 **FAX:** (718) 852-1290

DATE: September/October

FREQUENCY: Monthly

COVER PRICE: $2.75

SUBSCRIPTION PRICE: $18.00

TOTAL NUMBER OF PAGES: 140

TOTAL NUMBER OF AD PAGES: 37

EDITOR: Melissa Ennen

EDITORIAL CONCEPT: "A magazine for Brooklyn," with articles about music, food, photography, film, books, art and more.

Health Pages

PUBLISHED BY: Health Pages

135 Fifth Ave., 7th Floor

New York, NY 10010

TEL: (212) 505-0103

DATE: Winter

FREQUENCY: Quarterly

COVER PRICE: $3.95

SUBSCRIPTION PRICE: n/a

TOTAL NUMBER OF PAGES: 68

TOTAL NUMBER OF AD PAGES: 0

PUBLISHER: Martin I. Schneider

EDITOR: Martin I. Schneider

EDITORIAL CONCEPT: "Atlanta doctors, hospitals and insurance plans."

Florida Care Giver

PUBLISHED BY: Johnson Associates

P.O. Box 380108

Jacksonville, FL 32205

TEL: (904) 573-9466 **FAX:** (904) 771-5381

FREQUENCY: Bimonthly

COVER PRICE: $4.00

SUBSCRIPTION PRICE: n/a

TOTAL NUMBER OF PAGES: 16

TOTAL NUMBER OF AD PAGES: 3

PUBLISHER: Anne M. Johnson

EDITOR: n/a

EDITORIAL CONCEPT: Designed to answer "a need for news, information and support for caregivers, their families, seniors and people in the business of caring for them."

Low Country

PUBLISHED BY: Select Publishing Group

P.O. Box 23616

Hilton Head, SC 29925

TEL: (803) 837-5100 **FAX:** (803) 837-5300

FREQUENCY: Quarterly

COVER PRICE: $4.50

SUBSCRIPTION PRICE: $15.00

TOTAL NUMBER OF PAGES: 40

TOTAL NUMBER OF AD PAGES: 32

PUBLISHER: Albert Hendershot, Larry Hunter

EDITOR: Stephanie Herring

EDITORIAL CONCEPT: A look at the art, history, architecture and customs of the Southern Lowland region.

Georgia Country Life Magazine

PUBLISHED BY: 1994 Nail Publications

2875 Nail Rd.

Baxley, GA 31513

TEL: (912) 367-5777

DATE: Spring

FREQUENCY: Quarterly

COVER PRICE: $2.95

SUBSCRIPTION PRICE: $9.95

TOTAL NUMBER OF PAGES: 40

TOTAL NUMBER OF AD PAGES: 0

PUBLISHER: Chris Nail

EDITOR: Chris Nail

EDITORIAL CONCEPT: Descriptions of Georgia country life.

Manhattan File

PUBLISHED BY: News Communications

594 Broadway, Suite 500

New York, NY 10012

TEL: (212) 219-3453 **FAX:** (212) 219-3509

DATE: April

FREQUENCY: Monthly

COVER PRICE: $2.50

SUBSCRIPTION PRICE: $29.00

TOTAL NUMBER OF PAGES: 106

TOTAL NUMBER OF AD PAGES: 54

PUBLISHER: Julie Dannenberg

EDITOR: Cristina Greeven

EDITORIAL CONCEPT: Articles and photographs depicting Manhattan life.

New York Bar Guide '96

PUBLISHED BY: T.K. Publishers Inc.

349 Ave. of the Americas, Suite 3

New York, NY 10014

TEL: (212) 229-9527

DATE: Fall

FREQUENCY: Semiannually

COVER PRICE: $2.50

SUBSCRIPTION PRICE: n/a

TOTAL NUMBER OF PAGES: 60

TOTAL NUMBER OF AD PAGES: 0

PUBLISHER: Eric Berman

EDITOR: Eric Berman

EDITORIAL CONCEPT: *Featuring 600 reviews and listings of bars, pubs, cafes and clubs, this publication is THE resource for that New York night on the town.*

Q San Francisco

PUBLISHED BY: Q Communications Inc.

584 Castro St., Suite 521

San Francisco, CA 94114

TEL: (415) 764-0324

DATE: Fall

FREQUENCY: Bimonthly

COVER PRICE: $2.95

SUBSCRIPTION PRICE: $19.95

TOTAL NUMBER OF PAGES: 64

TOTAL NUMBER OF AD PAGES: 13

PUBLISHER: Don Tuthill

EDITOR: Robert Adams

EDITORIAL CONCEPT: *A San Francisco area magazine for gay men, lesbians and bisexuals, featuring interviews with city leaders and local personalities.*

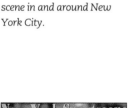

New York Living

PUBLISHED BY: Chiba Publications Inc.

20 W. 20th St., Suite 1005

New York, NY 10011-4213

TEL: (212) 727-1015   **FAX:** (212) 727-0838

DATE: June/July

FREQUENCY: Bimonthly

COVER PRICE: $3.95

SUBSCRIPTION PRICE: $16.50

TOTAL NUMBER OF PAGES: 116

TOTAL NUMBER OF AD PAGES: 18

EDITOR: n/a

EDITORIAL CONCEPT: *A guide to the residential real estate scene in and around New York City.*

Reckon

PUBLISHED BY: Center for the Study of Southern Culture

University of Mississippi

University, MS 38677

TEL: (601) 232-5997   **FAX:** (601) 232-7842

DATE: Summer

FREQUENCY: Quarterly

COVER PRICE: $5.95

SUBSCRIPTION PRICE: $21.95

TOTAL NUMBER OF PAGES: 164

TOTAL NUMBER OF AD PAGES: 14.33

PUBLISHER: William Ferris

EDITOR: Ann J. Abadie

EDITORIAL CONCEPT: *A magazine with articles on southern culture and the ways it is changing.*

New York Sportscene

PUBLISHED BY: New York Sportscene Enterprises Inc.

990 Motor Pkwy.

Central Islip, NY 11722

TEL: (516) 435-8890

DATE: May

FREQUENCY: Monthly

COVER PRICE: $2.95

SUBSCRIPTION PRICE: $29.95

TOTAL NUMBER OF PAGES: 64

TOTAL NUMBER OF AD PAGES: 20

PUBLISHER: Michael J. Cutino

EDITOR: Mark Sosna

EDITORIAL CONCEPT: *A magazine devoted to the sporting events happening in the New York metropolitan area.*

Seen

PUBLISHED BY: Seen Publishing

175 Fifth Ave., Suite 2126

New York, NY 10010

TEL: (212) 741-7336

FREQUENCY: Quarterly

COVER PRICE: $8.95

SUBSCRIPTION PRICE: n/a

TOTAL NUMBER OF PAGES: 98

TOTAL NUMBER OF AD PAGES: 1

EDITOR: Zachary Soreff

EDITORIAL CONCEPT: *A guide to the hot spots in New York City night life, including a section on the best restaurants and clubs for a variety of tastes.*

Southern New Mexico Destinations

PUBLISHED BY: Twin Publishing Inc.

425 W. Griggs Ave.

Las Cruces, NM 88005

TEL: (505) 524-1012

DATE: Summer

FREQUENCY: Quarterly

COVER PRICE: $2.50

SUBSCRIPTION PRICE: $8.00

TOTAL NUMBER OF PAGES: 56

TOTAL NUMBER OF AD PAGES: 12

PUBLISHER: Bonnie Drake

EDITOR: Keith Whelpley

EDITORIAL CONCEPT: *A travel and recreation magazine for southern New Mexico.*

Sports St. Louis

PUBLISHED BY: Sports St. Louis Inc.

11710 Administration Dr.

St. Louis, MO 63146

TEL: (314) 432-7787

DATE: September

FREQUENCY: Monthly

COVER PRICE: $3.25

SUBSCRIPTION PRICE: $28.00

TOTAL NUMBER OF PAGES: 36

TOTAL NUMBER OF AD PAGES: 15

PUBLISHER: Karen S. Hoffman

EDITOR: Sue Schneider

EDITORIAL CONCEPT: *For St. Louis sports enthusiasts ,with articles on local players and as the men and women who drive the St. Louis sports scene.*

St. Louis Magazine

PUBLISHED BY: Hartmann Publishing Co.

1221 Locust St., Suite 900

St. Louis, MO 63103

TEL: (314) 231-6661   **FAX:** (314) 231-9040

DATE: Spring

FREQUENCY: Quarterly

COVER PRICE: $2.95

SUBSCRIPTION PRICE: n/a

TOTAL NUMBER OF PAGES: 100

TOTAL NUMBER OF AD PAGES: 26

PUBLISHER: Cliff Froehlich

EDITOR: Tony DiMartino

EDITORIAL CONCEPT: *Features St. Louis hot spots and interviews with the people who shape the region.*

Style

PUBLISHED BY: Atlanta Jewish Times

1575 Northside Dr. NW, Suite 470

Atlanta, GA 30318

TEL: (404) 352-2400   **FAX:** (404) 609-7030

DATE: June/July

FREQUENCY: Bimonthly

COVER PRICE: $2.25

SUBSCRIPTION PRICE: $7.95

TOTAL NUMBER OF PAGES: 72

TOTAL NUMBER OF AD PAGES: 25

PUBLISHER: Charles A. Buerger

EDITOR: Francine Kaplan

EDITORIAL CONCEPT: *"Atlanta's magazine for smart living"* features articles on decorating, bridal preparations and general lifestyle topics.

Tennessee Living

PUBLISHED BY: ACE Communications

P.O. Box 2192

Cookeville, TN 38502

TEL: n/a

DATE: Fall

FREQUENCY: 3/year

COVER PRICE: $3.50

SUBSCRIPTION PRICE: n/a

TOTAL NUMBER OF PAGES: 56

TOTAL NUMBER OF AD PAGES: 30

PUBLISHER: Bill and Trish Monday

EDITOR: Ean Monday

EDITORIAL CONCEPT: *A travel guide with articles about state parks and historic places.*

Texas

PUBLISHED BY: Texas Water

Sports & Resorts Inc.

P.O. Box 340476

San Antonio, TX 78258

TEL: (210) 497-0627

DATE: Summer/Fall

FREQUENCY: 5/year

COVER PRICE: $3.50

SUBSCRIPTION PRICE: $9.95

TOTAL NUMBER OF PAGES: 48

TOTAL NUMBER OF AD PAGES: 10

PUBLISHER: Thomas J. Finn

EDITOR: Thomas J. Finn

EDITORIAL CONCEPT: *"A travel and recreation magazine"* for the state of Texas.

Time Out New York

PUBLISHED BY: Time Out New York Partners L.P.

627 Broadway, 7th Floor

New York, NY 10012

TEL: (212) 539-4444   **FAX:** (212) 673-8382

FREQUENCY: Weekly

COVER PRICE: $1.95

SUBSCRIPTION PRICE: n/a

TOTAL NUMBER OF PAGES: 130

TOTAL NUMBER OF AD PAGES: 39

PUBLISHER: Tony Elliot

EDITOR: Cyndi Stivers

EDITORIAL CONCEPT: *New York's new magazine of the night, featuring reviews of local events and personalities as well as general editorials.*

Today's Atlanta Woman

PUBLISHED BY: Women's News Media Inc.

P.O. Box 421666

Atlanta, GA 30342

TEL: (404) 303-7460

FREQUENCY: Quarterly

COVER PRICE: $2.95

SUBSCRIPTION PRICE: $12.00

TOTAL NUMBER OF PAGES: 44

TOTAL NUMBER OF AD PAGES: 16

PUBLISHER: Katherine Phelps

EDITOR: Katherine Phelps

EDITORIAL CONCEPT: *"The definitive guide to lifestyle, business, health and fashion for all Atlanta women!"*

Tribe

PUBLISHED BY: Big Mouth Media Inc.

2042 Magazine St.

New Orleans, LA 70130

TEL: (504) 524-5200   **FAX:** (504) 524-5242

DATE: October

FREQUENCY: Monthly

COVER PRICE: $2.50

SUBSCRIPTION PRICE: $18.00

TOTAL NUMBER OF PAGES: 68

TOTAL NUMBER OF AD PAGES: 17

PUBLISHER: Rand Ragusa

EDITOR: Yvette M. Beaugh

EDITORIAL CONCEPT: *Tribe aims to present the city of New Orleans and the state of Louisiana in a "provocative and daring" way, defining trends but not setting them.*

Whitefish: The Magazine Of Northwest Montana

PUBLISHED BY: Rising Wolf Inc.

127 Main St., Suite 200

Kalispell, MT 59903

TEL: (406) 755-2219

DATE: July

FREQUENCY: Quarterly

COVER PRICE: $3.95

SUBSCRIPTION PRICE: $13.45

TOTAL NUMBER OF PAGES: 76

TOTAL NUMBER OF AD PAGES: 24

PUBLISHER: Thom Harrop

EDITOR: Thom Harrop

EDITORIAL CONCEPT: *A magazine covering places to see in Montana. Includes color pictures and articles sent in by readers.*

Yippy-Yi-Yea Western Lifestyles

PUBLISHED BY: Long Publications Inc.

8393 E. Holly Rd., Holly, MI 48442

TEL: (313) 634-9675   **FAX:** (313) 634-0301

DATE: Fall

FREQUENCY: Quarterly

COVER PRICE: $3.95

SUBSCRIPTION PRICE: $12.00

TOTAL NUMBER OF PAGES: 132

TOTAL NUMBER OF AD PAGES: 70

PUBLISHER: Betty Long

EDITOR: John E. Long

EDITORIAL CONCEPT: *A magazine about western lifestyles, containing artwork, accessories and decorating ideas.*

ANNUAL, SPECIAL OR FREQUENCY UNKNOWN

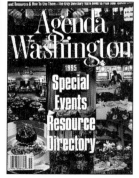

Agenda Washington

PUBLISHED BY: Agenda Washington Inc.

200 W. 57th St.

New York, NY 10019

TEL: (212) 399-1188   **FAX:** (212) 399-0070

FREQUENCY: Annually

COVER PRICE: $12.95

SUBSCRIPTION PRICE: n/a

TOTAL NUMBER OF PAGES: 164

TOTAL NUMBER OF AD PAGES: 66

PUBLISHER: Donna Uberman

EDITOR: Pamela Von Nostitz

EDITORIAL CONCEPT: *A special events resource directory for the executives responsible for Washington events of all kinds — philanthropic, civic, arts and corporate.*

All Florida Travel Directory

PUBLISHED BY: Destinations Florida Marketing Inc.

3238 Tamiami Tr. E.

Naples, FL 33962

TEL: (813) 744-4445

DATE: March

FREQUENCY: n/a

COVER PRICE: $5.50

SUBSCRIPTION PRICE: n/a

TOTAL NUMBER OF PAGES: 80

TOTAL NUMBER OF AD PAGES: 12

EDITOR: n/a

EDITORIAL CONCEPT: *"Information about hard-to-find properties all across Florida."*

Atlanta Guide Book For Kids

PUBLISHED BY: Kidz Books Co.

3046 Breckenridge Ln.

Louisville, KY 40220

TEL: (502) 491-5005   **FAX:** (502) 491-0805

FREQUENCY: n/a

COVER PRICE: $1.95

SUBSCRIPTION PRICE: n/a

TOTAL NUMBER OF PAGES: 36

TOTAL NUMBER OF AD PAGES: 8

EDITOR: n/a

EDITORIAL CONCEPT: *This puzzle-filled publication, featuring games and coupons, is published for children visiting Atlanta, Georgia.*

Basketball Time In Tennessee

PUBLISHED BY: Basketball Time In Tennessee

P.O. Box 5464

Knoxville, TN 37928

TEL: (423) 524-0933   **FAX:** (423) 546-2810

FREQUENCY: Special

COVER PRICE: $4.95

SUBSCRIPTION PRICE: n/a

TOTAL NUMBER OF PAGES: 68

TOTAL NUMBER OF AD PAGES: 22

PUBLISHER: Don Carringer

EDITOR: Don Carringer

EDITORIAL CONCEPT: *Reviews of the Tennessee Volunteer men's and women's basketball teams.*

Columbus Monthly's Wedding Planner

PUBLISHED BY: CM Media Inc.

5255 Sinclair Rd.

Columbus, OH 43229

TEL: (614) 888-4567

FREQUENCY: Annually

COVER PRICE: $2.95

SUBSCRIPTION PRICE: n/a

TOTAL NUMBER OF PAGES: 116

TOTAL NUMBER OF AD PAGES: 40

PUBLISHER: Max S. Brown

EDITOR: Adrienne Bosworth

EDITORIAL CONCEPT: *A wedding guide for central Ohio with articles on honeymoon trips and ideas for a perfect wedding.*

Design & Decoration: The South Florida Sourcebook

PUBLISHED BY: Designer Referral Service of Florida Inc.

1515 N. Federal Hwy., Suite 300

Boca Raton, FL 33432

TEL: (407) 998-0019   **FAX:** (407) 998-0190

FREQUENCY: Annually

COVER PRICE: $4.95

SUBSCRIPTION PRICE: n/a

TOTAL NUMBER OF PAGES: 180

TOTAL NUMBER OF AD PAGES: 122

PUBLISHER: Sharon Rosen

EDITOR: n/a

EDITORIAL CONCEPT: *"An annual reference book that identifies top quality sources and services for your home decorating and design needs."*

Downtown Atlanta

PUBLISHED BY: SouthComm Publishing

10 Church St.

Statesboro, GA 30458

TEL: (912) 489-1051   **FAX:** (912) 489-8191

FREQUENCY: Annually

COVER PRICE: $5.95

SUBSCRIPTION PRICE: n/a

TOTAL NUMBER OF PAGES: 96

TOTAL NUMBER OF AD PAGES: 26

PUBLISHER: Hope S. Merrill

EDITOR: Suzanne Walden

EDITORIAL CONCEPT: *The official resource guide and directory for downtown Atlanta.*

Flatiron News

PUBLISHED BY: Flatiron News Inc.

175 Fifth Ave., Suite 2327

New York, NY 10010

TEL: (212) 627-5400

FREQUENCY: n/a

COVER PRICE: $3.00

SUBSCRIPTION PRICE: n/a

TOTAL NUMBER OF PAGES: 98

TOTAL NUMBER OF AD PAGES: 47

PUBLISHER: Michael Abramson

EDITOR: Michael Abramson

EDITORIAL CONCEPT: *A very diverse publication aimed at serving the metro New York region featuring articles on movies, fiction, food, fashion and theater.*

Northern & Southern California Getaways

PUBLISHED BY: Anchor Communications

95 Chestnut St.

Providence, RI 02903

TEL: (401) 421-2552

FREQUENCY: Special

COVER PRICE: $3.95

SUBSCRIPTION PRICE: n/a

TOTAL NUMBER OF PAGES: 100

TOTAL NUMBER OF AD PAGES: 18

PUBLISHER: Dan Kaplan

EDITOR: Dan Kaplan

EDITORIAL CONCEPT: *Tells you where to stay and what to do for 65 romantic weekends.*

Golf New Mexico

PUBLISHED BY: Golf New Mexico

Rt. 9, Box 86 SA

Santa Fe, NM 87505

TEL: (505) 984-9978   **FAX:** (505) 984-0096

FREQUENCY: Special

COVER PRICE: $3.95

SUBSCRIPTION PRICE: n/a

TOTAL NUMBER OF PAGES: 48

TOTAL NUMBER OF AD PAGES: 29

PUBLISHER: Stan Jones

EDITOR: Ann Uhring

EDITORIAL CONCEPT: *A guide to golf courses in New Mexico.*

Northern California Bride

PUBLISHED BY: San Francisco Focus/KQED

2601 Mariposa St.

San Francisco, CA 94110

TEL: (415) 553-2800   **FAX:** (415) 553-2470

FREQUENCY: Special

COVER PRICE: n/a

SUBSCRIPTION PRICE: n/a

TOTAL NUMBER OF PAGES: 32

TOTAL NUMBER OF AD PAGES: 20

EDITOR: n/a

EDITORIAL CONCEPT: *A special supplement offering a collection of interesting wedding and bridal features.*

North Carolina's Taste Full *Special Issue: Summer Travel*

PUBLISHED BY: Summer Travel and Holiday

202 N. 3rd St., P.O. Box 1712

Wilmington, NC 28402

TEL: (910) 763-1601   **FAX:** (910) 763-0321

DATE: Summer

FREQUENCY: Special

COVER PRICE: $3.95

SUBSCRIPTION PRICE: $19.95

TOTAL NUMBER OF PAGES: 82

TOTAL NUMBER OF AD PAGES: 52

PUBLISHER: Elizabeth K. Norfleet

EDITOR: Elizabeth K. Norfleet

EDITORIAL CONCEPT: *This special edition of* North Carolina's Taste Full *focuses on restaurants, wine tours, brewpubs, festivals and shopping for summer visitors to the state.*

Outlook California

PUBLISHED BY: Afiniti Communications

2 Metro Square

2695 Villa Creek Dr., Suite 107

Dallas, TX 75234

TEL: (214) 241-1994   **FAX:** (214) 241-3858

FREQUENCY: n/a

COVER PRICE: $4.95

SUBSCRIPTION PRICE: n/a

TOTAL NUMBER OF PAGES: 84

TOTAL NUMBER OF AD PAGES: 25

PUBLISHER: Eric Kleinsorge

EDITOR: Eric Kleinsorge

EDITORIAL CONCEPT: *The guide for choosing business locations within the state of California.*

Outlook Texas

PUBLISHED BY: Afiniti Communications

1 Metro Square Building

2695 Villa Creek Dr., Suite 107

Dallas, TX 95234

TEL: (800) 632-9332

FREQUENCY: n/a

COVER PRICE: $4.95

SUBSCRIPTION PRICE: n/a

TOTAL NUMBER OF PAGES: 72

TOTAL NUMBER OF AD PAGES: 20

PUBLISHER: Eric Kleinsorge

EDITOR: Nancy Lapio

EDITORIAL CONCEPT: *"See for yourself why so many businesses have decided to hang their hats in the Lone Star State."*

Texas Our Texas

PUBLISHED BY: Texas Our Texas

P.O. Box 184

Mart, TX 76664

TEL: (817) 876-2617

DATE: October

FREQUENCY: Special

COVER PRICE: $2.95

SUBSCRIPTION PRICE: n/a

TOTAL NUMBER OF PAGES: 60

TOTAL NUMBER OF AD PAGES: 9

EDITOR: n/a

EDITORIAL CONCEPT: *"Featuring people, places, history and celebrations of the Lone Star State."*

Pittsburgh Magazine: Special Travel Publication

PUBLISHED BY: QED Communications

4802 Fifth Ave.

Pittsburgh, PA 15213

TEL: (412) 622-1360   **FAX:** (412) 622-7066

FREQUENCY: Special

COVER PRICE: $4.95

SUBSCRIPTION PRICE: n/a

TOTAL NUMBER OF PAGES: 82

TOTAL NUMBER OF AD PAGES: 38

PUBLISHER: Meg Cheever

EDITOR: Christopher Fletcher

EDITORIAL CONCEPT: *A special travel publication offering the best driving vacations for Pittsburgh residents.*

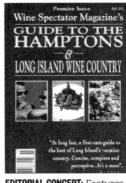

Wine Spectator Magazine's Guide To The Hamptons & Long Island Wine Country

PUBLISHED BY: M. Shanken Communications

387 Park Ave. S.

New York, NY 10016

TEL: (212) 684-4224   **FAX:** (212) 684-5424

FREQUENCY: Annually

COVER PRICE: $6.95

TOTAL NUMBER OF PAGES: 132

TOTAL NUMBER OF AD PAGES: 33

PUBLISHER: Marvin R. Shanken

EDITOR: Marvin R. Shanken

EDITORIAL CONCEPT: *Features on the wineries and restaurants of Long Island along with information about lodging, farmstands and other local attractions.*

Summertime

PUBLISHED BY: Southern Living

P.O. Box 523

2100 Lakeshore Dr.

Birmingham, AL 35201

TEL: (800) 272-4101

DATE: Summer

FREQUENCY: Special

COVER PRICE: $3.95

SUBSCRIPTION PRICE: n/a

TOTAL NUMBER OF PAGES: 146

TOTAL NUMBER OF AD PAGES: 51

PUBLISHER: Scott Sheppard

EDITOR: Dana Adkins Campbell

EDITORIAL CONCEPT: *Idea-packed issue to help the reader celebrate summer.*

Zia Magazine's Southern New Mexico Traveler

PUBLISHED BY: Zia Publishing Corp. of Southern New Mexico

400 N. Arizona St.

Silver City, NM 88061

TEL: (505) 388-3966   **FAX:** (505) 388-8784

FREQUENCY: Annually

COVER PRICE: $2.00

SUBSCRIPTION PRICE: n/a

TOTAL NUMBER OF PAGES: 20

TOTAL NUMBER OF AD PAGES: 17

PUBLISHER: Joseph Burgess

EDITOR: Joseph Burgess

EDITORIAL CONCEPT: *"The guide through southern New Mexico."*

Air Fan International

PUBLISHED BY: Publitek Ltd.

120 East Ave.

Norwalk, CT 06851

TEL: (203) 838-7979 **FAX:** (203) 838-7344

DATE: October

FREQUENCY: Bimonthly

COVER PRICE: $3.95

SUBSCRIPTION PRICE: n/a

TOTAL NUMBER OF PAGES: 68

TOTAL NUMBER OF AD PAGES: 10

PUBLISHER: Mel Williams

EDITOR: Rene J. Francillon

EDITORIAL CONCEPT: *The international journal of military aviation.*

Combat Handguns Buyer's Guide 1995

PUBLISHED BY: Harris Publications Inc.

1115 Broadway

New York, NY 10010

TEL: (212) 807-7100 **FAX:** (212) 627-4678

FREQUENCY: Annually

COVER PRICE: $5.50

SUBSCRIPTION PRICE: n/a

TOTAL NUMBER OF PAGES: 100

TOTAL NUMBER OF AD PAGES: 17

PUBLISHER: Stanley R. Harris

EDITOR: Harry Kane

EDITORIAL CONCEPT: *Features descriptions and price listings for every combat handgun.*

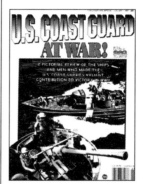

Military Technical Journal

PUBLISHED BY: Starlog Entertainment Inc.

475 Park Ave. S.

New York, NY 10016

TEL: (212) 689-2830 **FAX:** (212) 889-7933

FREQUENCY: Bimonthly

COVER PRICE: $6.99

SUBSCRIPTION PRICE: n/a

TOTAL NUMBER OF PAGES: 84

TOTAL NUMBER OF AD PAGES: 8

PUBLISHER: Norman Jacobs

EDITOR: Michael Benson

EDITORIAL CONCEPT: *The very best in blueprints, schematic drawings, diagrams and raw technical information regarding military hardware."*

U.S. Coast Guard At War!

PUBLISHED BY: Challenge Publications Inc.

7950 Deering Ave.

Canoga Park, CA 91304

TEL: (818) 887-0550 **FAX:** (818) 884-1343

FREQUENCY: Special

COVER PRICE: $6.95

SUBSCRIPTION PRICE: n/a

TOTAL NUMBER OF PAGES: 100

TOTAL NUMBER OF AD PAGES: 3

PUBLISHER: Edwin A. Schnepf

EDITOR: Edwin A. Schnepf

EDITORIAL CONCEPT: *"A pictorial review of the ships and men who made the U.S. Coast Guard's valiant contribution to victory in WWII."*

Soldier Of Fortune's Fighting Firearms

PUBLISHED BY: Soldier of Fortune

P.O. Box 693

Boulder, CO 80306

TEL: (303) 449-3750

DATE: Spring

FREQUENCY: Quarterly

COVER PRICE: $3.95

SUBSCRIPTION PRICE: n/a

TOTAL NUMBER OF PAGES: 84

TOTAL NUMBER OF AD PAGES: 11

PUBLISHER: Robert K. Brown

EDITOR: Peter G. Kokalis

EDITORIAL CONCEPT: *"The journal of armed professionals," featuring an operator's guide to the Uzi, an article on how to get into the gunfighting mindset and information on Beretta's super submachine guns."*

Victory Over Europe

PUBLISHED BY: Challenge Publications Inc.

7950 Deering Ave.

Canoga Park, CA 91304

TEL: (818) 887-0550 **FAX:** (818) 884-1343

FREQUENCY: Special

COVER PRICE: $5.95

SUBSCRIPTION PRICE: n/a

TOTAL NUMBER OF PAGES: 88

TOTAL NUMBER OF AD PAGES: 16

PUBLISHER: Edwin A. Schnepf

EDITOR: Michael O'Leary

EDITORIAL CONCEPT: *Commemorating the "50th anniversary of air power's victory over Hitler!"*

A PICTORIAL TRIBUTE TO ALL AMERICANS
WHO FOUGHT THE GREATEST WAR IN EUROPE

V-E DAY 1945-1995

50TH ANNIVERSARY

8 MAY 1945:
THE COLLAPSE OF NAZI GERMANY
FROM THE NORMANDY INVASION TO
THE FALL OF BERLIN, ALLIED FIGHTING
MEN WROTE A BATTLE HISTORY
NEVER TO BE FORGOTTEN

EDITORIAL CONCEPT: *"A pictorial tribute to all Americans who fought the greatest war in Europe."*

War Combat Special: V-E Day 50th Anniversary

PUBLISHED BY: Challenge Publications Inc.

7950 Deering Ave.

Canoga Park, CA 91304

TEL: (818) 887-0550   **FAX:** (818) 884-1343

FREQUENCY: Special

COVER PRICE: $5.95

SUBSCRIPTION PRICE: n/a

TOTAL NUMBER OF PAGES: 96

TOTAL NUMBER OF AD PAGES: 4

PUBLISHER: Edwin A. Schnepf

EDITOR: Blaine Taylor

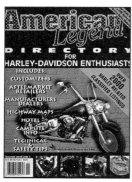

American Legend Directory

PUBLISHED BY: Absolute Digital Publishing

9587-A Arrow Route

Rancho Cucamonga, CA 91730

TEL: (909) 987-7137   **FAX:** (909) 987-4627

FREQUENCY: Semiannually

COVER PRICE: $6.95

SUBSCRIPTION PRICE: n/a

TOTAL NUMBER OF PAGES: 164

TOTAL NUMBER OF AD PAGES: 12

PUBLISHER: Michael T. McCoy, Sr.

EDITOR: William D. Rose

EDITORIAL CONCEPT: *"A directory for Harley-Davidson enthusiasts."*

Cycle Enthusiast Directory

PUBLISHED BY: Absolute Digital Publishing

9587-A Arrow Route

Rancho Cucamonga, CA 91730

TEL: (909) 987-7137   **FAX:** (909) 987-4627

DATE: April

FREQUENCY: Semiannually

COVER PRICE: $6.95

SUBSCRIPTION PRICE: n/a

TOTAL NUMBER OF PAGES: 162

TOTAL NUMBER OF AD PAGES: 2

PUBLISHER: Michael T. McCoy, Sr.

EDITOR: William D. Rose

EDITORIAL CONCEPT: *"A national directory of sales, service, parts and accessories for motorcycle enthusiasts."*

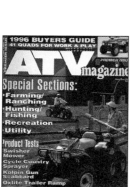

ATV Magazine

PUBLISHED BY: Ehlert Publishing Group

601 Lakeshore Pkwy., Suite 600

Minnetonka, MN 55305

TEL: (612) 476-2200   **FAX:** (612) 476-8065

DATE: November/December

FREQUENCY: 3/year

COVER PRICE: $3.50

SUBSCRIPTION PRICE: $10.50

TOTAL NUMBER OF PAGES: 92

TOTAL NUMBER OF AD PAGES: 20

PUBLISHER: Dick Henderson

EDITOR: Curt Bennink

EDITORIAL CONCEPT: *A magazine which features ATVs on the market, with special sections on new products and riding tips.*

Hot Rod Bikes

PUBLISHED BY: Peterson Publishing Co.

6420 Wilshire Blvd.

Los Angeles, CA 90048-5515

TEL: (213) 782-2000

DATE: March

FREQUENCY: Bimonthly

COVER PRICE: $2.95

SUBSCRIPTION PRICE: $13.95

TOTAL NUMBER OF PAGES: 92

TOTAL NUMBER OF AD PAGES: 22

PUBLISHER: Robert E. Peterson

EDITOR: Frank Kaisler

EDITORIAL CONCEPT: *Formerly known as Hot Rod Harleys, this magazine for motorcycle enthusiasts features buyer's guides and articles on different biking events happening around the country.*

Chrome Pony

PUBLISHED BY: Absolute Digital Publishing

9587-A Arrow Route

Rancho Cucamonga, CA 91730

TEL: (909) 987-7137   **FAX:** (909) 987-4627

DATE: June

FREQUENCY: Quarterly

COVER PRICE: $3.50

SUBSCRIPTION PRICE: n/a

TOTAL NUMBER OF PAGES: 74

TOTAL NUMBER OF AD PAGES: 1

EDITOR: Buck Lovell

EDITORIAL CONCEPT: *For riders of American-made motorcycles.*

Motocross Journal

PUBLISHED BY: Daisy/Hi-Torque Publishing

10600 Sepulveda Blvd.

Mission Hills, CA 91345-1936

TEL: (818) 365-6831

FREQUENCY: Bimonthly

COVER PRICE: $4.95

SUBSCRIPTION PRICE: $18.98

TOTAL NUMBER OF PAGES: 116

TOTAL NUMBER OF AD PAGES: 37

PUBLISHER: Roland Hinz

EDITOR: Timmy Mar

EDITORIAL CONCEPT: *Features the people, images and history of motocross racing.*

Quick Throttle

PUBLISHED BY: Paisano Publications Inc.

28210 Dorothy Dr.

Agoura Hills, CA 91301

TEL: (818) 889-8740

FREQUENCY: Bimonthly

COVER PRICE: $3.95

SUBSCRIPTION PRICE: $16.50

TOTAL NUMBER OF PAGES: 96

TOTAL NUMBER OF AD PAGES: 21

PUBLISHER: Joe Teresi

EDITOR: Keith R. Ball

EDITORIAL CONCEPT: *"Articles and photos of the world's best show-and-go Harley-Davidsons."*

American Iron Christmas

PUBLISHED BY: TAM Communications Inc.

1010 Summer St.

Stamford, CT 06905

TEL: (203) 425-8777

FREQUENCY: Annually

COVER PRICE: $4.99

SUBSCRIPTION PRICE: n/a

TOTAL NUMBER OF PAGES: 100

TOTAL NUMBER OF AD PAGES: 37

PUBLISHER: Buzz Kanter

EDITOR: Buzz Kanter

EDITORIAL CONCEPT: *"A Harley lover's buyer's guide for all budgets."* Lists hundreds of deals on America's favorite motorcycles.

Street Bike Magazine

PUBLISHED BY: RPM Publishing

1339 Mission St.

San Francisco, CA 94103

TEL: (415) 252-6669 **FAX:** (415) 252-6664

DATE: February

FREQUENCY: Monthly

COVER PRICE: $1.75

SUBSCRIPTION PRICE: $10.00

TOTAL NUMBER OF PAGES: 84

TOTAL NUMBER OF AD PAGES: 28

PUBLISHER: S. Alan Melaned

EDITOR: Cynthia Marsh

EDITORIAL CONCEPT: *Former magazines US Bike and Independent Biker join forces to bring you the latest information on new technologies while also looking back at some of the great bikes from the past.*

American Thunder

PUBLISHED BY: McMullen & Yee Publications

774 S. Placentia Ave.

Placentia, CA 92670

TEL: (714) 572-2255

FREQUENCY: Annually

COVER PRICE: $3.95

SUBSCRIPTION PRICE: n/a

TOTAL NUMBER OF PAGES: 116

TOTAL NUMBER OF AD PAGES: 24

EDITOR: Bob Clark

EDITORIAL CONCEPT: *A look at some of the finest custom bikes from the pages of Hot Bike magazine.*

ANNUAL, SPECIAL OR FREQUENCY UNKNOWN

All Sporties For Every Harley-Davidson Sportster Rider

PUBLISHED BY: Hatton-Brown Publishers

225 Hanrick St.

Montgomery, AL 36102

TEL: (334) 834-1170

FREQUENCY: Annually

COVER PRICE: $4.95

SUBSCRIPTION PRICE: n/a

TOTAL NUMBER OF PAGES: 100

TOTAL NUMBER OF AD PAGES: 19

PUBLISHER: Dennis Stemp

EDITOR: Terry Smith

EDITORIAL CONCEPT: *Pictures and articles about Harley-Davidson sportsters, past and present.*

Easyriders Roadware

PUBLISHED BY: Paisano Publications

P.O. Box 1025

Agoura Hills, CA 91376-9905

TEL: (818) 889-8740 **FAX:** (818) 889-4726

FREQUENCY: n/a

COVER PRICE: $5.00

SUBSCRIPTION PRICE: n/a

TOTAL NUMBER OF PAGES: 100

TOTAL NUMBER OF AD PAGES: 97

EDITOR: Joe Teresi

EDITORIAL CONCEPT: *A catalog for the Harley-Davidson rider.*

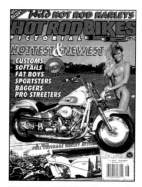

Hot Rod *Bikes Pictorial*

PUBLISHED BY: Peterson Publishing Co.

6420 Wilshire Blvd.

Los Angeles, CA 90048-5515

TEL: (213) 782-2000

FREQUENCY: Special

COVER PRICE: $4.95

SUBSCRIPTION PRICE: n/a

TOTAL NUMBER OF PAGES: 100

TOTAL NUMBER OF AD PAGES: 12

PUBLISHER: John Dianna

EDITOR: Frank Kaisler

EDITORIAL CONCEPT: *Photos of some of the nicest rides on two wheels.*

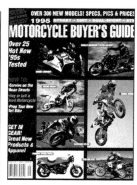

1995 Motorcycle Buyer's Guide

PUBLISHED BY: Petersen Publishing Co.

6420 Wilshire Blvd.

Los Angeles, CA 90048-5515

TEL: (213) 782-2000

FREQUENCY: Annually

COVER PRICE: $3.95

SUBSCRIPTION PRICE: n/a

TOTAL NUMBER OF PAGES: 100

TOTAL NUMBER OF AD PAGES: 28

PUBLISHER: Richard P. Lague

EDITOR: Richard P. Lague

EDITORIAL CONCEPT: *A compilation of over 300 motorcycle reviews with "specs, pics and prices."*

Motorcycle Milestones

PUBLISHED BY: Trader Publishing Co.

P.O. Box 9059

Clearwater, FL 34618-9059

TEL: (813) 538-1800

FREQUENCY: Special

COVER PRICE: $3.95

SUBSCRIPTION PRICE: n/a

TOTAL NUMBER OF PAGES: 92

TOTAL NUMBER OF AD PAGES: 12.5

EDITOR: Jason Scott

EDITORIAL CONCEPT: *A collector's edition devoted to great Harley-Davidsons of the past.*

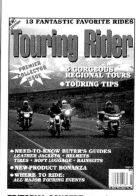

Touring Rider

PUBLISHED BY: TL Enterprises Inc.

3601 Calle Tecate

Camarillo, CA 93012

TEL: (805) 389-0300

FREQUENCY: Annually

COVER PRICE: $3.95

SUBSCRIPTION PRICE: n/a

TOTAL NUMBER OF PAGES: 100

TOTAL NUMBER OF AD PAGES: 32

PUBLISHER: Joseph E. McNeill, Jr.

EDITOR: Bill Stermer

EDITORIAL CONCEPT: *Equipment tips and touring routes for those people who like to experience the open road on a bike.*

Bass Frontiers

PUBLISHED BY: Information Revolution

6739 Sun Acer Way

Rio Linda, CA 95673

TEL: (916) 992-0233

FREQUENCY: Bimonthly

COVER PRICE: $3.50

SUBSCRIPTION PRICE: $16.44

TOTAL NUMBER OF PAGES: 52

TOTAL NUMBER OF AD PAGES: 18

PUBLISHER: Jim Hyatt

EDITOR: Jim Hyatt

EDITORIAL CONCEPT: *A magazine aimed at "fulfilling the need for a voice in the community for bassists everywhere." Features interviews with the world's top players.*

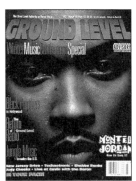

Ground Level

PUBLISHED BY: Ground Level Magazine

115 Allen St., 2nd Floor

New York, NY 10002

TEL: (212) 254-4500   **FAX:** (212) 254-0100

FREQUENCY: Bimonthly

COVER PRICE: $2.95

SUBSCRIPTION PRICE: $25.00

TOTAL NUMBER OF PAGES: 56

TOTAL NUMBER OF AD PAGES: 25

PUBLISHER: Oscar Poche

EDITOR: Oscar Poche

EDITORIAL CONCEPT: *"The street level authority on dance music."*

Fingerstyle Guitar

PUBLISHED BY: Fingerstyle Guitar Publications

7620 Delmonico Dr.

Colorado Springs, CO 80919

TEL: (719) 599-5076

DATE: March/April

FREQUENCY: Bimonthly

COVER PRICE: $4.95

SUBSCRIPTION PRICE: $28.00

TOTAL NUMBER OF PAGES: 72

TOTAL NUMBER OF AD PAGES: 20

PUBLISHER: John Schroeter

EDITOR: John Schroeter

EDITORIAL CONCEPT: *Sheet music and tips for fingerstyle guitarists.*

How To Play Blues

PUBLISHED BY: Miller Freeman Inc.

600 Harrison St.

San Francisco, CA 94107

TEL: (415) 905-2200   **FAX:** (415) 905-2233

FREQUENCY: 10/year

COVER PRICE: $4.95

SUBSCRIPTION PRICE: $29.95

DISCOUNT SUBSCRIPTION PRICE: $18.00

TOTAL NUMBER OF PAGES: 82

TOTAL NUMBER OF AD PAGES: 11

PUBLISHER: Pat Cameron

EDITOR: Dominic Milano

EDITORIAL CONCEPT: *For those interested in learning the tricks of the legendary blues performers, with lessons and editorials for guidance.*

Global Culture Rhythm Music Magazine

PUBLISHED BY: World Marketing Corp.

872 Massachusetts Ave., Suite 2-2

P.O. Box 391894

Cambridge, MA 02139

TEL: (617) 497-0356   **FAX:** (617) 497-0675

FREQUENCY: 11/year

COVER PRICE: $3.00

SUBSCRIPTION PRICE: $20.00

TOTAL NUMBER OF PAGES: 72

TOTAL NUMBER OF AD PAGES: 24

PUBLISHER: Kyle F. Russell

EDITOR: Joel Segel

EDITORIAL CONCEPT: *Formerly entitled RMM, this magazine reports on culture through travel, books, poetry and dance.*

How To Play Guitar

PUBLISHED BY: Miller Freeman Inc.

600 Harrison St.

San Francisco, CA 94107

TEL: (415) 905-2200   **FAX:** 415) 905-2233

FREQUENCY: 10/year

COVER PRICE: $4.95

SUBSCRIPTION PRICE: n/a

TOTAL NUMBER OF PAGES: 76

TOTAL NUMBER OF AD PAGES: 22

PUBLISHER: Marshall W. Freeman

EDITOR: Richard Johnston

EDITORIAL CONCEPT: *The publishers of Guitar Player present a new magazine with "loads of lessons and songs you can play."*

Lollipop

PUBLISHED BY: Lollipop Magazine

P.O. Box 147

Boston, MA 02123

TEL: (617) 623-5319

DATE: October

FREQUENCY: Monthly

COVER PRICE: $2.00

EDITORIAL CONCEPT: *"Sounds from the underground." The magazine focuses on up-and-coming bands in the underground music scene.*

SUBSCRIPTION PRICE: $15.00

TOTAL NUMBER OF PAGES: 48

TOTAL NUMBER OF AD PAGES: 15

PUBLISHER: Scott Hefflon

EDITOR: Scott Hefflon

The Tracking Angle

PUBLISHED BY: Too Many Brochures! Publishing Co.

P.O. Box 6449

San Jose, CA 95150-6449

TEL: (914) 361-3001   **FAX:** (914) 361-2332

FREQUENCY: Bimonthly

COVER PRICE: $5.00

EDITORIAL CONCEPT: *"Dedicated to telling you the truth as we hear it about the musical and sonic qualities of the recordings we review."*

SUBSCRIPTION PRICE: $30.00

TOTAL NUMBER OF PAGES: 74

TOTAL NUMBER OF AD PAGES: 18

PUBLISHER: Nick Despotopoulos

EDITOR: Michael Fremer

Music Confidential

PUBLISHED BY: LGA Publications

5000 Santa Rosa, Suite B-12

Camarillo, CA 93010

TEL: (805) 445-8310   **FAX:** (805) 445-8314

DATE: March

FREQUENCY: Monthly

COVER PRICE: $2.95

EDITORIAL CONCEPT: *A look into the lives of the musicians in the news today; includes interviews with artists like as Coolio and gossip about Paul McCartney's alleged love child.*

SUBSCRIPTION PRICE: 18.00

TOTAL NUMBER OF PAGES: 84

TOTAL NUMBER OF AD PAGES: 25

PUBLISHER: Toni Allen

EDITOR: Gina McHatton

Wolf Marshall's Guitar One

PUBLISHED BY: Cherry Lane Magazines Inc.

10 Midland Ave.

Port Chester, NY 10573-1490

TEL: (914) 935-5200   **FAX:** (914) 937-0614

FREQUENCY: Quarterly

COVER PRICE: $4.95

EDITORIAL CONCEPT: *A dynamic way to learn how to play the guitar and learn the songs you want to play at the same time."*

SUBSCRIPTION PRICE: n/a

TOTAL NUMBER OF PAGES: 106

TOTAL NUMBER OF AD PAGES: 10

PUBLISHER: Howard Cleff

EDITOR: Wolf Marshall

Shout !

PUBLISHED BY: Connell Communications

86 Elm St.

Peterborough, NH 03458

TEL: (603) 924-7271   **FAX:** (603) 924-7013

DATE: Summer

FREQUENCY: Monthly

COVER PRICE: $3.95

EDITORIAL CONCEPT: *Focuses on contemporary Christian music.*

SUBSCRIPTION PRICE: n/a

TOTAL NUMBER OF PAGES: 66

TOTAL NUMBER OF AD PAGES: 21

PUBLISHER: Ellen A. Holmes

EDITOR: Angela M. Casteel

ANNUAL, SPECIAL OR FREQUENCY UNKNOWN

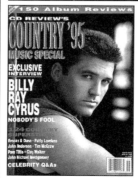

CD Review's Country '95

PUBLISHED BY: Connell Communications

86 Elm St.

Peterborough, NH 03458

TEL: (603) 924-7271   **FAX:** (603) 924-7013

FREQUENCY: Special

COVER PRICE: $4.95

EDITORIAL CONCEPT: *A year end look at country music, featuring exclusive interviews and reviews of 150 CDs.*

SUBSCRIPTION PRICE: $12.97

TOTAL NUMBER OF PAGES: 82

TOTAL NUMBER OF AD PAGES: 8

PUBLISHER: Ellen A. Holmes

EDITOR: Lou Waryncia

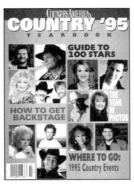

Country America Magazine's *Country '95 Yearbook*

PUBLISHED BY: Meredith Corp.

1716 Locust St.

Des Moines, IA 50309-3023

TEL:(515) 284-3000   **FAX:** (515) 284-3343

FREQUENCY: Annually

COVER PRICE: $3.95

SUBSCRIPTION PRICE: $14.00

TOTAL NUMBER OF PAGES: 148

TOTAL NUMBER OF AD PAGES: 16

PUBLISHER: Gail C. Healy

EDITOR: Danita Allen

EDITORIAL CONCEPT: *A photo review of the year in country music, plus a guide to the folks who sing it.*

Eye Deal

PUBLISHED BY: Eye Deal

355 E. 4th St., #18

New York, NY 10009

TEL: (212) 673-3063

FREQUENCY: n/a

COVER PRICE: $1.50

SUBSCRIPTION PRICE: n/a

TOTAL NUMBER OF PAGES: 36

TOTAL NUMBER OF AD PAGES: 5

PUBLISHER: Connie Garcia

EDITOR: Connie Garcia

EDITORIAL CONCEPT: *Focuses on the alternative music scene.*

Country Mirror

PUBLISHED BY: Country Mirror Publications

6 W. 18th St.

New York, NY 10011

TEL: (212) 242-5734

FREQUENCY: Special

COVER PRICE: $3.95

SUBSCRIPTION PRICE: n/a

TOTAL NUMBER OF PAGES: 84

TOTAL NUMBER OF AD PAGES: 4

PUBLISHER: Gerald Rothberg

EDITOR: Gerald Rothberg

EDITORIAL CONCEPT: *Articles and pictures of stars "reflecting the heart and soul of country music."*

4080

PUBLISHED BY: 4080 Publishing

2550 Shatluck Ave., Suite 107

Berkeley, CA 94704

TEL: (510) 644-9708

FREQUENCY: Special

COVER PRICE: $2.50

SUBSCRIPTION PRICE: n/a

TOTAL NUMBER OF PAGES: 64

TOTAL NUMBER OF AD PAGES: 24

PUBLISHER: Lauchlan McIntyre

EDITOR: Lauchlan McIntyre

EDITORIAL CONCEPT: *A special collector's magazine on hip-hop.*

Cover

PUBLISHED BY: Cover Magazine

P.O. Box 1215

Cooper Station

New York, NY 10276

TEL: (212) 673-1152

DATE: March

FREQUENCY: n/a

COVER PRICE: $2.00

SUBSCRIPTION PRICE: n/a

TOTAL NUMBER OF PAGES: 68

TOTAL NUMBER OF AD PAGES: 17

PUBLISHER: Jeffrey C. Wright

EDITOR: Jeffrey C. Wright

EDITORIAL CONCEPT: *Profiles of rising bands in the underground music world.*

Green Day

PUBLISHED BY: Starline Publications Inc.

210 Rt. 2 E., Suite 401

Paramus, NJ 07652

TEL: (201) 843-4004

FREQUENCY: Special

COVER PRICE: $3.95

SUBSCRIPTION PRICE: n/a

TOTAL NUMBER OF PAGES: 80

TOTAL NUMBER OF AD PAGES: 8

EDITOR: Anne M. Raso

EDITORIAL CONCEPT: *Articles about the personalities and the history of Green Day and other popular bands.*

EDITORIAL CONCEPT: *"Complete guide to guitars, basses, amps, FX, pickups, strings and much more."*

Guitar & Bass Buyer's Guide 1995-96

PUBLISHED BY: Miller Freeman Inc.

600 Harrison St.

San Francisco, CA 94107

TEL: (415) 905-2200   **FAX:** (415) 905-2233

FREQUENCY: Annually

COVER PRICE: $5.95

SUBSCRIPTION PRICE: n/a

TOTAL NUMBER OF PAGES: 210

TOTAL NUMBER OF AD PAGES: 32

PUBLISHER: Pat Cameron

EDITOR: Jim Roberts

Murderous Intent

PUBLISHED BY: Madison Publishing Co.

P.O. Box 5947

Vancouver, WA 98668-5947

TEL: (360) 695-9004

DATE: Fall

FREQUENCY: Quarterly

COVER PRICE: $5.00

SUBSCRIPTION PRICE: $15.00

TOTAL NUMBER OF PAGES: 68

TOTAL NUMBER OF AD PAGES: 6

PUBLISHER: Margo Power

EDITOR: Margo Power

EDITORIAL CONCEPT: *A magazine of mystery and suspense publishing stories written by readers.*

Oi, Robot

PUBLISHED BY: Mercury Press Inc.

143 Cream Hill Rd.

West Cornwall, CT 06796

TEL: (203) 672-6376

FREQUENCY: n/a

COVER PRICE: $5.95

SUBSCRIPTION PRICE: n/a

TOTAL NUMBER OF PAGES: 178

TOTAL NUMBER OF AD PAGES: 6

TOTAL NUMBER OF AD PAGES: 1

EDITOR: Edward L. Ferman

EDITORIAL CONCEPT: *"Competitions and cartoons from fantasy and science fiction."*

Red Herring

PUBLISHED BY: Potpourri Publications Co.

P.O. Box 8278

Prairie Village, KS 66208

TEL: (913) 642-1503   **FAX:** (913) 642-3128

DATE: Summer

FREQUENCY: Quarterly

COVER PRICE: $3.95

SUBSCRIPTION PRICE: $15.00

TOTAL NUMBER OF PAGES: 90

TOTAL NUMBER OF AD PAGES: 0

EDITOR: Sherri Armel

EDITORIAL CONCEPT: *A magazine showcase different mystery writers from around the U.S.*

Bears Magazine

PUBLISHED BY: Brad Garfield

11110 N. 5600 W.

Tremonton, UT 84337

TEL: (800) 934-3634

DATE: Fall

FREQUENCY: Quarterly

COVER PRICE: $3.95

SUBSCRIPTION PRICE: $14.95

TOTAL NUMBER OF PAGES: 48

TOTAL NUMBER OF AD PAGES: 7

PUBLISHER: Brad Garfield

EDITOR: Drew Ross

EDITORIAL CONCEPT: *"A wealth of knowledge about bears and their world, from the grizzlies and black bears, to the spectacled and sloth bears."*

Nature's Best

PUBLISHED BY: National Wildlife Federation

8925 Leesburg Pike

McLean, VA 22184

TEL: (703) 790-4000

FREQUENCY: Annually

COVER PRICE: $4.95

SUBSCRIPTION PRICE: n/a

TOTAL NUMBER OF PAGES: 100

TOTAL NUMBER OF AD PAGES: 5

EDITOR: Stephen B. Freligh

EDITORIAL CONCEPT: *"To create and encourage an awareness among the people of the world of the need for conservation and proper management of the Earth's resources."*

The Commercial Image

PUBLISHED BY: PTN Publishing

445 Broad Hollow Rd.

Melville, NY 11747

TEL: (516) 845-2700 **FAX:** (516) 845-2797

DATE: February

FREQUENCY: Monthly

COVER PRICE: $5.00

SUBSCRIPTION PRICE: $60.00

TOTAL NUMBER OF PAGES: 76

TOTAL NUMBER OF AD PAGES: 23

PUBLISHER: Pat Bernardo

EDITOR: Steven Shaw

EDITORIAL CONCEPT: *Reflects the changes in the image arena and makes a statement about how we see the world of the commercial image now and into the next century.*

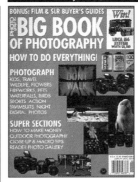

Big Book Of Photography

PUBLISHED BY: Petersen's Publishing Co.

6420 Wilshire Blvd., 6th Floor

Los Angeles, CA 90048

TEL: (213) 782-2800

FREQUENCY: Special

COVER PRICE: $5.95

SUBSCRIPTION PRICE: n/a

TOTAL NUMBER OF PAGES: 304

TOTAL NUMBER OF AD PAGES: 65

PUBLISHER: Paul Tzimoulis

EDITOR: Paul Tzimoulis

EDITORIAL CONCEPT: *Photo Graphic magazine revives the Big Book of Photography from the 1970s. Includes equipment tests and tips on better photography.*

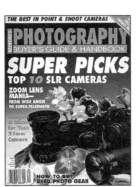

DoubleTake

PUBLISHED BY: Center for Documentary Studies at Duke University

1317 W. Pettigrew St.

Durham, NC 27705

TEL: (919) 660-3669 **FAX:** (919) 681-7600

DATE: Summer

FREQUENCY: Quarterly

COVER PRICE: $10.00

SUBSCRIPTION PRICE: $32.00

DISCOUNT SUBSCRIPTION PRICE: $24.00

TOTAL NUMBER OF PAGES: 132

TOTAL NUMBER OF AD PAGES: 12

EDITOR: Robert Coles, Alex Harris

EDITORIAL CONCEPT: *Photographic essays, fiction, poetry and book reviews make this magazine "a home where image and word have equal weight."*

Photography Buyer's Guide & Handbook

PUBLISHED BY: Bedford Communications

150 Fifth Ave., Suite 714

New York, NY 10011

TEL: (212) 807-8220 **FAX:** (212) 807-8737

DATE: Winter

FREQUENCY: Special

COVER PRICE: $4.95

SUBSCRIPTION PRICE: n/a

TOTAL NUMBER OF PAGES: 100

TOTAL NUMBER OF AD PAGES: 28

PUBLISHER: Edward D. Brown

EDITOR: Jules H. Gilder

EDITORIAL CONCEPT: *Features include "The Best in Point & Shoot Cameras" and "How To Buy Used Photo Gear."*

Shooter's Rag

PUBLISHED BY: Havelin Communications

P.O. Box 8509

Asheville, NC 28814

TEL: (704) 254-6700

DATE: January/February

FREQUENCY: Bimonthly

COVER PRICE: $3.00

SUBSCRIPTION PRICE: $16.00

TOTAL NUMBER OF PAGES: 28

TOTAL NUMBER OF AD PAGES: 6

PUBLISHER: Michael F. Havelin

EDITOR: Michael F. Havelin

EDITORIAL CONCEPT: *"A practical gazette for silver and digital photgraphers," containing articles on new equipment and tips for better shots.*

Popular Photography's Photo Information Handbook

PUBLISHED BY: Hachette Filipacchi

1633 Broadway

New York, NY 10019

TEL: (212) 767-6677 **FAX:** (212) 489-4217

FREQUENCY: Annually

COVER PRICE: $3.95

SUBSCRIPTION PRICE: n/a

TOTAL NUMBER OF PAGES: 236

TOTAL NUMBER OF AD PAGES: 110

PUBLISHER: Richard Rabinowitz

EDITOR: Harold O. Martin

EDITORIAL CONCEPT: *Purely practical information to address the hundreds of questions that photographers need answered.*

Shutterbug's
Outdoor And Nature Photography

PUBLISHED BY: Patch Publishing

5211 S. Washington Ave.

Titusville, FL 32780

TEL: (407) 268-5010 **FAX:** (407) 267-7216

DATE: Summer

FREQUENCY: Special

COVER PRICE: $3.95

SUBSCRIPTION PRICE: n/a

TOTAL NUMBER OF PAGES: 116

TOTAL NUMBER OF AD PAGES: 42

PUBLISHER: Christi Ashby

EDITOR: Peter K. Burian

EDITORIAL CONCEPT: *"Insights, recommendations and images of some 30 photographers," covering such topics as outdoor equipment, location information, aesthetics and technique.*

George

PUBLISHED BY: Hachette Filipacchi

1633 Broadway

New York, NY 10019

TEL: (212) 767-6000   **FAX:** (212) 489-4590

DATE: September

FREQUENCY: Bimonthly

COVER PRICE: $2.95

SUBSCRIPTION PRICE: $9.97

TOTAL NUMBER OF PAGES: 284

TOTAL NUMBER OF AD PAGES: 175

PUBLISHER: Michael J. Berman

EDITOR: John F. Kennedy, Jr.

EDITORIAL CONCEPT: *"Not just politics as usual," this magazine blends the worlds of politics and entertainment to form a new niche in the publishing industry.*

New Age Patriot

PUBLISHED BY: New Age Patriot

P.O. Box 419

Dearborn Heights, MI 48127

TEL: (313) 563-3192

DATE: Spring

FREQUENCY: Quarterly

COVER PRICE: $2.50

SUBSCRIPTION PRICE: $15.00 (6 issues)

TOTAL NUMBER OF PAGES: 24

TOTAL NUMBER OF AD PAGES: 8

EDITOR: n/a

EDITORIAL CONCEPT: *"The magazine for drug, environmental and social reform activists."*

The Limbaugh Letter

PUBLISHED BY: EFM Publishing Inc.

366 Madison Ave., 7th Floor

New York, NY 10017

TEL: (800) 457-4141   **FAX:** (212) 563-9166

DATE: November

FREQUENCY: Monthly

COVER PRICE: $2.95

SUBSCRIPTION PRICE: $29.95

TOTAL NUMBER OF PAGES: 16

TOTAL NUMBER OF AD PAGES: 0

EDITOR: Rush Limbaugh

EDITORIAL CONCEPT: The Limbaugh Letter *makes the transition from newsletter to four-color magazine but still dubs itself "the best political newsletter on the market — beyond a reasonable doubt."*

The Weekly Standard

PUBLISHED BY: News America Publishing

1150 Seventeenth St. NW, Suite 505

Washington, DC 20036

TEL: (202) 293-4900

DATE: September

FREQUENCY: Weekly

COVER PRICE: $2.95

SUBSCRIPTION PRICE: $79.96

DISCOUNT SUBSCRIPTION PRICE: $29.00

TOTAL NUMBER OF PAGES: 76

TOTAL NUMBER OF AD PAGES: 28

PUBLISHER: William Kristol

EDITOR: William Kristol

EDITORIAL CONCEPT: *A weekly with a conservative viewpoint, featuring articles on the ever-changing microcosm called Washington, D.C.*

Modern America

PUBLISHED BY: Modern America Publishing

1075 NW Murray Rd., Suite 196

Portland, OR 97229-5501

TEL: (800) 220-8541

DATE: Summer

FREQUENCY: Quarterly

COVER PRICE: $3.00

SUBSCRIPTION PRICE: $10.00

TOTAL NUMBER OF PAGES: 78

TOTAL NUMBER OF AD PAGES: 8

PUBLISHER: David W. Edwards

EDITOR: David W. Edwards

EDITORIAL CONCEPT: *"Politics, Art & Culture"*

Bent

PUBLISHED BY: Bent Pages Publishing

1887 Ingleside Terr. NW

Washington, DC 20010

TEL: (202) 319-9553

FREQUENCY: Bimonthly

COVER PRICE: $2.50

SUBSCRIPTION PRICE: $12.00

TOTAL NUMBER OF PAGES: 60

TOTAL NUMBER OF AD PAGES: 13

PUBLISHER: Scott Crawford

EDITOR: Eric Gladstone

EDITORIAL CONCEPT: *A Generation X music magazine with profiles on alternative bands.*

Eye

PUBLISHED BY: Eye

Box 303

New York, NY 10009

TEL: (910) 370-1702 **FAX:** (910) 370-1603

FREQUENCY: Quarterly

COVER PRICE: $3.95

SUBSCRIPTION PRICE: $14.95

TOTAL NUMBER OF PAGES: 52

TOTAL NUMBER OF AD PAGES: 0

PUBLISHER: L. Crosby

EDITOR: L. Crosby

EDITORIAL CONCEPT: *"An independent publication originating from a dissatisfaction with corporate mainstream media's narrow viewpoints and prevalent censorship."*

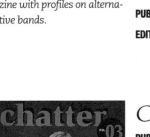

Chatter

PUBLISHED BY: Chatter Magazine

P.O. Box 692026

Los Angeles, CA 90069

TEL: (310) 657-8618

DATE: Spring/Summer

FREQUENCY: Bimonthly

COVER PRICE: $2.95

SUBSCRIPTION PRICE: $12.00

TOTAL NUMBER OF PAGES: 64

TOTAL NUMBER OF AD PAGES: 7.5

PUBLISHER: Michael P. Rouche

EDITOR: Michael P. Rouche

EDITORIAL CONCEPT: *Articles on famous celebrities, along with interviews, art and photography.*

Forehead Magazine

PUBLISHED BY: Forehead Magazine

32 Gramercy Park S., #17D

New York, NY 10003-1713

TEL: (212) 979-5106 **FAX:** (212) 460-5138

DATE: May

FREQUENCY: Bimonthly

COVER PRICE: $1.95

SUBSCRIPTION PRICE: $6.00

TOTAL NUMBER OF PAGES: 64

TOTAL NUMBER OF AD PAGES: 7

EDITOR: Alison M. McGonigal

EDITORIAL CONCEPT: *A glossy magazine featuring art, music, poems, fashion and culture.*

The Excluded Middle

PUBLISHED BY: The Excluded Middle

P.O. Box 1077

Los Angeles, CA 90048

TEL: n/a

FREQUENCY: Quarterly

COVER PRICE: $4.00

SUBSCRIPTION PRICE: n/a

TOTAL NUMBER OF PAGES: 60

TOTAL NUMBER OF AD PAGES: 7.5

PUBLISHER: Gregory Bishop, Robert Larson

EDITOR: Gregory Bishop, Robert Larson

EDITORIAL CONCEPT: *A magazine which ponders the existence of life as we know it and explores the possibilities of life on other planets.*

Freedom Rag

PUBLISHED BY: Freedom Rag Magazine

267 Fifth Ave., Suite 801-17

New York, NY 10016

TEL: n/a

DATE: Summer

FREQUENCY: Quarterly

COVER PRICE: $3.00

SUBSCRIPTION PRICE: n/a

TOTAL NUMBER OF PAGES: 62

TOTAL NUMBER OF AD PAGES: 5

PUBLISHER: Kelli Curry

EDITOR: Kelli Curry

EDITORIAL CONCEPT: *Intelligent literature and articles for the new generation of popular culture.*

International Virus

PUBLISHED BY: The Ninth Decade Coalition

P.O. Box 313

Farmington, MI 48332-0313

TEL: n/a

FREQUENCY: Quarterly

COVER PRICE: $2.75

SUBSCRIPTION PRICE: $12.00

TOTAL NUMBER OF PAGES: 84

TOTAL NUMBER OF AD PAGES: 9

PUBLISHER: O'Brian

EDITOR: David B. Livingstone

EDITORIAL CONCEPT: *"The self-actualization through fire-power magazine" contains interviews with Helmet and a look at society today.*

OneWorld

PUBLISHED BY: OneWorld Magazine Inc.

352 Fulton Ave.

Hempstead, NY 11550

TEL: (516) 485-8681   **FAX:** (516) 485-8684

DATE: Spring

FREQUENCY: Quarterly

COVER PRICE: $3.95

SUBSCRIPTION PRICE: $15.00

TOTAL NUMBER OF PAGES: 68

TOTAL NUMBER OF AD PAGES: 10

PUBLISHER: John N. Pasmore, Eddison Bramble

EDITOR: John N. Pasmore

EDITORIAL CONCEPT: *A magazine for people who are "white, black, straight, gay and all others," featuring art, fashion and music.*

Jack Magazine

PUBLISHED BY: Scenic Publications Inc.

2001 Chamisa St.

Santa Fe, NM 87505

TEL: (505) 984- 8192   **FAX:** (505) 984-5023

DATE: Summer

FREQUENCY: Bimonthly

COVER PRICE: $3.00

SUBSCRIPTION PRICE: $12.00

TOTAL NUMBER OF PAGES: 76

TOTAL NUMBER OF AD PAGES: 15

PUBLISHER: Richard N. Maslow

EDITOR: Richard N. Maslow

EDITORIAL CONCEPT: *"A magazine for lazy hedonists and the company they keep."*

Permission

PUBLISHED BY: Jayson Elliot and The Shame Club

1800 Market St., #777

San Francisco, CA 94102

TEL: (415) 469-2001

FREQUENCY: Quarterly

COVER PRICE: $4.00

SUBSCRIPTION PRICE: $15.00

TOTAL NUMBER OF PAGES: 100

TOTAL NUMBER OF AD PAGES: 18

PUBLISHER: Jayson Elliot

EDITOR: Jayson Elliot

EDITORIAL CONCEPT: *A magazine presented from the dark side of human nature, with editorials and articles on the macabre and the mysterious.*

New Thought Journal

PUBLISHED BY: Diversified Printing

P.O. Box 700754

Tulsa, OK 74146

TEL: (918) 299-7330

DATE: July/September

FREQUENCY: 5/year

COVER PRICE: $2.50

SUBSCRIPTION PRICE: $15.00

TOTAL NUMBER OF PAGES: 28

TOTAL NUMBER OF AD PAGES: 2.5

EDITOR: Ed Wincentsen

EDITORIAL CONCEPT: *A magazine with features on philosophy, religion, dialogue and book reviews.*

Popcorn

PUBLISHED BY: Pisces Productions

325 Edgewood Ave.

Atlanta, GA 30312

TEL: (404) 577-2632

FREQUENCY: Monthly

COVER PRICE: $2.00

SUBSCRIPTION PRICE: n/a

TOTAL NUMBER OF PAGES: 40

TOTAL NUMBER OF AD PAGES: 9

PUBLISHER: Chuck Morgan

EDITOR: Chuck Morgan

EDITORIAL CONCEPT: *A magazine for cross-dressers, transvestites and transsexuals.*

Speak

PUBLISHED BY: Speak Magazine Inc.

5150 El Camino Real, Suite B-24

Los Altos, CA 94022

TEL: (414) 428-0150

FREQUENCY: Bimonthly

COVER PRICE: $3.95

SUBSCRIPTION PRICE: $15.95

TOTAL NUMBER OF PAGES: 76

TOTAL NUMBER OF AD PAGES: 16

PUBLISHER: Dan Rolleri

EDITOR: Scott Marion

EDITORIAL CONCEPT: *Fashion and modern culture for the twenty-something generation.*

Tart

PUBLISHED BY: Tart Magazine

214 E. 24th St., Suite 4G

New York, NY 10010

TEL: (212) 802-7496

DATE: Summer

FREQUENCY: n/a

COVER PRICE: $3.00

SUBSCRIPTION PRICE: n/a

TOTAL NUMBER OF PAGES: 66

TOTAL NUMBER OF AD PAGES: 2

PUBLISHER: Riza Cruz, Aimee Shieh

EDITOR: Lynn Moloney

EDITORIAL CONCEPT: *An alternative lifestyle magazine with articles on strippers and S&M clubs.*

Strength

PUBLISHED BY: Delinquent Publicity

5050 Section Ave.

Cincinnati, OH 45212

TEL: (513) 531-0202   **FAX:** (513) 731-5513

DATE: Winter

FREQUENCY: Bimonthly

COVER PRICE: $3.25

SUBSCRIPTION PRICE: $17.00

TOTAL NUMBER OF PAGES: 120

TOTAL NUMBER OF AD PAGES: 27

EDITOR: n/a

EDITORIAL CONCEPT: *"Quality boards and noise." A magazine on snowboarding, surfing, skating and music.*

Thicker

PUBLISHED BY: Thicker World Enterprises

P.O. Box 881983

San Francisco, CA 94188-1983

TEL: n/a

DATE: March

FREQUENCY: n/a

COVER PRICE: $2.75

SUBSCRIPTION PRICE: n/a

TOTAL NUMBER OF PAGES: 84

TOTAL NUMBER OF AD PAGES: 20.5

PUBLISHER: Eric Bradford

EDITOR: Chuck Buckley

EDITORIAL CONCEPT: *An alternative rock magazine with interviews and stories on underground bands in the U.S.*

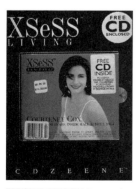

XSeSS Living

PUBLISHED BY: Proving Ground Publications

P.O. Box 504

Beverly Hills, CA 90213-0504

TEL: (310) 470-9917   **FAX:** (310) 441-8871

FREQUENCY: Quarterly

COVER PRICE: $8.95

SUBSCRIPTION PRICE: $30.50

TOTAL NUMBER OF PAGES: 170

TOTAL NUMBER OF AD PAGES: 22

PUBLISHER: Sean Perkin

EDITOR: Sean Perkin

EDITORIAL CONCEPT: *Devoted to a myriad of subjects — including fashion, music and computers — running the gamut of "Pop Culture."*

Word Up! Presents Summer Preview

PUBLISHED BY: Word Up! Publications Inc.

210 Rt. 4 E., Suite 401

Paramus, NJ 07652

TEL: (201) 536-0755

DATE: July

FREQUENCY: Special

COVER PRICE: $3.95

SUBSCRIPTION PRICE: n/a

TOTAL NUMBER OF PAGES: 84

TOTAL NUMBER OF AD PAGES: 14

EDITOR: Kate Ferguson

EDITORIAL CONCEPT: *The publishers of Word Up! preview the best music, television productions and films coming out during the summer.*

Angels

EDITORIAL CONCEPT: *For people fascinated by angels.*

PUBLISHED BY: GCR Publishing Group Inc.

1700 Broadway

New York, NY 10019

TEL: (212) 541-7100

FREQUENCY: Quarterly

COVER PRICE: $4.95

SUBSCRIPTION PRICE: n/a

TOTAL NUMBER OF PAGES: 68

TOTAL NUMBER OF AD PAGES: 13

PUBLISHER: Charles Goodman

EDITOR: Mary Arrigo

Christianity And The Arts

EDITORIAL CONCEPT: *America's guide to Christian expression.*

PUBLISHED BY: Christianity and the Arts

P.O. Box 118088

Chicago, IL 60611

TEL: (312) 642-8606

FREQUENCY: Quarterly

COVER PRICE: $4.50

SUBSCRIPTION PRICE: $15.00

TOTAL NUMBER OF PAGES: 40

TOTAL NUMBER OF AD PAGES: 10

PUBLISHER: Marci Whitney-Schenck

EDITOR: Marci Whitney-Schenck

Angels On Earth

EDITORIALCONCEPT: *Inspirational stories about works of angels done on earth.*

PUBLISHED BY: Guideposts

39 Seminary Hill Rd.

Carmel, NY 10512

TEL: (914) 225-3681

FREQUENCY: Bimonthly

COVER PRICE: $1.95

SUBSCRIPTION PRICE: n/a

TOTAL NUMBER OF PAGES: 48

TOTAL NUMBER OF AD PAGES: 0

PUBLISHER: Ruth Stafford Peale

EDITOR: Fulton Oursler, Jr.

Clarity

EDITORIAL CONCEPT: *"To inspire and equip contemporary Christian women to celebrate their passion for God, influence their world for Him and experience life to the fullest."*

PUBLISHED BY: Guideposts

39 Seminary Hill Rd.

Carmel, NY 10512

TEL: (914) 225-3681

FREQUENCY: Bimonthly

COVER PRICE: $3.50

SUBSCRIPTION PRICE: $18.97

TOTAL NUMBER OF PAGES: 68

TOTAL NUMBER OF AD PAGES: 12

PUBLISHER: John F. Temple

EDITOR: Judith Couchman

Books & Culture: A Christian Review

EDITORIAL CONCEPT: *Discusses cultural issues from the Christian perspective.*

PUBLISHED BY: Christianity Today Inc.

465 Gundersen Dr.

Carol Stream, IL 60188

TEL: (708) 260-6200   **FAX:** (708) 260-0114

DATE: November/December

FREQUENCY: Bimonthly

COVER PRICE: $3.50

SUBSCRIPTION PRICE: $24.95

TOTAL NUMBER OF PAGES: 32

TOTAL NUMBER OF AD PAGES: 6

PUBLISHER: Harold L. Myra

EDITOR: John Wilson

Essential Connection

EDITORIAL CONCEPT: *"A leisure and devotional magazine" that strives to be a spiritual guide for everyday life.*

PUBLISHED BY: Sunday School Board of the Southern Baptist Convention

127 Ninth Ave. N.

Nashville, TN 37234

TEL: (615) 251-3649   **FAX:** (615) 251-2795

DATE: October

FREQUENCY: Monthly

COVER PRICE: n/a

SUBSCRIPTION PRICE: n/a

TOTAL NUMBER OF PAGES: 60

TOTAL NUMBER OF AD PAGES: 2

PUBLISHER: James T. Draper

EDITOR: Cheryl D. Lewis

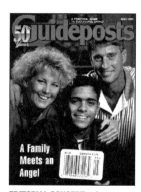

Guideposts

PUBLISHED BY: Guideposts Associates Inc.

39 Seminary Inc.

Carmel, NY 10512

TEL: (914) 225-3681

FREQUENCY: Monthly

COVER PRICE: $1.35

SUBSCRIPTION PRICE: $10.97

TOTAL NUMBER OF PAGES: 48

TOTAL NUMBER OF AD PAGES: 0

PUBLISHER: Ruth Stafford Peale

EDITOR: Fulton Ousler Jr.

EDITORIAL CONCEPT: *The "practical guide to successful living" celebrates its 50th year with its first newsstand issue.*

Miracles Inspirational Magazine

PUBLISHED BY: Miracles Inspirational

P.O. Box 40086

Jacksonville, FL 32203

TEL: (904) 384-9140

DATE: Summer

FREQUENCY: Quarterly

COVER PRICE: $2.95

SUBSCRIPTION PRICE: $12.95

TOTAL NUMBER OF PAGES: 52

TOTAL NUMBER OF AD PAGES: 13

PUBLISHER: Sally J. Holmes

EDITOR: Terry Fugate

EDITORIAL CONCEPT: *True stories of divine intervention.*

Kaleidoscope

PUBLISHED BY: Conference of the United Methodist Church Inc.

5124 Greenwich Ave.

Baltimore, MD 21229-2393

TEL: (410) 362-4700   **FAX:** (410) 362-4714

DATE: December

FREQUENCY: Bimonthly

COVER PRICE: $3.00

SUBSCRIPTION PRICE: $18.00

TOTAL NUMBER OF PAGES: 44

TOTAL NUMBER OF AD PAGES: 8.5

PUBLISHER: James E. Skillington, III

EDITOR: James E. Skillington, III

EDITORIAL CONCEPT: *A Christian lifestyle magazine with articles on successful living and reviews of CDs and books.*

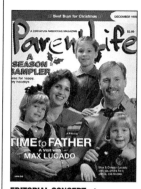

Parent Life

PUBLISHED BY: Lifeway Press

127 Ninth Ave. N.

Nashville, TN 37234

TEL: (800) 458-2772

DATE: December

FREQUENCY: Monthly

COVER PRICE: $2.95

SUBSCRIPTION PRICE: $19.95

TOTAL NUMBER OF PAGES: 52

TOTAL NUMBER OF AD PAGES: 0

EDITOR: Ellen Oldacre

EDITORIAL CONCEPT: *A Christian magazine for parents of children age 12 and younger.*

Luminarios

PUBLISHED BY: Guideposts Associates Inc.

39 Seminary Hill Rd.

Carmel, NY 10512

TEL: (914) 225-3681

DATE: January

FREQUENCY: Monthly

COVER PRICE: $1.75

SUBSCRIPTION PRICE: $16.95

TOTAL NUMBER OF PAGES: 48

TOTAL NUMBER OF AD PAGES: 0

EDITOR: Abraham Feldman

EDITORIAL CONCEPT: *An inspirational magazine for Spanish-speaking readers.*

Positive Living

PUBLISHED BY: Peale Center for Christian Living

66 E. Main St.

Pawling, NY 12564-1409

TEL: (914) 855-5000   **FAX:** (914) 855-1462

DATE: January/February

FREQUENCY: Bimonthly

COVER PRICE: n/a

SUBSCRIPTION PRICE: $12.95

TOTAL NUMBER OF PAGES: 40

TOTAL NUMBER OF AD PAGES: 0

PUBLISHER: Elizabeth Peale Allen

EDITOR: Elizabeth Peale Allen

EDITORIAL CONCEPT: *Articles on how to live a good Christian life and be a positive person.*

A Positive Note

PUBLISHED BY: The Gatling Printing Co.

10053 S. Halsted

Chicago, IL 60628

TEL: (800) 795-9379

DATE: January/February

FREQUENCY: Bimonthly

COVER PRICE: $2.50

SUBSCRIPTION PRICE: $12.95

DISCOUNT SUBSCRIPTION PRICE: $9.95

TOTAL NUMBER OF PAGES: 64

TOTAL NUMBER OF AD PAGES: 14

PUBLISHER: Lafayette Gatling, Sr., Marguerite Gatling

EDITOR: Maxine Walker

EDITORIAL CONCEPT: *A religious magazine for African-Americans.*

Release Ink

PUBLISHED BY: Royal Magazine Group

404 BNA Dr., Suite 600

Building 200

Nashville, TN 37217

TEL: (615) 872-8080

DATE: June/July

FREQUENCY: Bimonthly

COVER PRICE: $2.00

SUBSCRIPTION PRICE: $12.00

TOTAL NUMBER OF PAGES: 36

TOTAL NUMBER OF AD PAGES: 14

PUBLISHER: Timothy L. Gilmour

EDITOR: Roberta Croteau

EDITORIAL CONCEPT: *A Christian authors magazine about books and personalities in the market.*

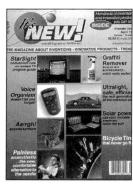

It's New

PUBLISHED BY: Sunshine Publishing Co.

7060 Convoy Ct.

San Diego, CA 92111

TEL: (619) 278-9080

DATE: April

FREQUENCY: Bimonthly

COVER PRICE: $3.95

SUBSCRIPTION PRICE: n/a

TOTAL NUMBER OF PAGES: 84

TOTAL NUMBER OF AD PAGES: 4

PUBLISHER: Sam Solana

EDITOR: Ian McLean

EDITORIAL CONCEPT: *The magazine about inventions, innovative products and trends.*

Science Spectra

PUBLISHED BY: The Gordon and Breach Publishing Group

2 Gateway Ctr.

Newark, NJ 07102-0301

TEL: (201) 643-7500 **FAX:** (201) 643-7676

FREQUENCY: Quarterly

COVER PRICE: $9.50

SUBSCRIPTION PRICE: $38.00

TOTAL NUMBER OF PAGES: 76

TOTAL NUMBER OF AD PAGES: 9

PUBLISHER: Ashley Crawford

EDITOR: Dr. Gerhart Friedlander

EDITORIAL CONCEPT: *A magazine by and for scientists, covering the spectrum of emerging scientific thought.*

21•C

PUBLISHED BY: Gordon & Breach Publishing Group

P.O. Box 200029

Riverfront Plaza Station

Newark, NJ 07102-0301

TEL: (201) 643-7500 **FAX:** (201) 643-7676

FREQUENCY: Quarterly

COVER PRICE: $6.95

SUBSCRIPTION PRICE: $21.00

TOTAL NUMBER OF PAGES: 86

TOTAL NUMBER OF AD PAGES: 10

PUBLISHER: Ashley Crawford

EDITOR: Ray Edgar

EDITORIAL CONCEPT: *"A magazine of culture, technology and science,"* featuring editorials on the impact of today's technology on tomorrow's society.

Apollo Thirteen: Collector's Edition

PUBLISHED BY: Magnolia Media Group

1227 W. Magnolia Ave.

Garden Level Suite

Fort Worth, TX 76104

TEL: (800) 856-8060

FREQUENCY: Special

COVER PRICE: $4.95

SUBSCRIPTION PRICE: n/a

TOTAL NUMBER OF PAGES: 68

TOTAL NUMBER OF AD PAGES: 0

PUBLISHER: Mark Hume

EDITOR: Joel C. Gregory

EDITORIAL CONCEPT: *"The story of American heroism,"* recounting NASA's near-tragedy, presented in chronological and photographic form.

Astronomy Presents Observer's Guide 1995

PUBLISHED BY: Kalmbach Publishing Co.

21027 Crossroads Cir.

P.O. Box 1612

Waukesha, WI 53187

TEL: (414) 796-8776

FREQUENCY: Annually

COVER PRICE: $4.95

SUBSCRIPTION PRICE: n/a

TOTAL NUMBER OF PAGES: 104

TOTAL NUMBER OF AD PAGES: 25

PUBLISHER: Russell G. Larson

EDITOR: Robert Burnham

EDITORIAL CONCEPT: *A stargazer's guide to viewing the night sky and buying astronomy-related products.*

Explorations In Artificial Life

PUBLISHED BY: Miller Freeman

600 Harrison St.

San Francisco, CA 94107

TEL: (415) 905-2200 **FAX:** (415) 905-2234

FREQUENCY: n/a

COVER PRICE: $9.95

SUBSCRIPTION PRICE: n/a

TOTAL NUMBER OF PAGES: 68

TOTAL NUMBER OF AD PAGES: 4

PUBLISHER: Peter Westerman

EDITOR: Kay Keppler

EDITORIAL CONCEPT: *Presents research on artificial life.*

Skeptical Inquirer

PUBLISHED BY: Committee for the
Scientific Investigation of
Claims of the Paranormal
3965 Rensch Rd.
Amherst, NY 14228-2713

TEL: (716) 636-1425

DATE: January/February

FREQUENCY: Special

COVER PRICE: $4.95

SUBSCRIPTION PRICE: n/a

TOTAL NUMBER OF PAGES: 76

TOTAL NUMBER OF AD PAGES: 4

PUBLISHER: Barry Karr

EDITOR: Kendrick Frazier

EDITORIAL CONCEPT: *A magazine that explores investigations of paranormal activity.*

Smithsonian Institution's Ocean Planet

PUBLISHED BY: Times Mirror Magazines
2 Park Ave.
New York, NY 10016

TEL: (212) 779-5000

FREQUENCY: Special

COVER PRICE: $5.95

SUBSCRIPTION PRICE: n/a

TOTAL NUMBER OF PAGES: 68

TOTAL NUMBER OF AD PAGES: 15

EDITOR: Robin McMillan

EDITORIAL CONCEPT: *A souvenir magazine that "covers the major marine issues while presenting, as vividly as possible, the wealth of nature to be found beneath the waves."*

Adam Gay Video Pictorial

PUBLISHED BY: Knight Publishing Corp.

8060 Melrose Ave.

Los Angeles, CA 90046

TEL: (213) 653-8060

FREQUENCY: Bimonthly

COVER PRICE: $4.95

SUBSCRIPTION PRICE: n/a

TOTAL NUMBER OF PAGES: 68

TOTAL NUMBER OF AD PAGES: 11

EDITOR: Dave Kinnick

EDITORIAL CONCEPT: *"The most comprehensive, accurate, entertaining and useful tool for attaining an insider's look at the world of video erotica."*

Asian Lace

PUBLISHED BY: WBC Publishing

P.O. Box 1292

New York, NY 10013

TEL: (212) 925-3115

FREQUENCY: Quarterly

COVER PRICE: $5.00

SUBSCRIPTION PRICE: $20.00

TOTAL NUMBER OF PAGES: 100

TOTAL NUMBER OF AD PAGES: 21

EDITOR: Chino Chinowitz

EDITORIAL CONCEPT: *A pictorial look at Asian women, all scantily clad in lingerie.*

Amateur Sex Videos

PUBLISHED BY: Eton Publishing Co. Inc.

1775 Broadway, Suite 604

New York, NY 10019

TEL: (212) 262-1773

DATE: July

FREQUENCY: Bimonthly

COVER PRICE: $5.99

SUBSCRIPTION PRICE: n/a

TOTAL NUMBER OF PAGES: 84

TOTAL NUMBER OF AD PAGES: 35

EDITOR: Marc Verlaine

EDITORIAL CONCEPT: *An adult magazine featuring clips from amateur sex films and profiles on the people in them.*

Badboy

PUBLISHED BY: Killer Joe Productions Inc.

801 Second Ave.

New York, NY 10017

TEL: (212) 661-7878

FREQUENCY: Bimonthly

COVER PRICE: $3.95

SUBSCRIPTION PRICE: n/a

TOTAL NUMBER OF PAGES: 115

TOTAL NUMBER OF AD PAGES: 13

EDITOR: Christopher Morgan

EDITORIAL CONCEPT: *An erotic, sexually explicit magazine targeted at gay men.*

Amateurs In Action

PUBLISHED BY: Ultracolor Publications

256 S. Robertson Blvd., Suite 3901

TEL: n/a

DATE: April

FREQUENCY: Bimonthly

COVER PRICE: $5.95

SUBSCRIPTION PRICE: $29.95

TOTAL NUMBER OF PAGES: 100

TOTAL NUMBER OF AD PAGES: 17

EDITOR: Robyn K. Wyatt

EDITORIAL CONCEPT: *"A reader participation magazine,"* featuring pictures from amateur home sex movies.

Bang

PUBLISHED BY: Sportmatic Ltd.

P.O. Box 470

Port Chester, NY 10573

TEL: (914) 939-2111

DATE: December

FREQUENCY: 8/year

COVER PRICE: $3.50

SUBSCRIPTION PRICE: n/a

TOTAL NUMBER OF PAGES: 100

TOTAL NUMBER OF AD PAGES: 26

EDITOR: Dan Maxwell

EDITORIAL CONCEPT: *A magazine of sex tales involving strangers and forbidden lovers.*

EDITORIAL CONCEPT: A gay sex magazine with a "country boy" motif.

Beau *Presents Country Boys*

PUBLISHED BY: Sportmatic Publishing Ltd.

P.O. Box 470

Port Chester, NY 10573

TEL: (914) 939-2111

DATE: July

FREQUENCY: Quarterly

COVER PRICE: $4.95

SUBSCRIPTION PRICE: n/a

TOTAL NUMBER OF PAGES: 148

TOTAL NUMBER OF AD PAGES: 32

EDITOR: Dan Maxwell

EDITORIAL CONCEPT: Pictures of women with very large breasts and reviews of sex videos that emphasize sizable busts.

Boob Tube Busters

PUBLISHED BY: Relim Publishing Co. Inc.

550 Miller Ave.

Mill Valley, CA 94941

TEL: (415) 383-5464 FAX: (415) 383-5312

FREQUENCY: Quarterly

COVER PRICE: $6.95

SUBSCRIPTION PRICE: n/a

TOTAL NUMBER OF PAGES: 88

TOTAL NUMBER OF AD PAGES: 13

EDITOR: Arv Miller

EDITORIAL CONCEPT: A magazine for bisexuals, with sexually explicit stories and black-and-white photographs.

Bi-Curious

PUBLISHED BY: Killer Joe Productions Inc.

801 Second Ave.

New York, NY 10017

TEL: (212) 661-7878

DATE: February/March

FREQUENCY: Bimonthly

COVER PRICE: $3.50

SUBSCRIPTION PRICE: n/a

TOTAL NUMBER OF PAGES: 116

TOTAL NUMBER OF AD PAGES: 13

EDITOR: Christopher Morgan

EDITORIAL CONCEPT: Pictorials of "newd" women in unnatural positions; also features letters from models describing how easy they are.

Cheri *Undercover*

PUBLISHED BY: Cheri Magazine Inc.

801 Second Ave.

New York, NY 10017

TEL: (212) 661-7878 FAX: (212) 687-2993

DATE: June

FREQUENCY: Bimonthly

COVER PRICE: $5.99

SUBSCRIPTION PRICE: n/a

TOTAL NUMBER OF PAGES: 130

TOTAL NUMBER OF AD PAGES: 49

EDITOR: Emil Ihasz, Jr.

EDITORIAL CONCEPT: "Mahogany and silk get kinky!"

Black Pleasure International

PUBLISHED BY: Black Pleasure Inc.

139 Fourth St.

Wood Ridge, NJ 07075-2064

TEL: n/a

DATE: October

FREQUENCY: Bimonthly

COVER PRICE: $5.25

SUBSCRIPTION PRICE: n/a

TOTAL NUMBER OF PAGES: 74

TOTAL NUMBER OF AD PAGES: 6

EDITOR: Maria Ewen

EDITORIAL CONCEPT: An adult magazine featuring letters from readers who want to share their sexual experiences.

Confidential Letters

PUBLISHED BY: AJA Publishing Corp.

P.O. Box 470

Port Chester, NY 10573

TEL: (914) 939-2111

DATE: July

FREQUENCY: 8/year

COVER PRICE: $3.50

SUBSCRIPTION PRICE: n/a

TOTAL NUMBER OF PAGES: 100

TOTAL NUMBER OF AD PAGES: 13

PUBLISHER: Jack Dean

EDITOR: Max Daniels

Down-n-Nasty

PUBLISHED BY: Vanity Publishing Co.

1775 Broadway, Suite 604

New York, NY 10019

TEL: (212) 262-1773

DATE: July

FREQUENCY: Bimonthly

COVER PRICE: $4.75

SUBSCRIPTION PRICE: n/a

TOTAL NUMBER OF PAGES: 112

TOTAL NUMBER OF AD PAGES: 22

PUBLISHER: J.P. Smith

EDITOR: Clint Hammer

EDITORIAL CONCEPT: *"The best in one-handed reading."*

ForePlay

PUBLISHED BY: Rem-Mer Ltd.

P.O. Box 700

Canal Street Station

New York, NY 10013

TEL: (212) 924-1278

FREQUENCY: Monthly

COVER PRICE: $5.95

SUBSCRIPTION PRICE: $50.00

TOTAL NUMBER OF PAGES: 132

TOTAL NUMBER OF AD PAGES: 20

PUBLISHER: Richard Shore

EDITOR: Victoria G. Reeves

EDITORIAL CONCEPT: *A magazine filled with steamy, sultry stories and letters, complete with correlating pictures.*

Easy Girls

PUBLISHED BY: Eton Publishing Co. Inc.

1775 Broadway, Suite 604

New York, NY 10019

TEL: (212) 262-1773

DATE: August

FREQUENCY: Bimonthly

COVER PRICE: $5.99

SUBSCRIPTION PRICE: n/a

TOTAL NUMBER OF PAGES: 84

TOTAL NUMBER OF AD PAGES: 30

EDITOR: Marc Verlaine

EDITORIAL CONCEPT: *Features heterosexual and lesbian sex.*

Golden Beauties

PUBLISHED BY: Onyx Publishing

55 Ave. of the Americas

New York, NY 10013

TEL: n/a

FREQUENCY: Bimonthly

COVER PRICE: $5.99

SUBSCRIPTION PRICE: $30.00

TOTAL NUMBER OF PAGES: 108

TOTAL NUMBER OF AD PAGES: 21

EDITOR: n/a

EDITORIAL CONCEPT: *"World-class women of color" posing for nude photographs.*

Forbidden

PUBLISHED BY: Vanity Publishing Co.

1775 Broadway, Suite 604

New York, NY 10019

TEL: (212) 262-1773

DATE: February

FREQUENCY: Bimonthly

COVER PRICE: $5.50

SUBSCRIPTION PRICE: n/a

TOTAL NUMBER OF PAGES: 210

TOTAL NUMBER OF AD PAGES: 26

EDITOR: Sally Wright

EDITORIAL CONCEPT: *A magazine comprised of letters about people having sex: sex with neighbors, sex with strangers and sex with friends.*

Group Gropers

PUBLISHED BY: Eton Publishing Co. Inc.

1775 Broadway, Suite 604

New York, NY 10019

TEL: (212) 262-1773

DATE: July

FREQUENCY: Bimonthly

COVER PRICE: $5.99

SUBSCRIPTION PRICE: n/a

TOTAL NUMBER OF PAGES: 84

TOTAL NUMBER OF AD PAGES: 30

EDITOR: Marc Verlaine

EDITORIAL CONCEPT: *A sex magazine specializing in orgies.*

Gruf Magazine

PUBLISHED BY: Gruf Magazine

2235-A Market St.

San Francisco, CA 94114

TEL: (415) 863-0212

FREQUENCY: Quarterly

COVER PRICE: $5.00

SUBSCRIPTION PRICE: n/a

TOTAL NUMBER OF PAGES: 56

TOTAL NUMBER OF AD PAGES: 10

PUBLISHER: Sam A. Zifferblatt

EDITOR: Jeff Lettow

EDITORIAL CONCEPT: *"A forum for and about men with facial hair and the guys who are turned on by them."*

Jack

PUBLISHED BY: Candy Publications Ltd.

310 Cedar Ln.

Teaneck, NJ 07666

TEL: (201) 836-9177

FREQUENCY: Bimonthly

COVER PRICE: $3.99

SUBSCRIPTION PRICE: n/a

TOTAL NUMBER OF PAGES: 164

TOTAL NUMBER OF AD PAGES: 33.5

PUBLISHER: Jackie Lewis

EDITOR: Jackie Lewis

EDITORIAL CONCEPT: *A collection of sexy letters, steamy articles and sultry illustrations.*

Hot Chix !

PUBLISHED BY: Eton Publishing Co.

475 Park Ave. S.

New York, NY 10016

TEL: (212) 213-8620

DATE: May

FREQUENCY: 9/year

COVER PRICE: $4.99

SUBSCRIPTION PRICE: n/a

TOTAL NUMBER OF PAGES: 84

TOTAL NUMBER OF AD PAGES: 31

EDITOR: n/a

EDITORIAL CONCEPT:
"America's most obscene magazine!"

Juniors

PUBLISHED BY: Canterbury Publishing

438 West 37th St., Suite 400

New York, N.Y. 10018

TEL: n/a

DATE: March

FREQUENCY: Bimonthly

COVER PRICE: $5.95

SUBSCRIPTION PRICE: $35.70

TOTAL NUMBER OF PAGES: 98

TOTAL NUMBER OF AD PAGES: 16

EDITOR: n/a

EDITORIAL CONCEPT: *A sex magazine for gay men.*

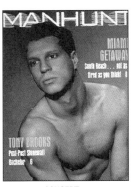

Hustler *Hard Drive*

PUBLISHED BY: L.F.P. Inc.

8484 Wilshire Blvd.

Beverly Hills, CA 90211

TEL: n/a

DATE: September

FREQUENCY: Bimonthly

COVER PRICE: $5.99

SUBSCRIPTION PRICE: $29.95

TOTAL NUMBER OF PAGES: 96

TOTAL NUMBER OF AD PAGES: 35

PUBLISHER: Larry Flynt

EDITOR: Michelle Marks

EDITORIAL CONCEPT: *"Where sex and technology interface."* A guide to some of the best cyber sex on the market.

Manhunt

PUBLISHED BY: Manhunt Magazine Corp.

101 Lafayette St., Suite 5

New York, NY 10013

TEL: (212) 226-0720   **FAX:** (212) 226-2777

DATE: May

FREQUENCY: Biweekly

COVER PRICE: $2.50

SUBSCRIPTION PRICE: n/a

TOTAL NUMBER OF PAGES: 32

TOTAL NUMBER OF AD PAGES: 12

PUBLISHER: Robert Block

EDITOR: Jonathan Eric Johnson

EDITORIAL CONCEPT: *A gay lifestyle magazine featuring vacation spots, horoscopes and dating and fiction departments.*

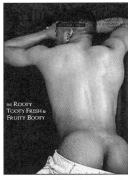

Millennium

PUBLISHED BY: Be Open Corp.

1730 K St. NW, Suite 304

Washington, DC 20006

TEL: (202) 466-0967 **FAX:** (202) 331-3759

FREQUENCY: Monthly

COVER PRICE: $3.75

SUBSCRIPTION PRICE: $23.00

TOTAL NUMBER OF PAGES: 44

TOTAL NUMBER OF AD PAGES: 4

PUBLISHER: John Bernard Jones

EDITOR: John Bernard Jones

EDITORIAL CONCEPT: A sexually explicit gay magazine featuring black men in black-and-white photographs and homoerotic fiction.

Naughty Neighbors

PUBLISHED BY: Quad International Inc.

214 W. Grant Rd.

Tucson, AZ 857050

TEL: (800) 367-3359 **FAX:** (800) 769-8324

DATE: September

FREQUENCY: Monthly

COVER PRICE: $5.99

SUBSCRIPTION PRICE: $36.00

TOTAL NUMBER OF PAGES: 100

TOTAL NUMBER OF AD PAGES: 16

PUBLISHER: Sam Lessner

EDITOR: John Fox

EDITORIAL CONCEPT: A men's magazine featuring female amateurs posing nude and letters from readers.

Naked Magazine

PUBLISHED BY: Naked Magazine

7985 Santa Monica Blvd., #109-232

West Hollywood, CA 90046

TEL: (800) 796-2533

FREQUENCY: Monthly

COVER PRICE: $4.95

SUBSCRIPTION PRICE: $43.00

TOTAL NUMBER OF PAGES: 52

TOTAL NUMBER OF AD PAGES: 15

EDITOR: Doug DiFranco

EDITORIAL CONCEPT: A magazine for "men who like to get naked."

Naughty Nights

PUBLISHED BY: Vanity Publishing Co.

1775 Broadway, Suite 604

New York, NY 10019

TEL: (212) 262-1773

DATE: August

FREQUENCY: Bimonthly

COVER PRICE: $5.99

SUBSCRIPTION PRICE: n/a

TOTAL NUMBER OF PAGES: 262

TOTAL NUMBER OF AD PAGES: 23

PUBLISHER: J.P. Smith

EDITOR: Clint Hammer

EDITORIAL CONCEPT: An adult storybook where "kinky lovers go wild," designed for reading on those naughty nights alone.

Nasty Women

PUBLISHED BY: Eton Publishing Co. Inc.

475 Park Ave. S.

New York, NY 10016

TEL: (212) 213-8620

DATE: February

FREQUENCY: Bimonthly

COVER PRICE: $5.50

SUBSCRIPTION PRICE: n/a

TOTAL NUMBER OF PAGES: 100

TOTAL NUMBER OF AD PAGES: 32

EDITOR: Jan Landay

EDITORIAL CONCEPT: Pictures of nude women who like to have sex.

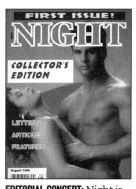

Night

PUBLISHED BY: Candy Publications Ltd.

310 Cedar Ln.

Teaneck, NJ 07666

TEL: (201) 836-9177

DATE: August

FREQUENCY: Bimonthly

COVER PRICE: $3.99

SUBSCRIPTION PRICE: $18.25

TOTAL NUMBER OF PAGES: 164

TOTAL NUMBER OF AD PAGES: 32

PUBLISHER: Jackie Lewis

EDITOR: Lisa Rosen

EDITORIAL CONCEPT: Night is an adult magazine filled with letters and stories about people's sexual encounters.

Orgy Girls

PUBLISHED BY: Eton Publishing Co. Inc.

1775 Broadway, Suite 604

New York, NY 10019

TEL: (212) 262-1773

DATE: September

FREQUENCY: Bimonthly

COVER PRICE: $5.99

SUBSCRIPTION PRICE: n/a

TOTAL NUMBER OF PAGES: 84

TOTAL NUMBER OF AD PAGES: 32

EDITOR: Marc Verlaine

EDITORIAL CONCEPT: *An adult men's magazine featuring the men and women of porno movies engaged in what they do best.*

Pure Pink

PUBLISHED BY: Paradise Magazines

350 Fifth Ave., Suite 2208

New York, NY 10118

TEL: (212) 630-0242

FREQUENCY: Monthly

COVER PRICE: $5.99

SUBSCRIPTION PRICE: n/a

TOTAL NUMBER OF PAGES: 40

TOTAL NUMBER OF AD PAGES: 22

EDITOR: n/a

EDITORIAL CONCEPT: *Men and women having sex, plus more than a handful of phone sex ads.*

Oui International

PUBLISHED BY: Laurent Publishing Ltd.

28 W. 25th St., 7th Floor

New York, NY 10010

TEL: (212) 647-0222   **FAX:** (212) 647-0236

FREQUENCY: Bimonthly

COVER PRICE: $5.95

SUBSCRIPTION PRICE: n/a

TOTAL NUMBER OF PAGES: 132

TOTAL NUMBER OF AD PAGES: 34

PUBLISHER: Anthony Destefano

EDITOR: Anthony Destefano

EDITORIAL CONCEPT: *A sampling of some of the easiest women from around the world, brought to you by the editors of Oui magazine.*

Rainbow Tales

PUBLISHED BY: Firsthand Ltd.

310 Cedar Ln.

Teaneck, NJ 07666

TEL: (201) 836-9177   **FAX:** (201) 836-5055

DATE: February

FREQUENCY: Monthly

COVER PRICE: $4.95

SUBSCRIPTION PRICE: n/a

TOTAL NUMBER OF PAGES: 132

TOTAL NUMBER OF AD PAGES: 34

PUBLISHER: Jackie Lewis

EDITOR: Bob Harris

EDITORIAL CONCEPT: *A sexually explicit, multi-cultural, gay magazine with stories and black-and-white drawings.*

Party Chicks

PUBLISHED BY: Eton Publishing Co. Inc.

1775 Broadway, Suite 604

New York, NY 10019

TEL: (212) 262-1773

DATE: September

FREQUENCY: Bimonthly

COVER PRICE: $5.99

SUBSCRIPTION PRICE: n/a

TOTAL NUMBER OF PAGES: 84

TOTAL NUMBER OF AD PAGES: 30

EDITOR: Marc Verlaine

EDITORIAL CONCEPT: *All about those "girls who get drunk and horny," with articles like "Meet Babes Who Have Sex With the First Guy Who Buys Them a Drink."*

Raw Sex

PUBLISHED BY: Swank Publications Inc.

210 Rt. 4 E., Suite 401

Paramus, NJ 07652-5116

TEL: (201) 843-9068

DATE: July

FREQUENCY: 8/year

COVER PRICE: $5.99

SUBSCRIPTION PRICE: n/a

TOTAL NUMBER OF PAGES: 84

TOTAL NUMBER OF AD PAGES: 24

EDITOR: n/a

EDITORIAL CONCEPT: *Explicit photographs of women in various unnatural sexual positions.*

Real Affairs

PUBLISHED BY: Vanity Publishing Co. Inc.

1775 Broadway, Suite 604

New York, NY 10019

TEL: (212) 262-1773

DATE: January

FREQUENCY: Bimonthly

COVER PRICE: $5.50

SUBSCRIPTION PRICE: n/a

TOTAL NUMBER OF PAGES: 212

TOTAL NUMBER OF AD PAGES: 31

EDITOR: Paula Townsend

EDITORIAL CONCEPT: "200+ pages of raunchy reading." Sexually explicit stories with black-and-white photographs.

Savage Male

PUBLISHED BY: Savage Male

564 Mission St., Box 345

San Francisco, CA 94105-2918

TEL: n/a

DATE: March

FREQUENCY: Bimonthly

COVER PRICE: $4.95

SUBSCRIPTION PRICE: $20.00

TOTAL NUMBER OF PAGES: 100

TOTAL NUMBER OF AD PAGES: 18.5

PUBLISHER: R.C. Thompson

EDITOR: Thom Proco

EDITORIAL CONCEPT: A full-color, gay sex magazine featuring sexually explicit photographs, homoerotic fiction and a special commemorative calendar.

Risqué

PUBLISHED BY: Risqué Publications

564 Mission St., Box 345

San Francisco, CA 94105-2918

TEL: (800) 323-6481

FREQUENCY: Bimonthly

COVER PRICE: $5.95

SUBSCRIPTION PRICE: $25.00

TOTAL NUMBER OF PAGES: 158

TOTAL NUMBER OF AD PAGES: 60

PUBLISHER: R.C. Thompson

EDITOR: Chris Dotson

EDITORIAL CONCEPT: Presented in rich color, "Risqué lets you explore the wonderful world of phone sex ."

Secrets From Sexy People

PUBLISHED BY: Vanity Publishing Co.

1775 Broadway, Suite 604

New York, NY 10019

TEL: (212) 262-1773

DATE: January

FREQUENCY: Bimonthly

COVER PRICE: $5.99

SUBSCRIPTION PRICE: n/a

TOTAL NUMBER OF PAGES: 292

TOTAL NUMBER OF AD PAGES: 20

PUBLISHER: Jane White

EDITOR: Brian Maxwell

EDITORIAL CONCEPT: The biggest magazine ever of sexually explicit stories and black-and-white photographs.

Rude & Lewd

PUBLISHED BY: Eton Publications Co. Inc.

1775 Broadway, Suite 604

New York, NY 10019

TEL: (212) 262-1773

DATE: July

FREQUENCY: Bimonthly

COVER PRICE: $5.99

SUBSCRIPTION PRICE: n/a

TOTAL NUMBER OF PAGES: 84

TOTAL NUMBER OF AD PAGES: 32

EDITOR: Marc Verlaine

EDITORIAL CONCEPT: A hardcore porno magazine that focuses on the raunchiest stuff it can find.

Sex Fever

PUBLISHED BY: Swank Publications Inc.

210 Rt. 4 E., Suite 401

Paramus, NJ 07652-5116

TEL: (201) 843-9068

DATE: December

FREQUENCY: Bimonthly

COVER PRICE: $6.99

SUBSCRIPTION PRICE: n/a

TOTAL NUMBER OF PAGES: 84

TOTAL NUMBER OF AD PAGES: 25

EDITOR: n/a

EDITORIAL CONCEPT: Sexually explicit, full-color photographs featuring heterosexual and lesbian sex.

Sex Scandals

PUBLISHED BY: Vanity Publishing Co.

1775 Broadway, Suite 604

New York, NY 10019

TEL: (212) 262-1773

DATE: December

FREQUENCY: Bimonthly

COVER PRICE: $6.50

SUBSCRIPTION PRICE: n/a

TOTAL NUMBER OF PAGES: 260

TOTAL NUMBER OF AD PAGES: 14

PUBLISHER: H.N. Smith

EDITOR: Shana Vista

EDITORIAL CONCEPT: *A sex magazine where readers write about their strange and erotic sex stories, both straight and lesbian .*

Shocking Stories

PUBLISHED BY: Vanity Publishing Co.

1775 Broadway, Suite 604

New York, NY 10019

TEL: (212) 262-1773

DATE: January

FREQUENCY: Bimonthly

COVER PRICE: $5.99

SUBSCRIPTION PRICE: n/a

TOTAL NUMBER OF PAGES: 292

TOTAL NUMBER OF AD PAGES: 23

PUBLISHER: Jane White

EDITOR: Brian Maxwell

EDITORIAL CONCEPT: *A jumbo package featuring heterosexual sex stories with black-and-white photography.*

Sexiest Women In X-Films

PUBLISHED BY: Eton Publishing Co.

475 Park Ave. S.

New York, NY 10016

TEL: (212) 213-8620

DATE: January

FREQUENCY: 9/year

COVER PRICE: $4.99

SUBSCRIPTION PRICE: n/a

TOTAL NUMBER OF PAGES: 84

TOTAL NUMBER OF AD PAGES: 23

EDITOR: Keith Applegate

EDITORIAL CONCEPT: *The stars of X-rated movies grace the pages of this magazine, which also includes articles such as "So You Want to be a Porn Stud."*

Sista !

PUBLISHED BY: Onyx Publishing

55 Avenue of the Americas

New York, NY 10013

TEL: n/a

FREQUENCY: Bimonthly

COVER PRICE: $5.99

SUBSCRIPTION PRICE: $30.00

TOTAL NUMBER OF PAGES: 100

TOTAL NUMBER OF AD PAGES: 15

PUBLISHER: Jackson Glenville

EDITOR: Leroy Sampson

EDITORIAL CONCEPT: *For lovers of tan and brown women.*

Shaved Orientails

PUBLISHED BY: WBC Publishing

55 Avenue of the Americas

New York, NY 10013

TEL: (212) 925-3115

DATE: February

FREQUENCY: Bimonthly

COVER PRICE: $5.99

SUBSCRIPTION PRICE: n/a

TOTAL NUMBER OF PAGES: 100

TOTAL NUMBER OF AD PAGES: 23

EDITOR: Chino Chinowitz

EDITORIAL CONCEPT: *Sexually explicit pictures of shaved Asian women; includes bilingual writing.*

Skinz

PUBLISHED BY: Swank Publications Inc.

210 Rt. 4 E., Suite 401

Paramus, NJ 07652-5116

TEL: (201) 843-9068

DATE: December

FREQUENCY: 8/year

COVER PRICE: $6.99

SUBSCRIPTION PRICE: n/a

TOTAL NUMBER OF PAGES: 80

TOTAL NUMBER OF AD PAGES: 25

EDITOR: n/a

EDITORIAL CONCEPT: *Women of color posing in the nude.*

Stag's Original Porn Legends

PUBLISHED BY: Stag Publishing Inc.

210 Rt. 4 E., Suite 401

Paramus, NJ 07652-5116

TEL: (201) 843-9068

FREQUENCY: 16/year

COVER PRICE: $5.99

SUBSCRIPTION PRICE: n/a

TOTAL NUMBER OF PAGES: 100

TOTAL NUMBER OF AD PAGES: 37

EDITOR: n/a

EDITORIAL CONCEPT: A sexually explicit magazine "devoted solely to preserving the legacy of the most famous porn queens to ever grace the blue screen."

Tight Cheeks

PUBLISHED BY: Eton Publishing Co.

1775 Broadway, Suite 604

New York, NY 10019

TEL: (212) 262-1773

DATE: August

FREQUENCY: Bimonthly

COVER PRICE: $5.99

SUBSCRIPTION PRICE: n/a

TOTAL NUMBER OF PAGES: 84

TOTAL NUMBER OF AD PAGES: 32

EDITOR: Marc Verlaine

EDITORIAL CONCEPT: "America's only all-butt adult magazine," with articles such as "Buttslammers 8," "Making Butt Detective" and "Battle of the Buns."

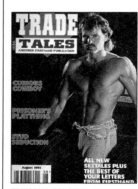

Stroke-Off Tales

PUBLISHED BY: Vanity Publishing Co.

1775 Broadway, Suite 604

New York, NY 10019

TEL: (212) 262-1773

DATE: July

FREQUENCY: Bimonthly

COVER PRICE: $5.99

SUBSCRIPTION PRICE: n/a

TOTAL NUMBER OF PAGES: 292

TOTAL NUMBER OF AD PAGES: 18

EDITOR: Sally Wright

EDITORIAL CONCEPT: Stroke-Off Tales is a magazine of stories that people have sent in about their sex lives.

Trade Tales

PUBLISHED BY: First Hand Ltd.

310 Cedar Ln.

Teaneck, NJ 07666

TEL: (201) 836-9177

DATE: August

FREQUENCY: Monthly

COVER PRICE: $4.95

SUBSCRIPTION PRICE: n/a

TOTAL NUMBER OF PAGES: 132

TOTAL NUMBER OF AD PAGES: 20

PUBLISHER: Jackie Lewis

EDITOR: Jerry Douglas

EDITORIAL CONCEPT: A gay men's magazine that features stories from people who write in.

T&A

PUBLISHED BY: Candy Publications Inc.

310 Cedar Ln.

Teaneck, NJ 07666

TEL: (201) 836-9177

DATE: December

FREQUENCY: 9/year

COVER PRICE: $3.99

SUBSCRIPTION PRICE: $25.97

TOTAL NUMBER OF PAGES: 100

TOTAL NUMBER OF AD PAGES: 23

EDITOR: Jackie Lewis

EDITORIAL CONCEPT: A magazine which focuses on the finer points of the female body.

Urge

PUBLISHED BY: Urgent Media

7080 Hollywood Blvd. #1104

Hollywood, CA 90028

TEL: (213) 896-9778

DATE: May/June

FREQUENCY: Bimonthly

COVER PRICE: $5.95

SUBSCRIPTION PRICE: $30.00

TOTAL NUMBER OF PAGES: 64

TOTAL NUMBER OF AD PAGES: 10.66

EDITOR: Mickey Skee

EDITORIAL CONCEPT: An adult magazine featuring photos of gay men and their lovers.

Wet Lips

PUBLISHED BY: Eton Publishing Co.

1775 Broadway, Suite 604

New York, NY 10019

TEL: (212) 262-1773

DATE: August

FREQUENCY: Bimonthly

COVER PRICE: $5.99

SUBSCRIPTION PRICE: n/a

TOTAL NUMBER OF PAGES: 86

TOTAL NUMBER OF AD PAGES: 35

EDITOR: Keith Applegate

EDITORIAL CONCEPT: *"The only magazine devoted to oral sex," full of illustrations.*

The Best Of Score

PUBLISHED BY: Quad International Inc.

214 W. Grant Rd.

Tucson, AZ 85705

TEL: (800) 367-3359

FREQUENCY: Special

COVER PRICE: $5.95

SUBSCRIPTION PRICE: n/a

TOTAL NUMBER OF PAGES: 100

TOTAL NUMBER OF AD PAGES: 12

EDITOR: n/a

EDITORIAL CONCEPT: *A pictorial magazine of very large-breasted women.*

Women Of Color

PUBLISHED BY: Heartland Publications Inc.

462 Broadway, 4th Floor

New York, NY 10013

TEL: (212) 966-8400

FREQUENCY: Quarterly

COVER PRICE: $6.99

SUBSCRIPTION PRICE: n/a

TOTAL NUMBER OF PAGES: 100

TOTAL NUMBER OF AD PAGES: 0

PUBLISHER: Jay Epstein

EDITOR: Savannah Dahl

EDITORIAL CONCEPT: *"Black vixens and Latina spitfires mix it up!"*

Busty & Black

PUBLISHED BY: B&B

P.O. Box 7394

New York, NY 10017

TEL: n/a

FREQUENCY: n/a

COVER PRICE: $5.99

SUBSCRIPTION PRICE: n/a

TOTAL NUMBER OF PAGES: 88

TOTAL NUMBER OF AD PAGES: 5

PUBLISHER: H. Robert Shapiro

EDITOR: Johnnie Cockring

EDITORIAL CONCEPT: *A sex magazine featuring black women in many different positions.*

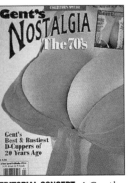

Women's Forum

PUBLISHED BY: Forum International Ltd.

277 Park Ave.

New York, NY 10172-0003

TEL: (212) 702-6000   **FAX:** (212) 873-4071

FREQUENCY: Monthly

COVER PRICE: $4.99

SUBSCRIPTION PRICE: $30.00

TOTAL NUMBER OF PAGES: 164

TOTAL NUMBER OF AD PAGES: 25

PUBLISHER: James B. Martise

EDITOR: Susan Crain Bakos,

John Heidenry

EDITORIAL CONCEPT: *Featuring articles like "The Pleasuring of America."*

Gent's Nostalgia: The 70s

PUBLISHED BY: Dugent Publishing Corp.

2600 Douglas Rd.

Coral Gables, FL 33134

TEL: (305) 443-2378

DATE: July

FREQUENCY: Special

COVER PRICE: $4.95

SUBSCRIPTION PRICE: n/a

TOTAL NUMBER OF PAGES: 100

TOTAL NUMBER OF AD PAGES: 23

EDITOR: n/a

EDITORIAL CONCEPT: *A Gent's collection from Dugent's archives of naked, big-breasted women of the 70s.*

High Society Insider

PUBLISHED BY: Crescent Publishing

801 Second Ave.

New York, NY 10017

TEL: (212) 661-7878

FREQUENCY: n/a

COVER PRICE: $5.99

SUBSCRIPTION PRICE: n/a

TOTAL NUMBER OF PAGES: 132

TOTAL NUMBER OF AD PAGES: 51

EDITOR: n/a

EDITORIAL CONCEPT: *"America's sex scene magazine."*

Passion Partners

PUBLISHED BY: Swank Publications Inc.

210 Rt. 4 E., Suite 401

Paramus, NJ 07652-5116

TEL: (201) 843-9068

FREQUENCY: Special

COVER PRICE: $5.99

SUBSCRIPTION PRICE: n/a

TOTAL NUMBER OF PAGES: 100

TOTAL NUMBER OF AD PAGES: 24

EDITOR: n/a

EDITORIAL CONCEPT: *Strictly pictorials in a full-page, adults-only format.*

Hustler's *Voyeur*

PUBLISHED BY: L.F.P. Inc.

8484 Wilshire Blvd., Suite 900

Beverly Hills, CA 90211

TEL: (800) 999-1170

DATE: Winter

FREQUENCY: n/a

COVER PRICE: $5.00

SUBSCRIPTION PRICE: n/a

TOTAL NUMBER OF PAGES: 100

TOTAL NUMBER OF AD PAGES: 15

PUBLISHER: Larry Flynt

EDITOR: Larry Flynt

EDITORIAL CONCEPT: *Hustler's speciality magazine ,devoted to women who like to be seen in public and the people who like to watch.*

Penthouse *Erotica*

PUBLISHED BY: Girls of Penthouse Publishing Inc.

277 Park Ave.

New York, NY 10172-0003

TEL: (212) 702-6000

DATE: November

FREQUENCY: Special

COVER PRICE: $5.50

SUBSCRIPTION PRICE: n/a

TOTAL NUMBER OF PAGES: 108

TOTAL NUMBER OF AD PAGES: 15

PUBLISHER: Bob Guccione

EDITOR: Don Myrus

EDITORIAL CONCEPT: *"Sexy stories with a few editorials and plenty of sexually explicit pictures."*

Joy Toys

PUBLISHED BY: Secondwind Publications

P.O. Box 1314

Teaneck, NJ 07666

TEL: (717) 224-6972

DATE: Summer

FREQUENCY: Special

COVER PRICE: $3.99

SUBSCRIPTION PRICE: n/a

TOTAL NUMBER OF PAGES: 98

TOTAL NUMBER OF AD PAGES: 32

PUBLISHER: Jackie Lewis

EDITOR: Jackie Lewis

EDITORIAL CONCEPT: *A magazine for those who prefer loving to be battery-powered. Covers a full assortment of toys for the home and office.*

Penthouse *Lingerie*

PUBLISHED BY: Hot Talk Magazines

277 Park Ave.

New York, NY 10172-0003

TEL: (212) 702-6000

FREQUENCY: Special

COVER PRICE: $5.00

SUBSCRIPTION PRICE: n/a

TOTAL NUMBER OF PAGES: 116

TOTAL NUMBER OF AD PAGES: 17

EDITOR: Bob Guccione

EDITORIAL CONCEPT: *A special issue produced by Penthouse to bring you some of the hottest women with very little on.*

Penthouse VP

PUBLISHED BY: Hot Talk Publications Ltd.

277 Park Ave.

New York, NY 10172-0003

TEL: (212) 702-6000

DATE: January

FREQUENCY: Special

COVER PRICE: $5.00

SUBSCRIPTION PRICE: n/a

TOTAL NUMBER OF PAGES: 114

TOTAL NUMBER OF AD PAGES: 19

PUBLISHER: Bob Guccione

EDITOR: Bob Guccione

EDITORIAL CONCEPT: *"Hot talk and photographs of Penthouse video pets."*

Playboy's *College Girls*

PUBLISHED BY: Playboy Press

608 N. Lake Shore Dr.

Chicago, IL 60611

TEL: (312) 751-8000   **FAX:** (312) 751-2818

FREQUENCY: Special

COVER PRICE: $5.95

SUBSCRIPTION PRICE: n/a

TOTAL NUMBER OF PAGES: 116

TOTAL NUMBER OF AD PAGES: 6

PUBLISHER: Jeff Cohen

EDITOR: Jeff Cohen

EDITORIAL CONCEPT: *"The best-looking girls from 30 colleges and universities."*

Playboy's *Anna Nicole Smith*

PUBLISHED BY: Playboy Press

680 N. Lake Shore Dr.

Chicago, IL 60611

TEL: (312) 751-8000   **FAX:** (312) 751-2818

FREQUENCY: Special

COVER PRICE: $6.95

SUBSCRIPTION PRICE: n/a

TOTAL NUMBER OF PAGES: 100

TOTAL NUMBER OF AD PAGES: 5

PUBLISHER: Jeff Cohen

EDITOR: Jeff Cohen

EDITORIAL CONCEPT: *"Her complete story in pictures."*

Playboy's *Hot Denim Daze*

PUBLISHED BY: Playboy Press

680 N. Lake Shore Dr.

Chicago, IL 60611

TEL: (312) 751-8000   **FAX:** (312) 751-2818

FREQUENCY: Special

COVER PRICE: $6.95

SUBSCRIPTION PRICE: n/a

TOTAL NUMBER OF PAGES: 100

TOTAL NUMBER OF AD PAGES: 6

PUBLISHER: Jeff Cohen

EDITOR: Jeff Cohen

EDITORIAL CONCEPT: A Playboy *pictorial with emphasis on denim, in honor of button-flies, copper rivets and leather patches.*

Playboy's *Blondes*

PUBLISHED BY: Playboy Press

608 N. Lake Shore Dr.

Chicago, IL 60811

TEL: (312) 751-8000   **FAX:** (312) 751-2818

FREQUENCY: Special

COVER PRICE: $6.95

SUBSCRIPTION PRICE: n/a

TOTAL NUMBER OF PAGES: 100

TOTAL NUMBER OF AD PAGES: 5

PUBLISHER: Jeff Cohen

EDITOR: Jeff Cohen

EDITORIAL CONCEPT: Playboy *celebrates blondes in the traditional Playboy pictorial fashion.*

Playboy's *Nude Celebrities*

PUBLISHED BY: Playboy Press

680 N. Lake Shore Dr.

Chicago, IL 60611

TEL: (312) 751-8000   **FAX:** (312) 751-2818

DATE: June

FREQUENCY: Special

COVER PRICE: $6.95

SUBSCRIPTION PRICE: n/a

TOTAL NUMBER OF PAGES: 100

TOTAL NUMBER OF AD PAGES: 5

PUBLISHER: Jeff Cohen

EDITOR: Jeff Cohen

EDITORIAL CONCEPT: A *pictorial look at the celebrities who have posed nude for* Playboy.

Playboy's Pocket Playmates

PUBLISHED BY: Playboy Press

680 N. Lake Shore Dr.

Chicago, IL 60611

TEL: (312) 751-8000 **FAX:** (312) 751-2818

FREQUENCY: Special

COVER PRICE: $3.95

SUBSCRIPTION PRICE: n/a

TOTAL NUMBER OF PAGES: 98

TOTAL NUMBER OF AD PAGES: 0

PUBLISHER: Jeff Cohen

EDITOR: Jeff Cohen

EDITORIAL CONCEPT: *All the best of Playboy in a pocket-sized package.*

Scream Beat

PUBLISHED BY: Market Square Productions

20 Market Sq.

Pittsburgh, PA 15222

TEL: (412) 471-1511

FREQUENCY: Irregular

COVER PRICE: $6.95

SUBSCRIPTION PRICE: n/a

TOTAL NUMBER OF PAGES: 64

TOTAL NUMBER OF AD PAGES: 8

PUBLISHER: John A. Russo

EDITOR: John A. Russo

EDITORIAL CONCEPT: *"Exclusive scream queen and fantasy girl pin-up issue!"*

Playboy's Supermodels

PUBLISHED BY: Playboy Press

680 N. Lake Shore Dr.

Chicago, IL 60611

TEL: (312) 751-8000 **FAX:** (312) 751-2818

DATE: February

FREQUENCY: Special

COVER PRICE: $5.95

SUBSCRIPTION PRICE: n/a

TOTAL NUMBER OF PAGES: 100

TOTAL NUMBER OF AD PAGES: 5

PUBLISHER: Jeff Cohen

EDITOR: Jeff Cohen

EDITORIAL CONCEPT: *Revealing photos of supermodels from around the world.*

Video Stars

PUBLISHED BY: n/a

ADDRESS: n/a

TEL: n/a

FREQUENCY: Special

COVER PRICE: $4.95

SUBSCRIPTION PRICE: n/a

TOTAL NUMBER OF PAGES: 68

TOTAL NUMBER OF AD PAGES: 7

EDITOR: n/a

EDITORIAL CONCEPT: *A special collector's edition featuring black-and-white photographs and interviews with female porn stars.*

Salsa Tales

PUBLISHED BY: First Hand Ltd.

310 Cedar Ln.

Teaneck, NJ 07666

TEL: (201) 836-9177

DATE: June

FREQUENCY: Special

COVER PRICE: $4.95

SUBSCRIPTION PRICE: n/a

TOTAL NUMBER OF PAGES: 132

TOTAL NUMBER OF AD PAGES: 22

PUBLISHER: Jackie Lewis

EDITOR: Jackie Lewis

EDITORIAL CONCEPT: *A gay men's magazine featuring Latino men and all the crazy sex stories they have to tell.*

Wet Dreams

PUBLISHED BY: Montcalm Publishing Corp.

401 Park Ave. S.

New York NY 10016

TEL: (212) 779-8900

DATE: Summer

FREQUENCY: Special

COVER PRICE: $5.95

SUBSCRIPTION PRICE: n/a

TOTAL NUMBER OF PAGES: 100

TOTAL NUMBER OF AD PAGES: 12

EDITOR: n/a

EDITORIAL CONCEPT: *"Features some of the sexiest, most alluring and, of course, wettest women to be featured in Gallery."*

EDITORIAL CONCEPT: X-Rated Close-Ups lives up to its name as it brings you right into the action.

X-Rated Close-Ups

PUBLISHED BY: Swank Publications

210 Rt. 4 E., Suite 401

Paramus, NJ 07652-5116

TEL: (201) 843-9068

DATE: April

FREQUENCY: Special

COVER PRICE: $5.99

SUBSCRIPTION PRICE: n/a

TOTAL NUMBER OF PAGES: 95

TOTAL NUMBER OF AD PAGES: 20

EDITOR: n/a

America Latina

PUBLISHED BY: America Latina

P.O. Box 2426

Salt Lake City, UT 84110

TEL: (801) 537-1510 **FAX:** (801) 537-1450

DATE: April/May

FREQUENCY: Bimonthly

COVER PRICE: $2.50

SUBSCRIPTION PRICE: n/a

TOTAL NUMBER OF PAGES: 52

TOTAL NUMBER OF AD PAGES: 12.5

EDITOR: Manuel Gomez Solano

EDITORIAL CONCEPT: *A magazine that deals with the issues that face Latinos in America.*

Country Heart

PUBLISHED BY: The Alliance Press

1320 N. Stewart

Springfield, MO 65802

TEL: (417) 831-8182 **FAX:** (417) 831-8184

DATE: Fall

FREQUENCY: Quarterly

COVER PRICE: $2.95

SUBSCRIPTION PRICE: $11.80

TOTAL NUMBER OF PAGES: 60

TOTAL NUMBER OF AD PAGES: 20

PUBLISHER: Timothy S. McDonald

EDITOR: Nancy R. Brueck

EDITORIAL CONCEPT: *A lifestyles magazine for country people and for people who are country at heart.*

Arts & Understanding

PUBLISHED BY: Arts & Understanding Inc.

25 Monroe St., Suite 205

Albany, NY 12210

TEL: (518) 426-9010 **FAX:** (518) 436-5354

DATE: September/October

FREQUENCY: Bimonthly

COVER PRICE: $3.95

SUBSCRIPTION PRICE: $24.95

TOTAL NUMBER OF PAGES: 60

TOTAL NUMBER OF AD PAGES: 16.3

EDITOR: David Waggoner

EDITORIAL CONCEPT: *A magazine that brings you personalities and art from around the world and confronts the subject of AIDS.*

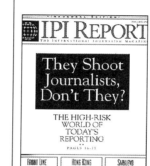

IPI Report

PUBLISHED BY: International Press Institute

Times Mirror Sq.

Los Angeles, CA 90053

TEL: (213) 237-2900 **FAX:** (213) 237-4677

DATE: May/June

FREQUENCY: Quarterly

COVER PRICE: $4.00

SUBSCRIPTION PRICE: n/a

TOTAL NUMBER OF PAGES: 36

TOTAL NUMBER OF AD PAGES: 2

PUBLISHER: David Laventhol

EDITOR: Alvin Shuster

EDITORIAL CONCEPT: *A journalism magazine with articles on hotspots for journalists and cameramen as well as information on the changing industry.*

Country Connections

PUBLISHED BY: Country Connections

P.O. Box 6748

Pine Mountain, CA 93222

TEL: (805) 242-1047 **FAX:** (805) 242-5704

DATE: March

FREQUENCY: Monthly

COVER PRICE: $2.50

SUBSCRIPTION PRICE: $28.00

TOTAL NUMBER OF PAGES: 32

TOTAL NUMBER OF AD PAGES: 6

PUBLISHER: Catherine Roberts Leach, Britt Leach

EDITOR: Catherine Roberts Leach

EDITORIAL CONCEPT: *A magazine of "opinions, reviews, essays, foolishness, poetry and fiction."*

Lefthander Magazine

PUBLISHED BY: Lefthanders International

P.O. Box 8249

Topeka, KS 66608

TEL: (913) 234-2177

FREQUENCY: Bimonthly

COVER PRICE: $3.00

SUBSCRIPTION PRICE: $15.00

TOTAL NUMBER OF PAGES: 32

TOTAL NUMBER OF AD PAGES: 5

PUBLISHER: Dean R. Campbell

EDITOR: Kim Kipers

EDITORIAL CONCEPT: *"The world's only magazine for left-handers."*

My Life As A Girl

EDITORIAL CONCEPT: *Stories to help you find your own fierce inner-girl.*

PUBLISHED BY: Bust Magazine

P.O. Box 319, Ansonia Station

New York, NY 10023

TEL: (212) 533-5134

DATE: Winter/Spring

FREQUENCY: Quarterly

COVER PRICE: $2.50

SUBSCRIPTION PRICE: $10.00

TOTAL NUMBER OF PAGES: 74

TOTAL NUMBER OF AD PAGES: 21

PUBLISHER: Betty Boob

EDITOR: Celina Hex

Prevailing Winds

PUBLISHED BY: The Center for the Preservation of Modern History

P.O. Box 23511

Santa Barbara, CA 93121

TEL: (805) 899-3433   **FAX:** (805) 899-4773

FREQUENCY: Quarterly

COVER PRICE: $4.95

SUBSCRIPTION PRICE: $20.00

TOTAL NUMBER OF PAGES: 98

TOTAL NUMBER OF AD PAGES: 6.5

EDITORIAL CONCEPT: *Devoted to exposing hidden history, intelligence abuses, the threat of resurgent facism and related issues.*

EDITOR: Martin Cannon

National Crime Monthly

EDITORIAL CONCEPT: *America's #1 crime awareness magazine with articles on the current events in the United States. Stories include coverage of the O.J. Simpson trial and the Unabomber.*

PUBLISHED BY: Gentry Publications and Productions

P.O. Box 90328

Gainesville, FL 32607

TEL: (904) 371-1800

FREQUENCY: Monthly

COVER PRICE: $2.25

SUBSCRIPTION PRICE: $16.95

TOTAL NUMBER OF PAGES: 64

TOTAL NUMBER OF AD PAGES: 18

PUBLISHER: Dave Gentry

EDITOR: Benjamin Gross

Si

PUBLISHED BY: Si Magazine L.P.

6464 Odin St.

Los Angeles, CA 90068

TEL: (213) 975-9313   **FAX:** (213) 957-1114

FREQUENCY: Bimonthly

COVER PRICE: $2.95

SUBSCRIPTION PRICE: $8.95

TOTAL NUMBER OF PAGES: 98

TOTAL NUMBER OF AD PAGES: 17.3

EDITORIAL CONCEPT: *"For Latinos, Latin lovers and lovers of Latinos."*

PUBLISHER: Joie Davidow

EDITOR: Michael Lassell

Non-Stop Magazine

EDITORIAL CONCEPT: *Features different science-fiction short stories sent in by readers.*

PUBLISHED BY: Non-Stop Magazine

P.O. Box 981, Peck Slip Station

New York, NY 10272-0981

TEL: n/a

DATE: Winter

FREQUENCY: Quarterly

COVER PRICE: $4.95

SUBSCRIPTION PRICE: $18.00

TOTAL NUMBER OF PAGES: 52

TOTAL NUMBER OF AD PAGES: 0

PUBLISHER: K.J. Cypret

EDITOR: K.J. Cypret

Single Styles

PUBLISHED BY: Single Styles Inc.

1001 Ave. of the Americas, 7th Floor

New York, NY 10018

TEL: (212) 780-3232

DATE: April

FREQUENCY: Monthly

COVER PRICE: $2.95

SUBSCRIPTION PRICE: n/a

TOTAL NUMBER OF PAGES: 100

TOTAL NUMBER OF AD PAGES: 26

PUBLISHER: Kevin McGarry

EDITOR: Robert Yehling

EDITORIAL CONCEPT: *Devoted to "the art of single living." The magazine includes articles about relationships, health, fashion and travel.*

Singles

PUBLISHED BY: Tedel Inc.

130 Durst Pl.

Yonkers, NY 10704

TEL: (800) 735-2832

DATE: October

FREQUENCY: 10/year

COVER PRICE: $2.95

SUBSCRIPTION PRICE: $25.00

TOTAL NUMBER OF PAGES: 68

TOTAL NUMBER OF AD PAGES: 20

PUBLISHER: Delia Passi

EDITOR: Joseph Scott

EDITORIAL CONCEPT: *"The monthly magazine for independent living," with articles on celebrity singles and meeting the right people.*

The Singles Resource

PUBLISHED BY: The Singles Resource

P.O. Box 695

Yonkers, NY 10704

TEL: (800) 735-2832

FREQUENCY: Monthly

COVER PRICE: $2.95

SUBSCRIPTION PRICE: $25.00

TOTAL NUMBER OF PAGES: 52

TOTAL NUMBER OF AD PAGES: 17

PUBLISHER: Delia Passi

EDITOR: Joseph Scott

EDITORIAL CONCEPT: *A singles magazine that offers advice on dating as well as great places to meet other singles.*

Smoke

PUBLISHED BY: Lockwood Trade Journal

660 Mayhew Lake Rd. NE

St.Cloud, MN 56302

TEL: (212) 391-2060

FREQUENCY: Quarterly

COVER PRICE: $3.95

SUBSCRIPTION PRICE: $14.00

TOTAL NUMBER OF PAGES: 184

TOTAL NUMBER OF AD PAGES: 52

PUBLISHER: Robert L. Lockwood, George E. Lockwood

EDITOR: Aaron L. Sigmond

EDITORIAL CONCEPT: *"Cigars, pipes and life's other burning desires." Reviews of some of the finest cigars and tobaccos at the best prices.*

Sufism

PUBLISHED BY: International Association of Sufism

P.O. Box 2382

San Rafael, CA 94912

TEL: (415) 472-6959

FREQUENCY: Quarterly

COVER PRICE: $5.00

SUBSCRIPTION PRICE: $16.00

TOTAL NUMBER OF PAGES: 54

TOTAL NUMBER OF AD PAGES: 7

EDITOR: Ali Kianfar

EDITORIAL CONCEPT: *Expores issues related to the Islamic religion of Sufism.*

Transformation

PUBLISHED BY: Transformation/Spartacus Publishing

13331 Garden Grove Blvd., #6

Garden Grove, CA 92643

TEL: (714) 971-9877   **FAX:** (714) 971-3206

FREQUENCY: Quarterly

COVER PRICE: $8.95

SUBSCRIPTION PRICE: $40.00

TOTAL NUMBER OF PAGES: 84

TOTAL NUMBER OF AD PAGES: 22

PUBLISHER: Jeri Lee

EDITOR: Jeri Lee

EDITORIAL CONCEPT: *A magazine for men who like to cross-dress.*

Unexplained Universe

PUBLISHED BY: GCR Publishing Group Inc.

1700 Broadway

New York, NY 10019

TEL: (212) 541-7100

FREQUENCY: Quarterly

COVER PRICE: $4.95

SUBSCRIPTION PRICE: n/a

TOTAL NUMBER OF PAGES: 68

TOTAL NUMBER OF AD PAGES: 7

PUBLISHER: Charles Goodman

EDITOR: Timothy Green Beckley

EDITORIAL CONCEPT: *Unexplained Universe presents new concepts that try to further explain the mysteries of the universe.*

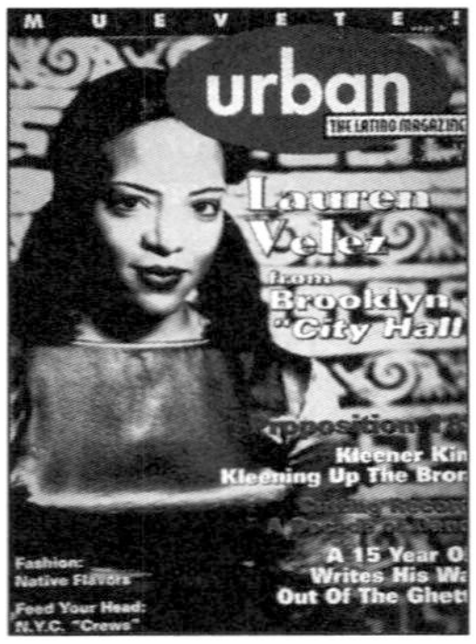

EDITORIAL CONCEPT: Urban *focuses on the Latino experience in New York.*

Urban: The Latino Magazine

PUBLISHED BY: Urban: The Latino Magazine Inc.

35-20 Leverich St., Suite C641

Jackson Heights, NY 11372

TEL: (212) 780-3316 **FAX:** (212) 335-0521

DATE: May/June

FREQUENCY: Bimonthly

COVER PRICE: $1.50

SUBSCRIPTION PRICE: n/a

TOTAL NUMBER OF PAGES: 32

TOTAL NUMBER OF AD PAGES: 7

EDITOR: Rodrigo Salazar

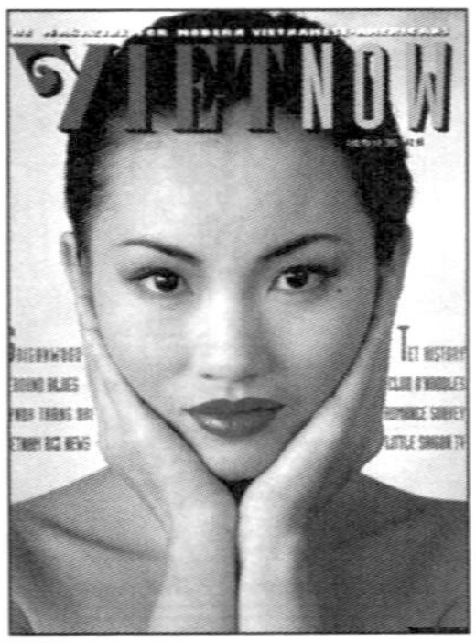

EDITORIAL CONCEPT: "Vietnow *explores the evolving presence of Vietnamese-Americans in the arts, commerce and society, as well as their balancing of American and Vietnamese values."*

Vietnow

PUBLISHED BY: Vietnow Publications

P.O. Box 4134

Westminster, CA 92684

TEL: (714) 841-0709

DATE: February/March

FREQUENCY: Bimonthly

COVER PRICE: $32.95

SUBSCRIPTION PRICE: n/a

TOTAL NUMBER OF PAGES: 60

TOTAL NUMBER OF AD PAGES: 7

EDITOR: Trung Pham

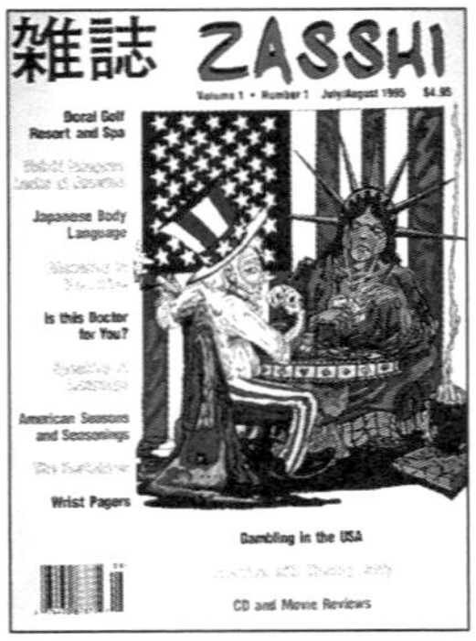

EDITORIAL CONCEPT: *A Japanese-American magazine dealing with arts and entertainment as well as social and political issues relevant to Japanese-Americans.*

Zasshi

PUBLISHED BY: Worthington Publishing

201 E. Main St., Suite 100

Murfreesboro, TN 37130

TEL: (615) 893-9788 **FAX:** (615) 893-9717

DATE: July/August

FREQUENCY: Bimonthly

COVER PRICE: $4.95

SUBSCRIPTION PRICE: $22.27

TOTAL NUMBER OF PAGES: 68

TOTAL NUMBER OF AD PAGES: 7

PUBLISHER: Steve Saunders, Carylee Caputo

EDITOR: Steve Saunders

ANNUAL, SPECIAL OR FREQUENCY UNKNOWN

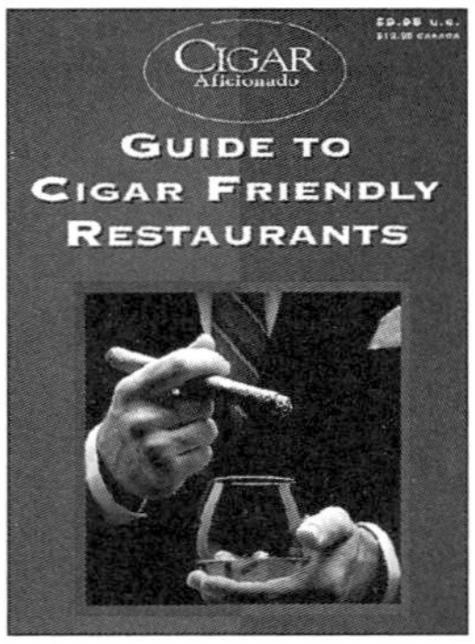

EDITORIAL CONCEPT: *A guide to cigar-friendly restaurants around the United States.*

Cigar Aficionado: Guide To Cigar Friendly Restaurants

PUBLISHED BY: M. Shanken Communications

387 Park Ave. S.

New York, NY 10016

TEL: (212) 684-4224 **FAX:** (212) 684-5424

FREQUENCY: Annually

COVER PRICE: $9.95

SUBSCRIPTION PRICE: n/a

TOTAL NUMBER OF PAGES: 244

TOTAL NUMBER OF AD PAGES: 25

PUBLISHER: Marvin R. Shanker

EDITOR: Marvin R. Shanker

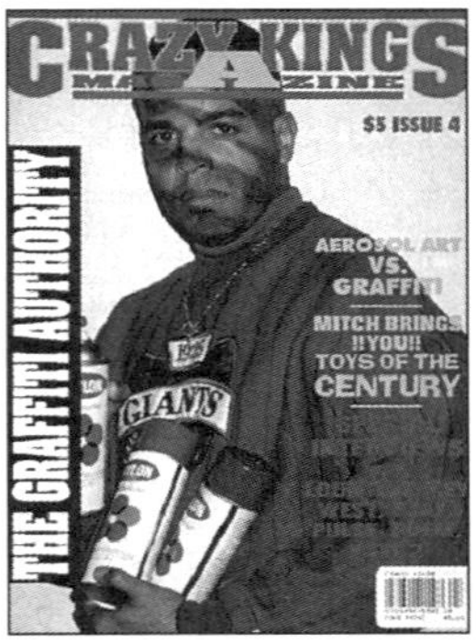

EDITORIAL CONCEPT: *"The first all-color graffiti magazine from the state of New Jersey."*

Crazy Kings Magazine

PUBLISHED BY: Crazy Kings Magazine

417 Straight St.

Paterson, NJ 07501

TEL: (201) 742-9064

FREQUENCY: n/a

COVER PRICE: $5.00

SUBSCRIPTION PRICE: n/a

TOTAL NUMBER OF PAGES: 36

TOTAL NUMBER OF AD PAGES: 4

PUBLISHER: Mitch Santiago

EDITOR: Mitch Santiago

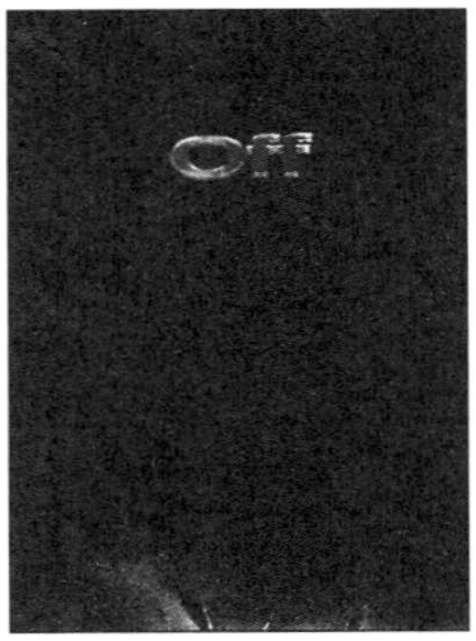

EDITORIAL CONCEPT: *"A magazine committed to affording consumers discriminating discounts on a variety of quality products and services."*

Off

PUBLISHED BY: Off Magazine

231 Viste del Mar, Suite B

Redondo Beach, CA 90277

TEL: (310) 792-1568 **FAX:** (310) 792-1567

DATE: April

FREQUENCY: n/a

COVER PRICE: n/a

SUBSCRIPTION PRICE: n/a

TOTAL NUMBER OF PAGES: 16

TOTAL NUMBER OF AD PAGES: 15

PUBLISHER: John Michel, Chris Hardwich

EDITOR: John Michel

Psychedelic Illuminations

PUBLISHED BY: Panther Press

1032 Irving, #514A

San Francisco, CA 94122

TEL: (415) 753-6481

FREQUENCY: n/a

COVER PRICE: $6.95

SUBSCRIPTION PRICE: $14.95

TOTAL NUMBER OF PAGES: 112

TOTAL NUMBER OF AD PAGES: 12

PUBLISHER: Ron Piper

EDITOR: James L. Kent

EDITORIAL CONCEPT: *A magazine for and about psychedelic drug use.*

American Cheerleader

PUBLISHED BY: Lifestyles Publications Inc.

3350 W. 50th St., Suite 2AA

New York, NY 10019

TEL: (212) 861-8108 **FAX:** (212) 988-0621

DATE: February

FREQUENCY: Bimonthly

COVER PRICE: $2.95

SUBSCRIPTION PRICE: $16.95

TOTAL NUMBER OF PAGES: 80

TOTAL NUMBER OF AD PAGES: 18

PUBLISHER: Michael Weiskopf

EDITOR: Julie Davis

EDITORIAL CONCEPT: *A magazine which focuses on different aspects of cheerleading, with articles on topics from looking good for competitions to celebrity cheerleaders.*

Box

PUBLISHED BY: Critical Mass Inc.

1223 Wilshire Blvd., #893

Santa Monica, CA 90403

TEL: (310) 451-8061

DATE: Fall

FREQUENCY: Quarterly

COVER PRICE: $2.95

SUBSCRIPTION PRICE: n/a

TOTAL NUMBER OF PAGES: 64

TOTAL NUMBER OF AD PAGES: 24

PUBLISHER: Chris Mitchell

EDITOR: Neil Feineman

EDITORIAL CONCEPT: *A magazine devoted to skateboarding and the skateboarder lifestyle.*

Back Country

PUBLISHED BY: Back Country Publishing

7065 Dover Way

Arvado, CO 80004

TEL: (303) 424-5858 **FAX:** (303) 424-4063

DATE: October

FREQUENCY: Quarterly

COVER PRICE: $3.50

SUBSCRIPTION PRICE: $9.95

TOTAL NUMBER OF PAGES: 64

TOTAL NUMBER OF AD PAGES: 14

PUBLISHER: David Harrower

EDITOR: John Dostal

EDITORIAL CONCEPT: *A magazine for back country skiers featuring a gear guide and strategies for steeps.*

Boxing Illustrated

PUBLISHED BY: Warner Publishing Services

530 Fifth Ave.

New York, NY 10036

TEL: (212) 730-1374

FREQUENCY: 10/year

COVER PRICE: $3.00

SUBSCRIPTION PRICE: $30.00

TOTAL NUMBER OF PAGES: 72

TOTAL NUMBER OF AD PAGES: 10

PUBLISHER: John G. Ledes

EDITOR: Herbert G. Goldman

EDITORIAL CONCEPT: *A magazine bringing you the latest in boxing news as well as the current rankings and decisions.*

Blunt

PUBLISHED BY: Dickhouse Publishing Group

815 N. Nash

El Segundo, CA 90245

TEL: (310) 640-3066

FREQUENCY: 5/year

COVER PRICE: $3.95

SUBSCRIPTION PRICE: $19.95

TOTAL NUMBER OF PAGES: 104

TOTAL NUMBER OF AD PAGES: 36

PUBLISHER: Steve Rocco

EDITOR: Marc McKee

EDITORIAL CONCEPT: *A high-gloss, photo-filled publication for snowboarders, featuring editorials, letters and interviews with snowboarding greats.*

Caged!

PUBLISHED BY: Titansports Inc.

P.O. Box 420174

Palm Coast, FL 32142-9814

TEL: n/a

DATE: Winter

FREQUENCY: Semiannually

COVER PRICE: $4.95

SUBSCRIPTION PRICE: n/a

TOTAL NUMBER OF PAGES: 36

TOTAL NUMBER OF AD PAGES: 5

EDITOR: Vince Russo

EDITORIAL CONCEPT: *World Wrestling Federation Magazine presents a semi-annual volume of body-slamming, action-packed, historically-themed wrestling information.*

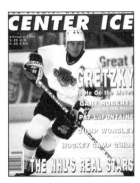

Center Ice

PUBLISHED BY: Center Ice Hockey

2719 Grant Ave., Suite 1

Redondo Beach, CA 90278

TEL: (310) 318-5444   **FAX:** (310) 318-0474

DATE: November

FREQUENCY: Monthly

COVER PRICE: $3.25

SUBSCRIPTION PRICE: $18.00

TOTAL NUMBER OF PAGES: 60

TOTAL NUMBER OF AD PAGES: n/a

EDITOR: n/a

EDITORIAL CONCEPT: *All the news you need to know about hockey's favorite teams.*

Golf Illustrated

PUBLISHED BY: NatCom Inc.

5300 CityPlex Tower

2448 E. 81st St.

Tulsa, OK 74137-4207

TEL: (918) 491-6100

DATE: June

FREQUENCY: Bimonthly

COVER PRICE: $2.95

SUBSCRIPTION PRICE: $13.95

TOTAL NUMBER OF PAGES: 100

TOTAL NUMBER OF AD PAGES: 28

PUBLISHER: Gerald W. Poper

EDITOR: Al Barkow

EDITORIAL CONCEPT: *A golf magazine with articles on choosing equipment and tips for improving your game.*

East Infection Snowboard Magazine

PUBLISHED BY: Green Design

P.O. Box 1395

Burlington, VT 05402-1395

TEL: n/a

FREQUENCY: Quarterly

COVER PRICE: $2.50

SUBSCRIPTION PRICE: $7.95

TOTAL NUMBER OF PAGES: 36

TOTAL NUMBER OF AD PAGES: 12

EDITOR: Mark Sullivan

EDITORIAL CONCEPT: *Snowboarding pictures — mostly from the eastern United States.*

GunGames

PUBLISHED BY: Wallyworld Publishing

P.O. Box 516

Moreno Valley, CA 92556

TEL: (909) 485-7986   **FAX:** (909) 485-6628

FREQUENCY: Bimonthly

COVER PRICE: $3.50

SUBSCRIPTION PRICE: $16.95

DISCOUNT SUBSCRIPTION PRICE: $44.95 (3 years)

TOTAL NUMBER OF PAGES: 90

TOTAL NUMBER OF AD PAGES: 22

PUBLISHER: Wally Arida

EDITOR: Wally Arida

EDITORIAL CONCEPT: *"America's handgun sports and recreation magazine."*

Fitness Swimmer

PUBLISHED BY: Rodale Press Inc.

33 E. Minor St.

Emmaus, PA 18098

TEL: (610) 967-5171

DATE: Summer

FREQUENCY: Quarterly

COVER PRICE: $2.95

SUBSCRIPTION PRICE: $19.94 (6 issues)

TOTAL NUMBER OF PAGES: 76

TOTAL NUMBER OF AD PAGES: 5.25

PUBLISHER: Heidi Rodale

EDITOR: Mary Bolster

EDITORIAL CONCEPT: *A magazine dedicated to fitness through swimming. Contains articles on exercises and proper diets.*

Knockouts

PUBLISHED BY: Umi Khandu Productions

8 W. 118th St., #5E

New York, NY 10029

TEL: n/a

DATE: July/August

FREQUENCY: Bimonthly

COVER PRICE: $2.95

SUBSCRIPTION PRICE: $15.00

TOTAL NUMBER OF PAGES: 52

TOTAL NUMBER OF AD PAGES: 5

PUBLISHER: Pamela Blue

EDITOR: Lynne Christensen

EDITORIAL CONCEPT: *"For the woman with the will to win." The first magazine for and about women in boxing.*

Martial Arts Ultimate Warriors

PUBLISHED BY: C.F.W. Enterprises Inc.

4201 Vanowen Pl.

Burbank, CA 91505

TEL: (818) 845-2656 **FAX:** (818) 845-7761

DATE: February

FREQUENCY: Monthly

COVER PRICE: $3.00

SUBSCRIPTION PRICE: n/a

TOTAL NUMBER OF PAGES: 80

TOTAL NUMBER OF AD PAGES: 28

PUBLISHER: Mark Komuro

EDITOR: Dave Carter

EDITORIAL CONCEPT:. *A martial arts magazine that focuses on the full-contact UFC tournaments.*

Paintball Player's Bible

PUBLISHED BY: American Paintball Media

15507 S. Normandie Ave., #487

Gardena, CA 90247

TEL: (310) 323-1021 **FAX:** (310) 323-7642

DATE: May/June

FREQUENCY: Bimonthly

COVER PRICE: $2.95

SUBSCRIPTION PRICE: $19.95 (2 years)

TOTAL NUMBER OF PAGES: 88

TOTAL NUMBER OF AD PAGES: 30

PUBLISHER: Mike Henry

EDITOR: Mike Henry

EDITORIAL CONCEPT: *"The player's complete guide to paintball guns, games and gear."*

Multisport

PUBLISHED BY: Multisport Media Inc.

475 Gate Five Rd., Suite 210-A

Sausalito, CA 94965

TEL: (415) 289-1710 **FAX:** (415) 331-0523

DATE: October/November

FREQUENCY: Bimonthly

COVER PRICE: $2.95

SUBSCRIPTION PRICE: $17.70

TOTAL NUMBER OF PAGES: 60

TOTAL NUMBER OF AD PAGES: 14

PUBLISHER: William R. Katovsky

EDITOR: William R. Katovsky

EDITORIAL CONCEPT: *"The magazine for endurance athletes," with tips on maintaining your body's top fitness.*

PowerPlay

PUBLISHED BY: Quarton Group Inc.

888 W. Big Beaver, Suite 600

Troy, MI 48084

TEL: (810) 362-7400

DATE: November/December

FREQUENCY: Quarterly

COVER PRICE: $2.95

SUBSCRIPTION PRICE: $9.95

TOTAL NUMBER OF PAGES: 76

TOTAL NUMBER OF AD PAGES: 20.3

PUBLISHER: James C. Small

EDITOR: Vince Aversano

EDITORIAL CONCEPT: *A rundown of the players and teams of the NHL, including articles and interviews.*

New Cyclist

PUBLISHED BY: Rodale Press Inc.

33 E. Minor St.

Emmaus, PA 18098

TEL: (610) 967-5171

DATE: Spring

FREQUENCY: 11/year

COVER PRICE: $3.95

SUBSCRIPTION PRICE: n/a

TOTAL NUMBER OF PAGES: 100

TOTAL NUMBER OF AD PAGES: 15

PUBLISHER: Mike Greehan

EDITOR: Ed Pavelka

EDITORIAL CONCEPT: *A bicycling magazine for beginning riders.*

Skier Magazine

PUBLISHED BY: All Weather Publishing Co.

P.O. Box 305

Stowe, VT 05672

TEL: (802) 253-8282 **FAX:** (802) 253-6236

DATE: Fall

FREQUENCY: Quarterly

COVER PRICE: $2.50

SUBSCRIPTION PRICE: $5.95

TOTAL NUMBER OF PAGES: 50

TOTAL NUMBER OF AD PAGES: 17.5

PUBLISHER: Paul Piccirillo

EDITOR: Kimberly Fredrick

EDITORIAL CONCEPT: *A publication for outdoor enthusiasts with articles on the best gear to buy and the best places to ski.*

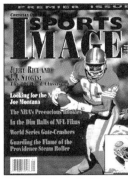

Sports Image

PUBLISHED BY: Sports Image

940 E. Alosta Ave.

Azusa, CA 91702

TEL: (818) 969-1339

DATE: November

FREQUENCY: Monthly

COVER PRICE: $2.95

SUBSCRIPTION PRICE: $8.95

TOTAL NUMBER OF PAGES: 54

TOTAL NUMBER OF AD PAGES: 6

PUBLISHER: Christian Okoye

EDITOR: Phil Barber

EDITORIAL CONCEPT: *A sports magazine with articles on sports stars from different fields of competition.*

The Surfwriter's Quarterly

PUBLISHED BY: Surfwriter's Quarterly

P.O. Box 700

Ventura, CA 93002

TEL: (805) 987-7286

DATE: Summer

FREQUENCY: Quarterly

COVER PRICE: $3.50

SUBSCRIPTION PRICE: $10.95

TOTAL NUMBER OF PAGES: 52

TOTAL NUMBER OF AD PAGES: 5.3

PUBLISHER: Phil Wikel

EDITOR: Phil Wikel

EDITORIAL CONCEPT: *A surfing magazine featuring great surf spots, a poetry contest and a women's forum.*

Sports Scene

PUBLISHED BY: One Look Publications

10340 Camino Santa Fe, Suite A

San Diego, CA 92121

TEL: n/a

FREQUENCY: Quarterly

COVER PRICE: $3.95

SUBSCRIPTION PRICE: $19.95

TOTAL NUMBER OF PAGES: 66

TOTAL NUMBER OF AD PAGES: 12

PUBLISHER: Gary R. Dubie

EDITOR: Gary R. Dubie

EDITORIAL CONCEPT: *The world's hottest sports magazine for men, formerly known as* Men's Sports Magazine.

Tandem Magazine

PUBLISHED BY: Petzold Publishing

26895 Petzold Rd.

Eugene, OR 97402

TEL: (503) 485-5262

DATE: Spring

FREQUENCY: Quarterly

COVER PRICE: $3.95

SUBSCRIPTION PRICE: $12.95

TOTAL NUMBER OF PAGES: 68

TOTAL NUMBER OF AD PAGES: 13

PUBLISHER: Marlen Shepherd

EDITOR: Greg Shepherd

EDITORIAL CONCEPT: *A magazine for tandem bicycle enthusiasts.*

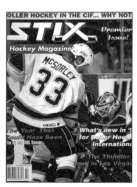

Stix

PUBLISHED BY: Stix Magazine

P.O. Box 90455

Industry, CA 91715

TEL: (800) 784-9624

DATE: June/July

FREQUENCY: Bimonthly

COVER PRICE: $3.50

SUBSCRIPTION PRICE: $15.95

TOTAL NUMBER OF PAGES: 48

TOTAL NUMBER OF AD PAGES: 10

PUBLISHER: Alex E. Bergidis, Nicholas L. Bergiadis

EDITOR: John P. Geanakos

EDITORIAL CONCEPT: *A magazine that covers both roller hockey and ice hockey. Includes articles on players, coaches and teams.*

3-D Times

PUBLISHED BY: Hickory Hills Publishing Co.

702 E. Archer Ave.

Monmouth, IL 61462

TEL: (702) 323-6828

DATE: February/March

FREQUENCY: Bimonthly

COVER PRICE: $2.95

SUBSCRIPTION PRICE: $14.95

TOTAL NUMBER OF PAGES: 68

TOTAL NUMBER OF AD PAGES: 18

PUBLISHER: Royce Armstrong

EDITOR: Royce Armstrong

EDITORIAL CONCEPT: *The official publication of the Association of Professional Archers features "the most complete shoot schedule anywhere."*

Wahine

PUBLISHED BY: Wahine Magazine

5520 E. 2nd St., Suite K

Long Beach, CA 90803

TEL: (310) 434-9444 **FAX:** (310) 434-9444

FREQUENCY: Quarterly

COVER PRICE: $2.95

SUBSCRIPTION PRICE: $11.50

TOTAL NUMBER OF PAGES: 34

TOTAL NUMBER OF AD PAGES: 5

PUBLISHER: Marilyn J. Edwards

EDITOR: Elizabeth A. Glazner

EDITORIAL CONCEPT: *A surfing magazine for women with articles on the different personalities in the sport.*

Above The Rim

PUBLISHED BY: College Sports Communications

4099 Mcewen Dr., #350

Dallas, TX 75244

TEL: (214) 742-2000 **FAX:** (214) 490-9333

FREQUENCY: Special

COVER PRICE: $4.99

SUBSCRIPTION PRICE: n/a

TOTAL NUMBER OF PAGES: 100

TOTAL NUMBER OF AD PAGES: 18

PUBLISHER: Robert Bennett

EDITOR: Chris Greer

EDITORIAL CONCEPT: *A look at the up-and-coming players in the NBA, including their stats and career history.*

Wave Rider

PUBLISHED BY: L.F.P. Inc.

8484 Wilshire Blvd., Suite 900

Beverly Hills, CA 90211

TEL: (916) 244-1063

DATE: July

FREQUENCY: Bimonthly

COVER PRICE: $3.50

SUBSCRIPTION PRICE: $9.95

TOTAL NUMBER OF PAGES: 80

TOTAL NUMBER OF AD PAGES: 19.25

PUBLISHER: Larry Flynt

EDITOR: Chris Davidson

EDITORIAL CONCEPT: *A magazine focusing on personal watercraft like the Sea Doo. Offers tips on riding as well as new products and equipment.*

Bicycle Repair Illustrated

PUBLISHED BY: Rodale Press

33 E. Minor St.

Emmaus, PA 18098

TEL: (610) 967-5171 **FAX:** (610) 967-8963

FREQUENCY: Special

COVER PRICE: $3.95

SUBSCRIPTION PRICE: n/a

TOTAL NUMBER OF PAGES: 100

TOTAL NUMBER OF AD PAGES: 20

PUBLISHER: Mike Greehan

EDITOR: Geoff Drake

EDITORIAL CONCEPT: *"A collection of basic, intermediate and advanced procedures designed for people who want to care for their bikes, not just ride them."*

Women Of Action Sports Magazine

PUBLISHED BY: Phillips Publishing Group

6524 San Felipe, Suite 354

Houston, TX 77057

TEL: n/a

FREQUENCY: 10/year

COVER PRICE: $3.50

SUBSCRIPTION PRICE: $35.00

TOTAL NUMBER OF PAGES: 68

TOTAL NUMBER OF AD PAGES: 26.5

PUBLISHER: Gwendolyn Phillips

EDITOR: Dr. R. Scott Yarnish

EDITORIAL CONCEPT: *"Women of Action Sports Magazine is about women who take life as it comes and make it work on their terms." Features articles on women who have successfully managed their lives.*

Blitz

PUBLISHED BY: Harris Publications Inc.

1115 Broadway

New York, NY 10010

TEL: n/a

FREQUENCY: Annually

COVER PRICE: $4.95

SUBSCRIPTION PRICE: n/a

TOTAL NUMBER OF PAGES: 132

TOTAL NUMBER OF AD PAGES: 30

PUBLISHER: Dennis S. Page

EDITOR: Tony Gervino

EDITORIAL CONCEPT: *Blitz takes you into the locker rooms and away from the stadiums with coverage of professional, college and high school football.*

BMX Special '95 Buyer's Guide

PUBLISHED BY: Challenge Publications Inc.

7950 Deering Ave.

Canoga Park, CA 91304

TEL: (818) 887-0550   **FAX:** (818) 883-3019

FREQUENCY: Special

COVER PRICE: $3.95

SUBSCRIPTION PRICE: n/a

TOTAL NUMBER OF PAGES: 96

TOTAL NUMBER OF AD PAGES: 28

PUBLISHER: Edwin A. Schnepf

EDITOR: Brian Hemsworth

EDITORIAL CONCEPT: *A guide to BMX freestyle and mountain bikes, including articles on the best equipment to use and tips from the pros.*

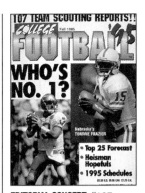

College Football '95

PUBLISHED BY: London Publishing Co.

7002 W. Butler Pike

Ambler, PA 19002

TEL: (215) 643-6385

FREQUENCY: Annually

COVER PRICE: $2.95

SUBSCRIPTION PRICE: n/a

TOTAL NUMBER OF PAGES: 132

TOTAL NUMBER OF AD PAGES: 2

PUBLISHER: Stuart M. Saks

EDITOR: Roger Mooney

EDITORIAL CONCEPT: *"107 team scouting reports."*

Body Building News

PUBLISHED BY: Body Building News Inc.

1596 Carey Pl.

Fredrick, MD 21701

TEL: n/a

DATE: January

FREQUENCY: Special

COVER PRICE: $2.50

SUBSCRIPTION PRICE: n/a

TOTAL NUMBER OF PAGES: 32

TOTAL NUMBER OF AD PAGES: 6

EDITOR: Carol Ann Marshall

EDITORIAL CONCEPT: *Body Building News includes contest coverage packed with color photos, the latest gossip and industry information and interviews with top athletes.*

Dr. J's Pro Basketball Yearbook '95

PUBLISHED BY: C.S. Communications L.P.

Rt. 22 E. , 1 Salem Sq.

Whitehouse Station, NJ 08889

TEL: (908) 534-5390   **FAX:** (908) 534-5308

FREQUENCY: Annually

COVER PRICE: $4.95

SUBSCRIPTION PRICE: n/a

TOTAL NUMBER OF PAGES: 164

TOTAL NUMBER OF AD PAGES: 16

PUBLISHER: Paul Abramson

EDITOR: Norb Garrett

EDITORIAL CONCEPT: *Dr. J gives the reader a prognosis and the inside scoop on the NBA.*

College Basketball Madness

PUBLISHED BY: College Sports Communications

4099 Mcewen Dr., Suite 350

Dallas, TX 75244

TEL: (214) 851-1770   **FAX:** (214) 490-9333

FREQUENCY: Annually

COVER PRICE: $4.95

SUBSCRIPTION PRICE: n/a

TOTAL NUMBER OF PAGES: 104

TOTAL NUMBER OF AD PAGES: 23

PUBLISHER: Robert Bennett

EDITOR: Chris Greer

EDITORIAL CONCEPT: *College Basketball Madness brings you the teams and players on the NCAA Road to the Final Four. Includes team stats and articles .*

Easy Golf

PUBLISHED BY: Werner Publishing Corp.

12121 Wilshire Blvd., Suite 1220

Los Angeles, CA 90025-1175

TEL: (310) 820-1500

FREQUENCY: Special

COVER PRICE: $3.95

SUBSCRIPTION PRICE: n/a

TOTAL NUMBER OF PAGES: 100

TOTAL NUMBER OF AD PAGES: 3

PUBLISHER: Steven D. Werner

EDITOR: Steven D. Werner

EDITORIAL CONCEPT: *Designed to teach you how to play better golf, with tips on improving your swing and setting up your shots.*

ESPN College Basketball '95

PUBLISHED BY: The Hearst Corp.

959 Eighth Ave.

New York, NY 10019

TEL: (212) 649-2208   **FAX:** (212) 247-1804

FREQUENCY: Special

COVER PRICE: $4.95

SUBSCRIPTION PRICE: n/a

TOTAL NUMBER OF PAGES: 156

TOTAL NUMBER OF AD PAGES: 26

PUBLISHER: John Mack Carter

EDITOR: Gary Hoenig

EDITORIAL CONCEPT: *Packed with info on the 64 best teams, the 15 top players, 29 conference picks, 50 prep stars and the publisher's #1 pick .*

ESPN The Year In Sports

PUBLISHED BY: The Hearst Corp.

959 Eighth Ave.

New York, NY 10019

TEL: (212) 649-2208   **FAX:** (212) 247-1804

FREQUENCY: Special

COVER PRICE: $4.95

SUBSCRIPTION PRICE: n/a

TOTAL NUMBER OF PAGES: 156

TOTAL NUMBER OF AD PAGES: 22

PUBLISHER: John Mack Carter

EDITOR: Gary Hoenig

EDITORIAL CONCEPT: *Highlights of the most dramatic moments in sports during 1995.*

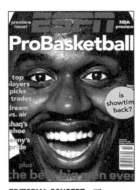

ESPN ProBasketball '95

PUBLISHED BY: The Hearst Corp.

959 Eighth Ave.

New York, NY 10019

TEL: (212) 649-3135   **FAX:** (212) 247-1804

FREQUENCY: Special

COVER PRICE: $4.95

SUBSCRIPTION PRICE: n/a

TOTAL NUMBER OF PAGES: 156

TOTAL NUMBER OF AD PAGES: 21

PUBLISHER: John Mack Carter

EDITOR: Gary Hoenig

EDITORIAL CONCEPT: *The complete resource for those seeking the inside line on NBA basketball, with previews and scouting reports.*

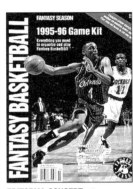

Fantasy Basketball

PUBLISHED BY: Fantasy Season

P.O. Box 29288

Columbus, OH 43229

TEL: (614) 899-2632

DATE: Fall

FREQUENCY: Annually

COVER PRICE: $5.95

SUBSCRIPTION PRICE: n/a

TOTAL NUMBER OF PAGES: 28

TOTAL NUMBER OF AD PAGES: 0

EDITOR: n/a

EDITORIAL CONCEPT: *Everything you need to know about organizing and playing fantasy basketball, with rules and stats on players.*

ESPN ProFootball '95

PUBLISHED BY: The Hearst Corp.

959 Eighth Ave.

New York, NY 10019

TEL: (212) 649-3135   **FAX:** (212) 247-1804

FREQUENCY: Special

COVER PRICE: $4.95

SUBSCRIPTION PRICE: n/a

TOTAL NUMBER OF PAGES: 164

TOTAL NUMBER OF AD PAGES: 26

PUBLISHER: John Mack Carter

EDITOR: Gary Hoenig

EDITORIAL CONCEPT: *The complete resource for those seeking the inside line on NFL football, with previews and scouting reports.*

Fantasy Football

PUBLISHED BY: Fantasy Season

P.O. Box 29288

Columbus, OH 43229

TEL: (614) 899-2632

DATE: Fall

FREQUENCY: Annually

COVER PRICE: $5.95

SUBSCRIPTION PRICE: n/a

TOTAL NUMBER OF PAGES: 28

TOTAL NUMBER OF AD PAGES: 5

EDITOR: n/a

EDITORIAL CONCEPT: *Everything you need to know about organizing and playing fantasy football, with rules and stats on players.*

Greg LeMond: The Official Story

PUBLISHED BY: Inside Communications

1830 N. 55th St.

Boulder, CO 80301

TEL: (303) 440-0601 **FAX:** (303) 444-6788

DATE: Spring

FREQUENCY: Special

COVER PRICE: $5.00

SUBSCRIPTION PRICE: n/a

TOTAL NUMBER OF PAGES: 84

TOTAL NUMBER OF AD PAGES: 10

PUBLISHER: Nancy Grimes

EDITOR: John Wilcockson

EDITORIAL CONCEPT: *Photographs and articles about one of the best cyclists in the world.*

How To Surf Your Best

PUBLISHED BY: Western Empire Publications

950 Calle Amanecer, Suite C

San Clemente, CA 92673

TEL: (714) 492-7873 **FAX:** (714) 498-6485

FREQUENCY: Special

COVER PRICE: $4.95

SUBSCRIPTION PRICE: n/a

TOTAL NUMBER OF PAGES: 83

TOTAL NUMBER OF AD PAGES: 21

PUBLISHER: Bob Mignogna

EDITOR: Nick Carroll

EDITORIAL CONCEPT: *"Every surfer's ultimate high-performance guide" focuses on great techniques for surfing your best.*

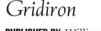

Gridiron

PUBLISHED BY: William Byrd Press

2901 Byrdhill Rd.

Richmond, VA 23228

TEL: (804) 264-2711

DATE: Fall

FREQUENCY: Special

COVER PRICE: $3.95

SUBSCRIPTION PRICE: n/a

TOTAL NUMBER OF PAGES: 100

TOTAL NUMBER OF AD PAGES: 21

PUBLISHER: James D. Causey

EDITOR: Larry Canale

EDITORIAL CONCEPT: *"Your complete guide to football collectibles," with a full-color price guide.*

In-line Skater 1995 Buyer's Guide

PUBLISHED BY: College Sports Communications

4099 Mcewen Dr., Suite 350

Dallas, TX 75244

TEL: (214) 851-1770 **FAX:** (214) 490-9333

FREQUENCY: Special

COVER PRICE: $2.95

SUBSCRIPTION PRICE: n/a

TOTAL NUMBER OF PAGES: 78

TOTAL NUMBER OF AD PAGES: 18

PUBLISHER: Robert Bennett

EDITOR: Paula Caballero

EDITORIAL CONCEPT: *A buyer's guide to over 140 new in-line skates, also featuring articles on better skating.*

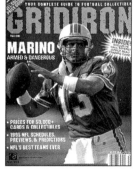

Hockey Greats

PUBLISHED BY: London Publishing Co.

7002 W. Butler Pike

Ambler, PA 19002

TEL: (215) 643-6385 **FAX:** (215) 628-3571

FREQUENCY: Special

COVER PRICE: $3.95

SUBSCRIPTION PRICE: n/a

TOTAL NUMBER OF PAGES: 76

TOTAL NUMBER OF AD PAGES: 4

PUBLISHER: Stuart M. Saks

EDITOR: Dave Rosenbaum

EDITORIAL CONCEPT: *A rating of hockey's greatest players to determine who should be the most eligible for the Hall of Fame.*

Inside College Basketball

PUBLISHED BY: London Publishing Co.

7002 W. Butler Pike

Ambler, PA 19002

TEL: (215) 643-6385

FREQUENCY: Annually

COVER PRICE: $2.95

SUBSCRIPTION PRICE: n/a

TOTAL NUMBER OF PAGES: 132

TOTAL NUMBER OF AD PAGES: 0

PUBLISHER: Stuart M. Saks

EDITOR: Vincent Paterno

EDITORIAL CONCEPT: *A rundown of all 305 VCAA Division 1 college basketball teams, with stats and team profiles.*

Inside Line: Special Red Wings Playoff Issue

PUBLISHED BY: Detroit Red Wings Inc.

600 Civic Center Dr.

Joe Louis Arena

Detroit, MI 48226

TEL: (313) 396-7600

FREQUENCY: Special

COVER PRICE: $3.00

SUBSCRIPTION PRICE: n/a

TOTAL NUMBER OF PAGES: 52

TOTAL NUMBER OF AD PAGES: 26

PUBLISHER: Jeanne Tower

EDITOR: Ruth Benedict

EDITORIAL CONCEPT: *The goal of "the official publication of the Detroit Red Wings" is to give fans the latest news and profiles on the team.*

Ironman: The Road To Kona

PUBLISHED BY: Inside Communications

1830 N. 55th St.

Boulder, CO 80301

TEL: (303) 440-0601   **FAX:** (303) 444-6788

FREQUENCY: Special

COVER PRICE: $3.95

SUBSCRIPTION PRICE: n/a

TOTAL NUMBER OF PAGES: 64

TOTAL NUMBER OF AD PAGES: 28

PUBLISHER: Felix Magowan

EDITOR: Chris Newbound

EDITORIAL CONCEPT: *A supplement to Inside Triathlon magazine's May issue, featuring descriptions of all 22 qualifying athletes.*

Jam 1995

PUBLISHED BY: William Byrd Press

2901 Byrdhill Rd.

Richmond, VA 23228

TEL: (804) 264-2711

FAX: (804) 264-4290

FREQUENCY: Special

COVER PRICE: $3.95

SUBSCRIPTION PRICE: n/a

TOTAL NUMBER OF PAGES: 100

TOTAL NUMBER OF AD PAGES: 21.5

PUBLISHER: Frank Finn

EDITOR: Larry Canale

EDITORIAL CONCEPT: *The complete guide to basketball collectibles, including a full-color price guide.*

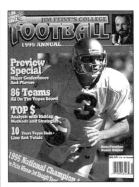

Jim Feist's College Football Magazine

PUBLISHED BY: National Sports Services

3110 Polaris, Suite 24

Las Vegas, NV 89102

TEL: (702) 873-3677

FREQUENCY: Annually

COVER PRICE: $4.95

SUBSCRIPTION PRICE: n/a

TOTAL NUMBER OF PAGES: 290

TOTAL NUMBER OF AD PAGES: 43

PUBLISHER: Jim Feist

EDITOR: Nils Holt

EDITORIAL CONCEPT: *A sports information guide, with picks and predictions for the 1995 college football season.*

Jim Feist's Pro Football 1995 Annual

PUBLISHED BY: National Sports Services

3110 Polaris, Suite 24

Las Vegas, NV 89102

TEL: (702) 873-3677

FREQUENCY: Annually

COVER PRICE: $4.95

SUBSCRIPTION PRICE: n/a

TOTAL NUMBER OF PAGES: 290

TOTAL NUMBER OF AD PAGES: 43

PUBLISHER: Jim Feist

EDITOR: Nils Holt

EDITORIAL CONCEPT: *A sports information , guide with picks and predictions for 1995 pro football season.*

Jiu-Jitsu

PUBLISHED BY: C.F.W. Enterprises Inc.

4201 Vanowen Pl.

Burbank, CA 91505

TEL: (818) 845-2656   **FAX:** (818) 845-7761

DATE: October

FREQUENCY: Special

COVER PRICE: $4.95

SUBSCRIPTION PRICE: n/a

TOTAL NUMBER OF PAGES: 110

TOTAL NUMBER OF AD PAGES: 20

EDITOR: n/a

EDITORIAL CONCEPT: *Martial Arts Legends brings you a total guide to grappling arts, with articles on form and execution.*

Las Vegas Handicapper Jeff Allen's College & NBA Basketball Preview And Betting Guide

PUBLISHED BY: Allen Communications

5025 S. Eastern, #19

Las Vegas, NV 89119

TEL: n/a

FREQUENCY: Annually

COVER PRICE: $6.95

TOTAL NUMBER OF PAGES: 132

TOTAL NUMBER OF AD PAGES: 43

PUBLISHER: Jeff Allen

EDITOR: Jeff Allen

EDITORIAL CONCEPT: "Complete analysis of 151 college teams and all 29 NBA teams."

Mountain Biking How-To's

PUBLISHED BY: Challenge Publications Inc.

7950 Deering Ave.

Canoga Park, CA 91304

TEL: (818) 887-0550 **FAX:** (818) 884-1343

FREQUENCY: Special

COVER PRICE: $4.95

SUBSCRIPTION PRICE n/a

TOTAL NUMBER OF PAGES: 80

TOTAL NUMBER OF AD PAGES: 7

PUBLISHER: Edwin A. Schnepf

EDITOR: Mark Langton

EDITORIAL CONCEPT: Includes shop tricks, trail-side tips, set-up secrets, advice from the pros and more.

Mountain Biking's Racing Special

PUBLISHED BY: Challenge Publications Inc.

7950 Deering Ave.

Canoga Park, CA 91304

TEL: (818) 887-0550 **FAX:** (818) 883-3019

FREQUENCY: Special

COVER PRICE: $3.95

SUBSCRIPTION PRICE: n/a

TOTAL NUMBER OF PAGES: 88

TOTAL NUMBER OF AD PAGES: 26.3

PUBLISHER: Edwin A. Schnepf

EDITOR: Brian Hemsworth

EDITORIAL CONCEPT: This special edition of Mountain Biking is devoted to racers and racing events. It includes racer profiles and technical information.

The 1955 Brooklyn Dodgers

PUBLISHED BY: The New York Daily News

450 W. 33rd St.

New York, NY 10001-2681

TEL: (212) 210-2100

FREQUENCY: Special

COVER PRICE: $4.95

SUBSCRIPTION PRICE: n/a

TOTAL NUMBER OF PAGES: 196

TOTAL NUMBER OF AD PAGES: 7

PUBLISHER: Mortimer B. Zuckerman, Fred Drasner

EDITOR: Kevin Whitmer

EDITORIAL CONCEPT: "A 40th anniversary collector's edition," with articles on the great players from the past and the history of the New York team.

1995 AVP Yearbook & Tour Guide

PUBLISHED BY: Faircount International Inc.

3816 W. Linebaugh Ave., Suite 401

Tampa, FL 33624

TEL: (813) 961-0006 **FAX:** (813) 264-4237

FREQUENCY: Special

COVER PRICE: $4.95

SUBSCRIPTION PRICE: n/a

TOTAL NUMBER OF PAGES: 132

TOTAL NUMBER OF AD PAGES: 30

PUBLISHER: Ross W. Johnson

EDITOR: Robert L. Yehling Jr.

EDITORIAL CONCEPT: The Association of Volleyball Professionals strives to provide to on-site fans and television audiences the best that professional beach volleyball has to offer.

1995 Coca-Cola ASP World Tour Guide

PUBLISHED BY: Faircount International Inc.

3816 W. Linebaugh Ave., Suite 401

Tampa, FL 33624

TEL: (813) 961-0006 **FAX:** (813) 264-4237

FREQUENCY: Special

COVER PRICE: $4.95

SUBSCRIPTION PRICE: n/a

TOTAL NUMBER OF PAGES: 148

TOTAL NUMBER OF AD PAGES: 22

PUBLISHER: Ross W. Jobson, Peter M. Antell

EDITOR: Robert L. Yehling Jr.

EDITORIAL CONCEPT: The official publication of the Association of Surfing Professionals.

Phenoms

PUBLISHED BY: College Sports
Communications

4099 Mcewen Dr., Suite 350

Dallas, TX 75244

TEL: (214) 742-2000 **FAX:** (214) 490-9333

FREQUENCY: Special

COVER PRICE: $4.99

SUBSCRIPTION PRICE: n/a

TOTAL NUMBER OF PAGES: 104

TOTAL NUMBER OF AD PAGES: 20

PUBLISHER: Robert Bennett

EDITOR: Chris Greer

EDITORIAL CONCEPT: *A look at the players, coaches and teams in the 1995 college football season.*

Pull Your Own Weight

PUBLISHED BY: Chelo Publishing Inc.

350 Fifth Ave., Suite 3323

New York, NY 10118

TEL: (212) 947-4322 **FAX:** (212) 563-4774

FREQUENCY: Special

COVER PRICE: $4.95

SUBSCRIPTION PRICE: n/a

TOTAL NUMBER OF PAGES: 164

TOTAL NUMBER OF AD PAGES: 16

PUBLISHER: Cheh Low

EDITOR: Steve Downs

EDITORIAL CONCEPT: *"A new workout philosphy that guarantees results." Features articles on proper techniques for a great workout.*

Phil Steele's 1995 College Football Preview

PUBLISHED BY: North Coast Sports

P.O. Box 35126

Cleveland, OH 44135

TEL: (800) 654-3448

FREQUENCY: Annually

COVER PRICE: $6.95

SUBSCRIPTION PRICE: n/a

TOTAL NUMBER OF PAGES: 196

TOTAL NUMBER OF AD PAGES: 6

PUBLISHER: Phil Steele

EDITOR: Phil Steele

EDITORIAL CONCEPT: *Phil Steele puts together a 196-page magazine filled with stats and predictions for the 1995 college football season.*

Sports Illustrated Presents College Football

PUBLISHED BY: Time Inc.

8 Bond St.

Great Neck, NY 11021-2471

TEL: (516) 243-6751

FREQUENCY: Annually

COVER PRICE: $4.95

SUBSCRIPTION PRICE: n/a

TOTAL NUMBER OF PAGES: 186

TOTAL NUMBER OF AD PAGES: 26

PUBLISHER: David L. Long

EDITOR: David Bauer

EDITORIAL CONCEPT: *College football articles and pictures.*

Power Golf

PUBLISHED BY: Werner Publishing Corp.

12121 Wilshire Blvd., Suite 1220

Los Angeles, CA 90025-1175

TEL: (310) 820-1500

FREQUENCY: Annually

COVER PRICE: $3.99

SUBSCRIPTION PRICE: n/a

TOTAL NUMBER OF PAGES: 100

TOTAL NUMBER OF AD PAGES: 3

PUBLISHER: Steven D. Werner

EDITOR: Steven D. Werner

EDITORIAL CONCEPT: *Your complete guide to a better golf game, with tips from the professionals that unlock their secrets.*

Sports Illustrated Presents NFL '95

PUBLISHED BY: Time Inc.

8 Bond St.

Great Neck, NY 11021-2471

TEL: (516) 243-6751

DATE: Summer

FREQUENCY: Annually

COVER PRICE: $4.95

SUBSCRIPTION PRICE: n/a

TOTAL NUMBER OF PAGES: 196

TOTAL NUMBER OF AD PAGES: 30

PUBLISHER: David L. Long

EDITOR: David Bauer

EDITORIAL CONCEPT: *A rundown on all of the NFL teams for the coming season, filled with stats on the teams and interviews with the players.*

Sports Illustrated Presents Pro Basketball '95 - '96

PUBLISHED BY: Time Inc.

8 Bond St.

Great Neck, NY 11021-2471

TEL: (516) 243-6751

FREQUENCY: Special

COVER PRICE: $4.95

SUBSCRIPTION PRICE: n/a

TOTAL NUMBER OF PAGES: 196

TOTAL NUMBER OF AD PAGES: 20

PUBLISHER: David L. Long

EDITOR: David Bauer

EDITORIAL CONCEPT: *"A special magazine brought to you by SI, with all the stats, moves and news you need to know for the upcoming basketball season."*

Sports Mirror Football

PUBLISHED BY: Sports Mirror Publications

6 W. 18th St.

New York, NY 10011

TEL: (212) 242-4902

FAX: (212) 242-5734

DATE: April

FREQUENCY: Special

COVER PRICE: $4.95

SUBSCRIPTION PRICE: n/a

TOTAL NUMBER OF PAGES: 100

TOTAL NUMBER OF AD PAGES: 0

PUBLISHER: Gerald Rothberg

EDITOR: Gerald Rothberg

EDITORIAL CONCEPT: *A run-down of the players and teams on the road to the Super Bowl.*

Superfit Cyclist

PUBLISHED BY: Rodale Press Inc.

33 E. Minor St.

Emmaus, PA 18098

TEL: (610) 967-5171

FREQUENCY: Special

COVER PRICE: $3.95

SUBSCRIPTION PRICE: n/a

TOTAL NUMBER OF PAGES: 100

TOTAL NUMBER OF AD PAGES: 17.5

PUBLISHER: Mike Greehan

EDITOR: Ed Pavelka

EDITORIAL CONCEPT: *This magazine is for every rider who wants to know how to excel. It includes articles on programs to increase your endurance and to become a better rider.*

The 31st Ryder Cup Matches

PUBLISHED BY: NYT Special Services

ADDRESS: n/a

TEL: n/a

FREQUENCY: Special

COVER PRICE: $6.00

SUBSCRIPTION PRICE: n/a

TOTAL NUMBER OF PAGES: 198

TOTAL NUMBER OF AD PAGES: 82

EDITOR: Robert J. LaMarche

EDITORIAL CONCEPT: *A look at the players, the course and the history of the Ryder Cup.*

The View

PUBLISHED BY: BSD Publishing Group Inc.

8306 Mills Dr., Suite 638

Miami, FL 33183

TEL: (305) 233-9523

FREQUENCY: Special

COVER PRICE: $5.95

SUBSCRIPTION PRICE: n/a

TOTAL NUMBER OF PAGES: 140

TOTAL NUMBER OF AD PAGES: 13

PUBLISHER: Joseph Hart

EDITOR: Michael Graff

EDITORIAL CONCEPT: *A magazine "for the hard-core fantasy football coach" with stats on players and overviews of strategies.*

All About You

PUBLISHED BY: Petersen Publishing Co.

6420 Wilshire Blvd.

Los Angeles, CA 90048-5515

TEL: (213) 649-0660

DATE: September

FREQUENCY: Bimonthly

COVER PRICE: $2.95

SUBSCRIPTION PRICE: $15.97

TOTAL NUMBER OF PAGES: 100

TOTAL NUMBER OF AD PAGES: 12

PUBLISHER: Jay N. Cole

EDITOR: Roxanne Camron

EDITORIAL CONCEPT: *The editors of* Teen *magazine present "contests, guys, fashion, advice and answers."*

react

PUBLISHED BY: Advance Magazine

Publications Inc.

711 Third Ave.

New York, NY 10017

TEL: (212) 450-7000   **FAX:** (212) 450-0975

FREQUENCY: Weekly

COVER PRICE: Free

SUBSCRIPTION PRICE: n/a

TOTAL NUMBER OF PAGES: 16

TOTAL NUMBER OF AD PAGES: 7

PUBLISHER: Carlo Vittorini

EDITOR: Lee Kravitz

EDITORIAL CONCEPT: *"The interactive news magazine for America's youth" offers young people a place to have their say. Included as a Sunday supplement in newpapers throughout the country.*

Grassroots Youth Magazine

PUBLISHED BY: Partners for the Planet

136 Main St., Suite A

El Segundo, CA 90245

TEL: (310) 322-0263   **FAX:** (310) 322-4482

FREQUENCY: Bimonthly

COVER PRICE: $3.95

SUBSCRIPTION PRICE: $16.00

TOTAL NUMBER OF PAGES: 16

TOTAL NUMBER OF AD PAGES: 2

PUBLISHER: Rick McLean

EDITOR: Wendy Rennison

EDITORIAL CONCEPT: *An insert in* Grassroots *magazine, written by and for youths. Covers a wide variety of environmental issues and what young people are doing about them.*

Real

PUBLISHED BY: Elbert/Alan Publishing Co.

4747 Troost Ave.

Kansas City, MO 64110

TEL: (816) 931-8336

DATE: Winter

FREQUENCY: Bimonthly

COVER PRICE: $2.95

SUBSCRIPTION PRICE: n/a

TOTAL NUMBER OF PAGES: 66

TOTAL NUMBER OF AD PAGES: 12

PUBLISHER: Alan Harris

EDITOR: Susan Campbell

EDITORIAL CONCEPT: *The magazine for growing teen minds.*

Affordable Travel

PUBLISHED BY: Aster Publishing Corp.

845 Williamette St.

Eugene, OR 97401

TEL: (503) 345-3800

DATE: July/August

FREQUENCY: 9/year

COVER PRICE: $3.95

SUBSCRIPTION PRICE: n/a

TOTAL NUMBER OF PAGES: 100

TOTAL NUMBER OF AD PAGES: 13

PUBLISHER: Edward Aster

EDITOR: Sarah T. Evans

EDITORIAL CONCEPT: *"The magazine for value-conscious travelers" offers articles about tour packages, cruise tips and traveling with teens.*

Costa Rica Adventure & Business

PUBLISHED BY: Publications & Communications

12416 Hymeadow Dr.

Austin, TX 78750

TEL: (512) 250-9023

DATE: June

FREQUENCY: Bimonthly

COVER PRICE: $3.95

SUBSCRIPTION PRICE: $19.95

TOTAL NUMBER OF PAGES: 48

TOTAL NUMBER OF AD PAGES: 10

PUBLISHER: Gary L. Pittman

EDITOR: Larry Storer

EDITORIAL CONCEPT: *The magazine about Costa Rican tourism.*

Baja Life

PUBLISHED BY: Baja Communications Group

23172 Alcade Dr., Suite 13

Lagima Hills, CA 92653

TEL: (714) 470-9086

FREQUENCY: Quarterly

COVER PRICE: $4.95

SUBSCRIPTION PRICE: $18.95

TOTAL NUMBER OF PAGES: 84

TOTAL NUMBER OF AD PAGES: 21

EDITOR: Robin Cox

EDITORIAL CONCEPT: *"The magazine of Mexico's magnificent peninsula."*

GuestWest

PUBLISHED BY: Dynacom

2180 Jefferson St.

Napa, CA 94558

TEL: (707) 255-7545   **FAX:** (707) 255-7589

DATE: October

FREQUENCY: Monthly

COVER PRICE: $2.95

SUBSCRIPTION PRICE: n/a

TOTAL NUMBER OF PAGES: 64

TOTAL NUMBER OF AD PAGES: 28

PUBLISHER: Dyan C. Lasch

EDITOR: Dyan C. Lasch

EDITORIAL CONCEPT: *"Your passport to the wine country" tells you where to go to have a good time and great wines.*

Club Villas International

PUBLISHED BY: Club Villas International

1329 Whirlaway Cir.

Helena, AL 35080

TEL: (205) 664-9728   **FAX:** (205) 664-3023

DATE: Spring/Summer

FREQUENCY: Semiannually

COVER PRICE: $9.95

SUBSCRIPTION PRICE: $19.95

TOTAL NUMBER OF PAGES: 84

TOTAL NUMBER OF AD PAGES: 8

PUBLISHER: Rodney E. May

EDITOR: n/a

EDITORIAL CONCEPT: *"Your complete guide to luxury lodging and lifestyle in exotic locations"* such as the Caribbean, Mexico, Central America, the South Pacific and Hawaii.

Honeymoon

PUBLISHED BY: Travel Publishing Group

4977 SW 74th Ct.

Miami, FL 33155

TEL: (305) 662-5589   **FAX:** (305) 662-8991

FREQUENCY: 3/year

COVER PRICE: $4.95

SUBSCRIPTION PRICE: $11.00

TOTAL NUMBER OF PAGES: 100

TOTAL NUMBER OF AD PAGES: 24

PUBLISHER: Adam Sandow

EDITOR: Karen Payne

EDITORIAL CONCEPT: *" The magazine dedicated to planning the perfect romantic adventure."*

MapEasy Traveler

PUBLISHED BY: MapEasy Inc.

P.O. Box 1889

Amagansett, NY 11930-1889

TEL: (516) 324-1804   **FAX:** (516) 324-2263

DATE: July

FREQUENCY: Monthly

COVER PRICE: $3.95

SUBSCRIPTION PRICE: $36.00

TOTAL NUMBER OF PAGES: 16

TOTAL NUMBER OF AD PAGES: 0

EDITOR: n/a

EDITORIAL CONCEPT: *Highlights hotels, restaurants, attractions, sights and retail shops in four different cities each month.*

Caribbean For Two

PUBLISHED BY: Caribbean Travel and Life

8403 Colesville Rd, Suite 830

Silver Spring, MD 20910

TEL: (301) 588-2300

FREQUENCY: Annually

COVER PRICE: $4.95

SUBSCRIPTION PRICE: n/a

TOTAL NUMBER OF PAGES: 106

TOTAL NUMBER OF AD PAGES: 44

PUBLISHER: Joseph N. DiMarino, Jr.

EDITOR: Veronica Gould Stoddart

EDITORIAL CONCEPT: *A complete guide to romantic getaways in the Caribbean, with articles on resorts and places to see.*

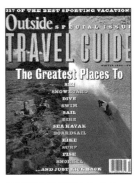

Southern Inns And Bed & Breakfasts

PUBLISHED BY: Whitline Ink Inc.

P.O. Box 24683

Winston-Salem, NC 27114

TEL: (910) 961-6803

DATE: September

FREQUENCY: Quarterly

COVER PRICE: $2.50

SUBSCRIPTION PRICE: $9.00

TOTAL NUMBER OF PAGES: 30

TOTAL NUMBER OF AD PAGES: 9

PUBLISHER: Emily Sarah Lineback

EDITOR: Emily Sarah Lineback

EDITORIAL CONCEPT: *"Exploring charming getaways and restful retreats."*

Outside Travel Guide

PUBLISHED BY: Mariah Media Inc.

400 Market St.

Sante Fe, NM 87501

TEL: (505) 989-1996

DATE: Winter

FREQUENCY: Special

COVER PRICE: $3.99

SUBSCRIPTION PRICE: n/a

TOTAL NUMBER OF PAGES: 142

TOTAL NUMBER OF AD PAGES: 53

PUBLISHER: Lawrence J. Burke

EDITOR: Leslie Weeden

EDITORIAL CONCEPT: *An information-packed compendium of the best sporting vacations from the South Pacific to the Alps.*

The Audio Adventure

PUBLISHED BY: Tomart Publishing Inc.

P.O. Box 15256

Chevy Chase, MD 20825

TEL: (301) 588-6870

DATE: October

FREQUENCY: Monthly

COVER PRICE: $3.50

SUBSCRIPTION PRICE: $21.00

TOTAL NUMBER OF PAGES: 88

TOTAL NUMBER OF AD PAGES: 25

PUBLISHER: Art Lafionatis

EDITOR: Tom Miller

EDITORIAL CONCEPT: *An audio review magazine aimed at "exploring frontiers of sound."*

Audio • Video Home Theater Buyer's Guide

PUBLISHED BY: Bedford Communications

150 Fifth Ave.

New York, NY 10011

TEL: (212) 807-8220

FREQUENCY: Annually

COVER PRICE: $4.95

SUBSCRIPTION PRICE: n/a

TOTAL NUMBER OF PAGES: 100

TOTAL NUMBER OF AD PAGES: 21

PUBLISHER: Edward D. Brown

EDITOR: Ephraim Schwartz

EDITORIAL CONCEPT: *An annual magazine previewing the best new home theater equipment on the market.*

Car Sound Stereo & Security Buyer's Guide

PUBLISHED BY: MP&A Editorial/Design Inc.

939 Port Washington Blvd.

Port Washington, NY 11050

TEL: (516) 944-5940 **FAX:** (516) 767-1745

DATE: Summer

FREQUENCY: Bimonthly

COVER PRICE: $4.95

SUBSCRIPTION PRICE: $17.95

TOTAL NUMBER OF PAGES: 138

TOTAL NUMBER OF AD PAGES: 31

PUBLISHER: Eric Schwartz

EDITOR: Martin Porter

EDITORIAL CONCEPT: *A guide to new stereos and security systems on the market.*

Car Stereo Buyer's Guide And Handbook

PUBLISHED BY: Bedford Communications

150 Fifth Ave.

New York, NY 10011

TEL: (212) 807-8220

DATE: Fall

FREQUENCY: Special

COVER PRICE: $4.95

SUBSCRIPTION PRICE: n/a

TOTAL NUMBER OF PAGES: 100

TOTAL NUMBER OF AD PAGES: 20

PUBLISHER: Edward D. Brown

EDITOR: David Drucker

EDITORIAL CONCEPT: *Bedford's electronics buyer's guide features the best buys in cellular phones, compact discs, speakers and more.*

Power Source

PUBLISHED BY: AT&T Home Business

ADDRESS: n/a

TEL: (800) 383-6164

FREQUENCY: Quarterly

COVER PRICE: n/a

SUBSCRIPTION PRICE: n/a

TOTAL NUMBER OF PAGES: 32

TOTAL NUMBER OF AD PAGES: 4

EDITOR: Linda Schwartz

EDITORIAL CONCEPT: *Management, technical and financial information written for home-based business people.*

Home Theater Technology Buyer's Guide

PUBLISHED BY: CurtCo Publishing

29160 Heathercliff Rd., Suite 200

Malibu, CA 90265

TEL: (310) 589-3100 **FAX:** (310) 589-3131

FREQUENCY: Special

COVER PRICE: $4.95

SUBSCRIPTION PRICE: n/a

TOTAL NUMBER OF PAGES: 164

TOTAL NUMBER OF AD PAGES: 72

PUBLISHER: Megean Roberts

EDITOR: Brent Butterworth

EDITORIAL CONCEPT: *A complete guide for the audiophile on how to shop for a home theater system.*

EDITORIAL CONCEPT: *"Everything you need to know about home theater."*

Stereophile *Guide To Home Theater* 1995

PUBLISHED BY: Stereophile

208 Delgado

Sante Fe, NM 87501

TEL: (505) 989-8791

FREQUENCY: Annually

COVER PRICE: $6.95

SUBSCRIPTION PRICE: n/a

TOTAL NUMBER OF PAGES: 216

TOTAL NUMBER OF AD PAGES: 76

PUBLISHER: Larry Archibald

EDITOR: Lawrence B. Johnson

Eligible

PUBLISHED BY: Eligible Inc.

P.O. Box 17625

Encino, CA 91416-7625

TEL: (818) 709-1736

DATE: Summer

FREQUENCY: Quarterly

COVER PRICE: $2.95

SUBSCRIPTION PRICE: $11.50

TOTAL NUMBER OF PAGES: 74

TOTAL NUMBER OF AD PAGES: 18

PUBLISHER: Katherine Duliakas

EDITOR: Sada Volkoff

EDITORIAL CONCEPT: *Formerly LA's Eligible, the magazine features articles and information for the independent woman.*

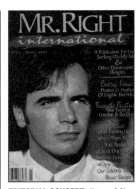

Mr. Right International

PUBLISHED BY: Mr. Right International

P.O. Box 3065-E105

Garden Grove, CA 92642

TEL: (714) 530-2225

FREQUENCY: Bimonthly

COVER PRICE: $4.95

SUBSCRIPTION PRICE: n/a

TOTAL NUMBER OF PAGES: 64

TOTAL NUMBER OF AD PAGES: 11

PUBLISHER: Randi Alam

EDITOR: Ellen A. Diamond

EDITORIAL CONCEPT: *"A publication for ladies seeking worldly men and other quintessential delights."*

Hues

PUBLISHED BY: Hues Inc.

P.O. Box 7787

Ann Arbor, MI 48107

TEL: (800) 483-7482

FREQUENCY: Semiannually

COVER PRICE: $3.95

SUBSCRIPTION PRICE: $14.99 (2 years)

TOTAL NUMBER OF PAGES: 64

TOTAL NUMBER OF AD PAGES: 13.3

PUBLISHER: Ophira Edut, Dyann Logwood, Tali Edut

EDITOR: Ophira Edut

EDITORIAL CONCEPT: *A magazine promoting women in a positive light.*

Women's Sports Traveler

PUBLISHED BY: Sports Traveler

167 Madison Ave., Suite 405

New York, NY 10016

TEL: (212) 759-1357 **FAX:** (212) 759-1282

DATE: Fall/Winter

FREQUENCY: Quarterly

COVER PRICE: $2.95

SUBSCRIPTION PRICE: $9.97

TOTAL NUMBER OF PAGES: 114

TOTAL NUMBER OF AD PAGES: 32

PUBLISHER: Polly Perkins

EDITOR: Karen Walden

EDITORIAL CONCEPT: *"A sports participation magazine"* designed to capture the total sports experience for women.

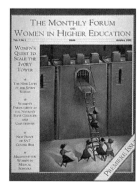

The Monthly Forum On Women In Higher Education

PUBLISHED BY: Women's Forum Publishers

200 W. 57th St., 15th Floor

New York, NY 10019

TEL: (212) 399-1087 **FAX:** (212) 245-1973

DATE: October

FREQUENCY: Monthly

COVER PRICE: $5.00

SUBSCRIPTION PRICE: $36.00

TOTAL NUMBER OF PAGES: 52

TOTAL NUMBER OF AD PAGES: 1

PUBLISHER: Mary Cross

EDITOR: Marina Budhos

EDITORIAL CONCEPT: *"The latest statistics and in-depth features on topics in academia and profiles of women academics doing fascinating research, book reviews and essays."*

ANNUAL, SPECIAL OR FREQUENCY UNKNOWN

American Woman Love Guide

PUBLISHED BY: GCR Publishing Group

1700 Broadway

New York, NY 10019

TEL: (212) 541-7100

FREQUENCY: Special

COVER PRICE: $3.50

SUBSCRIPTION PRICE: $19.97

DISCOUNT SUBSCRIPTION PRICE: $12.97

TOTAL NUMBER OF PAGES: 84

TOTAL NUMBER OF AD PAGES: 21

PUBLISHER: Charles Goodman

EDITOR: Lynn Varacalli

EDITORIAL CONCEPT: *A magazine for those looking for love, in love or wanting to keep love alive.*

Love & Sex

EDITORIAL CONCEPT: *Your 1995 guide to finding, keeping and making love.*

PUBLISHED BY: GCR Publishing Group

1700 Broadway

New York, NY 10019

TEL: (212) 541-7100

FREQUENCY: Special

COVER PRICE: $2.95

SUBSCRIPTION PRICE: n/a

TOTAL NUMBER OF PAGES: 84

TOTAL NUMBER OF AD PAGES: 15

PUBLISHER: Charles Goodman

EDITOR: Lynn Varacalli

A Woman's Guide To Personal Security

EDITORIAL CONCEPT: *Articles on how to stay safe, with tips and reviews of new products, methods and techniques.*

PUBLISHED BY: Challenge Publications Inc.

7950 Deering Ave.

Canoga Park, CA 91304

TEL: (818) 887-0550 **FAX:** (818) 884-1343

FREQUENCY: Special

COVER PRICE: $5.95

SUBSCRIPTION PRICE: n/a

TOTAL NUMBER OF PAGES: 88

TOTAL NUMBER OF AD PAGES: 10

PUBLISHER: Edward Schnepf

EDITOR: Brian Hemsworth

Prevention's Guide To Age Erasers

EDITORIAL CONCEPT: *"Everything you need to know to look and feel young."*

PUBLISHED BY: Rodale Press Inc.

33 E. Minor St.

Emmaus, PA 18098

TEL: (610) 967-5171

FREQUENCY: Special

COVER PRICE: $2.95

SUBSCRIPTION PRICE: n/a

TOTAL NUMBER OF PAGES: 100

TOTAL NUMBER OF AD PAGES: 8

PUBLISHER: Richard Alleger

EDITOR: Catherine M. Cassidy

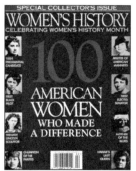

Women's History

EDITORIAL CONCEPT: *A special collector's issue celebrating Women's History Month.*

PUBLISHED BY: Cowles History Group

741 Miller Dr. SE, #D2

Leesburg, VA 22075

TEL: (703) 771-9400

FAX: (703) 779-8345

FREQUENCY: Special

COVER PRICE: $3.95

SUBSCRIPTION PRICE: n/a

TOTAL NUMBER OF PAGES: 76

TOTAL NUMBER OF AD PAGES: 12

EDITOR: Margaret Fortier

Control

PRODUCED BY: Light Rail Communications

625 Second St.

San Francisco, CA 94107-9439

TEL: (800) 741-3337

FREQUENCY: Quarterly

COVER PRICE: $15.95

SUBSCRIPTION PRICE: $49.95

EDITORIAL CONCEPT: *This CD-ROM magazine focusing on the equipment of the music industry offers reviews and demos of the latest software for musicians.*

Home PC Sneak Peeks

PRODUCED BY: CMP Media

600 Community Dr.

Manhasset, NY 11030

TEL: (516) 562-5000

DATE: Winter

FREQUENCY: n/a

COVER PRICE: $9.95

SUBSCRIPTION PRICE: n/a

EDITORIAL CONCEPT: *"Your guide to over 1,500 entertainment and educational CD-ROMs."*

Digizine

PRODUCED BY: Ahrens Interactive Inc.

ADRESS: n/a

TEL: n/a

FREQUENCY: Quarterly

COVER PRICE: $9.95

SUBSCRIPTION PRICE: n/a

PUBLISHER: Bob Aherns

EDITORIAL CONCEPT: *A CD-ROM magazine bringing you entertainment news and features on your computer.*

Multimedia World Live!

PRODUCED BY: Multimedia World Live!

501 Second St.

San Francisco, CA 94107

TEL: (800) 604-9555

FREQUENCY: n/a

COVER PRICE: $9.95

SUBSCRIPTION PRICE: n/a

EDITORIAL CONCEPT: *"Provides an interactive experience for the multimedia PC enthusiast."*

ANNUAL, SPECIAL OR FREQUENCY UNKNOWN

Go Digital

PRODUCED BY: ElectroMedia

1223 Wilshire Blvd., Box E

Santa Monica, CA 90403

TEL: (310) 829-5457

FREQUENCY: n/a

COVER PRICE: $14.95

SUBSCRIPTION PRICE: n/a

EDITORIAL CONCEPT: *An interactive magazine.*

Trouble & Attitude

PRODUCED BY: Marinex Multimedia Corp.

The SoHo Building

110 Greene St., Suite 800

New York, NY 10012

TEL: (212) 334-6700

FREQUENCY: n/a

COVER PRICE: $9.95

SUBSCRIPTION PRICE: n/a

EDITORIAL CONCEPT: *"The multimedia magazine for men."*

Blender

PRODUCED BY: Dennis Publishing Inc.

25 W. 39th St.

New York, NY 10018

TEL: (212) 302-2626

DATE: 1994

FREQUENCY: n/a

COVER PRICE: $19.95

SUBSCRIPTION PRICE: n/a

EDITORIAL CONCEPT: *"Your interactive guide to pop culture."*

Metatec's Nautilus CD

PRODUCED BY: Metatec Corp.

7001 Metatec Blvd.

Dublin, OH 43017

TEL: (800) 637-3472

DATE: 1994

FREQUENCY: n/a

COVER PRICE: $6.95

SUBSCRIPTION PRICE: n/a

EDITORIAL CONCEPT: *"Your multimedia guide to interactive music."*

Concept

PRODUCED BY: Concept Interactive Inc.

9101 Nantwick Ridge

Brooklyn Park, MN 55443

TEL: (612) 424-9438

DATE: 1994

FREQUENCY: n/a

COVER PRICE: $19.95

SUBSCRIPTION PRICE: n/a

EDITORIAL CONCEPT: *"This publication is for everyone who uses the creative arts to promote goods and services."*

Online Access BBS Phone Book

PRODUCED BY: Chicago Fine Print Inc.

ADRESS: n/a

TEL: (312) 573-1700 **FAX:** n/a

DATE: 1994

FREQUENCY: n/a

COVER PRICE: $2.50

SUBSCRIPTION PRICE: n/a

EDITORIAL CONCEPT: *"10,000 new BBS numbers."*

Digital Culture Stream

PRODUCED BY: Mixed Media Productions

6 Sentry Pkwy.

Building 660, Suite 102

Blue Bell, PA 19422

TEL: (800) 578-7326

DATE: 1994

FREQUENCY: n/a

COVER PRICE: $19.95

SUBSCRIPTION PRICE: n/a

EDITORIAL CONCEPT: *"Interactive entertainment and emerging trends."*

Acoustic Musician Magazine

PUBLISHED BY: Border Crossing Publications

P.O. Box 1349

New Market, VA 22844

TEL: (703) 740-4005   **FAX:** (703) 740-4006

DATE: March 1994

FREQUENCY: Monthly

COVER PRICE: $2.95

SUBSCRIPTION PRICE: $29.95

TOTAL NUMBER OF PAGES: 64

TOTAL NUMBER OF AD PAGES: 22

PUBLISHER: Jim Jesson

EDITOR: Steve Spence

EDITORIAL CONCEPT: *A magazine to help make you a better musician and a better music businessperson, while having a little fun along the way.*

The Bachelorette Book

PUBLISHED BY: Bachelor International

8222 Wiles Rd., Suite 111

Coral Springs, FL 33067

TEL: (305) 341-8801   **FAX:** (305) 341-8982

DATE: 1994

FREQUENCY: 5/year

COVER PRICE: $5.95

SUBSCRIPTION PRICE: $31.25

DISCOUNT SUBSCRIPTION PRICE: $26.25

TOTAL NUMBER OF PAGES: 64

TOTAL NUMBER OF AD PAGES: 7

PUBLISHER: Mindi F. Rudan

EDITOR: Paul Gallotta

EDITORIAL CONCEPT: *A magazine for single gentlemen looking for female companions.*

Adoptive Families

PUBLISHED BY: Adoptive Families of America Inc.

3333 Hwy. 100 N.

Minneapolis, MN 55422

TEL: (612) 535-4829

DATE: July/August 1994

FREQUENCY: Bimonthly

COVER PRICE: $4.00

SUBSCRIPTION PRICE: $24.00

TOTAL NUMBER OF PAGES: 80

TOTAL NUMBER OF AD PAGES: 27

EDITOR: Jolene Roehlkepartain

EDITORIAL CONCEPT: *Formerly* Ours *magazine, this publication deals with issues important to parents who have adopted a child.*

Biomechanics

PUBLISHED BY: I.F. Health Media Inc.

172 Rollins Ave.

Rockville, MD 20852

TEL: (301) 770-3333   **FAX:** (301) 770-7062

DATE: May/June 1994

FREQUENCY: Bimonthly

COVER PRICE: Free

SUBSCRIPTION PRICE: n/a

TOTAL NUMBER OF PAGES: 82

TOTAL NUMBER OF AD PAGES: 52

PUBLISHER: Edwin Black

EDITOR: Edwin Black

EDITORIAL CONCEPT: *The magazine of lower extremity movement.*

As You Were

PUBLISHED BY: Reiman Publications L.P

5400 S. 60th St.

Greendale, WI 53129

TEL: (414) 423-0100

DATE: 1994

FREQUENCY: Bimonthly

COVER PRICE: $2.95

SUBSCRIPTION PRICE: $16.98

DISCOUNT SUBSCRIPTION PRICE: $10.98

TOTAL NUMBER OF PAGES: 68

TOTAL NUMBER OF AD PAGES: 0

PUBLISHER: Roy J. Reiman

EDITOR: Clancy Strock

EDITORIAL CONCEPT: *"Great memories of military days shared by veterans in this one-of-a-kind, ad-free magazine."*

The Boston Book Review

PUBLISHED BY: Boston Book Service Inc.

P.O. Box 1322

Cambridge, MA 1322

TEL: (617) 497-0344

DATE: Winter 1994

FREQUENCY: Quarterly

COVER PRICE: $3.00

SUBSCRIPTION PRICE: $8.00

TOTAL NUMBER OF PAGES: 32

TOTAL NUMBER OF AD PAGES: 3

EDITOR: Lucinda Jewell

EDITORIAL CONCEPT: *Books and short stories with a New England flair are reviewed here.*

CCD Astronomy

PUBLISHED BY: Sky Publications Corp.

49 Bay State Rd.

Cambridge, MA 02138

TEL: (617) 864-7360   **FAX:** (617) 864-6117

DATE: Spring 1994

FREQUENCY: Quarterly

COVER PRICE: $5.00

SUBSCRIPTION PRICE: $20.00

TOTAL NUMBER OF PAGES: 46

TOTAL NUMBER OF AD PAGES: 11

EDITOR: Laurence A. Marshall

EDITORIAL CONCEPT: *"Devoted to the applications for digital imaging in astronomy,"* this magazine contains articles on new equipment and achievements in the field.

Famous Monsters Of Filmland

PUBLISHED BY: Dynacomm

P.O. Box 9669

North Hollywood, CA 91609

TEL: (818) 764-9400   **FAX:** (818) 764-1823

DATE: 1994

FREQUENCY: 10/year

COVER PRICE: $4.95

SUBSCRIPTION PRICE: n/a

TOTAL NUMBER OF PAGES: 76

TOTAL NUMBER OF AD PAGES: 13

PUBLISHER: Ray Ferry

EDITOR: Forrest J. Ackerman

EDITORIAL CONCEPT: *"The magazine of classic fantasticinema."*

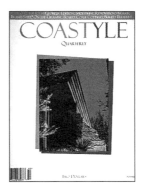

Coastyle Quarterly

PUBLISHED BY: Cannes Deux Colour

201 Redfern Village

St. Simons Island, GA 31522

TEL: (912) 638-8631

DATE: Summer 1994

FREQUENCY: Quarterly

COVER PRICE: $2.00

SUBSCRIPTION PRICE: $10.00

TOTAL NUMBER OF PAGES: 24

TOTAL NUMBER OF AD PAGES: 8

EDITOR: n/a

EDITORIAL CONCEPT: *Defines and captures the sights and sounds of the Georgia coast.*

The Flicker Magazine

PUBLISHED BY: The Hillview Lake Publishing Co. Inc.

Box 20544

Vestavia, AL 35216-0544

TEL: n/a

DATE: 1994

FREQUENCY: Bimonthly

COVER PRICE: $2.95

SUBSCRIPTION PRICE: $19.95

TOTAL NUMBER OF PAGES: 20

TOTAL NUMBER OF AD PAGES: 4

PUBLISHER: Ron Hill

EDITOR: Jeff Quick

EDITORIAL CONCEPT: *"Encouraging balanced growth in children."*

Combo

PUBLISHED BY: Century Publishing Co.

990 Grove St.

Evanston, IL 60201-4370

TEL: (708) 491-6440   **FAX:** (708) 491-0459

DATE: 1994

FREQUENCY: Monthly

COVER PRICE: $3.95

SUBSCRIPTION PRICE: $39.95

DISCOUNT SUBSCRIPTION PRICE: $19.97 (8 issues)

TOTAL NUMBER OF PAGES: 180

TOTAL NUMBER OF AD PAGES: 42

PUBLISHER: Norman Jacobs

EDITOR: Joseph A. Gallo

EDITORIAL CONCEPT: *A price guide for comic books, non-sport cards, action figures and gaming cards.*

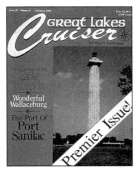

Great Lakes Cruiser

PUBLISHED BY: Great Lakes Cruiser Ltd.

P.O. Box 1722

Royal Oak, MI 48068-1722

TEL: (810) 545-5999   **FAX:** (810) 545-6992

DATE: February 1994

FREQUENCY: Monthly

COVER PRICE: $2.50

SUBSCRIPTION PRICE: $19.95

TOTAL NUMBER OF PAGES: 50

TOTAL NUMBER OF AD PAGES: 30

PUBLISHER: Bruce Jenvey

EDITOR: Bruce Jenvey

EDITORIAL CONCEPT: *The boater's travel guide to the Great Lakes.*

Guideposts For Kids

PUBLISHED BY: Guideposts Associates Inc.

39 Seminary Hill

Carmel, NY 10512-1999

TEL: (914) 225-3681

DATE: November/December 1994

FREQUENCY: Bimonthly

COVER PRICE: $2.95

SUBSCRIPTION PRICE: $15.95

TOTAL NUMBER OF PAGES: 32

TOTAL NUMBER OF AD PAGES: 0

EDITOR: Mary Lou Carney

EDITORIAL CONCEPT: *A children's general interest magazine.*

Malt Advocate

PUBLISHED BY: The Malt Society

3416 Oak Hill Rd.

Emmaus, PA 18049

TEL: (610) 967-1083

DATE: 1994

FREQUENCY: Quarterly

COVER PRICE: $2.95

SUBSCRIPTION PRICE: $11.95

TOTAL NUMBER OF PAGES: 52

TOTAL NUMBER OF AD PAGES: 14

PUBLISHER: John Hansell

EDITOR: John Hansell

EDITORIAL CONCEPT: *"Dedicated to the discerning consumption of beer and whisky."*

Inquisitor

PUBLISHED BY: Luna Grafika Design

P.O. Box 132

New York, NY 10024

TEL: (212) 595-8370

DATE: Spring 1994

FREQUENCY: Quarterly

COVER PRICE: $5.00

SUBSCRIPTION PRICE: $18.00

TOTAL NUMBER OF PAGES: 48

TOTAL NUMBER OF AD PAGES: 0

PUBLISHER: Daniel Drennan

EDITOR: Daniel Drennan

EDITORIAL CONCEPT: *Focuses on technology, art and culture.*

Masala

PUBLISHED BY: Masala Magazine Inc.

43 W. 24th St., #913

New York, NY 10010

TEL: (212) 627-4465   **FAX:** (212) 627-5657

DATE: October 1994

FREQUENCY: Monthly

COVER PRICE: $2.25

SUBSCRIPTION PRICE: $19.00

TOTAL NUMBER OF PAGES: 56

TOTAL NUMBER OF AD PAGES: 12

PUBLISHER: Gopal Raju

EDITOR: Dilip N. Massand

EDITORIAL CONCEPT: *"A quality forum for the South Asian community to show itself to the rest of America."*

Killing Moon

PUBLISHED BY: Draculina Publishing

P.O. Box 969

Centralia, IL 62801

TEL: (618) 532-8813

DATE: 1994

FREQUENCY: Quarterly

COVER PRICE: $3.25

SUBSCRIPTION PRICE: n/a

TOTAL NUMBER OF PAGES: 36

TOTAL NUMBER OF AD PAGES: 4

PUBLISHER: Hugh Gallagher

EDITOR: Alex T. Low

EDITORIAL CONCEPT: *Reviews of horror movies, plus interviews with and stories on people in the horror film buisness.*

Mexico Business

PUBLISHED BY: Mexico Business Publishing Group Ltd.

3033 Chimney Rock, Suite 300

Houston, TX 77056

TEL: (713) 266-0861

DATE: May/June 1994

FREQUENCY: Bimonthly

COVER PRICE: $4.00

SUBSCRIPTION PRICE: $24.00

TOTAL NUMBER OF PAGES: 76

TOTAL NUMBER OF AD PAGES: 13

PUBLISHER: Chris Hearne

EDITOR: Chris Hearne

EDITORIAL CONCEPT: *"The magazine of business and travel in Mexico."*

Onsight!

PUBLISHED BY: Vertical World Publications

8516 W. Lake Mead Blvd., Suite 104

Las Vegas, NV 89128

TEL: (702) 255-8866   **FAX:** (702) 228-4340

DATE: Summer 1994

FREQUENCY: Quarterly

COVER PRICE: $3.95

SUBSCRIPTION PRICE: $14.50

TOTAL NUMBER OF PAGES: 48

TOTAL NUMBER OF AD PAGES: 4

PUBLISHER: Randy Faulk

EDITOR: Randy Faulk

EDITORIAL CONCEPT: *"The most current, up-to-date information about all aspects of climbing and extreme mountaineering."*

Tea : A Magazine

PUBLISHED BY: Olde English Tea Company

3 Devotion Rd., P.O. Box 348

Scotland, CT 06264

TEL: (203) 456-1145   **FAX:** (203) 456-1023

DATE: December 1994

FREQUENCY: Bimonthly

COVER PRICE: $4.95

SUBSCRIPTION PRICE: $29.70

TOTAL NUMBER OF PAGES: 36

TOTAL NUMBER OF AD PAGES: 5

PUBLISHER: Pearl Dexter

EDITOR: Pearl Dexter

EDITORIAL CONCEPT: *The past and present of all aspects of tea.*

Outre

PUBLISHED BY: Filmfax

1320 Oakton St.

Evanston, IL 60202

TEL: (708) 866-7155

DATE: 1994

FREQUENCY: Quarterly

COVER PRICE: $5.95

SUBSCRIPTION PRICE: n/a

TOTAL NUMBER OF PAGES: 84

TOTAL NUMBER OF AD PAGES: 9

PUBLISHER: Michael Stein

EDITOR: Michael Stein, Ted Okuda

EDITORIAL CONCEPT: *"The world of ultranation."*

Travel West

PUBLISHED BY: Infinite Loop Design

P.O. Box 15143

Las Vegas, NV 89114

TEL: (602) 565-3326

DATE: Winter 1994-95

FREQUENCY: Bimonthly

COVER PRICE: $2.50

SUBSCRIPTION PRICE: $12.50

TOTAL NUMBER OF PAGES: 44

TOTAL NUMBER OF AD PAGES: 15

PUBLISHER: Maggie Minton

EDITOR: Jeannie Inman

EDITORIAL CONCEPT: *A travel guide for the western states.*

Power Builder Developer's Journal

PUBLISHED BY: Sys-Con Publications Inc.

46 Holly St.,

Jersey City, NJ 07305

TEL: (201) 332-1515   **FAX:** (201) 333-7361

DATE: 1994

FREQUENCY: Monthly

COVER PRICE: $12.00

SUBSCRIPTION PRICE: $119.00

DISCOUNT SUBSCRIPTION PRICE: $188.00 (2 years)

TOTAL NUMBER OF PAGES: 56

TOTAL NUMBER OF AD PAGES: 30

PUBLISHER: Fuat A. Kirkaali

EDITOR: Steve S. Benfield

EDITORIAL CONCEPT: *A computer programmer's magazine with an emphasis on developmental training.*

TV Plus

PUBLISHED BY: Triple D Publishing Inc.

P.O. Box 2384

Shelby, NC 28151-2384

TEL: (800) 884-7077

DATE: 1994

FREQUENCY: Weekly

COVER PRICE: $1.95

SUBSCRIPTION PRICE: $52.00

DISCOUNT SUBSCRIPTION PRICE: $99.00 (2 years)

TOTAL NUMBER OF PAGES: 144

TOTAL NUMBER OF AD PAGES: 15

PUBLISHER: Douglas G. Brown

EDITOR: Jim H. Cothran

EDITORIAL CONCEPT: *The complete guide for users of the new Digital Satellite Service, providing listings with the schedules.*

The Washington Golf Monthly

PUBLISHED BY: News World Communications

3600 New York Ave. NE

Washington, DC 20002

TEL: (800) 318-4652

DATE: July 1994

FREQUENCY: Monthly

COVER PRICE: $3.00

SUBSCRIPTION PRICE: $19.95

TOTAL NUMBER OF PAGES: 52

TOTAL NUMBER OF AD PAGES: 19

PUBLISHER: Michael Keating

EDITOR: Jeff Thoreson

EDITORIAL CONCEPT: *"First-rate professional writing and photography on subjects and developments that affect and captivate the metropolitan-area golfer."*

Delaware Today Beach Guide

PUBLISHED BY: Suburban Publishing Inc.

201 N. Walnut St., Suite 1204

Wilmington, DE 19801

TEL: (302) 656-1809   **FAX:** (302) 656-5843

DATE: Summer 1994

FREQUENCY: Annually

COVER PRICE: $2.00

SUBSCRIPTION PRICE: n/a

TOTAL NUMBER OF PAGES: 40

TOTAL NUMBER OF AD PAGES: 21

PUBLISHER: Robert F. Martinelli

EDITOR: Lisa Monty

EDITORIAL CONCEPT: *A guide to the Delaware beach life.*

Writes Of Passage

PUBLISHED BY: Writes of Passage Inc.

P.O. Box 7676

Greenwich, CT 06836

TEL: n/a

DATE: Spring/Summer 1994

FREQUENCY: Semiannually

COVER PRICE: $5.95

SUBSCRIPTION PRICE: n/a

TOTAL NUMBER OF PAGES: 90

TOTAL NUMBER OF AD PAGES: 0

EDITOR: Wendy Mass, Laura Hoffman

EDITORIAL CONCEPT: *"The literary journal for teenagers,"* featuring the poetry and prose of teens from across America.

Highball Magazine

PUBLISHED BY: Highball Enterprises

1615 Chestnut St.

Philadelphia, PA 19106

TEL: n/a

DATE: 1994

FREQUENCY: n/a

COVER PRICE: $3.50

SUBSCRIPTION PRICE: n/a

TOTAL NUMBER OF PAGES: 32

TOTAL NUMBER OF AD PAGES: 0

PUBLISHER: Jeff Lush

EDITOR: Jeff Fox

EDITORIAL CONCEPT: *"The definitive guide to booze, cars and girls."*

ANNUAL, SPECIAL OR FREQUENCY UNKNOWN

Decorating The American Home

PUBLISHED BY: GCR Publishing Group

1700 Broadway

New York, NY 10019

TEL: (212) 541-7100

DATE: 1994

FREQUENCY: Special

COVER PRICE: $3.50

TOTAL NUMBER OF PAGES: 84

TOTAL NUMBER OF AD PAGES: 15

PUBLISHER: Charles Goodman

EDITOR: Richard M. Braun

EDITORIAL CONCEPT: *An abundance of ideas for decorating the American home, whether it is country, traditional, Colonial or Victorian.*

Images "Of War"

PUBLISHED BY: Images Inc.

P.O. Box 2058

Stillwater, MN 55082

TEL: (612) 439-9338

DATE: 1994

FREQUENCY: n/a

COVER PRICE: $2.95

SUBSCRIPTION PRICE: n/a

TOTAL NUMBER OF PAGES: 44

TOTAL NUMBER OF AD PAGES: 0

EDITOR: Mary E. Sharbono

EDITORIAL CONCEPT: *"The magazine where the reader is the writer"* contains numerous letters, poems and other writings by war veterans. Its purpose is to provide a wall on which to post memories.

Mortal Kombat II

PUBLISHED BY: Sendai Publishing Group

P.O. Box 1613

Lombard, IL 60148-8613

TEL: (310) 824-5297

DATE: 1994

FREQUENCY: Special

COVER PRICE: $4.99

SUBSCRIPTION PRICE: n/a

TOTAL NUMBER OF PAGES: 52

TOTAL NUMBER OF AD PAGES: 6

PUBLISHER: Steve Harris

EDITOR: Joe Funk

EDITORIAL CONCEPT: *The official magazine of Mortal Kombat II is full of secret tips and strategies for Kombat fans.*

Santana

PUBLISHED BY: Rock-It Comix

26707 W. Agoura Rd.

Calabasas, CA 91302-1960

TEL: (818) 878-7400

DATE: May 1994

FREQUENCY: Special

COVER PRICE: $3.95

SUBSCRIPTION PRICE: n/a

TOTAL NUMBER OF PAGES: 54

TOTAL NUMBER OF AD PAGES: 8

EDITOR: Timothy Truman

EDITORIAL CONCEPT: *A comic book tribute to guitar great Carlos Santana.*

NBA Superstars

PUBLISHED BY: Prima Publications

P.O. Box 1260

Rocklin, CA 95677

TEL: (916) 632-4400

DATE: 1994

FREQUENCY: Special

COVER PRICE: $6.99

SUBSCRIPTION PRICE: n/a

TOTAL NUMBER OF PAGES: 36

TOTAL NUMBER OF AD PAGES: 0

EDITOR: Vince Aversano

EDITORIAL CONCEPT: *"A live-action look at the heroes of the NBA." Includes a giant pull-out poster in full color.*

Shadis Presents The World Of Collectible Card Games

PUBLISHED BY: Alderac Entertainment Group

4045 Guasti Rd., Suite 212

Ontario, CA 91761

TEL: (909) 390-5444   **FAX:** (909) 390-5446

DATE: 1994

FREQUENCY: Special

COVER PRICE: $3.95

SUBSCRIPTION PRICE: n/a

TOTAL NUMBER OF PAGES: 84

TOTAL NUMBER OF AD PAGES: 20

EDITOR: Jolly R. Blackburn

EDITORIAL CONCEPT: *A supplementary publication to the usual offerings of Shadis.*

Radio!

PUBLISHED BY: Radio Shack

1 Tandy Ctr.

Fort Worth, TX 76102-2816

TEL: (817) 390-3011

DATE: Spring 1994

FREQUENCY: n/a

COVER PRICE: $1.95

SUBSCRIPTION PRICE: n/a

TOTAL NUMBER OF PAGES: 82

TOTAL NUMBER OF AD PAGES: 9

PUBLISHER: Robert B. Miller

EDITOR: Harold Ort

EDITORIAL CONCEPT: *Your comprehensive guide to the world of communications — available exclusively to Radio Shack customers.*

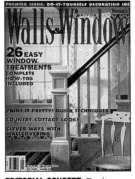

Walls & Windows

PUBLISHED BY: Hachette Filipacchi

1633 Broadway

New York, NY 10019

TEL: (212) 767-5611

DATE: 1994

FREQUENCY: Special

COVER PRICE: $3.50

SUBSCRIPTION PRICE: n/a

TOTAL NUMBER OF PAGES: 130

TOTAL NUMBER OF AD PAGES: 17

EDITOR: Olivia Monjo

EDITORIAL CONCEPT: *Do-it-yourself decorating ideas.*

EDITORIAL CONCEPT: *For the new generation of surfers.*

Wave Action Surf Magazine

PUBLISHED BY: Wave Action Surf Magazine

409 Monterey Ln., Suite A

San Clemente, CA 92674

TEL: (714) 361-7715   **FAX:** (714) 361-7716

DATE: 1994

FREQUENCY: Special

COVER PRICE: $2.95

SUBSCRIPTION PRICE: n/a

TOTAL NUMBER OF PAGES: 84

TOTAL NUMBER OF AD PAGES: 38

PUBLISHER: Mike Fry

EDITOR: Pete Rocky

A

Above the Rim, 225
Acoustic Musician, 242
Action Heroes, 163
Adam Gay Video Pictorial, 202
Additions & Decks, 154
Adobe, 101
Adoptive Families, 242
Adult PC Guide, 101
Adventures of Sword & Sorcery, 115
Affordable Travel, 234
African-American History, 91
Agenda Washington, 176
Air Fan International, 180
Alabama Teen Sports, 5, 172
All About You, 232
All-American Home Plans, 151
All Florida Travel Directory, 177
All Number Fill-It-Ins Special, 109
All Number-Finds, 115
All Sporties for Every Harley-Davidson
    Sportster Rider, 183
Alternative Medicine Digest, 149
Amateur Sex Videos, 202
Amateurs in Action, 202
Amazing Figure Modeler, 116
America Latina, 5, 216
America Online Guide Multimedia Online, 106
America's Favorite Home Plans, 151
American Baby: Baby Fair Special, 89
American Cake Decorating, 129
American Cheerleader, 27, 221
American Country Afghans, 122
American Hunter's Guide, 138
American Iron Christmas, 183
American Legend Directory, 182
American Patchwork & Quilting: Quilt Sampler, 122
American Photo: Jerry Garcia and the Grateful Dead, 164
American Style, 109
American Thunder, 183
American Woman Bridal Hair Guide, 92
American Women Love Guide, 238
Angels, 197
Angels on Earth, 197
Animerica: Anime & Manga Monthly, 98
Anvil, 144
Apollo 13: Collector's Edition, 200
Aqua-Field World of Hunting and Shooting, 137
Architect: Home Plans, 151
Architecture South, 172
Arizona Style, 172
Artnews for Students, 79
Arts & Understanding, 216
As You Were, 242
Asian Lace, 202
Astronomy Presents Observer's Guide 1995, 200
Atlanta Guide Book for Kids, 177
ATV, 182
Audio-Video Home Theater Buyer's Guide, 236
AudioAdventure, 236
AutoCAD Tech Journal, 101
Automobile Buying & Leasing '95, 84
Automobile Magazine's Great Drives, 84
Aveda, 28, 135
Aviation Art Showcase, 87

B

Baby Names, 89
Babylon 5, 125
Bachelorette Book, 242
Back Country, 221
Back Office, 101
Badboy, 202
Baffler, 159
Baja Life, 234
Bang, 202
Basketball Time in Tennessee, 177
Bass Frontiers, 185
Batman and Other Dark Heroes, 164
Batman Forever: Official Movie Magazine, 125
Batman Forever: Official Poster Magazine, 125
Bay Style, 172
Baywatch, 29, 163
B.B. King: The Best of Guitar Player, 163
Bears, 190
Beatles Forever, 164
Beckett Sports Heroes: Michael Jordan, 164
Ben Franklin Crafts, 116
Bent, 194
Best of Decks and Backyard Projects, 154
Best of Logic Puzzles, 109
Best of Low Rider, 8, 84
Best of PC Computing, 8
Best of Score, 211
Best of Things, 154
Best Value Home Plans, 154
Better Homes and Gardens Crafts Showcase, 109
Better Homes and Gardens' Home Buyer's Guide, 154
Better Homes and Gardens' Prizewinning Recipes, 131
Betty Crocker's Cooking Today, 131
Bi-Curious, 203
Bicycle Repair Illustrated, 225
Big Book of Photography, 191
Big Guy and Rusty the Boy Robot, 98
Biomechanics, 242
Birds & Blooms,30, 145
Bizára, 159
Bizarre, 109
Black Child, 90
Black College, 90
Black Elegance Presents Belle, 90
Black Pleasure International, 203
Black Professional, 90
Blackriders, 90
Blaster, 101
Blender, 241
Blitz, 225
Blunt, 221

BMX Special '95 Buyer's Guide, 226
Body Building News, 226
Bodywise: Diet & Exercise, 142
Boob Tube Busters, 203
Book of Lists, 172
Bookcase, 6, 31, 159
Bookforum, 159
Books & Culture: A Christian Review, 197
Bop's BB, 163
Boston Book Review, 242
Bovanti, 90
Box, 221
Boxing Illustrated, 221
Branson Living, 172
Brew Your Own, 32, 129
Brooklyn Bridge, 6, 173
Building Dioramas, 109
Building Ideas for Your New Home, 151
Busty & Black, 221
Buzz Daly's Player's Guide to Las Vegas Sports Books: 1995
    Football Edition, 144

C

Caged!, 221
Calling All Cars, 33, 81
Car Stereo Buyer's Guide and Handbook, 236
Car Sound Stereo & Security Buyer's Guide, 236
Car Toys, 110
Carabella, 135
Caribbean for Two, 235
CCD Astronomy, 243
CD Review's Country '95, 186
CD-ROM Advisor, 101
CD-ROM Power, 102
Celebrity Posters, 164
Celebrity Recipes, 131
Center Ice, 222
Century, 159
Chatter, 194
Cheri Undercover, 203
Chevy Truck, 81
Children's Book Review, 97
Christianity and the Arts, 97
Chrome Pony, 182
Chrysler Engines Etc., 84
Cigar Aficionado: Guide to Cigar Friendly Restaurants, 219
Cinescape's 1995 Science Fiction Television Yearbook, 125
Clarity, 197
Club Villas International, 234
Coastal Home, 5, 34, 151
Coastyle Quarterly, 243
Coffee Journal, 35, 129
Collecting, 110
Collectors' Bulletin, 110
Collector's World of Racing, 116
College Basketball Madness, 226
College Football '95, 226
Columbus Monthly's Wedding Planner, 177
Combat Handguns Buyer's Guide 1995, 180
Combo, 243

Comic Relief Presents Funny Stuff, 98
Comics Lit , 98
Commercial Image, 191
Complete Hair & Beauty Guide, 136
Computer Shopper Holiday Issue Buying Guide, 106
Conan the Savage, 98
Concept, 241
Confidential Letters, 203
Consultants Report, 93
Consumer Review Power Windows, 106
Control, 240
Cooking Light's Quick & Easy Weeknights, 131
Corvette Review, 81
Costa Rica Adventure & Business, 234
Country Accents: Decks and Gardening Ideas, 154
Country Accents' Today's Home, 152
Country Accents' White Christmas Crafts, 116
Country Accents' Soups, Stews & Chili, 132
Country America Magazine's Country '95 Yearbook, 187
Country Boys, 203
Country Collections, 152
Country Crafts, 110
Country Folk Art's Quick 'n' Easy Home Cooking, 129
Country Heart, 216
Country Home Holidays at Home, 155
Country Kitchens, 155
Country Mirror, 187
Country Sampler's Romantic Homes, 152
Countrybeat Presents Exclusive Interviews with Country's Top
    Stars! 163
Cover, 187
Crafting: Plastic Canvas, 116
Crafting Today Christmas Ornaments, 116
Crafting Traditions, 110
Crafting Wreaths, 177
Craftsman at Home: Decks and Outdoor Living, 152
Craftsman Practical Lawns & Gardens, 145
Crazy Kings, 219
Create, 36, 79
Cult Movies, 124
Cups, 129
Cyber Sports, 102
Cycle Enthusiast Directory, 182

D

Death of a Model: Linda Sobek, 164
Decorating the American Home, 246
Deer Hunter, 138
Delaware Today Beach Guide, 246
Delphi Informant, 102
Deluxe Variety Puzzles, 110
Dennis! 165
Development Design & Decoration: The South Florida
    Sourcebook, 177
Digit, 102
Digital Culture Stream, 241
Digizine, 240
Dimension 3, 111
Dimension PS-X, 111
Discover Horses, 158

Disney's Big Time, 97
Disney's Pocohontas, 99
DoubleTake, 6, 37, 191
Down-'n'-Nasty, 204
Downtown Attack, 177
Dr. Dobb's Sourcebook: Internet and Worldwide Web, 107
Dr. Dobb's the Interoperable Objects Special Report, 107
Dr. J's Pro Basketball Yearbook '95, 226
Dune Buggies & Hot VW's Presents The California Look and How
    to Get It! 85
duPont Registry: A Buyers Gallery of Fine Homes, 38, 152

E

East Infection Snowboard, 222
Easy Crochet, 122
Easy Girls, 204
Easy Golf, 226
Easy Wood, 111
Easyriders Roadware, 183
Eating Right, Feeling Fit, 132
Eating Well Holiday Recipes, 132
EGM Player's Guide to Playstation Video Games, 111
EGM Player's Guide to Sega Saturn Video Games, 111
EGM 3-D, 117
eligible, 39, 238
Elvis: An American Legend, 165
ESPN College Basketball, 40, 227
ESPN ProBasketball '95, 40, 227
ESPN ProFootball '95, 40, 227
ESPN Year in Sports '95, 40, 227
Essential Connection, 197
Excluded Middle, 194
Exotic Cars, 81
Explorations In Artificial Life, 200
Eye , 194
Eye Deal, 187

F

Fall Garden Planner, 146
Family Circle: You Do It! 117
Family Fun Crafts, 117
Family Next Door, 147
Famous Monsters of Filmland, 243
Fantasy Basketball, 227
Fantasy Football, 227
Fast Company, 5, 41, 93
50/50, 147
Figurines & Collectibles, 42, 111
Films of the Golden Age, 124
Fine Scale Modeler Presents: Modeling The Second
    World War, 117
Fingerstyle Guitar, 185
Fit, 141
Fit, Fresh and Fast: Flavors from Florida, 132
Fitness Swimmer: 222
5.0 Mustang Hop-Ups, 85
Flatiron News, 178
Flicker, 243

Floral & Nature Crafts Holiday Decorating, 117
Florida Care Giver, 173
Flower Gardening, 146
Flowerlover, 145
Fly Tyer, 137
Forbidden, 204
Ford High Performance, 81
Ford Truckin', 85
Forehead, 194
ForePlay, 204
Forever Beatles, 165
Forkroads, 159
4x4 Mechanix, 81
4080, 187
Freedom Rag, 194
Fusion, 43, 102

G

Gambero Rosso, 44, 129
Game Sport, 107
GamePro Official Player's Guide, 118
Gamer, 118
Garcia: Reflections, 165
Garden Gate, 145
Gardens, Decks & Patios, 146
Gent's Nostalgia: The '70s, 211
Gentleman's Club Guide, 171
George, 5, 45, 193
Georgia Country Life, 173
Global Culture Rhythm Music, 185
Glock Autopistols, 139
GM Collector's Guide, 82
Go Digital, 240
Golden Beauties, 204
Golf Illustrated, 222
Golf New Mexico, 178
Good Taste, 130
GrandParenting and Other Great Adventures, 162
Grassroots Youth, 233
Great Lakes Cruiser, 243
Great Outdoors: 1995 Annual Guide, 96
Green Day, 187
Green Giant's Dinner Tonight, 132
Greenthumb, 145
Greg LeMond: The Official Story, 228
Gridiron, 228
Griffey vs. Thomas '95 Showdown, 165
Ground Level, 185
Group Gropers, 204
Gruf, 205
GuestWest, 234,
Guideposts, 198
Guideposts for Kids, 244
Guitar & Bass Buyer's Guide 1995-96, 188
Gun News Digest, 137
GunGames, 46, 222
Guns & Ammo Firearms for Law Enforcement, 139
Guns & Weapons for Law Enforcement,139
Guns & Weapons for Self Defense, 139
GW2K: Gateway, 102

H

Handcannons, 137
Hastings Power Zone, 118
Health Digest, 149
Health Pages, 173
Healthy & Natural Journal, 149
Heavy Metal Overdrive, 99
Hemi Muscle, 85
Heroes of the Heartland, 148
High Adventure, 161
High Performance Kitbuilts, 87
High Society Insider, 212
High-Tech Performance, 82
Highball, 246
Hockey Greats, 228
HomeGarden, 5, 8, 47, 145
Home Improvement, 155
Home PC Sneak Peeks, 240
Home Plans Presents Country & Farmhouse Designs, 155
Home Theater Technology Buyer's Guide, 236
Homes from the Heartland, 155
Honeymoon, 234
Horse, 158
Hot Chix! 205
Hot Rod Bikes, 182
Hot Rod Bikes Pictorial, 184
Hot Shoebox Chevys, 85
Hot Hair, 136
How to Play Blues, 185
How to Play Guitar, 185
How to Surf Your Best, 228
Hues, 238
Hunt's Simple Meals, 132
Hustler Hard Drive, 205
Hustler's Voyeur, 212

I

I Have Seen the Mermaids Singing, 161
I'll Take Romance, 160
I-Way, 107
IBA Magazine, 91
Iké Udés aRUDE, 79
Images "of War," 246
Immature, 165
In-line Skater 1995 Buyer's Guide, 228
Inc. Special Issue: The State of Small Business, 95
Inc. Technology, 107
Income Plus Presents Success Secrets, 95
Individual Investor, 93
Indoor & Patio Gardening, 146
Infobahn, 48, 103
InQuest, 49, 112
Inquisitor, 244
Inside College Basketball, 228
Inside Line: Special Red Wings Playoff Issue, 229
Inside Racing, 82
InterActive Teacher, 123
International Virus, 195

Internet Underground, 103
IPI Report, 216
Ironman: The Road to Kona, 229
It's New, 200

J

Jack, 205
Jack Magazine, 195
Jam 1995, 229
Jerry Garcia, 166
Jerry Garcia: What a Long Strange Trip it Was, 166
Jet Classics, 87
Jim Feist's College Football, 229
Jim Feist's Pro Football 1995 Annual, 229
Jiu-Jitsu, 229
Joe Weider's Prime Fitness & Health, 149
John A. Russo's Making Movies, 124
Jordan: The Sequel, 166
Joy Toys, 212
JTT's Scrapbook, 166
Juice, 5, 50, 130
Juniors, 205
Just the Write Touch, 98
Juxtapoz, 79

K

Kaleidoscope, 198
Killing Moon, 244
Kitchen Planning Guide, 156
Knockouts, 222
Kraft Holiday Homecoming, 133

L

Large Fill-Ins Special! 112
Las Vegas Handicapper Jeff Allen's College & NBC Basketball Preview and Betting Guide, 230
Learn to Fly, 88
Learning from Today's Art Masters, 80
Lefthander, 5, 216
Lethal Force! 139
LFP Presents an Inside Look at Melrose Place, 166
LFP Presents O.J. Simpson Trial of the Century, 166
Life Extension, 149
Light, Lively & Low-Fat, 133
Limbaugh Letter, 193
Log Home Lifestyle, 156
Lollipop, 186
Lottery Winner's Weekly Lotto, 144
LottoWorld, 51, 144
Lotus Notes Advisor, 103
Love & Sex, 239
Low Budget Weekend Decorating Ideas, 156
Low Country, 173
Luminarios, 198

M

Mad Super Special Number 107, 100
Mad TV, 100
Madeleine, 136
Malt Advocate, 244
Manhattan File, 173
Manhunt, 205
Many Mountains Moving, 160
MapEasy Traveler, 235
Martha Stewart Living Weddings, 6, 92
Martial Arts Legends Presents Steven Seagal: Master of Harmony, 167
Martial Arts Movies, 126
Martial Arts Ultimate Warriors, 223
Masala, 244
Master's Variety Puzzles Plus Crostics, 112
Maximize, 103
Medizine Guidebook toWomen's Medications, 150
Meet Thy Doom, 118
Men's Perspective, 170
Men's Style, 147
Metatec's Nautilus CD, 241
Metropolitan Home Plans, 152
Mexico Business, 244
Michael Jackson: His Life in Pictures, 167
Michael Jordan Pro Basketball Illustrated, 167
Michael Jordan Returns, 167
Michael!, 167
Michael's Arts & Crafts Christmas Craft Preview, 118
Mickey Mantle: His Glorious Years, 167
Mighty I, 99
Military Surplus Warplanes, 87
Military Technical Journal, 180
Millennium, 206
Miniature Quilt Ideas, 112
Minnesota Fabrics: Home Expressions, 153
Miracles Inspirational, 198
MK3 Official Kollector's Book, 126
Mobile Computing, 108
Model Railroad Planning 1995, 118
Modern America, 52, 193
Modern Ferret, 5, 7, 53, 121
Money Card Collector, 112
Monster Bow Bucks, 139
Monthly Forum on Women in Higher Education, 238
More Michael Jordan Returns, 168
Mortal Kombat, 126
Mortal Kombat II, 247
Motocross Journal, 182
Motor Trend Performance Cars, 85
Motorcycle Milestones, 184
Motorist, 82
Mountain Biking How-To's, 230
Mountain Biking's Racing Special, 230
Mountain Living, 5, 54, 153
Mountain Pilot, 87
Mr. Right International, 238
Multimedia Producer, 103
Multimedia World Live!, 240
Multisport, 223
Murderous Intent, 189
Music & Computers, 103
Music Confidential, 186
Mustang Classics, 86
My Life as a Girl, 217

N

Naked, 206
Nascar Super Truck Racing, 82
Nasty Women, 206
National Crime Monthly, 55, 217
National Home Business Directory, 93
National O.J., 168
Natural Way, 149
Nature's Best, 190
Naughty Neighbors, 206
Naughty Nights, 206
NBA Superstars, 247
Nestle Toll House Best-Loved Cookies, 133
Net, 56, 104
New Age Patriot, 193
New Body's Low Fat, No Fat Cookbook, 133
New Body's Quick & Easy Diet & Exercise Guide, 150
New Body's Firm Butt, Thin Thighs in 30 Days, 142
New Body: The Super-Easy Weight Loss Guide Book, 142
New Cyclist, 223
New House '95, 156
New Thought Journal, 195
New York Bar Guide '96, 5, 174
New York Living, 174
New York Sportscene, 174
Next Generation, 104
Nick at Night, 126
Night, 206
Niko, 5, 135
1955 Brooklyn Dodgers, 230
1995 AVP Yearbook & Tour Guide, 230
1995 Coca-Cola ASP World Tour Guide, 230
1995 Motorcycle Buyer's Guide, 184
1995 Video Game Buyer's Guide, 119
Non-Stop, 217
North Carolina's Tasteful Special Issue: Summer Travel, 178
Northern California Bride, 178
Northern & Southern California Getaways, 178

O

Off, 219
Off-Road Racing Scene, 82
Official Congo Collector's Magazine, 126
Official GoldenEye Collector's Magazine, 127
Official's Logic Problems, 112
Official's Varieties and Crosswords, 113
Oi, Robot, 189
Oil Highlights I: Landscapes, 80
Old Farmer's Almanac Good Cook's Companion, 133
Old Farmer's Almanac Home Owners Companion, 156
Omni Comix, 100
OneWorld, 57, 195

100 Years of Moving Pictures, 127
1,001 Weight Loss Secrets, 141
Online Access BBS Phone Book, 241
Online User, 104
Onsight!, 245
Opportunist, 93
Orgy Girls, 207
Ornament Collector, 113
Oui International, 207
Outdoor Action, 96
Outdoor Gear, 96
Outlook Americas, 93
Outlook California, 178
Outlook Texas, 179
Outre, 245
Outside Buyer's Guide 1995, 96
Outside Travel Guide, 235

P

Paintball Player's Bible, 223
Parent Life, 198
Party Chicks, 207
Passion Partners, 212
Pasta Press, 130
Pastry Art & Design, 130
PC Magic, 108
PC Novice Guide to Going Online, 108
PC Sims Buyer's Guide, 104
Penthouse Erotica, 212
Penthouse Lingerie, 212
Penthouse Men's Adventure Comix, 99
Penthouse VP, 213
Permission, 195
Personal Database, 108
Personal Styles Fitness, 141
Phenoms, 231
Phil Steele's 1995 College Football Preview, 231
Photography Buyer's Guide & Handbook, 191
Photo Tribute to Eazy-E, 168
Picture Word-Finds, 113
Pittsburgh Magazine: Special Travel Publication, 179
Playboy's Blondes, 213
Playboy's College Girls, 213
Playboy's Anna Nicole Smith, 213
Playboy's Hot Denim Daze, 213
Playboy's Nude Celebrities, 213
Playboy's Pocket Playmates, 214
Playboy's Supermodels, 214
Popcorn, 5, 195
POPSCI, 97
Popular Photography's Photo Information Handbook, 191
Positive Living, 198
Positive Note, 199
P.O.V., 5, 58, 94
Power Builder Developer's Journal, 245
Power Golf, 231
Power Programmer, 104
Power Source, 236
PowerPlay, 223
Precious Collectibles, 113

Premium Crosswords, 113
Prevailing Winds, 217
Prevention's Guide: Personal Safety, 148
Prevention's Guide to Age Erasers, 239
Princess Di: A Look at the Royal Woman, 168
Provocateur, 147
P.S.X. Playstation Experience, 113
Psychedelic Illuminations, 220
Pull Your Own Weight, 231
Puppetry International, 119
Pure Pink, 207

Q

Q San Francisco, 174
Quick & Easy Painting, 114
Quick Knit & Crochet, 122
Quick Throttle, 183
Quilter's Gallery, 122

R

Rad!, 168
Radio!, 247
Ragtyme Sports, 114
Rainbow Tales, 122
Raw Sex, 207
react, 5, 59, 233
Real, 233
Real Affairs, 208
Reckon, 174
Red Herring, 189
Release Ink, 198, 199
Return of the Beatles, 168
Risqué, 60, 208
Road & Track Presents Open Road, 83
Rod & Customs Pictorial, 83
Rodale's Guide to Family Camping, 96
Rose Kennedy: The Legend and the Legacy, 169
Rude & Lewd, 208

S

Salsa Tales, 214
Saltwater Fly Fishing, 137
Santana, 247
Savage Male, 208
Scenario, 61, 160
Scenarios: Special Wired Edition, 108
Sci-Fi TV Fall Preview, 127
Science Spectra, 62, 200
Scientific American: The Computer In the 21st Century, 108
Score: 1995 Betting Guide for College and NFL, 144
Scratchbuilding Ship Models, 114
Scream Beat, 214
Script, 124
Season, 135
Secrets from Sexy People, 208
Seen, 174

Sensuous Muscle: The Women of Bodybuilding, 142
Serif, 79
Sex Fever, 208
Sex Scandals, 209
Sexiest Women in X-Films, 209
Sexual Health, New Body Health, 150
Shadis Presents the World of Collectible Card Games, 247
Shape Presents Fit Pregnancy, 141
Shaping Your Figure Through Health, 141
Shaq: The Magic Strikes, 169
Shocking Stories, 209
Shooter's Rag, 191
Shout!, 186
Shutterbug's Outdoor and Nature Photography, 192
Sí, 63, 217
Signal, 104
Simply Perfect Pasta, 133
Single Styles, 217
Singles, 218
Singles Resource, 218
Sista!, 209
Skeptical Inquirer, 201
Skier, 223
Skinz, 209
Slammer, 86
Smart Computer & Software Retailing, 105
Smith & Wesson Handguns '95, 140
Smithsonian Institution's Ocean Planet, 201
Smoke, 218
Soap Opera Spectacular, 169
Soap Opera Stars, 163
Soldier of Fortune's Fighting Firearms, 180
South Africa: The Journal of Trade, Industry & Investment, 94
Southern Inns and Bed & Breakfasts, 235
Southern New Mexico Destinations, 175
Speak, 5, 64, 196
Special! Superb Word-Find, 114
Special! Variety Word-Find Puzzles, 114
Species, 127
Speedway Pit Pass, 83
Spider-Man, 97
Spider-Man: The Lost Years, 99
Sport Truck Annual '95, 86
Sports Cards Presents the Comprehensive Guide to
   Fleer Trading Cards, 119
Sports Cards Presents the Comprehensive Guide to Topps
Trading Cards, 119
Sports Illustrated Presents College Football, 65, 231
Sports Illustrated Presents NFL '95, 65, 231
Sports Illustrated Presents Pro Basketball '95-'96, 65, 232
Sports Illustrated: The Best of the Swimsuit Super Models, 171
Sports Image, 224
Sports Mirror Football, 232
Sports St. Louis, 175
Sports Scene, 224
Sportsman's Journal Off-The-Road, 83
St. Louis, 175
Stable Companion, 5, 7, 66, 158
Stag's Original Porn Legends, 210
Star Magazine Special Star Diets, 142
Star Trek Voyager, 124
Starbase, 127

Starflash Poster, 169
Starlog Platinum Edition, 127
Starz!, 169
Stereophile Guide to Home Theater 1995, 237
Stitchery, 122
Stix, 224
Stock Car Superstars, 83
Street Bike, 183
Street Machine Special: Super Coupes, 86
Strength, 196
Stretching for Success, 142
Stroke-Off Tales, 210
Style, 175
Style 1900, 114
Su Casa, 153
Sufism, 218
Summer Cooking & Entertaining, 130
Summertime, 179
Summertime Grilling, 134
Sunsational Home Plans, 156
Super Mario World 2 Yoshi's Island, 119
Super Summer Movie Heroes, 128
Super Truck Spectacular, 83
Superb Crosswords and Varieties, 115
Superfit Cyclist, 232
Surfwriter's Quarterly, 6, 224

T

T&A, 210
Tactical Bowhunting, 140
Tactical Knives, 137
Talk About Pets, 67, 121
Tandem, 224
Tart, 196
Tea: A Magazine, 245
Television Today, 124
Tennessee Living, 175
Texas, 175
Texas Our Texas, 179
Thicker, 196
This Old House, 5, 68, 153
3-D Times, 105
3D Design, 105
30 Days to a Flatter Stomach, 143
30 Easy Menu Ideas, 134
31st Ryder Cup Matches, 232
Tight Cheeks, 210
Time for Kids, 697
Time Out New York, 69, 176
Today's Atlanta Woman, 176
Total Fitness for Men, 141
Touring & Tasting, 70, 130
Touring Rider, 184
Tracking Angle, 186
Trade Tales, 210
Traditional Home Renovation Style, 5, 71, 153
Transformation, 5, 218
Trauma, 125
Travel West, 245
Travelling Sportsman, 138

Tribe, 6, 176
Tribute to Mickey Mantle, 170
Trophy, 138
Trouble & Attitude, 240
Truckin' Presents Hot Mini-Trucks Pictorial, 86
Tuff Stuff's Guide To Starting Lineup, 119
TV Plus, 245
TV. Guide: Star Trek, 128
21-C, 72, 200
Two Girls Review, 160

U

U.S. Coast Guard at War! 180
Ultimate Body, 143
Ultimate Gamer, 115
Ultralights, 87
Unexplained Universe, 218
Urban, 5, 219
Urge, 210

V

Vantage Comic & Card Picks, 99
Varmit Masters, 138
VB Tech Journal, 105
Vegetarian Gourmet Presents Low-Fat Special, 134
Vegetarian Times' Low-Fat & Fast, 131
Ventura, 115
Victorian Bride, 92
Victorian Homes & Gardens, 153
Victory Over Europe, 180
Victory!, 147
Video Stars, 214
Vietnow, 5, 219
View, 232
Vignette, 160
Virtual City, 73, 105
Visions, 125
Visual Objects Advisor, 105
VR World, 105

W

Wahine, 225
Walls & Windows, 247
War Combat Special V-E Day 50th Anniversary, 181
Warbird, 88
Washington Golf Monthly, 246
Watercolor '95, 79
Wave Action Surf, 248
Wave Rider, 225
Weekend, 157
Weekly Standard, 5, 74, 193
Wes Craven's New Nightmare, 128
Western Deer Hunting, 138
Wet Dreams, 214
Wet Lips, 211
White's Guide to Collecting Figures, 115

Whitefish: The Magazine of Northwest Montana, 176
Wilde, 147
Windows NT, 106
Wine & Spirits Guide to Understanding Wine, 131
Wine Spectator Magazine's Guide to the Hamptons & Long
    Island Wine Country, 179
Winning Sports Gambling Illustrated, 144
Winning Strategies, 94
Wolf Clan, 121
Wolf Marshall's Guitar One, 186
Woman's Day Weekend Crafts, 120
Woman's Day Weekend Projects, 157
Woman's Guide to Personal Security, 239
Women's History, 239
Women of Action Sports, 225
Women of Color, 211
Women's Forum, 211
Women's Sports Traveler, 75, 238
Wood Magazine's Best Woodworking Tips, 120
Word Up! Presents Summer Preview, 196
Word Wrights!, 160
Working at Home, 94
World Business, 94
Writes of Passage, 246
WWWiz, 106

X

X-Files & Other Eerie TV, 128
X-Rated Close-Ups, 215
XSeSS Living, 196

Y

Yippy-Yi-Yea Western Lifestyles, 176
Your Future, 5, 76, 94

Z

Z Car, 84
ZD Internet Life, 6, 106
Zasshi, 5, 219
Zia Magazine's Southern New Mexico Traveler, 179
Zigzag, 97